Control of the Imaginary

Theory and History of Literature
Edited by Wlad Godzich and Jochen Schulte-Sasse

For other books in the series, see p. 251

Control
of the Imaginary:
Reason and Imagination
in Modern Times

Luiz Costa Lima
Translation by Ronald W. Sousa
Afterword by Jochen Schulte-Sasse

Theory and History of Literature, Volume 50

University of Minnesota Press, Minneapolis

Published by the University of Minnesota Press
2037 University Avenue Southeast, Minneapolis, MN 55414.
Published simultaneously in Canada by Fitzhenry & Whiteside
Limited, Markham.
Printed in the United States of America.

Library of Congress Cataloging-in-Publication Data

Lima, Luiz Costa, 1937-
  Control of the imaginary.

 √ (Theory and history of literature; v. 50)
  Translation of: O Controle do imaginário. 1984.
  Bibliography: p.
  Includes index.
  1. Literature—Philosophy. I. Title. II. Series.

PN49.L48513 1988   801   88-19154
ISBN 0-8166-1562-4
ISBN 0-8166-1563-2 (pbk.)

Contents

Preface

Control of the Imaginary is grounded in a dual articulation. The first element is constituted by the terms mimesis, imagination, and fiction. The second, operational in character, is formed by the hypothesis that, from the beginning of modern times, fictional texts have been subjected to either explicit or hidden forms of taming or control.

The basic terms in the first articulation deserve special attention. The first of those terms, mimesis, undergoes a significant reversal with respect to its common usage. We all know that from the Renaissance rediscovery of Aristotle's *Poetics* on, mimesis has been taken as the equivalent of the Latin word *imitatio*. What the prominent critic Ingemar Düring notes — "The artist, the musician, or the poet reproduces or imitates the things of the sensible world"[1] — could be repeated by the most undiscerning of commentators. That agreement, however, does not see that when mimesis and *imitatio* are taken as equivalents, with regard to the Greek outlook and especially with regard to Aristotle's thought, an irreparable deformation is established. If, to the Greek mind, mimesis presupposed a correspondence with the cosmic order, in Aristotle that correspondence also became dynamic in nature. That is, mimesis presupposed adequation not with the powerful, sensible appearance of things but rather with their internal potentialities. Its product, *mimema*, was not understood as the copy or imitation of something previously given, for, conversely, it presumed the actualization of the *dynamis* of a cosmos harmonic because ordered by laws. Even though that concept of a dynamic yet ordered universe was lost with the end of the ancient world, under-

standing mimesis as *imitatio* implies turning the former into a grotesque carica-
ture of what it was.

Using a logic like the one that A. MacIntyre develops about ethics in *After
Virtue*,[2] we can say that, at the outset of modern times, poetics suffers a catas-
trophe similar to the one that that English philosopher believes took place in moral
philosophy after the Enlightenment. For poetics too came to rely on a vocabulary whose systematicity had been lost. Obviously, there can be no way to recuperate it and restore the Greek sense of mimesis, for the very mentality of modern
times, and within it the way that *physis* is conceived, has dramatically changed.
It seems to me, then, that someone interested in art has at hand only two alter-
natives: either to abandon mimesis to the list of tools no longer serviceable or to
revive its sense. I have opted for the second route.

Let me explain in simple terms. In the Greek cosmological model, mimesis
presupposed an external modeling element to which the *mimema* naturally had
to subject itself, namely the ordering law of *physis*. As I use the term, mimesis
does not presume a cosmological conception but rather a network of psycho-so-
cial meaning. As Mauss and Durkheim demonstrated in "De Quelques formes
primitives de classification,"[3] every human society presupposes a classification
of beings and things by means of which those beings and things are invested with
meaning and value. To be socialized is, then, to internalize classificatory net-
works that locate the individual along the different scales (family, community,
professional milieu, social class, and so on) within the social environment.
Mimesis is, first and foremost, one — or *the* — mode of learning socialization, that
is, a mode of internalizing social values.

Mimesis, then, from the outset presupposes *identification* or *similarity*. But
that vector does not exhaust its import. To watch the socialization process of a
child, which any parent can do, is to see, on the one hand, the (social) force that
impels the child to mold his or her gestures, way of walking and talking, and
behavior according to models reasonably open to his or her "choice." But, on
the other hand, as the socialization process proceeds, the object of this education
manifests differences that are at first almost imperceptible. For socialization via
mimesis implies the exercise of a tense, often conflictive, dialectic between
assimilation and differentiation. Schematically, two outcomes are predictable; in
the first, difference does not advance and the pattern of similarity takes on so
much power that the new individual becomes the copy, albeit ever an imperfect
one, of the chosen model. (Anyone who was an adolescent in the early 1960s
surely recalls some futile Marilyn Monroe, noticed, pointed out, even admired
by those in her peer group!) The hypertrophy of the "similarity" vector thus produces the teratology of the mimetic process: the outcome of copy or imitation is
a pathological product. The "normal" resolving process has an opposite profile:
the "imitator" becomes autonomous — that is, he or she assumes the mark of his
or her difference. The real path of mimesis, therefore, supposes not copy but

difference. Rather than imitation, mimesis is the production of difference. It is, however, not an idiosyncratic difference similar to an idiolect but a socially recognizable, potentially acceptable difference. Recognizable and acceptable according to the expectations engendered in the members of a given community by the criteria of classification in force in that community.

No matter how simplified the above explanation may be, it suggests that I do not take mimesis to be something reducible to experience of the fictional. And, because I do not analyze it in itself but only as it relates to the fictional, my intent here is to indicate how I conceive the articulation between the two.

Between mimesis and fictional precipitation lies the imaginary. Along with Sartre[4] I take the imaginary to be one of the two forms of thematization of the world. Whereas the other form, the perceptual, locates things as present, the imaginary annihilates (*néantise*) them, thematizing them as absent. (I perceive what surrounds me, but I can imagine only what is absent.) To be sure, I agree with those who criticize Sartre because his criterion does not allow for distinction between day-to-day use of the imaginary and its specific use in the production and reception of the fictional. But, although I cannot develop the critique here, the problem is not insoluble. As Wolfgang Iser would say, because the fictional concretizes in a text that materializes in a signifying organization, the fictional negates the negation of the imaginary on which it is based.[5] The fictional is a critical use of the imaginary.

With that established, let us pass, with even greater brevity, to the notion of the fictional. As I understand it, the fictional is a *discursive* form, that is, a type of territoriality configured through signs; as such, it is governed by rules that are normally not conscious ones. Product of mimesis, actualized by the thematization of the imaginary, nourished by the negation of the negativity of the latter, the fictional takes on the appearance of a "game" that does not contain the choice between true and false. That does not mean, however, that it does not touch upon truths (pragmatic, religious, and so forth) but rather only that it is a game that puts truths into question; that is, it is a game that does not so much expand or apply truths as interrogate them.

Now that I have explained, albeit in a rudimentary manner, the first of *Control*'s articulations, my goal can be more directly grasped: I intend to pinpoint some moments in which, in very clear ways, the hostility and the endeavor employed by the dominant discourses to tame the questioning that can arise from the use of the fictional can be seen. In that way, it may perhaps be understood why the translation of mimesis into *imitatio* is by no means an innocent one: by means of that simple gesture the classical theorist could tame the poet's discourse. That discourse was legitimized at the same time that limits were imposed upon it.

What is the practical outcome of the foregoing analysis? Foremost, to show that what we fluidly and ambiguously call "literature" betokens a discursive practice subject to a powerful interplay of pressures. Only in appearance does literature seem a harmonious, pleasant, and disinterested form. The fictional is not that which estranges itself from the world, like a kind of legalized opiate; nor is it something that can be comprehended by means of a general interpretative scheme which, specifying the bases upon which a society rests, can explain all else that takes place within it as parts of its superstructure. The idea of the control of the imaginary, conversely, demonstrates the necessity for development of specific strategies of analysis that will capture in a subtler way the kind of counterposed interests that are configured in literary fiction.

The initial work of a series in progress, *Control of the Imaginary* is far from being an exhaustive book. At the moment when I write this note, a second volume is on the eve of publication and a third is in final stages. I therefore incur the temptation of communicating to my new reader what in fact I have concluded since *Control*'s initial publication. Were I to accede to that temptation, I would merely create an area of deception by announcing problems that either have not been treated here or have been broached in an unsatisfactory manner. Every book has its own life, independent of its creator. This volume now begins its American experience, at the moment when its author has concluded his.

Acknowledgments

Many people, by sending me books, chapters, articles, and essays, have placed themselves in my debt. At the great risk of creating omissions through fault of my memory, I must mention: Antônio Cândido, Bernard Cerquiglini, Hans Ulrich Gumbrecht, Jürgen Link, Ulla Link, Karlheinz Barck, Marlene Schwartz, Roberto Reis, Roberto Ventura, Ronald Sousa, Wlad Godzich, and Wolf-Dieter Stempel.

My gratitude necessarily extends in other directions as well, to include those who, through suggestions, critiques, and discussions about preliminary versions or sections of the chapters in this book, stimulated me to develop them further or to correct them: my students in the first semester of 1982 in the graduate program in psychology at the Pontifícia Universidade Católica of Rio de Janeiro—Hans Ulrich Gumbrecht, Haroldo de Campos, and Ricardo Benzagen.

Acknowledgment of a much greater kind must be given to my wife, Rebeca Schwartz, for her patience with me in daily life as well as for her generosity in systematically proofreading and criticizing every page of the manuscript.

My thanks as well to the Alexander von Humboldt-Stiftung, the Brazilian Conselho Nacional de Pesquisas, the Pontifícia Universidade Católica of Rio de Janeiro, and the Universidade Federal Fluminense, for having supported my contacts with, and participation in, the international meetings that have been indispensable in the reflection contained in the ensuing pages.

Translator's Introduction
"Mimesis, Why Can'cha be True?"

Control of the Imaginary will, I suspect, seem to many readers—especially North American and European readers—a highly unusual work, tracing as it does a problem-ordered pattern through an unlikely set of texts from late medieval times through classical Europe to late-nineteenth- and early-twentieth-century Brazil. The last two chapters, which deal with Brazil, will raise some questions on other scores as well. For, in contrast to the very general scope of what precedes them, each deals quite narrowly, in the language of contemporary professional debate, with an ongoing problem in Brazilian cultural and literary criticism. The book's general focus on the problems involved with reason and mimesis on the one hand, in opposition (and a far from simple opposition it is) to something called "imagination" on the other, is clear enough. But why, it will undoubtedly be asked, that particular choice of materials and why the summary, hopscotch treatment to which they are submitted? What, in sum, is this volume's overall purport, its "general interest"? It is a multifaceted question and one to which I shall return more than once in this short preliminary meditation.

There are a number of answers that might be assayed in response to such questions. In the ensuing pages I shall explore what is merely one avenue of response—one which in fact corresponds to what fascinated me about *Control of the Imaginary* when I first read it in its original Portuguese version, long before it was proposed to me that I undertake its translation.

I must, however, add two notes here before beginning my meditation. The first involves the nature of my undertaking itself. The translator's introduction is a curious form of writing, for it draws upon few of the closely directive genre markers that characterize other forms of writing and thus is highly variable; translators' introductions do indeed, in the midway hawker's jargon, come in all shapes and sizes. Perhaps this is the case because the translator is to some degree seen as speaking in the voice of a second author, having undergone the complex effort of attempting to grasp the details and idiosyncrasies of the original author's discourse and having produced, as the result of that process, the new but hybrid details and idiosyncrasies of the text that is about to be read. There is, then, a sense that two discourses have met, each activating the other in manifold ways, to a single end result of shared responsibility. I here avail myself of the freedom betokened by the presumptions surrounding that activity, and I do so to take up a line of thought that crystallized for me during that very translation process and to extend it beyond the frame of the translation itself to speak of some dimensions of *Control of the Imaginary* as they have entered into dialogue with my own thinking. Moreover, that analysis comes in a presentation that—as the reader will see—is a somewhat associative one. In short, I call upon the translator's position as license for a considerable amount of informality, license, ultimately, for my reading and systematization of some of my own reactions to the text. Some of the associations that suggested themselves to me as I worked through the Portuguese original, associations that clearly—perhaps, for me at least, even frighteningly, since they move from experimental literature to pop music—betray my own diverse cultural directions, are taken up and used in what follows.

Second, the issues that I shall be raising in my own voice are decidedly not ones that my friend Luiz Costa Lima was concerned with in writing the book. Indeed, as a cursory comparison between what follows and the argument of *Control of the Imaginary* makes amply clear, he does not accept great portions of my analysis. To be sure, my remarks do not constitute an attack on the book; nor, for that matter, do they amount to a defense of it. Instead they constitute a line of thought, quite apart from the book's own goals, that goes some way toward responding to the questions I have anticipated—as well as toward treatment of the issue, left dangling in my first paragraph, of the specificity of "general-interest readership" as it relates to such a work as this one.

* * *

An exceedingly pedantic note by Morelli: . . . *"Like all creatures of choice in the Western world, the novel is content in a closed order. Resolutely opposed to this, we should search here for an opening and therefore cut the roots of all systematic construction. . . . Method: irony, ceaseless self-criticism, incongruity, imagination in the service of no one."*

Julio Cortázar, *Hopscotch*

In order to leap into the matter that I wish to explore, let me, in one summary statement, cast a net that is not only much wider than the scope of Costa Lima's book but also extremely narrow both in its focus and in the implications that I shall be drawing from it. The statement is as follows: *Control of the Imaginary*, for all its effort to trace the lineaments of the culture of Aristotelian and post-Aristotelian mimesis in the realm of literary and historiographical theory, to point out the prescriptive gestures therein involved that have endeavored to exclude other possible bases for the organization and analysis of human experience, and to involve itself in the contemporary critique of that culture of mimesis, nonetheless itself falls into that very culture in many ways.

The tradition of academic publishing does, after all, depend to a great extent on such notions as language's ability to capture thought, to reproduce argument, and to inform readings that are primarily reproductive, among other similar notions. The traditional academic book is positioned as a sort of two-way mirror that presumes to guarantee a relatively distortion-free transmission first from the writer and his or her sources to itself (there may, of course, be other, intermediate sources that represent relays in a series seemingly originating in a set of paradigms analytical of human experience) and then from itself to the reader. What is presumed, then, is the smooth double transmission of relatively stable identity. To be sure, variation is admitted, perhaps even required, in the system, but the sense of transmission of identity from source to reader is the controlling concept involved. The self-arrogated viability of the very notion of such publishing depends upon acceptance of those stabilizing notions, and if any of the steps in that transmission come to be put into doubt, the entire enterprise so structured is threatened with collapse.

Some of the traditional guarantees of that smooth, multiply reproductive transmission include the scholarly activity of consultation, transmission, and referencing of sources, a principled, at least semitechnical language register, and a relatively consistent analytical attitude within that discourse on the part of the author, to "guarantee" relative uniformity of "treatment of the subject matter"—that is, relative reconcilability, via expository practice, of the divergent analytical paradigms from the various sources being incorporated into the text. The receiver/re-activator of the language so organized is, of course, the specific "general reader" to whom I have previously alluded, one in fact so specific as to have actually been trained in the reading techniques necessary to the presumably distortion-free reception of that purportedly stabilized language.

There can be no doubt that *Control of the Imaginary* intends to participate in that traditional stabilization of the academic discourse system—as does, in even more crucial ways, its translator, since, at least in contempory usage, translation is largely a genre-and decorum-stabilized language practice. The rule of a kind of mimesis and of reason is, then, unmistakably, and multiply, inscribed in the between-covers format in which *Control of the Imaginary* participates—and is so inscribed in ways that are wholly unavoidable if one chooses to participate in the academic enterprise in that manner.

To be sure, I do not precisely follow Costa Lima in my use of "mimesis," for he uses the concept in a broad manner to deal with the poetics of literature, literary theory, and historiography within a wide chronological frame, and he endows the term with the basic contours that it has in classical literary representation theories. My relocation of the term is nonetheless consonant with his usage, both in the analytical and the cultural-organizational import accorded mimesis, but I extend those values to a different bundle of interrelated discourses and genre markers, namely, those of the traditional academic study. And I allude to the Enlightenment-project organization of culture, of which that genre is a basic part. Simply put, I understand the purported stabilization of language in texts such as this one and consequently the supposed univocity, and hence analytical power, of the terminology therein employed as vouchsafed by a series of implicit arguments. Those arguments are grounded in one area of the culture of mimesis as it is formulated within the Enlightenment project of eventual historical sublimation of reason within human culture. The claims involved in a book like *Control of the Imaginary* ultimately involve faithful reproduction-with-change of phenomena of various sorts, from historical events to cultural processes to prior analyses of them, the last of those reproductions often effected with the stereotypical—and telltale—allied visual reference "thus we see in *X*'s work that . . . ".

There is some question, however, whether the process must in fact be carried out with the uniformity that it arrogates to itself or whether there is, or at least may be, even in its own terms, some degree of slippage, of subversion, within it.

And as regards *Control of the Imaginary*, the question is one of no small interest, for the degree of mimesis's inscription in/on the volume is far from clear. The space of subversion comes most obviously in the question of authorial attitude, for rather than adopting the theoretically uniform, magisterial attitude of the traditionally prescribed writer of works like this, Costa Lima engages in a rather more complex procedure. Whereas he guarantees technical-level consistency through analytical terminology, a discourse register well within the allowable bounds of the academic tradition, and other gestures to be expected in the genre, his point of view is far from consistent; it is, in fact, quite elusive. If one attempts to read *Control of the Imaginary* with an eye to deciding where its analytical discourse locates itself, one notices a fascinating process. Read that way, the text shows itself to be built to a great extent on a series of hanging attitudes, not only among the various chapters as they move in concentration from Guillaume de Machaut to Machado de Assis, but also within individual chapters. In fact, there seem to be key critical-theoretical turning points in the text, moments in which analysis becomes intense, argument deepens, and implications for the overall project multiply. In truth, the verbal realization of those moments is somewhat clearer in the original Portuguese than in the English, for, in obedience to the genre dictates involved and in consonance with the guidance they provide, I have, perhaps inevitably, masked those moments somewhat in the translation process. They are still strongly present, however, represented by several key theoretical figures. At the places in the text where those figures are invoked, their analytical import can be said to irradiate the text, the authorial voice seemingly taking up their position as well. Indeed, it is but a minimal exaggeration to suggest that the book's expository procedure—especially in its first three chapters—involves movement from one of those figures to the next, movement, then, from one focal point to another. It is a curious series of sojourns moving from Rosemond Tuve to Friedrich Schlegel to Wolfgang Iser to Alfred Schütz to Hannah Arendt to Ian Watt, with other stops of greater or lesser moment along the way—or, rather, to be sure, sojourns in aspects of the work of such figures, aspects invoked and developed under specific discursive circumstances. Each of those stopping places, however, takes on central analytical import for some portion of *Control of the Imaginary*, only then to be moved away from in its turn.

Now all but needless to say, even seen in respect to the reduced dimensionality of their appearance in this book, figures such as those just mentioned—and several others could easily be added to the list—are hardly compatible in and of themselves. And yet their import is by no means controlled by the technical authorial voice. The—as I call it—shuffling from one figure to the next that characterizes *Control of the Imaginary* does not, then, describe the traditionally prescribed academic-authorial stance.

Indeed, a similar tension between traditions from the culture of mimesis and procedures that seem to subvert that very culture can be seen at work on a general level in the book—in a way that ultimately proves to be structurally ironic. I refer to a dual attitude toward the discourse tradition of academic publication itself—that is, toward the very mimetic stabilization of language that I have just remarked on. Costa Lima, in analyzing the prescriptive power that has over time been assigned to various discourse functions grounded in mimesis, at the same time finds it very difficult not to reproduce a version of those same prescriptions in both the analytical and the discursive dimensions of his own work. Indeed, although there are instances where such is definitely not the case (e.g., the beginning of chapter 3), *Control of the Imaginary* seems intent, overall, on embracing the traditional academic enterprise—through deliberation over analytical terms, citing of field sources, and defense of historical reconstruction.

The clearest instance where that duality is profiled—in a complexity that I think to be the key interest of the book from the viewpoint of methodology—comes in relation to Costa Lima's attitude toward history. *Control of the Imaginary* is a book imbued with the methodology of German *rezeptionsästhetik* and most specifically in the line within that movement dedicated to reconceptualizing literary history. The number of references to *Poetik und Hermeneutik* and to works by a number of the collaborators in the Konstanz project clearly bespeak that orientation. That project has, of course, done much to change the way literary study looks at critical categories and to put into question the naive historicism that it has regularly cultivated, as Costa Lima in fact points out in his brief treatment of Hans-Robert Jauss. Nevertheless, as regards the aforementioned issue of analytical discourse, *rezeptionsästhetik* itself embraces the Enlightenment historical project in the presumption that, through its radical historicizing of immanentist critical categories, it has in effect created some sort of script according to which it can on the one hand simply indicate a historical text from a given period and on the other hand then stand apart from that text, at least momentarily, at the outset of analysis, and fashion/invoke, via contextual reconstruction, analytical discourse unproblematically adequate to the text. The much-proclaimed adequacy of literary works to their own historical horizon of expectations alone, becomes, then, nonetheless both analyzable, because that horizon is itself analyzable through an ecstatically initiated analytical discourse, and also subsumable into a historical series that is made transhistorical methodologically. Despite original statements seemingly to the contrary, then, works can finally be read in what is, in functional ways, an objective mode and can, in the last analysis, be organized historically.

To be sure, *Control of the Imaginary*, in its proclaimed intent to see if a specific analytical category, mimesis, can be accorded a transtemporal critical role (that statement of purpose is to be found in the Portuguese introduction, which has not survived the translation and editing process), flies in the face of the proclaimed intent of *rezeptionsästhetik*. It in fact, however, can also be seen to act as a kind of test of *rezeptionsästhetik*, for *Control of the Imaginary* admittedly pursues transtemporal goals and yet takes up major facets of the Konstanz critical project to explore the possibility of that transtemporality. Thus each of the two positions illuminates a complementary aspect of the other. Both, however, will obviously, as a part of their procedure, have to claim exemption from any ongoing critique of the transcendent elements that they hold in common. Much as *rezeptionsästhetik* has a conflictive investment in history, *Control of the Imaginary* both questions the historical place and critical potential of mimesis and ultimately relies upon it methodologically to carry out that very historical examination.

Such academic stabilization of discourse becomes most evident where *Control of the Imaginary* conflicts with a contrary position: in this case, with the possibility that language use and reception may be much more diverse than the academic project would like, rendering historical understanding more heterogeneous and terminology less centralizing and general than an approach such as *rezeptionsästhetik* would find comfortable. That possibility manifests itself in the passages in which the language of the book meets what Costa Lima calls, generically, the theories of *écriture*, which present themselves primarily in the work of

Roland Barthes. There *Control of the Imaginary's* stance is one that virtually proclaims its own interrogation by another mode of analysis, and it rejects the threat to its own integrity—albeit as a prelude to introduction of the work of such figures as Richard Harvey Brown, Robert Nisbet, and Hayden White, additional figures in the series of sojourns the text comprises. Costa Lima would have them approach what *Control of the Imaginary* sees as the abyss of *écriture* but only through the safety of *rezeptionsästhetik* and the Enlightenment project that it articulates.

What sort of discourse does all this ultimately describe? It is one that in the final analysis accepts—indeed, trades upon—academic stabilization but in a manner not wholly controlled by the discourse traditions of that genre. At the same time it even suggests the relativity of those traditions, both in direct thematic terms and in the process of shuffling from intellectual position to intellectual position in its own exposition and in the wider reverberations of that process within the text.

Moreover, there is in fact another sort of shuffling involved as well, one that is somewhat different schematically from the thematic and discursive ones but that ultimately contributes to their operation—indeed, I think, is ultimately their basis. For the texture of chapters and sections dealing with Brazil is remarkably different from those dealing with Europe. In the former, one senses an assured control of language analytical of the subject area, grounded in understanding of the cultural peculiarities and language-production systems of a society permeated by analytical categories transferred from the European culture sphere and unable to describe itself independently as a result. *Control of the Imaginary's* Brazil is a society living, in a hypersensitive way, what amounts to a dream of European cultural history, but whose very hypersensitivity bespeaks a degree of awareness that the dream is nothing but that, a dream. In the initial chapters dealing with Europe, by contrast, one senses not so much a deference toward the several figures of key critical import there invoked—although deference there is—as an unwillingness to operate in a similar manner, a hands-off attitude, perhaps multiply motivated, that simply does not engage the issues involved in the same way as it does with Brazil. It is as though those figures—with the notable exception of Friedrich Schlegel—must have their import transferred to the pages of *Control of the Imaginary*, located but unabsorbed culturally, relevant in a distant way not subject to close scrutiny. Thus is created another sense of shuffling, a culturally based one that has the ultimate effect of freeing the script of the "European" part of the book to act as the holder of a series of relatively discrete viewpoints on experience, identifiable as such in the final analysis because they come in one way or another to traverse the more tightly and quite differently held analytical space of Brazil.

Through that set of multiple shuffling processes in the book, critical terms are relativized and cultural operations are shown to be historical and local while at the same time being used quite traditionally to produce those very revelations. It is as though two partly conflicting imperatives were at work in the same text, producing a pattern of argument and simultaneous interference with that very argument. It is an interference that, paradoxically, also serves to direct the argument forward.

*   *   *

In a snatch of lyrics from Paul Simon's well-known popular song "Kodachrome," the (male) speaking voice contemplates coming face to face with the women he had known in his younger days. He realizes that they could "never match [his] sweet imagination," because (he summarizes by going on to compare that initial comparison to color versus black-and-white photography) "everything looks worse in black and white." Like the epigraph in the first part of this introduction, Simon's lyrics thematize the notion of imagination as something other than rationalistic and imitative, although, unlike the Cortázar passage, they do not relate the issue directly to language use. They do, however, bear immediately upon that issue: via a rather overblown comparison to a compartmentalized element of male fantasy, they suggest that, however grandiose the texture of that fantasy, imagination will still be other—and somehow greater. Additional textual analysis is unnecessary—and perhaps even perilous—in this context.

What is interesting about these lyrics for present purposes and relevant for questions raised by the "shuffling" outlook in *Control of the Imaginary* derives not from the rather safe location of mimesis and imagination that it performs, but rather from its subsequent relocation of them in a rather curious way. I have briefly quoted from Simon's standard lyrics of 1973, which is the text regularly replayed today. In their 1981 reunion concert in Central Park, however, Simon teamed with Art Garfunkel to give their audience an upbeat version of "Kodachrome" paired with an equally upbeat rendition of Chuck Berry's "Maybelline" (whence the subtitle I have given these introductory remarks). In the 1981 performance, one word was changed in the lyrics: "worse" became "better." Now, to be sure, the 1981 performance was, among other things, a celebration of New York City and thus very conscious of its own occasionality—indeed, the changed word, better, was punctuated in its oral delivery to call attention to the innovation that it represented and thereby to acknowledge and participate in that occasionality: in New York, "everything looks better in black and white." There is, then, a contextual explanation for the variant reading. The fact is, however, that the line including "better" makes no expository sense whatsoever—unless the "worse" line is read through it. In effect, "everything" can look "better" only after it has already looked "worse," indeed, its looking "better" depends on its having first looked "worse."

A number of relocations occur as a result of the "better" reading, the most important of which is that the entire verbal context in which it is inserted is in effect transformed; it is now suddenly not a series of images with primarily referential value but a discursive sequence that calls attention to itself as language: the word imagination and the notion of imitation that the passage trades upon lose their referential force to become analytical terms or maneuvers to be seen as such. For the effect of the one-word change has been to cause the removal of such terms from a practice involved in one sort of repetition—an exact, mechanical one, which despite the entropic implications that it entails nonetheless maintains the primacy of reference effect—and their grafting into another context grounded in a very different mode of repetition. The "visible" grafting process, moreover, leads to other implications: ones involving radical linguistic occasionality and at least one-way interdependence of readings.

One could go on at some length speaking about the many implications the change operates, but more to the present point is one of the most obvious of those implications: language can be understood at one and the same time in relation to more than one set of conditions, and it thus reveals itself as an opaque medium rather than as the neutral bearer of history or of reality. Moreover, that multiple understanding involves a modulation of modes of repetition in which one instance of language use may depend on another because of the latter's established priority or consecration and yet at the same time subvert and/or replace that supposedly primary instance. In Simon's lyrics, the "worse" reading can give rise to a locally understandable "better" reading that may not have the traditional stability of the former but, while depending on that reading, is viable both as its subversion and as its replacement. To be sure, Simon and Garfunkel, through their vocal emphasis on the grafting, in effect attempt to limit its implications to the realm of private communication, but that does nothing to diminish the principle involved—save that it allows me here to cease concentrating on "Kodachrome" now that its illustrative force is spent.

The point to be made is that the song lyric so understood recapitulates the complex duality observable in *Control of the Imaginary*: terms both reside, in multiple ways, within the discourse organization of the traditionally conceived academic project and, because of that very stabilization, can simultaneously stand partially free of it; therefore, they both reinforce that project and, by their very separability from it, call its self-arrogated power into question. And the disjunction seems ultimately to derive from a culturally keyed outlook. It reproduces the Europe-Brazil cultural dilemma in the realm of language. Costa Lima's outlook upon European thought from within a Brazilian context—I mean these terms to describe the dynamics within *Control of the Imaginary* and nothing more—literally invokes in verbal detail a dual perspective upon that thought.

One of the issues raised by the duality that is multiply marked in the text is the issue of language itself. It bears upon Costa Lima as author, upon myself as traditional translator, and, as will shortly be apparent, upon you as specific "general reader." What Costa Lima has done in this book is to hold together a discourse that is in fact freighted with culturally based disintegrative forces. He has done so through recourse to the traditional discourse of the genre, and it has enabled him to complete his task. The disintegrative elements that show through, however, paradoxically lay claim to subversion of that discourse. Moreover, as we have already seen, the subject of the study is precisely the power, mimesis, that lies at the heart of the discourse system used for textual integration. Consequently, the very issue thematically held in question in the book is relied upon to hold the book itself together. This is especially true at the aforementioned point of confrontation between *rezeptionsästhetik* and *écriture*. There *Control of the Imaginary* must in essence protect its very integrity, divided though it may be, by rejecting Roland Barthes's appeal to the pleasure of the text—from Costa Lima's point of view, Barthes's threat to break down the mimetic normatizing that he needs at a procedural level. Thus, in the last analysis, in *Control of the Imaginary*, just as in Paul Simon's qualification of "imagination" through the grafting process, "mimesis" is doubly inflected—at one and the same time thematically and procedurally. It is that double inflection that allows the book to open mimesis up to general questioning and to do so in a way that is not a simple reversal of the dominant mode of analysis, itself grounded in mimesis. Such a reversal would run the risk of merely reinscribing the dominance of that mode. Costa Lima's is instead a position grounded in a dualism that, at some level in its process, both acknowledges that dominance and aggresses against it at the same time. Moreover, that critique is, very clearly, methodological only as it appears to us; it is instead culturally based—an ultimate indicator that diversity of cultural experience can itself inform intellectual critique in quite thoroughgoing ways.

Another implication, however, approaches this same issue from the point of view of the other key term in the book, namely, imagination. If we look at *Control of the Imaginary*'s use of "imagination," another aspect of its self-protectiveness against the possible disintegration at the hands of *écriture* comes into play, one that indicates the ultimate priority of mimesis in the maintenance of the duality, of the shuffling process, I have noted as multiply inscribed in the book. According to the logic of discourse stabilization in *Control of the Imaginary*, it follows that imagination will have to be located somewhere other than in a sense of multiple capacities within language itself, for so located it would be . . . whatever is not mimesis in language, or, then, exactly the dimension that the book both invokes and must finally proscribe to maintain the integrity that enables the duality. And so it is that, despite all the language about language that surrounds recorded usages of the word imagination and such related terms as fantasy and fancy, *Control of the Imaginary* locates these terms in effect generically: in opposition to the genres grounded in mimesis. Both such terms and mimesis are conceived as having a territoriality about themselves. Thus the terms opposed to mimesis do represent the reinscription of the dominant. Paul Simon, with his wish to keep individual usages separate from each other, is thus accepted, whereas Julio Cortázar, with his proclamation of "irony, ceaseless self-criticism, incongruity, imagination in the service of no one," is, in the final analysis, proscribed.

Thus it is that *Control of the Imaginary* sets forth its remarkable textual fabric, one that carries out a highly productive program analytical of the tradition of mimesis and that simultaneously embodies a testing of that tradition. I have myself repeated that textual fabric with variation by translating in traditional ways. The last step in the communication sequence of academic publication, the final repetition, is reception, and that leaves the question to you, the reader. Now it is a much overworked commonplace to end an introduction with the observation that "the reader will have to judge." I shall, however, do so anyway. But it is not really a superficial, optional judgment of taste that you will have to perform as you read this book. It is something much more basic; and it is wholly inevitable. You are the specific, trained "general reader" necessary for completion of the traditional transmission process. The final question is how you will play your role in reception, since *Control of the Imaginary* in effect provides you with an option. Will you read mimesis thematically or procedurally, will you, in sum, play your part traditionally, or otherwise? The latter course, to be sure, requires inclusion of the former; the former, supression of the latter.

As a guide for your consultation, I give you the words of my subtitle, which themselves vary words from Simon and Garfunkel's 1981 rendition of Berry's "Maybelline." Will you, in your reading, starting from the need to "be true," have mimesis start back "doin' the things [it] used to do"?

*   *   *

There are a very few matters of which the reader of this translation should be aware. First, the base text is *O Controle do Imaginário* (São Paulo, 1984), but that text was corrected in some twenty places for me by its author. Costa Lima also made two minor changes in the actual reading of the original; in both cases the changes involved his quotation of different passages from the same source quoted in the original, for he found the new quotes bolstered his argument more strongly. None of those minor changes are noted in the text. Editorial matters have been held to a minimum; the only such issues worthy of note are that the unspaced ellipses (...) in quoted material indicate original punctuation, spaced ellipses(. . .) indicate an editorial omission, and brackets indicate an editorial addition. For both the omissions and the additions, even though they may at times merely replicate ones that Costa Lima supplied in the Portuguese text, the translator is ultimately responsible. All translations not otherwise noted are my own.

In carrying out this project I have greatly benefited from the aid of several individuals, among them Luiz Costa Lima, Giuliana Menozzi, and Brent Peterson. I thank them for all their help and patience.

Control of the Imaginary

The poetic imagination, which has one mortal enemy in prosaic thought, has—it is today more than ever necessary to bear in mind—two others as well: historical narration and eloquence.

André Breton, *Position politique du surréalisme*

Chapter 1
Controlling the Imaginary

While readiness to recognize alternative worlds may be liberating, and suggestive of new avenues of exploration, a willingness to welcome all worlds builds none. Mere acknowledgement of the many available frames of reference provides us with no map of the motions of heavenly bodies; acceptance of the eligibility of alternative bases produces no scientific theory or philosophical system; awareness of varied ways of seeing paints no pictures. A broad mind is no substitute for hard work.

Nelson Goodman, *Ways of Worldmaking*

The Itinerary of a Problem

What should we do when, in the course of life, a problem transfixes us, envelops us, obsesses us? A healthy constitution, one making its life between irony and irritation, would say: "Make it into a good steak and enjoy." But what if, because of either ambition on the one hand or laxity on the other, such a metamorphosis is not found to be a viable course of action—and if long walks, polite conversation, or the blue of the sea prove equally unproductive? And if the obsessed person, caught up in the web, is unable to transform the internal wolf

3

4 □ CONTROLLING THE IMAGINARY

into lambs and the problem into productive projects? Then that person simply has to live with it, like the patient with his bile, the gambler with his mania, or the dwarf with his stigma.

Some years ago a problem began to perplex me: even though the Italian *Cinquecento* had generated an extensive body of theorization on the poetic—one comparable in extent only to that produced in our own century—the more I read in its authors the more I became convinced that their common point of departure in fact amounted to a scandalous prohibition: a prohibition of fiction itself. But, as the rediscoverers of Aristotelian *Poetics*, the very thinkers who gave it to society and sought either to reconcile it with the Horatian and Platonic legacies or to combat those legacies in its name, how could they begin from that paradoxical position? The very question seemed nothing short of absurd. Unsure about how to get out of the circle thus created, I tried instead to acclimate myself. After all, one absurdity more or less brings no house down. Despite that approach, the circle's gravitation did not abate. After I had thus earned residency rights, the question, as though laughing at me, produced another: with what interests did this supposed prohibition correlate? Why should it have been promulgated precisely by those who dedicated themselves to the poetic and who therefore should have prized it most fully?

Although the question was still enigmatic for me, I began to see that it could at least be treated plausibly as the result of a line of thought opened up by my friend Hans Ulrich Gumbrecht in a course that he taught in Rio de Janeiro in August 1982. In one of his last sessions, Gumbrecht proffered a line of argument that analyzed the crisis that shook the late Middle Ages as the result of a relative lack of flexibility in the mental structure then predominant. That lack of flexibility, he argued, derived from two sources, namely, that the Christian cosmology of the time offered a single interpretation for every experience, and that it did not contain a temporal structure, and thus rendering itself incapable of dealing with change.

In support of the first point, we might do well to recall Huizinga's classical analysis: "So violent and motley was life that it bore the mixed smell of blood and of roses. The men of that time always oscillate between the fear of hell and the most naive joy, between cruelty and tenderness, between harsh asceticism and insane attachment to the delights of the world, between hatred and goodness, always running to extremes."[1]

In support of the second point, I would have recourse to Gumbrecht and his analysis of the Renaissance constitution of historical time as cyclical.

Given this atmosphere of crisis, the fourteenth and fifteenth centuries especially experienced the need to create mediating strategies. Among those that Gumbrecht examined in 1982, the one that will be key for the following discussion is the development of the experiencing of subjectivity. To the extent that the notion that truth had been inscribed by the Divinity in the things of this world and therefore revealed itself in unequivocal signs was being abandoned, phenomena were increasingly allowed multiple meanings; and it was the subject who was made responsible for apprehending the correct one. Subjectivity acquired what amounted to a supplementary function: because the traditional cosmic order, formulated theologically and grounded in the faith, was being found insufficient, the individual subject was charged with the discovery of a guiding logic.

I am well aware that the mode of exposition that I have adopted—one in which I endeavor to recall the moment when I began to comprehend a possible line of investigation for the problem that had so perplexed me—cannot itself communicate to the reader a sense of the articulation between the rediscovery of subjectivity and my hypothetical prohibition of fiction. Even so, I have chosen this development in homage to the colleague who opened the way for me, and I hope that, by the time I reach its conclusion, this chapter will have demonstrated that articulation.

Not being a medievalist myself, I did not control materials necessary for the development of the propositions that Gumbrecht had formulated. I held them in a kind of area of intuition that had to be developed by subsequent reading. What follows is a synthesis of the results of that undertaking. I began by trying to understand more fully the aforementioned appearance of subjectivity in the late Middle Ages, to analyze it in relation to poetic praxis, and to ascertain its accommodation within sociocultural circumstances, all to bring it more nearly completely into the ambit of my problem.

* * *

In his excellent study *Medieval French Literature and Law*, the American medievalist Howard Bloch observes that the recognition of subjectivity begins in the twelfth century and manifests itself over a large spectrum of areas of activity: "the writings of monastic reformers; the revival of Classical studies; renewed interest in letter writing and autobiography; the personalization of portraiture and sculpture; altered notions of intention, sin, and penance; the popularity of personal (mystical) religious experience; the appearance of the singular heroes of late epic and satirical forms; . . . the valorization of the individual within the courtly novel and lyric."[2]

Within that huge list, Bloch concentrates on changes in the judicial process, which he considers paradigmatic of the many other changes then taking place. In concert with the cosmology of the era, law in the early Middle Ages did not take the motivation of the offender into account because "under a system of immanent ordeal it is God, and not man, who alone is capable of assessing intent" (Bloch, 32). Therefore innocence or guilt would become apparent "only through the secondary effects, recompense or penalty, which they engender" (19). The truth or arbitrariness of an accusation would be proved, physically, by victory or defeat experienced by the accused or his or her representative in combat. God made the truth of what had happened manifest through visible and unequivocal signs, expressed in the outcome of the duel.

That mode of judicial resolution began to decay in the twelfth century and "significantly, the use of criminal expertise becomes increasingly frequent in the trial records of the late thirteenth and fourteenth centuries" (132). It was a change directly related to the contending political interests of the time:

> Judgment according to the notion of judicial truth depends upon the formulation of stable criteria independent of the act of judgment itself—and thus the existence of a state which, in contrast to feudal polity, could define itself through its laws as something more than a collection of separate subjective rights. Finally, judgment according a verbal rather than physical ordeal implies at least a modicum of civil organization, a state capable of enforcing its decisions without necessary recourse to arms. In general, the advent of inquest furthered the cause of political centralization, which emphasizes, once again, the impossibility of separating the evolution of judicial models from the historical struggle between monarchy and feudal aristocracy. (140-41)

The passage is reproduced at length because it demonstrates the connection between changes in judicial procedure on the one hand and the struggle between state centralization and feudal aristocracy on the other, the connection between the rise both of the individual and of the emphasis upon his or her subjectivity and an opposing resistance on the part of feudal-noble interests. Bloch can therefore argue that the medieval French epic, far from expressing the interests of the warlord aristocracy, is in fact the symptom of the crisis that it faced. It is a symptom that grew in dimension and took new directions with the "literary" forms that arose at that time or in the immediately subsequent period: "While in romance the rupture between individual and community is presented in terms of separation and reintegration and in the lyric it takes the form of a cyclical oscillation between unfulfilled expectations and short-lived satisfactions, the key concern within the explicitly bourgeois genres has to do with extracting the maximum of profit from the liberties that this peculiarly modern schism affords" (227).

In summary, Bloch stresses that, on the one hand, the emphasis placed on the individual subject pervades the "literary" and judicial manifestations of the era, and, on the other hand, it is related to interest in state centralization on the part of the royalty and the incipient bourgeoisie, in opposition to the principles and values of the feudal aristocracy, which functioned on the basis of group separateness articulated by blood kinship, preservation of tradition, and the concept of a divine justice made manifest through clear external signs—the defeat of the guilty party and the victory of the honest in combat, the last scene in the judicial process of medieval times.

Bloch's conclusions find support in Jacques Le Goff's monumental study on the establishment of the concept of purgatory. In his *La Naissance du purgatoire* [The Birth of Purgatory] he points out that, despite the "discovery's" preparation by Augustine, Pope Gregory, and Bernard de Clairvaux, purgatory, used as a noun designating a location, did not exist prior to 1170: "It was at the crossroads of the two milieus [Paris and Cîteaux], between 1170 and 1200, possibly in the decade from 1170 to 1180, surely by the last ten years of the century, when Purgatory appeared."[3]

The movement in support of individualistic justice that pervaded the century brought with it emphasis on the ecclesiastical law court and intervention in judicial matters by kings and local princes to the detriment of the feudal lords, who continued to rely on the old belief in the immanence of divine justice: "In opposition to the feudal lords, who monopolized both justice as law, instrument of domination over the members of their seigniories, and also justice as source of income, the kings and local princes laid claim to the ideal and reality of justice, and the ecclesiastics strengthened their influence over the collective aspirations of society by elaborating the Christian concept of justice" (Le Goff, 286).

It is most important here to emphasize the increasingly central role being played by the individual, a role already pointed to in the prior elaborations of the concept of sin, with their differentiation between guilt and penalty and their requirement of verbal confession:

> Purgatory depends on a less solemn verdict [than one between Salvation and the eternal fires of Hell], on an individualized judgement made at the time of death. . . . The length of condemnation depends, then, beyond Divine mercy as symbolized in the Angels' efforts to snatch souls away from the Demons, on personal merits acquired by the deceased during life and on commendations from the Church instigated by friends and relatives of the deceased. (285)

Thus celestial geography was enriched by the addition of a new place, a place of passage, the time spent in which depended on a detailed examination of each case and on the *intervention of personalized prayer*. In this sense, in contrast to heaven and hell, the right to purgatory implied a mitigation of the concept of a truth inscribed in things; it was supplemented, and thus made more flexible, by an "analysis" of the deceased sinner's intentions and by the ecclesiastically mediated intervention of his or her friends. The individual had begun to be heard in the celestial sphere.

Whereas the foregoing analyses demonstrate the increasing ascendancy of the individual on a general level, those that follow operate similarly on a more specific one.

Focusing on the presence of the "I" in medieval poetry, Paul Zumthor defines two basic situations. The first, and more common, involves an "I" that is essentially without referent, that is, an "I" whose entire value is exhausted in holding together the components of the poem itself. Within a "literature" of fixed roles corresponding to secular topoi and an impersonal tradition, the lexical "I" does not correspond to the "I" of the writer:

> The author's "person" appears for the purpose of confirming the text's objectivity, nothing more. His interventions represent before our eyes the textual projection of a situation. Normally transmitted orally, by a singer, recitant, or public reader, the medieval poetic work already possesses a concrete enunciator who is visually tangible—while it itself is not—but who in principle can change from performance to performance. If the author, who might be one of the many recitants, has made a specific poetic "I" the subject of the enunciation, that "I" functions as a virtual form the actualization of which varies according to the circumstances: it is highly unlikely that the medieval audience would have interpreted it in an autobiographical sense.[4]

Personal experience was not incorporated into textual experience during this time, but rather, it crossed it and was transcended by it, as though the former had no existential content of interest to the latter. The "I" was a vicarious, fluctuating form merely denoting the voice that pronounced it. It is in this sense that Zumthor declares this is "an almost totally objectivized poetry." Through a purely textual analysis that does not undertake to determine the social causation of the transformation, Zumthor shows how that general situation underwent changes during the fifteenth century:

> In the poetic forms that derived from it [i.e., the tradition of the courtly song] in the fifteenth century, we witness the invasion of a discourse of circumstance. The sign "I" comes to refer, in a wide, categorical manner, to the external subject that circumstance indicates; nothing further stands in the way of its identification with the person of the author. To be sure, moreover, that identification was often realized: in Eustache Deschamps, Christine de Pisan, Charles d'Orleans. The discourse is seldom narrative, however; it rather proceeds through descriptive allusions: it becomes conflated with the discourse of the *dits*, in the same ambiguity. (Zumthor, 179)

The tack taken by Zumthor, the identification of an "I" saturated with personality, is expanded on by Jacqueline Cerquiglini. In an essay dedicated solely to the genre of the *dit* in the work of Guillaume de Machaut (circa 1300-1377), Cerquiglini locates motivation for the presence of the extratextually referential "I" in the problematization of truth. In other words, the autobiographical "I" comes to the aid of a frame of reference that is no longer sufficient to assign meaning to specific acts:

> What is measured in Machaut's title, *Voir Dit*, is the path taken by that term since the beginning of the thirteenth century. The title in effect carries with it two premises. First and foremost, Machaut, in emphatically proclaiming the truth of his *dit*, leads us to the conclusion that the connection between the *dit* and truth is no longer an automatic one in his time. Second, in using a title . . . that eliminates allegory, Machaud makes it clear that for him—and here we see his great innovation—truth can no longer be guaranteed by recourse to an allegory but rather that it must be vouchsafed through appeal to lived experience. The *dit* is true only because *I* say that it is.[5]

Now whereas the medieval crisis in mental structures was by no means limited to the fourteenth and fifteenth centuries, the flexibilizing strategies then introduced, all of which revolved around the issue of subjectivity, were favored by the subsequent development and expansion of the printing press. As is attested in the work of one of the great specialists in the field—work wholly independent of the analyses heretofore reviewed—typographical reproduction in effect led to a break with the esoteric atmosphere bound up with culture based on the manuscript, no matter whether we see that culture in relation to the material or to the social conditions of its existence: "Advanced techniques could not be passed on without being guarded against contamination and hedged in by secrecy. To be preserved intact, techniques had to be entrusted to a select group of initiates who were instructed not only in special skills but also in the 'mysteries' associated with them."[6]

Culture gradually lost its initiatory character, and, at the same time, the strategies of flexibility that had been introduced were expanding and carrying the day in the late medieval world. While not specifically referring to the problem that occupies us here, Eisenstein nonetheless corroborates our approach to it by insisting on the influence that the printing press exerted on daily life, on the educational process, and on the options left to religion:

> Private life as well as public affairs underwent transformation; indeed the new medium encouraged a sharper division between these two zones. An unending stream of moralizing literature penetrated the privacy of the home and helped to precipitate a variety of domestic dramas. The "family" was not only endowed with new educational and religious functions . . . but the family circle also became the target of a complicated literary cross-fire. (Eisenstein, 133)
> Loss of confidence in God's words among cosmopolitan elites was coupled with enhanced opportunities for evangelists and priests to spread glad tidings and rekindle faith. (701)

Moreover, if we concentrate on the question per se, it should be noted that a corroboration of the thesis advanced by Zumthor and Cerquiglini is to be found in an earlier text by Menéndez Pidal, in which he demonstrated both the appearance of the empirical "I" in Castilian prose of the fourteenth century and the importance of fixing that "I" through the writing process. Contrasting the Arcipreste de Hita with don Juan Manuel (1282-1349), Pidal interprets the former as the prototype of the "sense of impersonality" that "dominated the jongleur"[7] and concludes that the latter, by naming himself directly and explicitly, confides to writing the wish that the transmission of his works remain forever accurate:

> And I don Juan, because I fear—I think quite rightly—that the books that I have written are not going to be copied over very frequently and because I have seen what often happens in the process of copying—namely that, either through the scribe's contrary opinions or the letters' resembling each other, a given thought comes to be replaced by another . . . to guard against this to the extent that I can, I have had this volume prepared, in which are inscribed all the books that I have heretofore written. (Quoted in Pidal, 247)

Reference to the individual "I" and need of a specific mode of fixation, namely, written form, thus appear in concert. What Cerquiglini would later say of Machaut, that "the *dit*, which prizes discontinuity, is inconceivable save through the mediation of writing" (Cerquiglini, 159), was, then, valid for the Castilian writer as well.

Written form provided the basis for establishment of a new set of values. It was not stressed simply because, as Pidal argued, don Juan Manuel was a learned writer whereas Juan Ruiz participated in the oral and popular tradition of the jongleurs. The opposition between learned and popular was not the basis of the question, for it was in fact merely a part of a larger conjuncture: while a link with music, with the memory, and with orality dominated in the poetry of the twelfth and thirteenth centuries, in the fourteenth and fifteenth centuries that "poetry founded upon song" gave way to one founded "on sentiment, on the I" as a sort of surrendering of the memory in order to constitute itself as a "chest or strongbox" given over to the written form.[8]

$$* \quad * \quad *$$

The analyses that I have outlined helped to germinate the seed that Hans Ulrich Gumbrecht had sown. They formed a decently coherent bundle, whose practical application I originally intended to assay in work on Fernão Lopes. Indeed, my first notion was to try to work out the general problem that I had with the Italian preceptors by examination of the work of the great Portuguese historiographer. I had to abandon the plan, however, for it would have led to a study unpublishable because of its great length. I shall therefore make extremely spare use of

Fernão Lopes, choosing for examination only those passages of his work that are absolutely indispensable to examination of the question at hand. The first of those passages involves the debate over the validity or lack thereof of the marriage between King Pedro and Inês de Castro and the arguments advanced by each side. Whereas chapters 27 and 28 of the *Crónica de D. Pedro* [Chronicle of King Pedro] deal with the king's deposition concerning his secret marriage and those who had witnessed it, chapter 29 focuses on the misunderstanding produced among those who had listened to him. Lopes, after dividing the people who disagreed into groups of those "of plain and simple understanding" and those "subtler," seems to hint at his own position:

When the disputation that you have just heard was done, there being present both learned persons and many of the general populace, those who were of plain and simple understanding and who therefore did not distinguish well the structure of such things gave facile acceptance, believing that all that they had heard was pure truth. Others, of subtler understandings, learned and quite wise, looked into all the aspects of that very delicate matter trying to see whether or not what they had heard could be true, and they decided to the contrary, since it seemed entirely illogical.[9]

Our suspicions about where the historiographer's judgment lies become stronger when we read: "Therefore, those who had exchanged these and other opinions amongst themselves in secret said that the truth, *which does not seek out beautiful words*, lay deeply concealed in those matters" (Lopes, 219; emphasis mine).

Indeed, were it not the case that it appears as the direct discourse of those who reject the argument for the validity of the marriage, this would be the author's own conclusion. Fernão Lopes in effect steps down from the position of omniscient narrator, limits his role to that of faithful chronicler of events, and assigns to the subjectivity of the individual reader the task of reaching a justifiable conclusion: "We, not in order to determine whether their conclusions were correct but rather only to note briefly what prior writers recorded, have put here a part of their deliberations, *leaving up to him who reads this which point of view he chooses to accept*" (219; emphasis mine).

The writer no longer feels himself in possession of the divine mandate, cornerstone of the cosmic and terrestrial order, that would establish univocal proofs of truth. What, however, does it mean to say that he leaves it up to the subjectivity of the hearer or reader to decide in situations of controversy or doubt? Doubtless that he assigns to that reader or hearer the role of supplementing the sense of things, which otherwise would not be revealed at all. The subjectivities, however, are not arranged uniformly on a single plane. Lopes, who may be considered the first European historian, clearly designated *his own place*, whether through primarily insinuating his own interpretation or deferring it in favor of a neutral transcription of his sources—"what prior writers recorded." Those two justificatory strategies, it must be added, are hierarchically ordered: the first has recourse to common judgment, allying itself with the analytical practice of those who form judgments according to the subtlest, or most discriminating, aspects of their understanding. *Over against* that backdrop, the historian's *own position* is constructed, a position defined as the one in which truth is to be declared. That implicit hierarchy is cemented in a phrase in the previous passage: "the truth, which does not seek out beautiful words." The user of beautiful words places himself or herself outside the realm of common judgment and thus constitutes the diametrical opposite of the historian. Represented in the practice of the poets in the early *cancioneiros* [songbooks], he would utilize his subjectivity for enthrallment and deception, whereas the historian would seek to neutralize his or her subjectivity to emerge as the controller of truth. To be sure, as Zumthor's analysis makes clear, I cannot say that the users of beautiful words employed their subjectivity to create deception. The historiographer's opinion on this score is anachronistic. Living within a different intellectual framework, he or she judged the poets according to a set of values that simply was not their own, which consisted of a tradition of anonymous themes and motifs. The historiographer's conclusion does not become less important as a result, however, for it exemplifies the suspicion and latent hostility that had come to weigh on poets. In the Portugal of the first half of the fifteenth century, therefore, subjectivity has ceased to play the part of mere supplement to meaning; instead it displays a hierarchically ordered range of possible attitudes. It can be used as a disservice to truth—sacrificing it to beautiful words—it can give rise to a clash in judgment, or, in a culminating attitude, it can be subordinated to truth. The last is an instance the conditions for which are met only when subjectivity is directed toward *reason* as put into operation by those who know how to examine and order "what prior writers recorded."

A passage from the *Crónica de D. Fernando* [Chronicle of King Fernando] shows how, to achieve his centrality, the historian had to be prepared to guard his position against both the creators of "fabulous and poetic fictions" (Augustine) and the installers of "empty opinion," such as one Martim Afonso de Melo, whom Lopes cites:

> There has been great damage created by some writers who have taken it
> upon themselves to write history having the kind of concept of history
> that they have had, for matters absolutely essential they have left with
> no mention whatsoever and to others they give only brief treatment,
> leaving them clouded in great confusion. If they were to write
> accurately and concisely, they would be praiseworthy, but as they omit
> much and remain so far from the truth, it would be better if they said
> none of the things that they do, especially since because of their words

some people are ill judged, which is an outcome much to be avoided in such an undertaking.[10]

Reason, then, during the era we are studying, constitutes itself in opposition to opinion and to beauty. Subjectivity admits of all three paths. But, if one chose to speak the truth, the correct option was foreordained. The crisis in Christian cosmology leads to a new centering, one less on humankind than on a specific area of human activity—the privileged area of reason.

That outcome is corroborated in a passage from the historiographer's most elaborate chronicle, dedicated to King John. The very outset of the prologue sets forth a univocal praise of the historian's activity: "Thus Generation, into which, in age-old process, mankind has been created, engenders so close a conformity between itself and human understanding that when we have to decide about something within it, be it praise or blame, we never recount that thing directly. This is because when it is praise we always exaggerate it and when it is the other we do not write of failings in the subtle forms in which they often occur."[11]

The passage is so explicit that a detailed commentary would be redundant. The profiled subjectivity belongs to others, to those who recount the facts in ways that they prefer or according to the customs of the time in which they live. Both practices are contrary to "human understanding." In the service of that understanding—of "reason"—the historian must comprehend those practices to avoid them just as the faithful must know the deceptions of the world to resist them. (The ambiguity proffered by the Arcipreste de Hita, according to which "good love" is reached through knowledge of the deceptions of "crazy love," is thus given up.) Curiously—or strangely—enough, the historian denies his own historicity to present himself as the transparent servant of truth. To consolidate his place in the hierarchy of knowledge, the historian denies the influence of his place in the world; he detemporalizes reason to present himself as dominated by it.

Later in the same prologue, Lopes reiterates the historian's opposition to those who "seek beauty and novelty of words" (3). The tripartite hierarchy apprehended in the two prior chronicles is here construed through focus on a fundamental opposition between those who seek beauty and those who listen only to the voice of reason: "And believe that I do not present something as true unless it is attested to by many and as well in writings of doubtless accuracy. I would prefer to remain silent rather than write falsehoods" (3).

It is clear, however, that the emphasis on the fundamental opposition does not annul the tripartite setup. Reason is located center stage. Opinion has no stable location and can either approach center stage as a function of the ingenuity of its user or be completely banished to the realm of the seekers of beauty. The realm of *doxa* is, then, Christianized as a purgatory. But its eventual entry into the celestial realm of the historian is far from a simple matter. Even though subtlety of understanding may direct the subject of *doxa* to center stage, the voice of reason and that of opinion are not to be confused, for the conformity engendered "in age-old process [in which] mankind has been created" renders the common human, even if astute, different from, and subordinate to, the agent of the "naked truth." The purgatory caused by "empty opinions" is overcome only in the historian's removal of himself from the world—that is, by his capacity to resist and overcome subjectivity. Thus my analysis of Fernão Lopes, slight though it may be, enables fuller understanding of the disruption created by the rediscovery of subjectivity documented in the literature of the fourteenth century. In the Middle Ages, poetic discourse was legitimated by a Christianized "Platonic holdover," which, in turn, carried with it the moral requirement of verisimilitude: "The rediscovery of poetic fiction in the Middle Ages proceeded, then, along two paths—the one, of ontology, the other of a fictionalization of the sensorially-experienced world; the former could be justified as a 'Platonic holdover,' the latter as the moral requirement of verisimilitude."[12]

Now, that legitimation would clearly be damaged by the introduction of a referential "I" because personalization would involve a variable totally incongruent with the two legitimizing criteria. Hence the opposition set up by Fernão Lopes, who, conceiving of objectivity on the basis of a subjective focus, saw three elements thereby produced: one involving beauty and song, another subordinated to the interests and customs of the agent, and reason. The last presumes an inquiry like judicial ones, with an enlisting and examination of the facts, analysis of the pros and cons with regard to a certain position, and the ultimate *unearthing* of the truth. The outcome which, as a historian, Fernão Lopes arrived at was, then, predictable from the moment he took up a concept of truth that involved evaluation of subjectivity, for "truth is relativized; and if the 'I' is deceitful, then truth becomes completely uncertain" (Cerquiglini, "Le Clerc et l'écriture," 167).

Reason, then, takes itself as the emblem of the truth that *inheres* in the facts as they are found recorded in written documents. And it is a truth that, conversely, is compromised by those who use their subjectivity to cultivate either opinion or beauty. History begins to be constituted, in an age significantly prior to the one that will be considered in chapter 2, as the discourse of reason *and* as a discourse disdainful of fictionality. Rhetoric will now be relegated to the domain of the latter: belles-lettres are ignorant of the path to center stage. How, then, could the fictional be accorded esteem, belles-lettres be defended, a poetology be created without either the denial of reason or the creation of a compact with it? The first of those possible options would not even be entertained by the poetologists of the immediately following centuries; their effort would in fact be directed at finding a route toward a compact. To that end, as we shall see, the contribution made by rhetoric would be decisive. It is noteworthy, however, that history opposed the middle discourse, founded on *doxai* (opinions). How, then, could the sin—admittedly, a minor one—on the part of these people destined for purgatory be avoided? Because the vice was characteristic of the common people, the historian's solution was to see himself as part of an elite. And there again rhetoric would give service, albeit in the process retarding acceptance of the practice of historiography as a science. A member of the elite would be one who could speak and write well. This criterion of judgment, outweighing the more "modern" criteria of Fernão Lopes, would make the "heaven" of discourse more open—and not dedicated solely to the sainthood of the historian. Even the poet would be saved, and the common people, so long as they wrote subtly, would be spared the pains of purgatory. It was necessary only that they should control their will to beauty.

If the historian thus postponed the recognition of his centrality, what would the poet have to lose to win salvation? Before I undertake an answer to the question, it must be recognized that one thing is certain: the salvation of a discourse would depend on the recognition that the subject being submitted to judgment is part of the higher estate of society.

The Compact with Reason

The thesis that begins to take shape—that classical theorization of the poetic had to start from the prohibition of the fictional—does not, however, appear to find corroboration in the work of the specialists on the era. The use I shall make of them will seem, then, a betrayal of sorts. My hypothesis will therefore have to find its support on the margins of their argumentation.

In the detailed description of the poetics written between 1250 and 1500, compiled by Concetta Carestia Greenfield, what is of present interest is her first point of articulation: the conflict between scholastic and humanistic poetics. Under attack by the clerics, especially the Dominicans, poetry had to secure its right to exist within Christendom. Therefore, a certain L. Ottimo, a fourteenth-century Dante commentator, denies that the value of poetry resides in its literality: "If the author believed in the literal level, there is no doubt that it would be heresy. . . but he poetizes. . . and painters and poets have such freedom."[13]

Therefore, too, in a line beginning with Dante and running through Mussato and Boccaccio, grounded in a misinterpretation of Aristotle's *Metaphysics*, poetry is defended as similar to theology, as an alternative means of access to the divine. But that tactic, although it did argue for one area of activity, could not but exasperate professional theologians. It is true, however, that the poet-theologian was legitimated as the annunciator of Christianity, in a posture always open to compromise. Greenfield summarizes:

> While the poets in ancient times knew that there was one God, they
> could not reveal these truths in plain words. They were speaking
> allegorically when they called Tethys and Ocean a god and a goddess

respectively. They communicated to the people hidden mysteries that could not be revealed to them but through poetical figures. They devised, then, fables and myths to explain truths about divine mysteries and primal causes that people were not prepared to understand. Thus, the poet-theologians invented allegories because the words of the mysteries attract good souls, while poetry, by filling them with wonder, makes the reader more attentive, since he understands things that are beyond the words. Figurative language allowed the presentation of mystical truths under the guise of pleasant fables. (Greenfield, 82)

Even this, however, would have seemed insufficient to those who defended a strict Christian order, for, as Greenfield also makes clear in specific regard to the polemic between Sautati and Domenici, the conflict did not have a merely intellectual dimension, it also included the practice of establishment of a pedagogical program to be developed: "Both, then, were concerned not only with literary issues, but with the civic and educational implications of these issues. It was not only a matter of proving the validity of poetry or even of the liberal arts; *what was at stake was the place of poetry within the curriculum of secondary schools"* (148; emphasis mine).

On the one hand, then, the humanist sought a reconciliation through conception of poetry as theology, whereas, on the other hand, an orthodox scholar like Domenici admitted the poetic only as an element in education (see Greenfield, 155).

The irreconcilability of the two positions is further demonstrated by the long polemic between the Ciceronians and the Augustinians, minutely analyzed by Marc Fumaroli. While the former, represented by Pietro Bembo (1470-1547), related the study of the classics to development of a personal style, which had as its corollary individualized knowledge — a position that would, then, lend autonomy to the search for a poetic language — the latter subordinated such study to its utility in service of the faith. The debate, very much as was the case with the one involving the Scholastics and the Humanists, did not so much question Christianity as it did the possibility, or lack thereof, of serving it in two different manners — as writer or as propagator of the faith — rather than through the direct religious path alone. Precisely because of this common ground, both the Humanists and the Ciceronians always ran the risk of being brought up short by accusations of heresy in their defense of the option that they followed, and consequently the risk of being condemned to the flames that had devoured Giordano Bruno and, in France, Etienne Dolet. Whether it was because of that pressure or because their focus of identity was the ancient world and not the cities and countries of their own time, it is noteworthy that both Bembo and his predecessor Petrarca made an effort to reconcile the principle of *imitatio*, cultivated in this regard from the first Humanists on, with expression of individuality. Hence Fumaroli's analysis in commenting on a passage from Bembo:

The theory of an innate idea that each person would have only to rediscover within himself and put into practice in the eclectic imitation of various models eliminates any notion of artistic perfection and, therefore, of a hierarchy between great artists and mediocre ones. Now imitation, which is itself a desire for perfection, establishes the distinction between those who are true artists and those who are not. If there is no longer an objective norm of beauty to refer to, mediocrity will know no bounds.[14]

It should be noted in Fumaroli's exegesis that, without the establishment of the model in which the power of *imitatio* is deposited, the "I" would become a *wild, uncontrollable* entity incapable of respecting any ordering principles, unable to determine whether its own legitimate place should come written in noble characters or lowly ones. Whereas the orthodox argument represented by the Scholastics and Augustinians solves the problem in one quick stroke—that writers gain value through the service that they perform to propagation of the faith—the Humanistic counterargument seeks to save an individuality that construes itself around a doubled center—one comprising both the Christian and the classical. We thus reach a key conclusion: the veto exercised against fiction is not directed categorically against subjectivity (indeed, as we shall see in chapter 2, *the pure expression of subjectivity can itself act as a veto of fictionality*). To the contrary, there exists a possible legitimation for the subjectivity to the extent that it presents itself according to a model acceptable to all, *doctores* and commons, Humanists and representatives of ecclesiastical thought alike. How was that form of presentation to be achieved? A point of general agreement immediately appears in the foregoing: both camps' positions consider nobility of language, *elegantia sermonis*, to be an indispensable condition for the literary work that they envision. Consequently, as Fumaroli polemically—and correctly—concludes, our concept of literature does not extend back to that period that lasted through the seventeenth century:

The status of what we call "literature" is, in the seventeenth century, greater than it will ever be again, for, under the far-reaching notion of Eloquence, it becomes the area of endeavor of all the "spokesmen" of the realm: aristocrats and men of law, ecclesiastics and magistrates, the "learned" and the "ignorant," and not only of specialists in "writing." But it is at the same time more lowly than we would like to allow, since, to the extent that "authors" wrote for the entertainment of an "ignorant" and "secular" public, they seemed like "sophists" among orators, working as they did in a sphere of activity that was useless to salvation, added little to knowledge, and offered nothing whatsoever to power save ornamentation. . . . *This "suspicion" is inherent to the very nature of Christian Humanist culture, to the very definition of* Eloquentia, *which is held in such high esteem only as an*

organ of Sapientia, *wisdom and knowledge, science and virtue,
responsibility and its exercise.* (Fumaroli, 23; emphasis mine)

The trumpeted polish of *elegantia sermonis* implied a divorce from the status
of fiction, the effective possibility of reconciling service to the faith with rever-
ence of classical models, and the necessity of bringing together individual expression and "objective parameters" — that is, those derived from the classics. Those
three principles are in fact closely interrelated, departing as they do from a
common pressure. As regards the first, it must be observed that while early
Humanism sought an autonomous place for poetry, therefore casting it as the
sister of theology, the "hard" Humanism of the sixteenth century, as we shall
see, abandoned that tactic and grounded its argumentation in the admission that
poetic discourse did not qualify as an expression of truth. As regards the second
principle and its impact on eloquence, let us reread the time-honored observation of Petrarca himself:

> Thus just as the true emanates only from the truth, so it is that only
> from eloquence can ornate and artful speech be learned; that poets and
> orators should have recourse to such eloquence not even Jerome denies,
> nor is any confirming proof necessary. . . . No, neither love of virtue
> nor thought of coming death should keep us from the study of letters,
> which, if it is carried out with good intentions, awakens the love of
> virtue and diminishes or destroys the fear of death.[15]

I will spend some time discussing the third principle. One of the greatest contemporary specialists on the Renaissance, Paul Oskar Kristeller, has called our
attention to the fact that the preeminence of rhetoric implied the creation of elegant phrases and of a "professional" language — that is, one from which the subjective conviction of the truth, or lack thereof, of what was being said was wholly
absent:

> They believed in the ancient rhetorical doctrine that a professional
> speaker and writer must acquire and show skill in making any idea that
> is related to his chosen topic plausible to his public. Consequently, a
> given idea is often expressed in phrases that aim at elegance rather than
> at precision, and many times, especially in a dialogue or in a speech,
> opinions may be defended with vigor and eloquence that are appropriate
> for the occasion, but do not express the author's final or considered
> view.[16]

But does this affirmation not conflict with the thesis, regularly advanced since
Burkhardt, which sees in the Renaissance the first full expression of individuality and therefore of subjectivity? Very aware of that question, Kristeller observes
that the forms through which subjectivity evinced itself during that time seem to
clash with the classicism and formalism also then evident: "In a curious way,

this individualism is blended in both art and literature with a strong classicism and formalism that might seem to be incompatible with it, but actually contributes to it a special color and physiognomy'' (Kristeller, 65).

The last part of the reproduced passage omits explanation for the clash that it pinpoints. It seems to me, in fact, that we can formulate that explanation only if we start from the notion that *imitatio* was the instrument for the reconciliation of the conflicting directions represented by the Ciceronians and the Augustinians. Moreover, that reconciliation was successful only if *imitatio* permitted the *control* of the individual subjectivity and if one of its possible discourses, the fictional, were controlled aprioristically as well, through its subjugation to legitimated models. Only thus could classicism and formalism be rendered compatible with expression of individuality.

The viability of that explanation is reinforced if we juxtapose it to interpretations advanced by two more renowned specialists. In his deservedly famous *Renaissance and Renascences*, Erwin Panofsky distinguishes the Carolingian Renaissance and the period of proto-Humanism from the Renaissance proper through the fact that in the first two the Medieval mentality created a *disjunction* within the classical legacy in which the pagan dimension was either suppressed or given the vestments of Christianized allegory, whereas Renaissance Humanism saw the classical world as so distant from its own that to seek inspiration in it should not constitute evidence of paganism and heresy:

We need only to look at Michelangelo's *Bacchus* and *Leda*, Raphael's Farnesina frescoes, Giorgione's *Venus*, Correggio's *Danae*, or Titian's mythological pictures to become aware of the fact that in the Italian High Renaissance the visual language of classical art had regained the status of an idiom in which new poems could be written—just as, conversely, the emotional content of classical mythology, legend and history could come to life in the dramas (non-existent as such throughout the Middle Ages), epics and, finally, operas devoted to such subjects as Orpheus and Eurydice, Cephalus and Procris, Venus and Adonis, Lucrece and Tarquin, Caesar and Brutus, Antony and Cleopatra.[17]

The examples that Panofsky cites, however, result from sporadic periods of liberalization, periods to be seen in counterposition to the more nearly constant zeal of the ecclesiastics.

The problem recurs in the work of the English scholar Walter Ullmann. As he demonstrates with elegance and precision, the rediscovery of subjectivity in the twelfth century was linked to the movement of secularization by means of which the century cast itself in opposition to the ecclesiological centrality characteristic of the Carolingian period. While in the latter period the church is seen as endeavoring to create a *Christianitas* involving ''baptism'' — the constitution of a ''new man"—the insuperable contradictions between civil and ecclesiastical powers might have been shown to demonstrate the necessity of combining *humanitas* and *Christianitas* through a reversal of the movement—through, that is, the secularization of power. Curiously, however, in various places in his work Ullmann emphasizes that the two directions did not conflict. While not considering the factors, political and practical in nature, that may have commended prudence to the Humanists—who would then be seen as having been pushed to justify their position as one complimentary to the ecclesiastical position—Ullmann writes:

> Otto of Freising is an early example of the new thought-patterns which see no conflict between the ecclesiological and the secular points of view. On the contrary, they are said to be in harmony with each other. One of the purposes of his writing *The Two Cities* was precisely to emphasize the permanence and immutability of the community in the *civitas Dei*, which stands in sharp contradistinction to the never ending change that occurred in the *civitas terrena*. . . . The observer here witnesses in Otto of Freising a cosmology that is in no wise opposed to the purely transcendental, religious or ecclesiologically oriented cosmology. On the contrary, both supplement each other.[18]

Panofsky and Ullmann have undeniably different concepts of the Renaissance. For the former, its ground lies in the rupture that its intellectual experiences with regard to the classical world; for the latter, it lies in the harmony between the humanistic and ecclesiological lines, which led it to the common project of exploration of the classical legacy. The two have in common, though, that both suppose that in the period no conflict existed between those two intellectually powerful sectors. My hypothesis, by contrast, partially supported by Kristeller, Fumaroli, and Greenfield, presumes just such a conflict. Moreover, it adds a new element to their work, namely the thesis that the reconciliation between the two parties was effected through a double operation: the choice of classical *imitatio* as the one criterion above all others, and at the same time the a priori ascription of inferior status to the poetic word. Thus was "competition" over theological truth avoided and, too, valorization of poetic products that did not subscribe to socially preestablished models effectively blocked.

We are now in a better position to discuss in direct terms the sources heretofore used. To that end we shall enlist the collaboration of the superb *A History of Literary Criticism in the Italian Renaissance* by Bernard Weinberg. The value of Weinberg's own commentary completely aside, his study will have immense value for us in its transcription of long passages from works either seldom reprinted or in fact never edited beyond their original manuscript form. As it is neither my ken nor my purpose to comment in detail on those authors but instead simply to see them in regard to the problem of the "veto of fiction," I shall make wide use of those transcriptions—as well as of passages from French and English theoreticians who belong to the same period and are therefore also useful for treatment of that problem.

Let us begin by concentrating on the basic category in classical theory: the category of *imitatio*. Without formally defining *imitatio*, Bernardino Parthenio, in *Della Imitatione Poetica* [Of Poetic Imitation] (1560), made a distinction between Aristotelian *imitatio*—that is, representation of the nature of human beings—and rhetorical *imitatio*: "It seems to me reasonable and necessary to recall that there are two kinds of poetic imitation. One, which consists in expressing in an excellent fashion the nature and characters of those persons whom we undertake to imitate. And this is the end of poetry. . . . But leaving this type of imitation to Aristotle, we shall treat only the other one, which consists in words and in figures of speech."[19]

The characterization advanced by Tommaso Correa in *De Antiquitate, Dignitateque Poesis & Poetarum Differentia* [Of Antiquity, the Dignity of Poetry, and Differences Among Poets] (1586) is much more ambitious, having *imitatio* cover such apparently contrary activities as the imitation of the thing "exactly as it in itself is" (*qualis ipsa est*) and of the thing "contrived and invented" (*simulata et ficta*), "a kind of true and exact imitation which renders each and every thing exactly as it is; the second, contrived and invented, expresses each thing not as it actually is but as it appears to be, or else can appear to the many" (quoted in Weinberg, *Literary Criticism* 1:321).

The third modality of classical *imitatio* is advanced by Varchi in *Lezioni della Poetica* [Lessons on Poetics] (1590). Men of genius, he says, are in themselves insufficient unless "they make use of imitation, that is, in their own compositions, go about imitating the compositions of good poets, for in that way it would be like using art; indeed, nothing can be done of greater usefulness than to look to the works of the perfect masters" (quoted in Weinberg, *Literary Criticism* 1:430).

This third sense of *imitatio* reappears in Pierre Delaudun's *Art Poétique François* [French Ars Poetica] (1597): "Homer in his *Iliad*, Vergil in his *Aeneid*, and Bartas in his *Sepmaine*, the reading of all of which will be highly useful; and observing them closely, seeing their manner of using language, will so incite the reader that it will make him become a poet—unless he is made of stone."[20] It also appears in Roger Ascham's *The Scholemaster* (1570):

> But to returne to *Imitation* agayne: There be three kindes of it in matters of learning.
> The whole doctrine of Comedies and Tragedies is a perfite *Imitation*, or faire livelie painted picture of the life of everie degree of man. . . .
> The second kind of *Imitation* is to folow for learning of tonges and sciences the best authors. . . . The third kinde of *Imitation* belongeth to the second: as, when you be determined whether ye will folow one or mo, to know perfitlie, and which way to folow, that one; in what place;

by what meane and order; by what tooles and instrumentes ye shall do it; by what skill and judgement ye shall trewlie discerne whether ye folow rightlie or no.[21]

In the light of the wide use of the concept of *imitatio*, it is hardly surprising that it became linked to criteria for excellence. Thus, in his *Oratione Contra gli Terentiani* [Oration against the Terentians] (1566), Benetto Grasso specifies: "One poet comes to be called more excellent than another insofar as he comes closer to what is natural, and this talent of expressing actions and characters and, in describing them, of representing faithfully the nature of things and their decorum, gives life, soul, and eloquence to the poet" (quoted in Weinberg, *Literary Criticism* 1:179).

Although this observation is hardly new, it might be noted that the criterion of proximity to the natural has nothing to do with what we now refer to as "naturalism" because the former is governed by a paradigm common to all these preceptors: the paradigm of "truth." That paradigm is not to be confused with proximity to the merely seen or observed. Partial though it be, that clarification leads us to the fragment that Weinberg attributes to Lorenzo Giaccomini: "If, then, poetry is an imitation, and the poet an imitator, and to imitate is to feign and compose fables, it follows that the poet can imitate even if he speaks in his own person. . . . Poetry is thus a feigned and mendacious form of speech [*orazione finta et mendace*], which by means of narrated discourses not true in themselves, and with a certain lying and falseness, imitates true actions and real things" (1:63).

The very subordination of the "feigned" to the true shows that the theoreticians with whom we are dealing, even when translating or commenting on Aristotle, maintained themselves radically estranged from him on key issues. Aristotelian mimesis presupposed a concept of *physis* (to simplify, let us say, of "nature") that contained two aspects: *natura naturata* and *natura naturans*, respectively, the actual and the potential. Mimesis had relation only to the possible, the capable of being created—to *energeia*; its limits were those of conceivability alone. Among the thinkers of the Renaissance, in contrast, the position of the possible would come to be occupied by the category of the verisimilar, which, of course, depended on what *is*, the actual, which was then confused with the true. The subject needs no prolonged discussion, for the authors that I here transcribe are, to put it diplomatically, quite explicit. In a passage from his *Lezioni* [Lessons] (composed some time after 1581), Agnolo Segni observes: "The fable is thus always lying and falseness, but it is divided into two; one is the false language, as Plato says. . .which contains within itself false things, whatever they may be; the other is those false things themselves and particularly false actions, not true but invented" (quoted in Weinberg, *Literary Criticism* 1:301-2).

Whatever poetry touches is, then, turned into falseness. As examples of its activity, there are matters that are naturally false because they belong to poetry, and, too, there are matters that become false simply from being treated poetically. Segni's declaration is by no means less condemnatory than one by the celebrated Robortello in *In Librum Aristotelis de Arte Poetica Explicationes* [Commentaries on Aristotle's Poetics] (1548): "Since, then, poetics has as its subject matter fictitious and fictional discourse, it is clear that the function of poetics is to invent in a proper way its fiction and its untruth; to no other art is it more fitting than to this one to intermingle lies. . . . In the lies used by the poetic art, false elements are taken as true, and from them true conclusions are derived" (quoted in Weinberg, *Literary Criticism* 1:391).

We have seen that the iron law of "truth" carved an abyss between the proponents of *imitatio* and Aristotle's *Poetics*, which, theoretically, they were making known. In the following passage (Lombardi and Maggi, *In Aristotelis Librum de Poetica Communes Explanationes* [Common Explanations of Aristotle's Poetics] (1550), the principle of verisimilitude is transformed into the rationale for the law of unity of time with which classical theater would be handcuffed: "Since, then, tragedy and comedy . . . attempt to approach as close to truth as is possible, if we were to hear things done in the space of a month presented in two or at most three hours, in which time certainly a tragedy or a comedy is acted, the thing will absolutely produce an effect of incredibility" (quoted in Weinberg, *Literary Criticism* 1:419).

From that position the prohibitions simply proliferate. The aforementioned Delaudun tries to prevent the placing of the fantastic on stage, with the allegation that "if a god or goddess, false entities, were to be introduced, the argument would itself also be false and consequently would not represent the deeds of illustrious men according to truth" (quoted in Weinberg, *Critical Prefaces*, 39).

And Jacques Grévin, in his *Théâtre* (1561), in the name of that same verisimilitude, is of the opinion that song should be banned from tragedies: "Since tragedy is nothing less than the representation of truth, or of that which has its appearance, it seems to me that wherever republics have experienced disruptions . . . the simple people have had little occasion to sing and that therefore they should be made to sing no more when acted on stage" (quoted in Weinberg, *Critical Prefaces*, 185).

Not much later, the influential Castelvetro would justify opposition to the time of action supposedly prescribed by Aristotle—a period of twelve hours—because, among other reasons, the spectator would be unable to spend that many hours in the theater, "because of bodily necessities, such as eating, drinking, eliminating waste substances from the stomach and the bladder, and sleeping[!]"[22] But why was so much care expended in restricting poetic fable to a reality marked by severe limitations? Why did the idealization of the model have to be carried out through progressive subtractions? A more extended consideration of Castelvetro may help answer such questions. It should be observed, first of all, that his theory, which would play a pivotal role in the French Renaissance, involves the explicit subordination of the poetic to the principle of reality. At the outset of his treatise, he declares: "Since truth is naturally prior to verisimilitude and the thing represented naturally prior to the representation, and verisimilitude therefore refers to, and depends entirely upon, the truth and the representation refers to, and depends entirely on, the thing represented . . . it is more necessary to have first of all a thorough and rational knowledge of the truth and of the thing represented than of verisimilitude and the representation" (Castelvetro, 3).

As an immediate consequence, poetry is made dependent on history, with "poetry taking all its light from the light of history" (4). Thus the writing of a poetics like Aristotle's has its only rationale in that there had been no history writing up to his time. When such logic is carried to its ultimate conclusion, poetics becomes "a superfluous and empty thing, to be laughed at" (4). What is more—and far from an arbitrary gesture—for Castelvetro poetry enjoys less freedom than science, history, and philosophy because it is conceived of for "the common people":

> Poetry was invented only to delight and to entertain, by which I mean
> to delight and entertain the souls of the rude multitude and the common
> people, who understand neither the reasonings nor the distinctions nor
> the arguments, subtle and far from the talk of the stupid, used by
> philosophers in investigating the truth of things and by artists in
> organizing the arts. Since they do not understand them, it is only natural
> that when others use them they feel annoyance and displeasure, for it is
> bothersome beyond all measure when others speak in a way that we
> cannot comprehend. (16-17)

We are, then, now in a position to answer that question of why this model for *imitatio* was constructed by subtraction. It is simply because it was grounded in the parameters of day-to-day reality—or, better yet, in the parameters of a pragmatic reason geared to the most routine aspects of daily life. It should not surprise us, then, that, taken to its ultimate consequences, that theorization implied a condemnation of the imaginary, enemy by definition of the routine. Cogent as he is, Castelvetro arrives at precisely that point. He expounds it first in relation to prose: "Not only should prose involve firm argumentation but also its subject should be truth, and not some imagined thing" (13).

And immediately afterward he expands on that interdiction through extension of it to poetry: "And how can we seek to have things we seek to dramatize seem to be true if we confess, still reasoning in our own minds, that they are in fact not true but rather imagined, or that we merely have others speak" (14).

The turn toward the concrete, which is so noticeable in the poetry of the fourteenth century and was so ingrained in the sensibility of the period that it permitted even someone like Fernão Lopes, who disdained "beauty," to envision the plight of the people of Lisbon when their city lay under seige by the Castilians (see *Crónica de D. João*, chap. 148), is now transformed through its restriction to sterile norms. The imagination comes to be seen as frightening, even when allowed into the author's internal stage and no farther because it distances us from the "truth"—for which, read "routine." For *"poetry is the similitude and resemblance of history"* (Castelvetro, 16; emphasis mine). The old fear of uncontrollable subjectivity and the constant need to temporize with the power of the church made the Renaissance poetologist in fact the enemy of his own field of endeavor.

A detailed examination of Castelvetro makes it clear that efforts to give primacy to reality and to limit expression of it to a narrow and idealized model through a process of subtraction are articulated by an *ethical rationalism* that attempts to expurgate the fictional of everything that threatens "honest" understanding. It is for that reason that verisimilitude refers back to the principle of decorum, a category that has the peculiar feature of combining the ethically good with the verisimilar. As Weinberg writes on the question, "according to that theory, poetry was by its nature an imitation or representation of reality, made to conform as nearly as possible to that reality in order to produce moral effects desirable both for the individual and for the state" (*Literary Criticism* 2:801). Hence the assignment of responsibility by Lodovico Dolce in his *Osservationi nella Volgar Lingua* [Observations about the Vulgar Language] (1550) is in fact very common among these theoreticians: "For the function of the poet is to imitate the actions of men, and his end, under lovely veils of useful and moral inventions, to delight the soul of him who reads" (quoted in Weinberg, *Literary Criticism* 1:127).

It is according to precisely the same line of thought that Ronsard, in the *Abbregé de l'Art Poëtique Français* [Summary of French Poetics] (1565), interpreted the poetry of the "first age" as "an allegorical theology" (quoted in Weinberg, *Critical Prefaces*, 196), in what amounts to the repetition of the old topos of poetry qua theology, now, however, purged of any risk of "competition." Reason and ethics pressed in on the poets, limited their use of imagination, forced them to approach the natural not through verism but rather, so that nature might be made sublime, through a rhetorical imitation of the ancients. Thus the poets' primacy presupposed their mastery of the sublime, which, in the final analysis, implied alleviating their readers of care and directing them to "the good path." Such principles are common to the Italians, French, and English of the period. In order not to weigh this text down with examples, I will leave to George Puttenham (*The Arte of English Poesie*, 1589) the task of speaking for all the others:

But the chief and principal [end of poetry] is the laud, honour, and glory of the immortall gods . . . secondly, the worthy gests of noble Princes, the memoriall and registry of all great fortunes, the praise of vertue and reproofe of vice, the instruction of morall doctrines, the revealing of sciences naturall and other profitable Arts, the redresse of boistrous and sturdie courages by perswasion, the consolation and repose of temperate myndes: finally, the common solace of mankind in all his travails and cares of this transitorie life. (Quoted in Hardison, 157)

Under the weight of such thinking, Sperone Speroni, in his *Dialogo dell' Historia* [Dialogue on History] (1595), cannot maintain the Aristotelian position except at the price of spiritualizing and moralizing the poetic:

The poet does not narrate the fact, but he imitates the fact as narrated in history; and he imitates it by abstracting it from the essence of the particular fact, that is, as it really happened, and he considers it as it could have come about according to reason and usage; therefore, although he does not desert the particular for the universal, nevertheless because he considers it as it could have or should have been, he abstracts himself from the particular and goes to the universal. (Quoted in Weinberg, *Literary Criticism* 2:688-89)

* * *

Up to this point, I have concentrated on the construction of the edifice of *imitatio* and on the part played therein by truth, adapted to that end by the category of verisimilitude and by ethics, the latter in its turn adapted through the category of decorum. The edifice reached its completion in the sublimation of nature through the operation of the idealized model—an operation, as I have shown, carried out by subtraction. The work of art is thus immunized, spiritualized, made impervious; and poetry, as Bacon says in *The Advancement of Learning* (1605), "serveth and conferreth to magnanimity, morality, and to delectation."[23] In completing the construct, however, it was necessary to maintain a special vigilance over its motive core, that is, over fiction. Pedemonte, in his *Ecphrasis in Horatii Flacci Artem Poeticam* [Description of the Ars Poetica of Horatius Flaccus] (1546), proffers the paradigmatic solution: fiction is conflated with the false and mendacious, and, to cure its original sin, the very poets who invented it also set forth the corresponding remedy, namely, that it had come "to envelop, in the wrappings of fables, doctrinal mysteries and moral instructions and a way of life" (quoted in Weinberg, *Literary Criticism* 1:115). According to Charles Estienne, in his 1542 preface to Terence's comedy *Andria*, awareness of fiction's poisonous effect had in fact been acknowledged by the Roman emperors, who imposed the change from tragedy to comedy and mandated that the latter treat its subject matter "as in the manner of historical faith," thereby making it "quite positive for the society" (quoted in Weinberg, *Critical Prefaces*, 91). In truth, declarations in restraint of fiction occur in almost all the authors of the time. I find only one brief passage in which poetic license is favored over the shackeling of fiction. I refer to a portion of Annibale Caro's *Apologia degli Academici di Banchi di Roma* [Apology by the Academicians of the *Banchi di Roma*](1558):

> Don't you know, nevertheless, that where opposite opinions exist the poets may attach themselves to one of them, whether it be the better or the worse? and that in different places they may use now the one, now the other? Don't you know, further, that they may follow not only the opinion of the wise but also the errors of the common people? . . . The license of the poets is such that they may use not only opposite opinions, but those which are clearly false and ridiculous, without being blamed for so doing. (Quoted in Weinberg, *Literary Criticism* 1:277)

While the passage is important as a virtual habeas corpus, the principle of poetic license that it sets forth does not really go beyond the status of a special grant always subject to the censors' scrutiny. Under normal conditions, at most it could be invoked for the prudent defense of the fantastic, such as is carried out by Torquato Tasso in his *Discorsi dell'Arte Poetica* [Discourses on Poetics] (1587): "Thus one and the same action may be marvelous and verisimilar, marvelous looking at it in itself and circumscribed within natural limits, verisimilar considering it removed from these limits in its cause, which is a supernatural force powerful and accustomed to produce marvels of this kind" (quoted in Weinberg, *Literary Criticism* 2:650).

*   *   *

To close this descriptive section of my investigation, I shall set forth a short inventory of what we have established. *Imitatio* was, unquestionably, the centerpiece of classical poetology. Estranged from Aristotle's sense, it came to imply the absolute privileging of similitude, represented terminologically in the category of verisimilitude. Moreover, Tasso shows us that the equation was a purposeful and conscious one, for, as he declares in the treatise just cited, "poetry is, in its nature, nothing but imitation," which "cannot exist without verisimilitude" because verisimilitude "is proper and intrinsic to its essence" (quoted in Weinberg, *Literary Criticism* 2:650). Therefore the verisimilar governed *inventio*—that is, it governed the essential issue for the orator and the poet. In a work of 1560, *The Arte of Rhetorique*, Thomas Wilson emphasizes the openness of invention to the verisimilar: "The finding out of apt matter, called otherwise Invention, is a searching out of things true, or things likely, the which may reasonablie set forth a matter, and make it appeare probable" (quoted in Hardison, 33).

The verisimilar was, however, still the mainspring which, released, would produce public credence and make its enjoyment possible. What remains for me to do is to deal briefly with the issue of decorum. As I have already said, it was through decorum that the verisimilar received its ethical charge. Nevertheless, it would seem that the poets' practice, not the theoreticians' words, should reveal that the ethical proposition came accompanied by an aesthetic counterpart. The vehement defense of the English poetry of the period that Rosamond Tuve engages in persuades me of that probability: "An Elizabethan or Jacobean poet . . . will make clear what a thing symbolizes to him by his manner of using it; a Symbolist poet does not do so. I am quite sure that an earlier poet would see this use of obscure symbols as a fault of *decorum*."[24]

It may be the case as well that, for the author, all this legislation did not appear oppressive, despite how it may seem to us today, for it may have weighed on his sphere of activity much less than it excluded from that sphere the vulgar, the masses, to whom the norms of humanism did not even reach. In other words, *the legislation just demonstrated directed itself to the functioning of an estate society*. It is, then, probable that the poets and the public that they projected did not feel constrained because they partook of the same ethical and aesthetic principles. Although she avoids recourse to Weberian terminology, Tuve supports us in that hypothesis, all the while explaining the difference between the artistic production involved therein and the poetry of modernity: "The most truly revolutionary change with respect to decorum in poetry must come when men are no longer able to accept the principle upon which it is erected, a principle which underlies both classical poetic and medieval culture. *When the notion of a hierarchy of values becomes suspect, the principle of decorum simply ceases to operate*" (Tuve, 234; emphasis mine).

Nevertheless, it is one thing to use the idea of estates to explain why legislation in favor of reason may not have created any unbearable sense of oppression among authors and public, and it is quite another to overlook in the process the motives that governed that legislation. Must it not of necessity be asked why the great representative, the chameleonlike ambassador, of *imitatio* was verisimilitude? Martin Fontius pinpoints the reason in explaining the importance of verisimilitude as a means of avoiding conflict with the church: "The fact that the concept of 'verisimilitude' had so extraordinary a significance for Aristotle's sixteenth- and seventeenth-century commentators was intimately related to the fact that through that category the risk of a possible conflict with the requirement of truth exacted of poetry by the Christian religion could be contained."[25]

It is obvious that the centrality of verisimilitude has roots in the very presence of the potential for conflict between secular and religious elites and therefore in the necessity of the compact of which I have spoken. But, rather than remain content with my findings up to now, I think it would be better to ask: why did Aristotelian mimesis come at this point to inform a model underlying the concept of *imitatio*? The beginnings of an answer are provided by Tuve. For her, our shock when confronted with Elizabethan poetics and our relative failure to understand the metaphysical poets stem from the fact that whereas we, as postromantics, concentrate on personal experience, those theoreticians and poets gave primacy to the need to affirm the universal: "Techniques vary extremely; what is shared is the common refusal to narrow the task of images to that of a truthful report of experience. Even when he writes on 'Going to Bed', Donne is ready to desert the particular for the personified universal" (Tuve, 42).

It is a difference in expectations between them and us, a difference grounded in different concepts of reality. Tuve approaches the concept held by the Elizabethans and Metaphysicals when she writes: "the poet as gardener assisting nature has but to make her intentions clearer and her fruits more sure" (147). As this is hardly the place to undertake a discussion of classical and modern concepts of reality, I shall merely refer to Foucault's analysis of the classical *episteme* and add that the estate society of the classical era favored the constitution, among its educated sectors, of a homogeneous frame of reference that had as its basis a specific concept of reality grounded in a continuity between the order of "words" and the order of "things," and the endowing of that continuity with a religious point of view. With respect to concepts of reality, it must also be added that the sixteenth and seventeenth centuries regarded the inalterability of humankind and of nature as given; both were governable by permanent laws on both the physical and the moral planes. Without that premise, the very principle of *imitatio*, the adoption of models furnished by selected works from antiquity, and the *organic* role of rhetoric would have been at best difficult to maintain. The ancients could not have been adduced as a model if human actions and passions had been considered culturally relative. The belief in immutability, by contrast, was in fact so strong that, as I will show in chapter 2, even when it had been overturned by the relativizing of values and by romanticism, it would continue to be defended by the traditionalists. Beyond that issue, too, the idealization of nature implicit in Renaissance *imitatio* hindered the exploration of any new directions, for the work of art, under the vigilance of decorum, could not escape from the prescribed ambit of the use of *figural language* (i.e., rhetorical imitation). In the light of these explanations, consider Tuve's defense: "The 'artificiality' is explicable by their [the Renaissance writers'] intention to imitate by making an artful construct, an artifact (to wrench the word somewhat). This artifact was designed to please on grounds of its formal excellence rather than by its likeness to the stuff of life—a relatively formless subject matter not to be identified with the poetic subject and evidently not even loosely identified with 'reality'" (25).

The following notions from that passage should be singled out: that the excellence attained by rhetorical devices did not depend on their similitude to life, which, in turn, should not be confused with reality—the former being fortuitous and personalized, the latter, constant and unrefined; and that coherence, considered a qualitative criterion for the work of art, depended on the author's ability *to select images in relation to their propriety in the verbal artifact*, an ability to be measured by that artifact's success in surpassing the individual dimension and entering into contact with the universal.

It is by means of the link between the homogeneity of representation carried out by the "cultured" estate and this universalizing vision of the laws that govern humankind and nature that the work of the metaphysical poets achieved its high degree of internal self-explanation, in contrast to the obscurity frequently encountered in the poetry of modernity.[26] I limit myself here to transcription of Tuve's remarks: "Few readers would dare claim that they surely read what Yeats surely wrote; more than that, these connections are seldom the same in two consecutive readings by the same reader. A great many connections are possible, and not any are surely intended" (Tuve, 270).

In summary, the universality presumed by the classical period provided the basis for the cult of reason that is transparent in its poetics; it was, moreover, a restrictive reason, both because of the interdictions raised by the theoreticians and also because of the necessity that the parameters of Christianity not be contradicted. But several questions might still be raised: How is it possible to postulate a collaboration between that rationality and the Christian-religious outlook without taking into account the sectarian disputes that characterized the era? In the specific case of England, how was it possible to overlook the battle launched by the various branches of Protestantism against the Roman Catholics? I will leave conclusive answers to specialists in the history of religion, but I shall point out that the religious differences between England and the Catholic city-states of Renaissance Italy and, indeed, of Renaissance France did not prevent the same rationalistic ambience from holding sway in the former as well: "As Leslie Stephen was to remark, Protestantism inevitably became a screen for rationalism."[27]

My reading of Keith Thomas's work leads me to conclude that the struggle carried out by various Protestant groups against the practice of magic and superstition, identified, by the assailants, with the interests of the Roman Catholic church, made them even more zealous in defense of reason:

Indeed the conventional distinction between a prayer and a spell seems to have been first hammered out, not by the nineteenth-century anthropologists, with whom it is usually associated, but by sixteenth-century Protestant theologians. It was well expressed by the Puritan Richard Greenham when he explained that parishioners should not assume that their ministers could give them immediate relief when their consciences were troubled. (Thomas, 61)

That emphasis on reason also served to reinforce the separation between the cultured estate and the rest of the population. Indeed, with regard to the latter, as Thomas declares, "fundamental changes are not accomplished overnight. 'Three parts at least of the people' were 'wedded to their old superstition still', declared a Puritan document of 1584" (73).

Be all this as it may, the answer here presented remains unsatisfactory. To justify *imitatio's* privileged status on the basis of immutable laws that govern humankind and nature and on the basis of the collaborative role of religion still seems more than a bit insubstantial. Why, after all, was this atemporal, restrictive version of reason taken up by the intellectuals of the era? And especially, why was it brought into harmony with the dominant political interests? Even though the France of the classical era has not been studied here—because, as regards the interests of this chapter, it represents little more than a torchbearer for the Italian preceptors—reference to that country now becomes necessary. Two matters stand out: (1) the cult of the imitated was not limited to the poetologists but indeed was taken up by the very court itself; (2) in France, the cult of classical laws led to and supported proclamations of national "superiority." Both factors are put in evidence through their apprehension by an author whose factualism disdained "interpretation"; I refer to René Bray. For proof of (1), Bray has recourse to a text of 1722, *Huetiana ou Pensées Diverses de M. Huet* [Huetiana or the Diverse Thoughts of M. Huet]; for (2), to a text of 1711, *De Quelques Livres* [On Certain Books]. Bray's first passage is as follows:

> If we believe Huet, the Court itself shared the writers'opinion on the matter: "Although natural beauties may be preferable to artistic ones, such is nonetheless not the taste of this century. Nothing is pleasing that is not costly. A spring bubbling up at the foot of a hill spilling upon golden sands the clearest and freshest water in the world would not please the members of the Court as much as a stream of stale, muddy water brought at considerable expense from some pond."[28]

Whence came the bestowal of such superiority on the imitated? Let us not forget that the two texts to which Bray turns for documentation were published either just before or just after the end of Louis XIV's reign (1714), at which time absolutist centralism had been achieved. The cult of a reason incarnating permanent, universal laws came in service to, and at the same time was the desideratum of, political centralization. The imitated bespoke the human capacity to control the world through obedience to laws that were themselves seen as central, that is to say, as universal. If the signs of Divine Will had long since ceased to manifest themselves immanently in things, then the use of the faculty of reason and the capacity for imitation were to be fomented, for they could reveal the truth hidden within things. As had been the case with the sixteenth-century preceptors, for whom *imitatio* played the role of reconciler with the church's pretentions to truth, so in France *imitatio*, rationally channeled, became an instrument of absolutist politics. *Imitatio* was, then, a principle that paralleled foundation of the political institution: both centralized, both mounted vigil against the unconverted, the unbeliever, the heretic. Further, so channeled into "norms," human behavior became subject to "objective" supervision, became open to judgment according to principles seen as "just."

Bray's second passage is self-explanatory: "The Chevalier de Méré speaks of the 'bizarre Spaniards'. Saint-Evremond is not satisfied with their nature and explains the irregularity of their poetry in his own way: 'Since all the gallantry of the Spaniards came from the Moors, it retains an undefinable flavor of Africa, different from other nations and too eccentric to adapt itself to the strictures of rules'" (Bray, 30-31).

Thus, it is argued, French drama's observance of the three unities proclaims a Europeanness superior to the Moorish barbarism of a Lope de Vega, who, although thoroughly acquainted with the best classical authors, preferred an undisciplined form of theater that would merely appeal to those who attended. The consequences of that argument will be revealed in chapter 2, when I discuss the polemics about Racine and Shakespeare in nineteenth-century France. Nevertheless, in speaking of France, Saint-Evremond was assuredly not speaking of its entire population but of only the upper estate, of those who participated in what we today would call "the apparatus of state." Analyzing that same period, and specifically the "literature" under Louis XIV, Auerbach has concluded, with his characteristic lucidity: "This notion of *vraisemblance* is typical of cultivated society. It combines the arrogant rationalism that refuses to be taken in by imaginative illusion with contempt for the *indocte et stupide vulgaire* which is perfectly willing to be taken in."[29]

It should be noted, however, that much as has been the case with the foregoing argument about the interests that favored emphasis on individual subjectivity, I do not here propose to take political centralization as the one and only cause for the character of French classical poetics after it freed itself from ecclesiastical vigilance. I merely point out, in opposition to purely aestheticist modes of inquiry, that the cult of reason, viewed as able to crystallize eternal norms to be obeyed by the poet, and as well the concomitant disdain for anything that transgressed its canon, were bound up with the form in which social power was organized, a form no longer grounded in medieval theocentrism. Is it really surprising that the church was able to adjust to changed times? (The question obviously does not address the situation of Italy, where lack of national unity aided in maintenance of ecclesiastical power.) "The patronage of the saints gave a sense of identity and of corporate existence to small and otherwise undifferentiated institutions. Hence their enduring popularity as names for colleges and schools even in a Protestant era" (Thomas, 28). Religion adapted itself to the new order to the extent that it continued to contribute to the formation of identity constructs, now national in character. Thus the above quotation from Martin Fontius is perfect for the *Cinquecento*: at that time verisimilitude was the recognized quantity enabling avoidance of conflict with religion. In the later, nationally constituted states, however, that concern became subordinate to motives of a more strictly political nature. Aside from that difference, explanation remains the same: verisimilitude was accepted in relation to the allegiance between the *cour et la ville*—that is, in relation to the upper estate of absolutist society—because nobles and wealthy bourgeois saw in the exercise of the imagination—in the exercise of a form of thematization of the world that might deny perceived reality rather than endorse it—both the presence of a barbarous, undisciplined mentality and a defiance of their own "arrogant rationalism." Thus was the receiver borne in mind— a fact implied in what I have written about Castelvetro—in absolutism's need to legislate him effectively. It should not come as a shock, then, that early romanticism produced the germ of a poetics that was not only antinormative but also what we would today call immanentist, that is, a poetics concerned only with the properties of the poetic text and not with the mode of its reception.

In summary, analysis of classical poetics can serve as a point of departure for opposite conclusions. For one of them, all but impervious to a historical inquiry into aesthetics, art is endowed with an internal energy that enables it to affirm itself in varying situations. After all, even if there did exist a veto of the fictional, even if hostility on the part of the church resulted in a compact incarnated in the concept of *imitatio*, what importance did those matters have? Who can deny the strong presence of the fictional in Racine and Molière? Art eternally holds out to man the possibility of his projection beyond the span of his short lifetime.

The other interpretation insists, by way of contrast, that human achievements are radically historical and that it is necessary to bear that fact in mind so that we resist making of the world a vast mirror in which we see only our own poor self. If mimesis was given by its commentators and interpreters of the sixteenth and seventeenth centuries a connotation contrary to that in Aristotelian thought, it was not because they were particularly narrow in outlook but rather because at that time reason had been given the charge to decide when the power of the individual subjectivity was correct and when it was in error. To take the fictional as *finto, favoloso* ("pretended," "fabulous"), as did Varchi (Weinberg, *Literary Criticism* 1:8), and have no contemporary oppose you, to have it identified, then, with the false and mendacious, implied taking the script out of the poet's hands and obliging him or her to behave as the legislators of subjectivity disposed. The theoretician of "literature" of that period began from a premise similar to the one we saw at work in Fernão Lopes. (If Renaissance historiography did not follow the path opened up for it by the Portuguese chronicler, it was because the criteria for truth in the classical age were not grounded in a logic of fact but rather in verbal, rhetorical justification having eloquence as its pinnacle. Therefore, history remained closely attached to poetry, as a part of the *studia humanitatis*.) Poetry does not possess truth; at most it approaches it, through verisimilitude. Its savage core is feigned and mendacious, and only beautiful composition vouchsafes it the right to exist at all. The Renaissance poetologists work like advocates who know beforehand that their case is lost. Their efforts consist in avoiding the maximum sentence, and they achieve that goal by locating the fictional on the lowest plane of human knowledge and restricting its field of operation.

As I initially proposed for this introductory development merely to understand what seemed to me a shocking hypothesis, and as that hypothesis now seems explained, I shall not undertake additional work on the further development of Renaissance poetics in the seventeenth century. Taking it as a background premise that matters remained relatively little changed in that era, let us instead turn to examination of how the problem of fictionality is presented in three essays written at the outset of the nineteenth century. And let us begin with the essay that radicalized the study of fiction by carrying it beyond the realm of belles-lettres, the *Theory of Fictions* by Jeremy Bentham.

The Inevitability of the Fictional

In 1814 the jurisconsult and philosopher Jeremy Bentham began the writing of an essay that he would never see published and which would advance his reputation as a thinker not in the least—not because *The Theory of Fictions* was a work to be ignored but because it was so far ahead of the concerns of its time. What Bentham proposed was, in fact, truly disorienting for the era: the grounding of philosophical inquiry in language itself. He thereby put into question the bases upon which the real and the fictional, the safe port of truth and the phantasmagorical, had been kept separate.

According to its modern editor, C. K. Ogden, the writing of the essay was motivated by Bentham's anguished recollections of an infancy dominated by an old aunt, fear of ghosts and specters, and a strong aversion to children's storybooks. As an old man, Bentham exacted his revenge, all the sweeter in that those early causes lay well hidden within it. They had been replaced by other, more recent annoyances: his experiences as a law student and his later law practice, at odds with the interpretive twists to which legal briefs were subjected. Be they remote or recent, the phantasms had to be exorcized.

Bentham takes as point of departure the concept of entity, "a denomination in the import of which every subject matter of discourse, for the designation of which the grammatical part of speech called a noun-substantive is employed, may be comprised."[30] Thence emerge his basic categories: entities can be real or fictitious; the real ones comprise perceptual and inferential categories; the latter can be either material or spiritual. Highlighting only those points relevant to the subject at hand, let me first establish that a real entity is defined as "an entity to which, on the occasion and for the purpose of discourse, existence is really meant to be ascribed" (Bentham, 10).

Immediately afterward comes the first collision with normal realist thought: because they can be either perceived or inferred, the class of real entities excludes anything deriving from mere mental apparatus: "Faculties, powers of the mind, dispositions: all these are unreal; all these are but so many fictitious entities" (10).

The origin of the presumption that those entities, which are really fictitious, are in fact real is lost in bygone ages, when a supposed equivalence between the real and the existence of a name for it was concretized. For it is the name that created the presumption of reality "between the idea of a name and that of the reality of the object to which it was applied, an association being thus formed, from a connexion thus intimate, sprung a very natural propensity, viz. that of attributing reality to every object thus designated; in a word, of ascribing reality to the objects designated by words" (17).

It is not Bentham's point, however, to attack this type of fictional entity. Carrying on his initial conceptualization, he continues: "A fictitious entity is an entity to which, though by the grammatical form of the discourse employed in speaking of it, existence be ascribed, yet in truth and reality existence is not meant to be ascribed" (12).

Moreover, he adds that it is characteristic of the fictional entity to exist as a shadow projected by a real entity: "Every fictitious entity bears some relationship to some real entity, and can no otherwise be understood than in so far as that relation is perceived—a conception of that relation is obtained" (12).

If that shadow—to use a metaphor not employed by Bentham himself—is immediately projected by the real entity that gives rise to it, it is designated a "fictitious entity of the first remove," which is "a fictitious entity, a conception of which may be obtained by the consideration of the relation borne by it to a real entity, without need of considering the relation borne by it to any other fictitious entity" (12).

It is a property of fictitious entities of the first remove to be treated *as if* they were real. They thereby belong to the class of ideas of movement and rest. In an explanation that is essential for the development of his thought, Bentham writes: "A body is said to be in motion. This, taken in the literal sense, is as much as to say—Here is a larger body, called a motion; in this larger body, the other body, namely, the really existing body, is contained" (13).

The root of fictionality is to be found, then, in language itself. Moreover, real fictionality does not constitute an error from which we must extricate ourselves. Such would be unthinkable—indeed, it would be so in the strictest of terms, for it is impossible for us to think without fictions: "To language, then—to language alone—it is, that fictitious entities owe their existence; their impossible, yet indispensable, existence" (15).

Making that analysis clearer, Bentham formulates the point with exemplary precision: "Of nothing that has place, or passes in our mind, can we give any account, any otherwise than by speaking of it as if it were a portion of space, with portions of matter, some of them at rest, others moving in it. Of nothing, therefore, that has place, or passes in our mind, can we speak, or so much as think, otherwise than in the way of *Fiction*" (17).

By way of contrast, the root of real entities is to be found in what we see. In its strict, basic sense, the real is very limited. In fact, at the outset of his chapter "Of Fictitious Entities," Bentham declares that of the Aristotelian categories—substance, quantity, quality, relation, and so on—only the first is not actually an example of a fictitious entity. The rationale on which the distinctions are based is to be inferred from prior definitions: real entities function like receptacles within which fictitious entities are held, their presence there being considered natural and self-evidently present. That argument, reiterated tirelessly throughout the treatise, is exemplified in the passage: "The ideas respectively designated by these corresponding words [i.e., matter and form] are fractional results, produced from the decomposition of the word *substance*" (24).

The concepts of matter and form, therefore, are mental projections imposed on the real receptacle, the substance; those projections, being immediately present within the horizon of the receptacle, become fictitious entities of the first remove. Such, for Bentham, is the mechanism through which the fictional receives its right to be, the right to its impossible yet indispensable existence. The fictional, one might say, derives from the fact that we cannot speak using only the substance that presents itself to us. (In other words, we are inhabited by a world that is not to be confused with its physical coordinates.) Bentham therefore takes the entity called "relation" as the first fictitious entity of the first remove: "Once introduced upon the carpet, the fictitious entity called relation swells into an extent such as to swallow up all the others. Every other fictitious entity is seen to be but a mode of this" (29).

As a consequence of its primacy, relation becomes an object of perception itself, that is, it comes to be "seen": "Whatsoever two entities, real or fictitious, come to receive names, and thus to receive their nominal existence, *Relation* would be the third; for, between the two—they being, by the supposition, different, and both of them actual objects of perception—the relation of difference or diversity would also become an object of perception" (29).

Whereas relation is therefore the first of the fictions that articulate our world, space presents itself as a mixed entity—one between the real and the fictional: "Substance being a real physical entity; perceptions real psychical entities; matter, form, quantity, and so on, so many fictitious entities: both descriptions being in part applicable to space, neither of them applicable entirely—space may be regarded and spoken of as a *semi-real entity*" (27).

It must be observed too that the area of the fictional is not to be confused with the field of the inferential real, which comprises "the soul in a state of separation from the body," God, and other lesser spiritual entities. (The development of this dimension is not of concern to us, especially because in it the philosopher becomes enmeshed in his own religious convictions.) This weak point, however, functions in such a manner as to make it clear that, despite the redemption that Bentham allows to fictitious entities of the first remove—I use the term redemption because I consider it an absolutely essential feature of his argument—he retains a degree of caution regarding that entity. That caution keeps him from classifying God as anything other than a real entity: "Author, and Creator—those alone, and not the word *cause*, can, with propriety, be employed in speaking of God. These, as well as God, are names of real entities, not names of fictitious entities" (44).

From the résumé here presented, it might be thought that the relative lack of recognition with which Bentham's treatise met resulted from its defense of fictionality. Although that analysis may have some merit, the fact is that Bentham did not endeavor to rescue poetic fiction from the secular prohibition that accompanied it. Indeed, he is quite harsh with that sort of fiction. It is not even identified with fictional entities of the second remove—that is, those that acquire their qualities via borrowing from those of the first remove. Poetic fictions instead receive the specific title fabulous fictions. If acceptable fictions—that is, those without which the "games of language" cannot function—presuppose a real entity, the "fabulous fictions" find their origin in entities unreal in themselves: "*Fabulous* may be the name employed for the designation of the other class of *unreal* entities" (17).

For Bentham, such "fabulous" entities are simply to be depreciated; they are to be seen as akin to the hypocrisy of the priest and the chicanery of the pettifogger, "very different the Fiction of the Logician from the Fictions of poets, priests, and lawyers" (18).

As the reader will have perceived, my purpose has not been to "popularize" a relatively little-known treatise but rather to show that Bentham's effort, with its attempt to ground discourse about reality in an explicitly established rational structure, was one of the first to radicalize thinking about truth. The fact that reason must recognize that it competes with necessary fictions, even though that recognition represents an important rejection of realist epistemology, offers no immediate surcease for poetic fiction. To reiterate, necessary fictions involve an operation that originates in the body of a real entity, of a real receptacle, of categorical "substance." Reason absorbs this impossible but necessary fictionality, naturalizes it, obliterates its bastard nature, and uses it to serve the discourses that deal with reality. In that operation no concessions are made to those spurious individuals who persist in dealing with fables and in adorning themselves with the "beauty" that is so suspect. If Bentham's treatise foreshadows Vaihinger's philosophy of the "as if," as Ogden notes, and anticipates the central role that language will command in the neopositivist circle and in analytical philosophy, by contrast it offers nothing anticipatory of a theory of poetic fictionality. To be sure, nothing would prevent our extracting from it ingredients in explanation of the sense of reality engendered by poetic fiction. Poetic fictionality crystallizes within an object, and its persuasive power would doubtless be diminished if it did not produce an illusion of reality. (As any casual observation shows, that illusion is the first effect produced by confrontation with an art object, and that effect, if it does not efface itself, negates the experience of the art itself.) Such results, however, would be marginal ones that would hardly require study of Bentham's treatise for their formulation. I have examined that treatise as a kind of end point in the historical construction of a reason, of a form of rationalism, that could justify its own existence only through depreciation of poetic fictionality. In the light of that history, the debt that we owe "advanced" romantic thought becomes all the more evident. It is a debt that traditional education, based as it is on the suspect practice of reading "selected texts," makes difficult to recognize. Early romanticism in fact squarely confronted the tradition I have outlined. Its success, or, rather, that of its sharpest cutting edge, was at best relative; that success was, however, great enough for us to become aware of the veto that our tradition practices with regard to the fictional.

The Reassumption of Subjectivity: Chateaubriand and Stendhal

When the *Essai sur la littérature anglaise* [Essay on English Literature] was published in 1836, romanticism was already fully consolidated in France. What is more, Chateaubriand's book vacillated between holdovers of classical patterns and ideas of a properly romantic stamp. I shall, therefore, ignore chronological order and consider it before I examine Stendhal's *Racine et Shakespeare* (1823). Just as in the preceding discussion, my purpose here will not be exhaustive exposition, for the two titles are of interest to us as symptoms of a new cultural scene.

One new element is obvious: the principle of the nation, the political criterion of nationality is no longer a secondary or correlative issue; it is now the very foundation of the machinery of judgment. The change is so pervasive that the anachronism of Chateaubriand's vision is in fact astonishing: he treats the medieval situation as though he were speaking of the Europe of his own time. It is through such leveling of the differences between historical periods that Chateaubriand not only takes the national spirit as an element productive of artistic quality but also accuses foreign influence of creating erroneous situations along the lines of what supposedly happened in medieval England, where, he says, Saxon writings lost their "native originality" because of the introduction of "French and Provençal poetry.'' In chapter 2 I will discuss the importance assumed at this time by the notion of nationality and its role in the constitution of the golden age of literary historiography, but for now I shall merely observe that Chateaubriand carried his conception of nationalities as self-enclosing, sealed compartments to such an extent that he actually came to doubt that one could understand a foreign author: ''In judging impartially the totality of foreign works as well as our own (if, after all, one can in fact judge foreign works, which I very much doubt), one will find that, although they are equal in strength of thought, we prevail as regards form and logic of composition.''[31]

The last part of the argument suggests that the hypothetical difficulty in interpretation may derive less from the declared reason than from Chateaubriand's retention of sixteenth- and seventeenth-century evaluative criteria. Moreover, at no time is he inclined to question the universality of the rules of classical poetics. The very fact that those rules reached their culmination in the France of Louis XIV—not to mention that the essay was written during the Restoration and its author had been one of the émigrés—made him all the more adverse to such questioning. He therefore contradicts the general direction of his own work when he declares in no uncertain terms that ''in a living literature no one is a competent judge save of works written in his own language'' (Chateaubriand, 261).

The feature that today seems to us the central one in romanticism, the *historicization of judgment*, Chateaubriand wholly bypasses. At the same time, his choice of *l'ordre et la raison de la composition* as typical French attributes suggests a pattern characteristic of the *restaurateurs* of the era and of the conservative thought that accompanied and/or followed that pattern: to condemn the literature and thought of the eighteenth century, which led to the Revolution, those of the seventeenth century were taken to constitute the mirror of what was truly French. Nationality is, then, exalted as a *defensive* principle, as a substance much in the sense in which Bentham used the term, that is, as the only strictly real entity. That very substantialization of nationality manifests how, in the nineteenth century, literary historiography became inextricably bound up with the interests and values of the national state.

At the same time that he preserves the old poetics, however, Chateaubriand also introduces elements foreign to it. Thus, however timidly, he recognizes the role played by the imagination, even though he reserves it—in a reservation that is of capital importance for my thesis—for the beguiling excesses of distant times or of young and naive peoples:

> The Middle Ages is not a time of style, properly so called, but it is a
> time of picturesque expression, naive painting, and fertile invention. We
> note with a smile of admiration what naive peoples produced from the
> beliefs that were taught them: to their great, lively, and far-reaching
> imagination, to their cruel customs, to their indomitable courage, to

their uncontrollable instinct for adventure and conquest, priests, missionaries, and poets offered marvellous torments, eternal perils, invasions to be attempted, but in some unknown locale without changing place. (36)

"Barbarians," then, have their allure for noble, civilized humans, who, correspondingly, maintain their reserve and recognize them as constituting an element to be kept a prudent distance away. The imagination is admired as the fruit of "early youth" that awakens in the writer of mature age—especially if he or she be *restauré*—a touch of envy but above all a goodly dose of caution. Admiration and caution: exactly the formula for exotic literature that Chateaubriand had used in *Renée* and *Atala*.

Couched in a more complex set of combinations, that same formula will be present in Chateaubriand's very approach to Shakespeare, which is an important issue since the *Essai* is basically a reflection on Milton and Shakespeare. The combinations are more complex because, although he takes up categories that had coin at his time—national spirit, barbarism, imagination—Chateaubriand still implies, in a passage that from the point of view of French classicism is quite daring, that Shakespeare's power stemmed from his raw material—life itself: "He mixes, *just as in the real world*, king and slave, patrician and plebeian, warrior and laborer, the prominent man and the anonymous man; he makes no distinctions of genre: he does not separate noble from ignoble, serious from comic, sad from merry, smiles from tears, happiness from misery, good from evil. He sets the entire society in motion, just as he sets out entirely the life of one man" (111; emphasis mine).

Does such language in fact explicitly deny categorizations of genre? Observant and nimble, Chateaubriand sees that he has to control the scope of the implications extractable from the above paragraph; he therefore immediately adds: "Let us be sure to affirm that writing is an art, that that art has genres, that each genre has its rules. Genres and their rules are not at all arbitrary; they spring from nature itself: art has merely made discrete what nature has thrown together. . . . Racine, in all the excellence of his *art*, is more *natural* than Shakespeare, just as Apollo, in all his divinity, has more of *human* form than an Egyptian colossus" (111).

While not wholly refractory to romantic innovation, Chateaubriand strives to maintain the profile of classicism. A perfect fit was unachievable, and the entire arsenal of classicism was therefore not saved. If the gravitation of a nature to be made sublime is retained through affirmation of a place for well-defined rules and genres, nonetheless *imitatio* is not spoken of. No matter the strength of our viscount's will to compromise, *imitatio* had to be banished. For, as we have seen, Renaissance *imitatio* presupposed an estate society with a homogeneity of representation that brought author and public together, thereby enabling the decoding of allusive literary tropes by means of references known beforehand. *Imitatio* did not presuppose life but rather a model of reality, not life as a model but rather a model of style. Now Chateaubriand is aware of the diversity of his time and of the fact that "literary society" had been invaded by alarming aliens. In that situation, a return to the old *imitatio* would imperil the fame that was his life goal. What seemed viable — indeed, necessary — to him, then, was to throw up a barricade against the barbarians: "Even so it is not my intent to contradict the forced changes that time and revolution have wrought upon literary opinion, as well as upon political opinion; those changes, however, do not justify the corruption of taste" (112).

It was a corruption that made him tremble with revulsion before "that love of the ugly," "that enrapturement with the bandy-legged, the crippled, the one-eyed, the dark-skinned (!), and the toothless" (112). The old, estate-based paradigm endeavors, then, to maintain the categories that we have seen at work, categories through which it governed, now not in the name of an objectivity for *imitatio* but in the name instead of an aristocracy of spirit. Therefore, Chateaubriand, as exponent of that outlook, says of Racine that "he purged his masterpieces of only such elements as ordinary spirits would have put there" (112). That is to say, the principle of decorum now assumes precisely the political function of differentiating between estates, if not between classes. The cornerstone, *imitatio*, had been pulled out from the old edifice, and a means was now being sought to keep that construction from falling in entirely. To the ex-émigré that task is the fundamental one, for, to his educated eyes, the barbarians had already broken into the house: "There do not even remain either actors to play Classical tragedy or a public to enjoy it, understand it, and judge it" (113).

How, then, could he reconcile all his objections with the high praise that he accords Shakespeare? Our essayist faced the challenge unabashed. For this task too his intimacy with classical eloquence served him well. The great English playwright was, simply put, a special sort of barbarian, "standing out amid the ranks of a civilization in progress and redirecting it toward the past" (125).

It is as a result of this special position that the admiration that Shakespeare incites, as well as the reserve that must be maintained with regard to his work, are justified. More so in fact because, even beyond ignoring decorum and rules of art, Shakespeare did not rise to the service of his country either, and praise of life, taken to be the proper function of artistic materials, is conditioned by a higher value: that of the state. The English playwright is therefore seen, in a comparative light, as inferior to such predecessors or contemporaries as Tasso, Lope de Vega, Calderón, Ercilla, Cervantes, and Camões, who had in their work something "that partakes of the beauty of their countries." Shakespeare, by contrast, "would have needed a different career," since if he is "enraptured in his work, he is seldom noble: his style frequently lacks dignity, just as does his life" (132). Consequently, it is for Milton that Chateaubriand reserves his categorical admiration. Is that not a strange choice, we might ask, since Milton was a republican and supporter of the regicidal Cromwell? No, the viscount answers, because at the bottom of it all Milton, "that fierce republican, was a noble" and had his arms (223).

In summary, Chateaubriand oscillates between the old set of precepts and the cult of life. As regards the former, he writes, in reinforcement of his praise of Racine and reservations against Shakespeare: "It must be said, however, to be honest, that if the criticism of detail has lost its power through the lapse of recognized rules, through the revolt of entrenched *amour-propre*, historical and general criticism has on the other hand made considerable progress" (260).

As regards the latter point, life is exalted in the hope of attaining individual salvation through expression of that life itself. It is doubtless an awkward hope to maintain, being, as it is, common to all *littérateurs*: "one after another, we each of us believe, with all candor and conscience, that we are the man of our century" (260). Perhaps because of its very struggle to maintain interchange between the old and the new, the *Essai* does not offer a thinker of the weight of a Coleridge or of the German romantic theoreticians. I have chosen it as an exemplary case—indeed, a somewhat tragic one—of the effort to sustain an impossible accommodation: one between the paradigms of an aesthetics that had rejected its own cornerstone and the vitalistic, particularistic, and individualized paradigm of romanticism.

* * *

When Chateaubriand's *Essai sur la littérature anglaise* appeared, thirteen years had already passed since Stendhal had scandalized *restaurateurs* and academicians alike with his short, ironic, aggressive *Racine et Shakespeare*. In my examination of the *Essai*, I showed quite clearly that allegiance to classical aesthetics was wholly consistent with Chateaubriand's political conservatism and with his effort not to be confused with the walking corpses from earlier times. The controversy sparked by Stendhal's manifesto of 1823 makes that relationship all the clearer—less, really, because of Stendhal's own words than because of the inflamed rejoinder that the then president of the French Academy, the long-forgotten Auger, directed against it. It is as defender of restored monarchical institutions that Auger undertakes to speak. The aesthetic principles that he defends are those that he thinks are endangered by the advent of the "nascent sect," the propagation of which could undermine established power. Therefore, the academy, as part of the established order, running the risk of giving too much attention to the adversary, takes up arms:

A new literary schism raises its head today. Many men, brought up with a religious respect for the old doctrines consecrated in innumerable masterpieces, are worried, indeed frightened, by the projects of the nascent sect and seem to call for reassurance. Shall the French Academy remain indifferent to their outcries? . . . The danger is perhaps not yet very great, and it might be feared that it will only be increased if too much importance is attached to it. Should we then wait until the sect of *Romanticism* (for that is what it calls itself), carried beyond the goals to which it tends—if indeed it proposes goals for itself—arrives there, casts doubt upon all our rules, insults all our masterpieces, and perverts, through some illegitimate successes, that mass of fluctuating opinions in which it is always fate that disposes?[32]

Few literary documents manifest their political correlatives so clearly. Indeed, they are so explicit that in his response Stendhal advises the classicists to "have a tender regard for the police. Otherwise, they will be ingrates."[33] Even though we can understand Auger's fears through a look at the political vicissitudes that France underwent during the decades in question, nonetheless, precisely whence came that danger that the president of the academy so needed to dispel? Notdisguising the nationalistic principle upon which he based himself, Auger saw his adversary as a member of an international conspiracy mounted by a barbarous people, the Germans (see Auger, 28). Recently over the Revolution that had shaken the entire continent, recently liberated from the "usurper" Bonaparte, France now spoke through the voice of the *restaurateurs*, who descried enemies everywhere. The Necker family, already suspect because of its illustrious relative who had not moved to save Louis XVI from bankruptcy and doubly feared as foreign and Protestant, had the misfortune of beginning, through one of its daughters, Mme. de Staël, the introduction of Germany and of German romantic ideas into the country. It little mattered that no precise political program accompanied those ideas, or that Mme. de Staël had in fact been banished under Bonaparte, or that Stendhal's first pamphlet dealt only with literature. The integrity of the restored state did not seem the less endangered for such reasons, for advocacy of freedom in matters of art was seen as equally threatening to that bourgeoisie that had quickly forgotten its alliance with the people. Over against freedom of production and evaluation, that is, over against the *relativization of values*, Auger insisted on the atemporality of humankind and of nature: "Truth, in the arts, consists first of all in representing nature and man just as they are in all countries and at all times; and secondarily in marking the accidental differences that modify their exteriors in accordance with their locale or era" (19).

Moreover, the atemporal perfection of genres is derived as a corollary from the general atemporality: "The genres have been identified and fixed; their nature cannot be changed or their number increased. Only if one jumbles them together and combines them in monstrous forms can one believe that he has created new ones" (24).

Auger's diatribe, in itself an insignificant piece, is nonetheless very valuable in that it manifests in obvious ways the direct link between normative aesthetics and political interests. That normativeness, albeit both diluted and shorn of the majority of its supporting categories, endured—and continues to endure—much beyond the ambience of the French Restoration. Its survival is achieved through the veto of fiction, a prohibition carried out in the name of common sense. We have seen Auerbach interpret the adoption of the unities of time, place, and action as the product of an arrogant rationalism cultivated by the members of *la cour et la ville*. To deal with the survival of the normativeness implicit in that rationalism, I must add that by the second half of the seventeenth century it had transformed its arrogance into a defense of mean, common reality: "Even though the formulae for imitation of nature seem all but identical from the start of the century to its close, the notion of nature tends to narrow around 1660 and to begin to apply less to the school of Boileau than to mean, everyday reality" (Bray, 148).

With that narrowing, it became possible for the veto of the fictional to be transmitted down to our own time, under the name of realism. Even in speaking of the most enduring aspect of the old normativeness, Stendhal did not foresee that his classicistic adversary would endure every bit as long as his own work: "The Academician [in defense of his principles]: Because it is not credible that an action represented in two hours should encompass a week or a month; or that in a few moments the actors should go from Venice to Cyprus, as in Shakespeare's *Othello*, or from Scotland to the English court, as in *Macbeth*" (Stendhal, 19).

In defense of what, then, did the young, then unknown author write? Of nothing less than the position that the articulating principle of literary production and reception should be the rendering of life itself: "What one should imitate in that great man [Shakespeare] is his manner of studying the world we live in and the art of giving to our contemporaries precisely the kind of tragedy they need but do not have the boldness to demand, because they are so terrified by the reputation of the great Racine" (42-43).

Romanticism, then, saw itself as characterized by a reflection carried out on the basis of the *hic et nunc* and no longer as a function of a verisimilitude with the permanently and universally present. If verisimilitude had had its ground in *imitation*, the resemblance now sought was one with the vicissitudes of a life that was social, individual, and everywhere differentiated. The latter could never be made synonymous with the former, for to abstract life and then frame it in a rhetorical treatment subject to models was in fact to break faith with that life. Therefore, the concept of *imitatio* would be replaced by the notion of *expression* by an individual. Subjectivity seemed to be rending the veil that had covered it over, and reason, identified with mean truth, that is, common sense, to be losing its position as guardian of the temple. A new principle was beginning to be raised, one founded on the explanation of the subjective richness of the individual: "Either I am mistaken, or these changes of the passions in the human heart are the most magnificent thing that poetry can hold up to be viewed by the eyes of men, whom it at once moves and instructs" (44).

* * *

My description of the struggle between classicism and romanticism in the French milieu may lead to the mistaken presumption that the struggle assumed the virulence that I have noted because of its articulation with political positions linked to the outcome of the French Revolution. If such were the case, how could one explain why the exile of *imitatio*, supposed translator of mimesis, took place throughout Europe, soon thereafter to be effected in the Americas as well? The theoretical elimination of the principle of imitation is bound up with life conditions in the modern era. If Schiller reserved "naive poetry" for the Greeks, it was because, as Fontius observes, the Greeks were unaware of a separation between the sensory and the intelligible, creating instead an "undivided sensory unity," whereas the modern science of nature emphasizes a dismembering analytical reason and that principle pervades the very organization of education: "Neither Antiquity nor the Middle Ages knew systematic instruction under State supervision. After the development of modern education, which emphasizes detailed analysis, a form of learning based on demonstration and imitation seems to belong to a historical stage profoundly separated from the life of modern civilization." (Fontius, 236)

Rather than by the actual fate of *l'ancien régime*, or the tedium and loss of opportunity for young people that came as a result of Napoleon's fall, the interment of *imitatio* was, then, in fact effected by the passage from an aristocratic, estate society to a national, class society articulated by the scientific spirit. But if it was thus that *imitatio* was led to its grave, what of the more distant concept of mimesis? Its ostracism by contemporary theoreticians is well known. And it is just as well known that the romantic cult of individual expression transformed itself into the immanentist aesthetics that dominated uncontested the first sixty years of the present century.[34] At the present moment, when signs are being seen of a crisis in that immanentism, signs all the more evident after the vogue of structuralism—and signs of which Hans Robert Jauss's well-known inaugural lecture at Konstanz in 1967 was the first overture—would it not be opportune to rethink that old concept? And would it not be appropriate to relate that reexamination to the clearly intriguing fact that, albeit under veto, fiction is recognized both in classical works and in realistic ones, that is, in precisely those works on which the veto most imposes itself?

The Imaginary and Mimesis

Among Saint Augustine's merits, those of defender of poetry and the arts cannot be counted. Very much to the contrary, his Christian zeal caused him to concentrate on one task alone: the employing of his undeniable gifts as writer and thinker for the strengthening of the church, making it the unifying institution amid the fragmentation that marked late antiquity. To the extent that classical thought had weight with him and the poets did not escape his scrutiny, they still were subordinate to that guiding purpose. In the very treatise to which I shall shortly be referring, he evidences his mode of thinking: Vergil is rejected because, in opposition to Christian tenets, he had said that the unburied could not enter the Stygian bark, while Lucan is praised for allowing that the heavens could serve as the required roof for the unburied. The classical legacy was, then, acceptable to Augustine in direct proportion to its correlation with ecclesiological thought. Despite that guiding direction in his work, however, it will be in Augustine that we shall find material to understand how works that either limited the use of the fictionality available to them—those of a Molière, for example—or actually rejected such use altogether because their author chose to remain shackled to reality—the supreme case coming in the works of Zola—are nonetheless still recognized as works of fiction. To mount such an inquiry, it will be necessary for me to violate the purpose, though to be sure not the spirit, of Augustine himself.

In his *De Cura Gerenda pro Mortuis* [On the Care to Be Taken for the Deceased], Augustine discusses the origin of the argument that the dead can appear to the living in dreams, asking something of them or pointing something out to them. His thesis is that, in that case, "it is not necessary to believe that the dead act as real, conscious beings. . . . For the living too appear to the living in dreams, and without knowing it."[35] He illustrates his position with an anecdote that one might very well imagine as the source for a Borges short story:

> While I was still in Milan, there occurred to Eulogius, rhetoric teacher at Carthage and my student in that art, the following event, as he himself told it to me when I returned to Africa. As his course dealt with Cicero's rhetorical works, he was preparing his lesson for the coming day when he came across an obscure passage of which he could make no sense. In his irritation, he had to use every device he knew to fall asleep. I then appeared to him during his sleep and explained the phrases that he had not been able to understand. It was not really I, of course, but rather my image, totally apart from myself. I was far away, on the other side of the ocean, involved in another matter or having another dream, totally unaware of his concern.
> How that happened I do not know. But no matter by what means, how can we not believe that the dead do not appear to us as images in our dreams just like the living? Who will see them and where no one either knows or cares. (Augustine, 494-95)

Whether we be alive or dead, we can therefore be the stimulus for someone else's dreams, all the while not being responsible for what we say therein, or do, or counsel. We are not responsible for images of ourselves, precisely because we are not to be identified with them.

Can the reader see what I am driving at or do doubts persist even where enough has been said? Dreams operate along a line like those established by poetic—if not all artistic—experience: they convert perceived material, the "day residue," into images that then assume their own activity, achieving an autonomy for which the originating material is not responsible. It is possible, then, to enter into communication with the fictional only when one learns to see it as a whole that one's imagination invokes. Or, rather, when one receives messages structured less through utterances than through images. To be sure, not all experience of the imaginary is aesthetic experience. The experience of hallucinations is, of course, wholly lacking in aesthetic content. While the imaginary presupposes the destruction of reality—that is, abandonment of the thematization of perception grounded in that concept—creating a diffuse magma in which anything can signify anything, aesthetic experience involves the negation of the negation of the imaginary: my interpretation of the poetry that I read cannot be strictly my own but must be formulated on the basis of the potential created by the schema contained in what I read.[36] What I wish to argue, then, is the following: it is proper to fictional discourse, be it aesthetic or other, that it be perceived as an articulation of images, that it be thematized by the imagination. Therefore, just like Augustine with regard to his disciple's dream, the author of such discourse does not control its reception, and it can be received as a fictional product, even though a veto may have been imposed on the use of fiction or the author in fact may have prohibited it.

The following options present themselves as consequences of this line of thought: one may either conclude that exhaustive analysis of the thematization of the imaginary represents a sufficient basis for a theory of the poetic or one may endeavor to link such an analysis to a reexamination of mimesis.[37] I opt here for the second of those courses, in the conviction that the ostracism of mimesis has depended more on historical reasons than on its internal exhaustion. I shall endeavor, then, to show what those historical reasons have been and how it would be possible to revivify the concept of mimesis.

* * *

We have seen, through recourse to the work of Martin Fontius, how the edifice of *imitatio* had become inadequate in relation to the institutions of modern life. The according of centrality to analytical, dismembering reason came at the time of the breakdown of the frames of reference supporting classical estate society and at the time of the rise of a new political institution, the nation-state, which, in the area of the arts, served as a pole around which society's legitimated historians and critics would revolve. It was in the light of that set of factors that the romantics proposed life itself as the new raw material for art. The work of art was to acquire veracity to the extent that it expressed life well. It was a mode of expression different, and distant, from the course of *imitatio* because it was not subordinated to significations previously established and socialized. Instead, expression involved personalized motifs and therefore became communication only when it touched on experiences that were intersubjectively common (as cultivated in the "normal" romanticism of a Lamartine, a Vigny, or a Musset, or even in that of Hugo). Beyond those boundaries, expression was enveloped in a necessarily faint aura, as Nerval's work clearly manifests. If, in *Racine et Shakespeare*, Stendhal was still battling to conquer the public for romantic art, and Hugo sustained that conquest throughout his long life, artists in general would soon abandon the cause. The artists' language began to retreat from communicative interchange and, as with Baudelaire, became an act of aggression, a "shock experience" (Walter Benjamin). This entire phenomenon is but one way of observing that the public had adopted the cause of the victorious entrepreneurial bourgeoisie, leaving the artists immersed in a marginalized subjectivity all their own. As a result, criticism, once it abandoned the hostility that it had directed against the rebellious poets, and after ascertaining that their rebellion could easily coexist with the politico-economical status quo, either took up biographical criticism, which kept faith with romantic pretensions by aestheticizing life itself or, in a gesture of rectification, rejected biographical criticism for concentration on study of the poetic process in a sort of revival of rhetoric, with the hope of describing the integrity of a new substance, the substance of the poetic.[38]

It is interesting to note — and in all likelihood has been noted — that this deprecation of common language did not arise only among artists and analysts of art at the beginning of the twentieth century. The very concept of the avant-garde, which at that time was expanding from the area of politics to that of art, shares in the same presupposition. Common usage and common values were also disdained by those involved in a new logic, formal and mathematical in character, as projected by the Vienna Circle on the one hand or, in far-off England, by Bertrand Russell on the other. The true producers, be they considered avant-garde artists or not, were to create either closed, clandestine political apparatuses or a purified language shorn of the ambiguities of daily usage. And even when one of those authors, Wittgenstein, changed his line of investigation, it took a long time for that change to be accepted and have its impact. In his later period:

> Wittgenstein focused his attention instead on *language as behavior*: concentrating his analysis on the pragmatic *rules* that govern the uses of different expressions, on the *language games* within which those rules are operative, and on the broader *forms of life* which ultimately give those language games their significance. The heart of the "transcendental" problem thus ceased (for Wittgenstein) to lie in the formal character of linguistic representations.[39]

Results, to be sure, of different conditioning factors, various areas of contemporary culture began from the premise that a new language should be created and that the public should receive from political and/or philosophical and/or artistic avant-gardes doctrines, manifestos, and studies that would liberate that public from oppression, misery, and automatism. As a consequence, it is not surprising that concern with mimesis did not appear in the field of art, in the strict sense of the term, for there it would be seen as representing an objectionable compromise with the figurative and the traditional; rather, it was taken up, albeit in a marginal way, within a project which was not supported by any previously constituted tradition and which, in requiring the presence and participation of an individual "of no special character," could not take part in the rejection of day-to-day language. The project was that of psychoanalysis. Elaboration of the subject will require a space other than this one, not to mention an author other than myself. I shall limit my development of it to some brief observations based on the work of Freud.

I shall take as my starting point the phenomenon of identification. Freud says that "identification is known to psychoanalysis as the earliest expression of an emotional tie with another person"; it can arise from a wish for identity, either positive or negative, with the object to be imitated.[40] That is, the symptom may be one involving identification with a rival object—the daughter coughs in the manner of the mother with whom she competes, thereby "bring[ing] about a realization, under the influence of a sense of guilt [*Schuldbewusstseins*], of her desire to take her mother's place: 'You wanted to be your mother, and now you *are*—anyhow so far as your sufferings are concerned'" (Freud, 106). Or it may involve identification with the love object, as with Dora, who imitates her father's cough (106). In a third possibility, "the identification leaves entirely out of account any object-relation to the person who is being copied," grounding the very mechanism of identification "upon the possibility or desire of putting oneself in the same situation [as the person being copied]" (107). The affective tie to a referent—to a person being copied—engenders a similitude of action or attitude, a similitude conceived only through the mediation of interpretation, that is, not based on a simple congruency of a visual nature. In many of Freud's cases, as Sérgio Paulo Rouanet observes, "The theory of identification is literally a theory of mimesis—a making-oneself-like through appropriation, be it partial or total, of the model."[41]

Even when similarity to the model is visual, it is not that visuality that is its basis; what is essential *is not its nature as copy or substantive trace but the process of transformation that is in operation*. That affirmation can be substantiated by supplementing the paraphrase of Freud's analysis with this one, which appeared in one of his earlier essays:

When, now, I perceive a movement like this of greater or lesser size in someone else, the securest way to an understanding (an apperception) of it will be for me to carry it out by imitation, and I can then decide from the comparison on which of the movements my expenditure [*Aufwand*] was the greater. An impulsion of this kind to imitation is undoubtedly present in perceptions of movements. But actually I do not carry the imitation through, any more than I still spell words out if I learnt to read by spelling. Instead of imitating the movement with my muscles, I have an idea of it through the medium of my memory-traces of expenditures on similar movements.[42]

Physically realized imitation—that is, one visibly evidenced—constitutes a stage preparatory to an imitation carried out through internal representation. What is decisive in the constitution of mimesis, then, is the creation of a *staging*, which is not so much the repetition of a model as *the organization of a response to that model carried out at the level of the sensorial*. Let us briefly recall the incident of the *fort-da*. A one-and-a-half-year-old boy, apparently mature enough not to cry when his mother left the house, instead exhibited the strange behavior pattern of scattering his toys at a great enough distance from himself that gathering them up again would require concerted effort. Moreover, in scattering them our small actor would voice a long "oooh" and, in gathering them together, would punctuate each recovery with a happy "*da.*"[43] The game symbolically staged the mother's leaving (her *Fortgehen*) and the joy at her return (*da*). In such analysis Freud took a step which, although compatible with the romantics' position, was not one that they contemplated. Psychoanalysis, one might say, is born of the horizon of inquiry opened up by the romantics. That inquiry was decisive in demonstrating that reason, as it was conceived by classical thought and classical poetics, could not serve as an explanatory criterion for art. Reason sets up *conscious* models to be internalized through either direct or sublimate action. It therefore confuses them with the *reality* to be imitated. Replacing the model of a conscious *imitatio* with reflection on scenes experienced in life, the romantics implicitly showed that reality does not become a *da* by the simple fact that it is formed of objects that offer themselves up before us [as *Gegenstände*].

As Schütz will observe (see chap. 3), man lives in contact with multiple realities, and each of them is constituted around a set of rules that enable his intersubjective experience. It is the case, however, that those multiple realities are constituted on the basis of one dominant reality, namely everyday reality, within which—I maintain, here independently of Schütz—perceptual thematization dominates over a thematization deriving from the imagination.[44] Hence the tendency to interpret the different *provinces* of the real—the provinces of dream, of art, of religion, and so on—as subcategories of the province of everyday reality alone, governed by its laws and thus explainable by recourse to the same rules that are applicable to everyday experience. (Parenthetically, we should note that whereas Schütz has the great merit of pointing out the simultaneous and multiple layers of reality, he nonetheless adheres to rationalistic tradition in binding the other provinces too closely to everyday reality. Thus, to my reading of him here, a very positive one for the construction of a basis for fiction, another reading could be counterposed emphasizing his continuation of the veto of the fictional.)

In opposition to the "arrogant rationalism" of the classical era, Stendhal foresaw a province of art possessing its own rules, as he demonstrates in discussing the problem of illusion: "When one says that the spectator imagines that the time necessary for the events represented on the stage has passed, one does not mean that the spectator's illusion extends to the point of believing that all this time has really elapsed" (Stendhal, 21).

Moreover, that observation was not entirely unprecedented. In 1719, in his *Réflexions critiques sur la poésie et la peinture* [Critical Reflections on Poetry and Painting], Jean-Baptiste Du Bos wrote:

People of spirit thought that the illusion was the prime cause of the pleasure that plays and paintings give us. According to that impression, the staging of the *Cid* gives us so much pleasure only through the illusion that it elicits. The poetry of the immortal Corneille, the theatrical apparatus, and the actors' declamation exercise such force on us that we believe that we are in the presence not of a representation of an event but rather of the event itself, that we are seeing the real action and not an imitation. That interpretation seems to me an untenable one.[45]

Du Bos's comments show that classicistic legislation presupposed that the reader or spectator was guided only by the principle of *perceived* time and operated on that premise. For the romantics — and Du Bos's sensualistic aesthetics as well — the basic premise was that the average spectator knew that stage time was not to be confused with time on the clock. Now I am not here arguing that among the ruins of *imitatio* the romantics discovered the figure of mimesis (it would be partially true in relation to Coleridge alone; see chap. 2). I do, however, wish to argue that, in the current crisis of the immanentist theory of poetics, it becomes both possible and desirable to reread the romantics with an eye to these lines of inquiry, which have heretofore been ignored. Especially those lines that, in giving specific definition to the province of art, do not divide it from the other provinces in life's repertoire. Now such specificity and interrelatedness can easily be apprehended from the point of view of mimesis. Our short incursion into Freud shows that psychoanalytic theory involves a mimesis that is carried out — and effaced — on a daily basis. What difference, then, can there be between those fields of its operation? The major difference seems to be the following: day-to-day mimesis operates within the province of everyday reality, thus obeying laws necessarily different from those governing artistic experience. That factor becomes evident in a comparison of the reading of a literary narrative with the compiling of a case history. As Hans Ulrich Gumbrecht writes:

Literary narratives—we can summarize—like all narratives, enable the receiver to experience life processes. Nevertheless, while, like all literary texts, they suggest by means of corresponding signs the neutralization of the question of their referentiality, they can act as representations of the (author's) imagination and as stimuli for the (reader's) imagination. Since these processes (and not an inventory of experiences or motivations to action) represent and stimulate the imagination, they can pre-direct the mode of their own realization through the receiver's imagination.[46]

When, by contrast, the psychoanalytic subject is a mimesis located in the province of the day-to-day, our relationship to it changes: "Referentiality and the loss of reference by the presentations of identity proffered by day-to-day fictions are equally relevant to the hearer. The referential passages serve as signs of the speaker's identity, the non-referential ones are symptoms of his or her hypertrophied self-evaluation. . . . Day-to-day fictions . . . are conventional signs or symptoms for the speaker's identity" (Gumbrecht, 417).

Therefore, whereas identification of a discourse as literary-fictional has an effect on the reader's constitution of the world, recognition of a psychoanalytical "case" as fictional leads to judgment of the subject: he or she is a storyteller, someone untrustworthy, a boaster.

With such issues in mind, let us look again at what happens in literary mimesis. Just as in day-to-day mimesis, it presupposes a correspondence between what it enunciates and the receiver's frame of reference. That correspondence is translated into a sense of *similarity* between the utterance and what the receiver can postulate as thinkable. In fact, then, the presumption of such a correspondence operates in both the receiver and the producer. From the point of view of the former, such is the case because his very perceptions have been oriented by the culturally socialized expectation of what he should see: "Perceptions are not discoveries, but instead they have an essentially prognostic character. The prognosis refers to the form that must arise if and when we act."[47]

From the point of view of the producer, the same central role for similitude results from: "The usual will always be the most seemly point of departure for the representation of the unusual; an already-existing representation will always exercise its ascendancy over the artist, even while that artist is seeking to capture the true" (Gombrich, 102).

Thus the experience of mimesis is historically and culturally variable because the first sensation that it produces, the sensation of similarity, stems from correspondence to frames of reference and expectations themselves historically and culturally variable. Nevertheless, the category of correspondence and its immediate corollary, "sensation of similarity," do not exhaust the area of experience of literary mimesis. Instead, it must be added that it is carried out within a specific sphere, that of aesthetic experience. That sphere, in its turn, presupposes that those who participate in it understand, as Stendhal argues, that time inside the theater is not the same as stage time, that time within a poem is not the same as the time in which the everyday, empirical "I" of the poet exists, that the experiences and values of narrators and characters are distinguishable from the experiences and values of the author. Between author and work there is neither a schizophrenic separation nor a simple continuity. The work of literature stages experiences imaginable on the basis of that aforementioned frame of reference and admissible on the basis of its author's values. (If Brecht is not Mother Courage, it is nonetheless still inconceivable that he would offer us a Nazi "hero.")

These are not rules dependent on formal education; if they were, only students of literature would be able to know and use them. Literary mimesis presupposes this sensation of similarity, to which a sense of difference is subsequently added.[48] To take up Searle's analysis—although our conclusions will be opposite to his—a fictional utterance supposes suspension of the vertical rules that, in linking the normal utterance to the province of day-to-day reality, subjects the reader to their sanctions. (Vertical rules are those that make us the object of either praise or censure according to whether we have acted in accordance with their sanctions or not.) That experiencing of the difference created by literarily articulated mimesis—that is, of a difference occasioned by aesthetic experience—seems to be normal in a reasonably prepared receiver.

That receiver also recognizes a second difference: while a quotidian narrative is prized to the extent that it is complete—that is, to the extent that it gives thorough and coherent information—a literary narrative exacts of its reader more than the mere capacity for verbal *decoding* of what he reads or hears. Since its constitutive elements do not possess the fluent, cogent concatenation of the quotidian—or scientific, or philosophical—narrative, since, in fact, those elements frequently conflict and contradict, *holes* are created, according to Wolfgang Iser, holes that must be filled by the reader's interpretation.[49] The reader's role is not limited to making sense of what the text already possesses as implicit form, for to affirm such a notion is to postulate the existence—at very least, the ideal existence—of a single correct interpretation. The receiver's role is, rather, a pluralizing one, for it depends on the activity of his own imagination. *Mimesis is, then, a process whose concretization is established under the form of fiction.* In the realm of day-to-day life, fiction is synonymous with deceit, fabrication, falseness, fantasy, or pretense. It is only within literary or artistic experience that it finds the desideratum necessary for the process of mimesis. It is a process that is therefore not to be confused with the expression of the "I," but, instead, must be seen in connection with its unfolding.

Chapter 2
The Fates of Subjectivity
History and Nature in Romanticism

*These days there is no longer any doubt that world history
must be rewritten from time to time. That necessity derives not,
for example, from the intervening discovery of numerous events
but rather from the advent of new ways of seeing, from the fact
that someone in a later time is led to vantage points on the
basis of which the past can be comprehended and evaluated in
a new manner. The same thing happens in the sciences.*

Johann Wolfgang von Goethe,
"Materialen zur Geschichte der Farbenlehre"

Nature

The Collapse of the Classical Universal

The classical period is so permeated by the idea of unity, progressively concretized with the development of the absolutist state, that we can capsule it in the
motto "only one God, only one King, only one law." In support of that uniformity came *reason*, which was to be studied by the theologian and by the philosopher so that, from the realm of politics to that of administration, the unity
between the human and the divine might be shown to be wholly justified. That

endeavor had as its desideratum the establishing of universal laws—the laws of reason. Reason revealed the world as a harmonious mosaic. To expend such effort in the maintenance and strengthening of the pact between God and humankind was to serve what was in effect the nature of things. The king that I revere is mine to the degree that I integrate myself into the universal order. Which is the same as saying that subjectivity was less negated by the classical order than it was subordinated and subsumed by supposedly natural principles. Universality of values and prior determination of the place that subjectivity might occupy were, then, the obverse and reverse of the same coin. As a result, the individual could feel repressed only when he or she did not accept the premise that the given order was indeed natural. If, conversely, he or she accepted the "natural" hierarchy and the modes of activity grounded in reason, the individual subject could not feel inhibited. The greatest wisdom of the classical period therefore consisted in learning little by little to control the rediscovery of the subjectivity, which had begun, long before, at the close of the twelfth century. It was, to be sure, a wisdom unaware of its own dimensions, having as its operational base the principle of analogy between the world of things and the world of words—a subject on which Foucault gave us his capital study *Les Mots et les choses*.[1] Analogy functioned as the tranquilizing *tertium comparationis*; it was prominent in the visual field—where, for example, a substance was considered beneficial in treating a certain disease because of its similarity in shape to the affected organ— but it had equal weight in abstract areas as well. In asking himself why his poetry was accepted by princes and peasants alike, Boileau implicitly utilizes the principle of similitude, taking it as the cause of his universal appeal: "It is that in them the true, vanquisher of the lie, / Displays itself to the eye throughout and seizes upon the heart, / For in them good and ill are given true appraisal."[2] What is true is clear to everyone's eyes and touches everyone's hearts, which know how to "see" the difference between good and evil. If the same epistle to the Marquis de Seignelay declares: "Only the true is possessed of beauty; the true alone is lovable" (Bloch, 102), it is precisely because the beautiful is similar to the true, the pinnacle of universal values. But to achieve that similitude promised by nature, the poet must know how to conduct himself, recognizing that his subject matter, fiction, is an elegant falsehood—or, better, a falsehood that he or she must make elegant, and clever, and correct: "The adroit untruth of all fiction / Only tends to make truth shine before our eyes" (102). The passage makes *imitatio's* function absolutely clear: it was through it that the poetic fable built its defenses against "conquering falsehood," only thus to be received by the reason inherent to all. Falsehood would indeed conquer if the author were to be guided only by his or her rebellious subjectivity and refused to adapt it to the "natural" order. Indeed, the veto against the fictional was aimed at control of the subjective. It was a control that would have been ineffective if it could not count on the consent of the agential subject or, more precisely, if it could not count on sufficiently persuasive sociopolitical conditions—that is, conditions that could both stifle open rebellion and remove any sense of slippage with regard to what norms should be obeyed. Now, by the end of the seventeenth century this laboriously constructed edifice founded on the principle of similitude, activated by the exercise of reason, and vigilant of a universal, atemporal legislation, began to be undermined. The travel accounts, real or invented, that proliferated in the century, taking China or Persia, Africa or America as their subjects, written by missionaries, explorers, or simple travelers, publicize a diversity of customs and values, casting doubt on the universality theretofore maintained. *Gulliver's Travels* (1726) represents only the best known of the fictional documents that satirize the presumed universality of classical patterns. If the relativism emphasized by the travel accounts attacked the external uniformity presumed by the classical era, in the sphere of philosophy Locke's *An Essay Concerning Human Understanding* attacked the basis of reason itself. For Locke, reason does not express the essence of our soul because our knowledge comes only from our senses, of which our thought, our reason, is a mere derivative. There is, then, nothing that can command the consensus of all human beings; instead of an innate reason, uneasiness and desire are the basic elements of our constitution. But do not such affirmations merely replace one source of the universal with another, retaining intact the program of universality? No, for the prominent place of uneasiness reveals something specific to the individual, even though it may be a something that all individuals have in common. The same cannot be claimed for the supposedly innate character of classical reason, for it eliminated the specificity of all individual "reasons."

While the philosophical debate is not of interest to us in and of itself, it is important to point out its impact in parallel fields of endeavor: the critique on which Locke's system is based implied the prominence of the individual. Now it would be foolish to think that the principle of individuality came *ex nihilo* to attack the whole edifice of universalizing reason. Indeed, we see it clearly at work in Leibniz's *Monadology* (1714). That brief treatise openly counterposed the idea of spiritual substance to the explanation based on mechanical causes supported by Cartesian thought. The monad, the individual's animating spirit, or, in the philosopher's own words, his entelechy, or soul (63), is a simple substance, indivisible, irreducible to itself alone, and not susceptible to being "inwardly altered or changed by some other being than itself. . . . The monads have no windows by which anything can enter in or go out."[3] Simply stated, monads change only through their own processes. The individual, a monad residing in an organic body, is, then, endowed with a spiritual principle rather than a mechanical one. That schematic statement allows us to pinpoint Leibniz's fierce defense of the individual subject against the universalizing *ratio* which determined the subject's place aprioristically. Leibniz, however, makes his argument acceptable to his time by joining the monodologic principle to the existence of God: "Thus

God alone is the primitive unity, or the simple original substance of which all the created or derivative monads are productions'' (Leibniz, 7:86).

God, then, becomes an indispensable condition for keeping the monads, self-enveloped as they are, from entering into conflict and, conversely, for allowing them to coexist in a perfect harmony. Only thus: "May [we] say indeed that in everything God the architect accords with God the law-giver'' (89:139).

These infinite, closed entities, the monads, are penetrated by that same ray of divinity that, on the one hand, orders them in a celestial harmony and, on the other, makes each of them the image of all the others: "As one and the same city looked at from different sides appears different and presents innumerable aspects, so likewise it comes about that there are as many different universes as there are simple substances the multitude of which is infinite. All those different universes are, however, only perspectives of one universe from the different viewpoints of each monad'' (57:99).

No matter how powerful such structures in maintenance of a criterion of universality may be, a destructive charge perforce operates within them. Individual subjectivity requires divine wisdom to explain why, monadic and privatized as that subjectivity is, it can *know* the universal. That is to say, the universal has now been interiorized and, making the individual into a potential, and multiple, mirror, converts its relationship to the divine into a dynamic that is similarly interiorized. The exterior world — nature — is, in turn, emptied of God. Those "simple substances" with voices, logically explained by recourse to a notion of divine action, the efficacy of which they in turn prove, become *in fact* the markers of God's existence. If they do not affirm that existence and, less Leibnizian than their creator would like, abandon the center from whence they came, the external world will seem empty, desacralized. On this general point, Leibniz's and Locke's thoughts move in the same direction: their common emphasis on the gravitation of the individual subjectivity leads toward the breakdown of the classical alliance between humans, nature, and God. Nature, which had acted as mediator for the meeting of Creator and created, as long as beauty accepted its similarity to truth and therefore completed itself within *imitatio*, now shows itself empty and hostile. Thus, as Cassirer emphasizes with respect to Rousseau: "there is now no longer any direct transition; not nature but morality, not any knowledge of the objective order of the world, but only conscience can show us the way to God."[4] From the end of the seventeenth century and throughout the eighteenth, then, signs of a crisis in the classical order become increasingly visible. Within the project this book envisions, it must be emphasized that to the classical mind the veto of fiction implied neither horror nor depreciation of an impractical discourse but rather hostility toward all formulations of experience incompatible with what was necessary to maintain the current political and religious forces in power. In the final analysis, control of fiction aimed at control of subjectivity, of what one might be able to do with it. Throughout the eighteenth century philosophical thought increasingly attributed an unprecedented importance to the senses, to consciousness, to the monodological basis of the individual, and religion began to lose its power as an instrument of socialization. The latter statement is amply testified to by an examination of the books published during the century in France. In the 1720s more than a third of the titles were religious; by the middle of the century, what were formerly the most popular works, "those of liturgy and devotion," had disappeared, and more "specialized" ones dealing with theology and apologetics remained.[5]

All these signals bespeak preparation for a change—a change which, it is easily seen today, would be a profound one. In furtherance of our investigation, let us look at one more of these sets of signals, namely, how the crisis affected the conceptualization and practice of history.

During the classical era, history, grounded in a catholic interpretation of the world, was conceived as universal history, within which particular histories were fitted. History was supported by an aprioristic schema that, on the one hand, separated it from the notion of investigation of facts and, on the other hand, assigned it to the area of rhetoric and belles-lettres. Hence the outraged criticism that Montaigne directed to historians:

> For the most part, and especially in these latter times, persons are picked out for this work from among the common people, on the sole consideration of skill in expression, as if we were trying to learn grammar from them! And having been hired to no other end and having put on sale only their gab, they are right to be chiefly solicitous only of that feature. And so, with an abundance of fine words, they concoct a pretty mess from the rumors they pick up in the city squares.[6]

By the second half of the eighteenth century, sacred history is severely disputed by the "antiquarians," who, like Leibniz, shut themselves up in archives and dedicate themselves to, or become specialists in, such until-then ancillary sciences as archeology, numismatics, and textual criticism. That immense documentary undertaking did not, however, affect the status of history, which remained in its location in the belles-lettres (see Furet, 105, 107).

In eighteenth-century France, in fact, the gulf between historian and antiquarian would actually be widened rather than diminished through the vogue enjoyed by "philosophical history," which was merely "a secularized 'discourse on universal history'" (Furet, 113). Located under the sign of transition, traditional historiography sought to patch the holes in the old universalizing paradigm through a mode of inquiry different from its predecessor only in its abandonment of the schema of religious interpretation. But that "only" bespeaks much: it declares that history was being desacralized. And it tells us too that the desacralizers believed they could attain their goals while maintaining their deprecation of the "manual" labor of the antiquarians. Nor would that situation change under the growing impact of the paradigm of the mathematical sciences. Indeed, to the contrary, the mathematical model led to the questioning of the historian's objectivity. And the situation was further complicated by the line of thought deriving from Locke and Leibniz, which emphasized the importance of empirical data and the irreducibility of the individual. This dilemma experienced by historiography at the outset of the eighteenth century has only one feature in common with the other signals previously referred to: it too is touched by the crisis in the universal, aprioristic conceptualization of reason—but it is not immediately aided by the intellectual currents that were lining up in opposition to the classical mentality. These currents were deployed on two fronts: that of mechanistic explanation, basically represented by the Cartesians, and that involving psychological explanation, which found its substantiation in features belonging to the individual subjectivity, when not in that subjectivity's very irreducibility to external activity. Neither line was of direct benefit to history, which, as we shall see in the second part of this chapter, would develop only in the final third of the century. The decisive element had not yet appeared: the struggle for national identity. Only in the light of that factor would history distance itself from any relationship with rhetoric and the belles-lettres.

This chapter is an inquiry into the relationships between the modern concept of history and fictional discourse, so let us pose the question of what was happening to fictional discourse during this period.

In absolute contrast to what was happening to history, the crisis of the classical mentality had an immediate effect both on literary expression and on modes of inquiry dedicated to it. In the latter area, it will suffice to recall the names Bouhours, Dubos, and Shaftesbury and the bases on which an aesthetics founded on the category of taste was proposed. On the literary front itself, let us remember the predominance of the expression of sentiment, in Prévost's *Manon*, Bernardin de Saint-Pierre's *Paul et Virginie*, Rousseau's *La Nouvelle Heloïse*, and Richardson's sentimental romances. I do not pretend to be writing a history of ideas, so I shall merely recite those names and currents and then dedicate subsequent development to examination of some assertions by Diderot. I wish to see how he approaches the question of the individual subject through consideration of the roles played by sentiment and by the now desacralized nature. As we shall have occasion to see, the individual and nature did not have to await romanticism to cement their relationship. With its old place no longer available, nature is ready to serve a new master.

In his famous "Essai sur la peinture" [Essay on Painting] (1765), Diderot evidences not only the low state in which he holds the model of *imitatio* but also the dilemma in which he finds himself with regard to two competing paradigms: one explains the quality of a work of art through the irradiation of an individual quality and the other explains it through its fidelity to nature. From the outset the author trains his artillery on the way artists are educated. The years given over to the academy do no more than teach the apprentice how to manipulate a "manner," an artificial technique of modeling forms in a way that "has nothing in common with natural positions and actions." For the apprentice to be free from the shackles of that "manner," it would be necessary for him or her to replace the academy's technique with the habit of observing life. Indeed, that alone would not be enough, for realization would remain imperfect without the aid of genius and refined sentiment: "It is not sufficient, however, to have laid the mass down well; it then becomes important to put in the details without destroying the whole. That is the work of spirit, of genius, of sentiment, of sentiment refined."[7]

It is clear that the condemnation of the "manner" manifests the rejection of the old *imitatio*. That *technique* is thought to be artificial and less rich than scenes of real life because the notion of an atemporal model of reality, the absorption of which by the individual artist would eliminate from his or her expression anything that might conflict with similitude between the beautiful and the true, is simply no longer believed in. The rejection of that old criterion is, however, not merely aesthetic. The attack on *imitatio* is made to parallel a virulence directed against religious hieratism: "the history of our religion and our God" would have another, figurative output: "If our priests had been more than stupid bigots, if this abominable Christianity had not been set up by blood and assassination, if the pleasures of our Paradise had not been reduced to a useless, beatific vision of I do not know what save that it is imperceivable and incomprehensible, if our Hell gave us something other than fiery abysses, hideous Gothic demons, shrieks, and teeth-grinding . . . " (Diderot, 1143).

In more direct terms, Christianity would be a source of inestimable value for plastic, poetic, or sculptural representation if it would renounce the model of ethereal reality in favor of expression of life. Now, even if someone of religious conviction, hearing Diderot, were to agree that the classical model of an atemporal reality had been converted into a stereotyped form, he or she would not be able to go along with Diderot in his praise of life, for that would imply the Virgin's loss of divinity for the image of seductress: "If the Virgin Mary had been the mother of pleasure, or else the mother of God; if she had had beautiful eyes, beautiful breasts, beautiful buttocks, that would have attracted the Holy Ghost to her, and if this were written in the book of her history . . . " (1143).

At this moment, when neither romanticism nor realism are yet being spoken of, Diderot's thought nonetheless moves in the direction of those two positions. At first reading, the essay seems to incline toward the realistic line. That is to say, with nature now become a vacant space, one not sacralized by a concept grounded in a proximity of the divine to the human, its power came to depend on its direct interchange with the human, whose interest, even enthusiasm, it would arouse by presenting scenes both alive and changeable into numberless combinations. But would the human envisioned in that interchange be just anyone? The passage transcribed above, in which it is explained that the artist needs a special talent, shows that such is not the case: the artist's powers of observation of the totality of nature must be aided by his or her verve, sentiment, and genius. Nor, for that matter, may the receiver possess merely the ability to observe well; he or she must have taste as well. Diderot, however, saw that the category of taste was too fluid. How could one work with so idiosyncratic a criterion? Better, how could one make it into an analytical instrument?

If taste is a matter of caprice, if there are no rules of the beautiful, whence, then, come these delightful emotions which arise so suddenly, so involuntarily, so tumultuously from the depths of our souls, which cause them to expand or contract, and which force from our eyes tears of joy, of sorrow, of admiration, be it at the presence of some great physical phenomenon or at the account of some great moral trait? *Apage, Sophista!* You will never persuade my heart that it is wrong in beating, nor my bowels that they are wrong in feeling. (1167)

The solution that our philosopher offers is less convincing than the question itself. Diderot explains taste from the receiver's viewpoint with the notion of habit and from the artist's viewpoint with the notion of a genius that manifests itself in actual anticipation of scientific discovery:

What, then, is taste? An ability, acquired through repeated experience, to capture the true or the good along with the circumstances that make it beautiful and to be immediately and vividly touched by it. . . . Michelangelo has given the dome of St. Peter's in Rome the most beautiful form possible. The geometrician of La Hire, impressed with that form, has traced out its plan and discovered that that plan is the curve of greatest resistance. What inspired Michelangelo to use that curve, among the infinite number of others that he could have chosen? Day-to-day experience of life. (1169)

In speaking of the individual and of the qualities to which creation and reception of art must correspond, Diderot touches lightly on particularistic considerations and quickly locates his reflection at a general level, the level of habit and anticipatory intuition. Whereas both of those areas presuppose everyday experience, they do not exist at the same general level. Habit inscribes itself directly at the general level—that is, it is sufficient to explain everyone's behavior. Anticipatory intuition, however, is particular to the individual endowed with genius. Instead of taking that concept as a *general definition* of the creative person, then, we must properly say that it involves a *generic trace* that is only vaguely defined in itself. Thus the question of taste leads to an imbalance in the fixing of the two poles that emerge in description of artistic experience. If it is understood as a function of habit, taste becomes operative; if it is related to the intuitive quality of genius, nothing further can be said of it save that it is the unexpected, the inexplainable, *the quality that anticipates what scientific discovery will reveal.* If we remove the issue of proximity to science, which Diderot himself does not develop, we see that genius is enclosed in a solipsistic conceptualization: genius is genius. That imbalance in analysis did not escape Diderot. The category of taste had served well in explaining the conditions of reception but not in explaining those of creation. If creation presupposes a special sensibility, he says, that sensibility seldom comes in concert with a corresponding taste. And from that regular incommensurability between innovative sensibility and taste necessary for its communication there arises an uncertainty about the acceptance of the work of art produced of genius. Acceptance is therefore ensured only through the intervention of—another genius: "Hence the uncertainty of any work of genius' success. It stands alone. It can be appreciated only if it is immediately related to nature. And who is capable of rising to the task of such a relating? Another man of genius" (1170). The interposed stipulation—that the products of genius are understood only through immediate relation to nature—reiterates the concept of nature as mediator. But that mediation is visible only to another genius. What at first seemed an obvious forerunner of realistic aesthetics is finally revealed as the anticipation of what will be defended by the least theoretically demanding romanticism. What is important, however, is not that outcome but rather the proof, implicit in Diderot's argument, that nature was no longer conceived at his time as a sphere separate from a symbolic network that gave it meaning. The realistic codification is favored by the removal of the old concept of a reality that abstracted and sublimated nature and made beings and events into figurations of a previously constituted truth. That conception now seems pale, false, and caricatural of the passionate truth of life. But transformation to a centering in life itself proves theoretically insufficient. The realistic codification runs into the thorny problem of imitation: to imitate what appears before one's eyes is still not to make life into art. To do that one must also be endowed with a particular individual ability. Abandonment of classical legislation leaves reflection on art revolving around the problem of idiosyncratic genius. What part, then, did "realism" play in Diderot's analytical thought? From my development of it here, it might be presumed that his annunciation of realism was no more than a preparatory stage, later to be subsumed into concentration on genius. But that impression is a false one. An article of four years earlier, "Éloge de Richardson" [Praise

of Richardson] (1761), shows more clearly both the tension between the romantic and realistic anticipations and also the reasons why Diderot did not attempt to
resolve that tension. He observes that Richardson

> never loses himself in magical realms. He sets his scenes in the world
> in which we live. The basis of his dramas is the true; his characters
> possess all possible reality. The personalities that he gives them are
> taken from the social milieu. The events that he depicts are within the
> customs of all civilized nations. The passions that he paints are those
> that I experience within myself. . . . He lays out for me the overall
> directions of the things that surround me. Without that art, since my
> soul inclines painfully toward chimerical states, the illusion would be
> but momentary and the impression weak and fleeting. (1060-61)

If the category of genius submerges the analyst of artistic experience in a darkness so great that no communication can be drawn from it, then the criterion of
realism becomes a necessary one: it provides the base from which the analyst
can explain both his evaluation of the work of art and also the enduring effect
that it has on the receiver. "Realism," therefore, becomes necessary less because
of any didactic dimension that it lends to art than because of the impossibility of
theorizing *operationally* about genius. When, then, Diderot goes on to write: "If
it is important to man to be persuaded that, independently of any consideration
beyond this life, we have nothing more to do to be happy than to be virtuous,
then what service will Richardson not have lent to the human race?" (1062), he
is not making a merely ethical judgment, because what is of importance ethically is equally so from an aesthetic point of view in ensuring the enduring nature
of the work's effect. The tension between romantic and realistic orientations,
then, represents less a prediction of what will be opposing movements than it
does a formulation of variables whose treatment becomes unavoidable in postclassical theories of art. In direct terms, the notion of genius seeks to describe
the conditions for the creative individual, whereas the notion of realism seeks to
describe the conditions for the circulation of the creative work. Total concentration on the former leads to the cult of a specific individual; total concentration
on the latter leads to the conceptualization of the relations between social reality
and the work of art, which will become rigidified in the concept of reflection. In
less general terms, romantic and realistic traces are anticipated in Diderot because
he foresees the necessity for a new theorization of art to take into account the
problems of the specificity of the work of art and its relationship to reality, without which the interest that it arouses cannot be explained.

Seen from this vantage, Diderot takes on the aspect of a microcosm of a problematic that will continue to develop through the end of the nineteenth century
in European literature, and to an even later date in the literature of the Americas.

That statement is not intended to turn the 150 years of development beginning in the mid-eighteenth century into one synchronic block. Such a gesture would be conceivable only if Diderot's language could be said to subsume all subsequent formulations during that period. If that very idea is absurd, especially in a time of such rapid change, a more modest proposition is still possible: the proposition that Diderot's anticipation of both romanticism and realism contains the questions that would be fundamental to the debate that would take place in the following decades.

To substantiate that proposition schematically, let us register the argument that Wolfgang Preisendanz develops with regard to the German novelists contemporary to naturalism (Stifter, Raabe, G. Keller, Fontane). The dissatisfaction that they all evidence with the directions of the novel in their time, Fontane's biting criticism of Zola and Turgeniev, result from their dislike of the way in which the "problematic articulation between subjective reality and objective facticity"[8] was effected. For Preisendanz, the question had arisen with romanticism, as a result of the emphasis on the role of a fantasy freed from its classical subjugation by *imitatio*: "It is well known that a fundamental principle of Romanticism was the emancipation of the fancy, of the imagination productive of the authority of relations in the empirical world. Precisely that principle, however, caused the Romantics to ask themselves with particular intensity about the relations between *mimesis* and *poiesis*" (Preisendanz, 458).

The emancipation of fantasy became problematic, then, because of the separation between the principle of mimesis and the principal of poiesis. Whereas the lyric poet takes the latter as his bastion, believing it sufficient for the expression of fantasy, the prose writer, for reasons yet to be discussed, opts for mimesis and makes history his muse. (The reader will perceive, in the absence of a more detailed commentary on my part, that the choice between poiesis or mimesis corresponds to the tension between genius and realism in Diderot.) Therefore, Preisendanz says that in the German prose writers' criticism of dominant realism, "the central question was always one of the nature of a poetic mimesis" (468). The very syntagm poetic mimesis bespeaks a will to balance counterposed directions, to unite "the prosaic consciousness of everyday life" (Hegel) with poetic imagination. The issue can be cast in general terms as follows: to achieve that desired unity in the field of art, the classical era subordinated poiesis to an understanding of mimesis that was simultaneously idealized and limited, which it named — as though simply offering a translation — *imitatio*. As we know, the entire edifice in which that concept figured admitted of the legitimacy both of only one authority, namely monarchical authority, and also of only one religion, which embodied and proclaimed the truth. In practice, that formulation involved the marginalization of such concepts as imagination, unless it was understood as a faint echo of *inventio*, which was in its turn the faint echo of poiesis. It also involved the depreciation of activities endeavoring to reconstitute the past because the sense of history had been priorly determined, in *Heiligsges-chichte*, sacred history. Life, then, had about it the aspect of a watertight ship, the passengers on which had no reason to feel suppressed — that is, those involved in art had no reason to be aware of the veto of fiction — for the voyage had been preplotted for all of them. Only when the capstone of the classical edifice, namely the atemporal universality of reason, is affected are the safety of the ship and well-being of the passengers put into question. That questioning, however, leads to the problem of subjectivity, of its role in the constitution of the world, its right to self-expression. In the case of art, the primacy of *imitatio* is countered with the aesthetics of taste and of genius.[9]

In this look at Diderot, I have shown a formulation that sought to give theoretical integrity to the understanding of art at the outset of modernity. I have also shown that his key concepts all verged on the same problem: expression of nature and of the individual within the systems of production and reception of art. Despite the fact that his thought on the subject would be surpassed by the best of romantic argumentation, that argumentation would itself nonetheless still deal with that same question to which Diderot attempted to respond. For that reason I have dedicated this space to the figure of the great *encyclopediste*, in the hope that an understanding of the tension between genius and "realism" in his work might help to orient us in the slippery field into which we now venture.

Subjectivity and Poetics in Early Romanticism

How is it that we can still refer to romanticism in the singular? As early as 1938 Huizinga asserted that "Romanticism has as many faces as it has voices."[10] An inventory of those voices will not be attempted here, for we do not even know how many there may be. Our inquiry will limit itself to the area occupied by theorization in early romanticism, with focus on Friedrich Schlegel and a small incursion into Wordsworth and Coleridge.

To avoid the erroneous impression that this study aspires to the status of a history of ideas — if it did it would be a history of the place either given or denied to fictional discourse — I shall begin with a look at the impact that the greatest event at the end of the eighteenth century had on the development of the romantic program. This direction, however, runs the risk of causing another error: the supposition that I take the French Revolution to be the originary event of romanticism. Although the foregoing pages should help prevent such an error, it is always well to guard against misunderstandings — at least those against which we *can* guard. The question of romanticism and that of the later realism sprang from the same soil: the necessity of offering art a new legitimation after the collapse of the classical order. It is well known that that necessity came at the same time as the change in the social function of art, for in the eighteenth century it had ceased to be an activity governed by, and directed to, specific roles — court entertainment, grandiose aristocratic or religious ceremonies, magnificent temples and palaces—and became, progressively, an autonomous commodity destined for the marketplace. That observation will function as a background premise, for it will have little direct role in our argument. The central question will be whether it is possible to lift the veto against fiction that was so solidly in force during the classical age. As we have noted, that veto was not even necessarily perceived. For that reason it was not perforce prejudicial from the point of view of the undertaking of artistic production. But from the moment when art ceased to have a fixed purpose and the alliance between God and humans no longer permitted the conceiving of universal values, the automatic subordination of the individual subjectivity to a preestablished order was considered to be an intolerable repression. And that general reaction was equally realized in the case of artistic experience: nature and life are raw materials that should no longer be expressed according to canons now repudiated. I shall now close these almost unnecessary preliminary observations and show how the French Revolution may be decisive for this inquiry.

The 1789 Revolution was greeted by the English and German intelligentsia as the principal event of the century. Some testimonies to the truth of that judgment follow.

"Day and night, my thought is today with France," the poet Wackenroder wrote in 1792, adding, "if France is unhappy, then I hate the whole world."[11] In a letter probably written in 1795, Fichte declared that his *Wissenchshaftlehre*, composed in 1794-95, "surged up in me" while "I was writing a work on the Revolution" and that his system was the metaphysical counterpart of the deliverance of humankind "from its material chains" accomplished by the Revolution.[12] In 1798, at the beginning of fragment 424 of his *Athenäum Fragments*, Friedrich Schlegel notes that it was a "usual" point of view to regard the French Revolution "as the greatest and most remarkable phenomenon in the history of states, as an almost universal earthquake, an immeasurable flood in the political world; or as a prototype of revolutions, as the absolute revolution per se."[13]

But the enthusiasm lasted only a few years. The Jacobin dictatorship, which began in 1793, the reign of terror under Robespierre, and the transformation of a defensive struggle into an offensive campaign would provoke a decrease in enthusiasm, discouragement, even reversal of sympathies in the same intelligentsia. "While Romanticism initially presented itself in Germany still involved with republican and liberal thoughts and even the Classicists sympathized with the ideas of the French Revolution, the triumphal march of the French armies engendered a considerable reversal" (Böttcher, 20). Even in an author like Coleridge, however, who became progressively conservative during the time, the change was not initially a radical one. In a letter to Wordsworth, probably dated 10 September 1799, Coleridge entreated his friend to write "a poem, in blank verse, addressed to those, who, in consequence of the complete failure of the French

Revolution, have thrown up all hopes of the amelioration of mankind, and are sinking into an almost epicurean selfishness, disguising the same under the soft titles of domestic attachment and contempt for visionary *philosophes*."[14]

Coleridge's *Biographia Literaria*, originally published in 1817, offers an important testimony to the later change of opinion: "The youthful enthusiasts who, flattered by the morning rainbow of the French revolution, had made a boast of *expatriating* their hopes and fears, now, disciplined by the succeeding storms and sobered by increase of years, had been taught to prize and honour the spirit of nationality as the best safeguard of national independence, and this again as the absolute pre-requisite and necessary basis of popular rights."[15]

Although that argument of nationalism was probably advanced at a date subsequent to the writing of the poem, the fact is that "France, an Ode," first published in 1798, shows that reversal already accomplished, in the cultivation of a sense of liberty that is now personal. The poem describes the poet's initial enthusiasm:

> When France in wrath her giant-limbs upreared,
> And with that oath which smote air, earth and sea
> Stamped her strong foot and said she would be free,
> Bear witness for me, how I hoped and feared!

That enthusiasm would leave him when he heard of the revolutionary troops' invasion of Switzerland:

> Forgive me, Freedom! Oh forgive those dreams!
> I hear thy voice, I hear thy loud lament,
> From bleak Helvetia's icy caverns, sent—
> I hear thy groans upon her blood-stained streams!

The poet then concludes by lamenting his confusion of desire for liberty with political events on the continent:

> The Sensual and the Dark rebel in vain,
> Slaves by their own compulsion! In mad game
> They burst their manacles and wear the name
> Of Freedom, graven on a heavier chain!

From those passages the direction that the reaction would assume becomes clearer. It would be important for the nature of romanticism and for the intellectual production of the time. The retreat into the self would stimulate the self-reflexive dimension of art. Thus, in the same ode, Coleridge finds anew the liberty that he seeks, in the contemplation of nature:

> And there I felt thee!—on that sea-cliff's verge,
> Whose pines, scarce travelled by the breeze above,
> Had made one murmur with the distant surge!

Yes, while I stood and gazed, my temples bare,

O liberty! my spirit felt thee there.[16]

Note the difference from the reason that led Diderot to give prominence to the realistic line. The poet now turns to nature not because he is dissatisfied with academic technique but because he must compensate himself for the failure of libertarian illusion. The same course will appear, in fictionalized form, in Hölderlin's *Hyperion* (1797-99). Hyperion breaks with his father and ends up losing Diotima because of his decision to fight against the Turks for the liberation of his Greece. But the war shows him a side of humankind that makes him quit the field of battle. The struggle for freedom thus becomes a paean to internal freedom, giving Hyperion's life an errant character. In a letter that will find Diodima still alive, Hyperion proclaims his change of conviction:

But let not pity, now or ever, lead you astray. Believe me, there is one joy left for us everywhere. True grief inspires. He who steps on his misery stands higher. And it is glorious that only in suffering do we truly feel freedom of soul. Freedom! if any understand the word—it is a deep word, Diotima. I am so inwardly assailed, so extraordinarily hurt, I am without hope, without a goal, utterly dishonored, and yet there is a power in me, something indomitable, that sets my frame sweetly trembling whenever it awakes in me.[17]

Thus are the first effects of political frustration attested to in two different, quite opposite ways, Hölderlin's distress contrasting with Coleridge's oratorical eloquence. In both cases, however, the solution is the same: refuge in poetic self-reflexivity. The Coleridge passages, however, manifest a second effect as well: if revolutionary enthusiasm led the young to expatriate their hopes, the Napoleonic Wars, disillusionment with Napoleon's expansionistic policies, his fall, and the advent throughout Europe of restoration repression, led to the swelling of nationalistic sentiments. Even though promulgated in this case by the same author, the two effects would lead to quite divergent paths in literature. In this chapter I will show that self-reflexivity would develop, especially in the lyric, whereas nationalistic sentiment would meld with the privileges accorded history to produce literary expression in the novel.

The repercussions of 1789 are revealed by two other authors as well. The first is important for his testimony that those repercussions were long-enduring, still felt in a year as far away from the revolutionary epicenter as 1816. In a letter of September 8 of that year to Lord Byron, Shelley tells of passing through Paris, and especially through the palace that had been ''the scene of some of the most interesting events of what may be called the master theme of the epoch in which we live—the French Revolution.''[18] The second, Wordsworth, provides one of the most vital testimonies to the reaction occasioned by the revolutionary years.

It is contained in his long *Prelude*, which will be examined here only as regards that subject.

Written between 1799 and 1805, although not published until 1850, *The Prelude* is, in the author's own words, "the history of a Poet's mind." It can therefore be seen as the poetic correlative of his friend Coleridge's *Biographia Literaria*, from which it differs only in having a more intimate and less intellectualized diction. As the history of a "mind"—seen from Wordsworth's rural infancy to passage through the benches of the university, wanderings in London, travel in France, where he payed witness to Robespierre's ascendancy and, friend of the Girondists, sensed the danger he was in and chose to return home, to continued aimlessness until his poetic vocation was revealed to him—as, then, the history of a life in search of its *raison d'être*, the poem can be taken as a *Bildungsgedichte*, the poem of a person's "education."

> Wordsworth's argument, like Milton's, is a theodicy which locates the justification for human suffering in the restoration of a lost paradise. In Milton's view, this event will not occur "till one greater Man/ Restore us, and regain the blissful Seat." Wordsworth's paradise, however, can be achieved simply by a union of man's mind with nature . . . without recourse, that is, either to an intervenient deity or to a heavenly kingdom to redress any imbalance between the good and the evil of our mortal state.[19]

We are dealing, then, as the same analyst points out, with "a theodicy without an operating *theos*." Therefore, as Abrams demonstrates in detail, both the *Bildungsgeschichte* and the *Bildungsroman* (and, I shall add, the *Bildungsgedichte* as well) are grounded in aspects of biography to treat a process of life resolution, of a reconquest of paradise, albeit now only a terrestrial one. The frequency of such forms in the romantic age accentuates the development of a secular view of the world, which had been in progress since the collapse of the classical era. It matters not that in his work the poet may confess religiosity; that religiosity is now a private one, and nature is no longer the point of encounter with God. For that very reason the event of the Revolution would take on the importance that every reader of *The Prelude* recognizes. Recalling his exultation at the triumph of the Revolution, Wordsworth writes:

> Trimphant looks
> Were then the common language of all eyes;
> As if awaked from sleep, the Nations hailed
> Their great expectancy.
>
> (6:756-58)[20]

It was a purely emotional enthusiasm unsupported by a political-social-economic examination, the practice of which was becoming common at this very time. Therefore, while wandering through the streets of Paris, Wordsworth voiced the hope that the present sacrifices might restore human dignity:

> And finally, as sum and crown of all,
> Should see the people having a strong hand
> In framing their own laws; whence better days
> To all mankind.
>
> (9:529-32)

If we today have some difficulty accepting that rhetoric, which seems to us highly declamatory, might it not be precisely because socioeconomic study of insurrections has become so normal a procedure that we automatically expect its homologue even in the most enthusiastic verses? Perhaps for that reason too the poet's disillusionment sounds a little suspect:

> When by the gliding Loire I paused, and cast
> Upon his rich domains, vineyard and tilth,
> Green meadow-ground, and many-coloured woods,
> Again, and yet again, a farewell look.
>
> (10:6-9)

But at least in this case our suspicions are not conclusive. Wordsworth has nothing to gain by speaking of the shame he feels in England—and this after his disillusionment—when finding her in league with the enemies of the Revolution:

> Britain put forth her freeborn strength in league,
> Oh, pity and shame! with those confederate Powers!
>
> (10:264-65)

It is thus consistent with his sentimental adherence to the revolutionary process that the poet refuses to become wholly disenchanted until he hears that the plan is for the pope to come and crown the Emperor:

> This last opprobrium, when we see a people,
> That once looked up in faith, as if to Heaven
> For man, take a lesson from the dog
> Returning to his vomit.
>
> (11:361-64)

Involvement with the revolutionary process ends there, and the autobiography takes another course. Nature had of course played a central role in Wordsworth's life since the days of his youth. And in section 4, which deals with his school holidays, there appears a fragment that another poetics would consider a separate poem:

> As one who hangs down-bending from the side

Of a slow-moving boat, upon the breast
Of a still water, solacing himself
With such discoveries as his eye can make
Beneath him in the bottom of the deep,
Sees many beauteous sights—weeds, fishes, flowers,
Grots, pebbles, roots of trees, and fancies more,
Yet often is perplexed and cannot part
The shadow from the substance, rocks and sky,
Mountains and clouds, reflected in the depth
Of the clear flood, from things which there abide
In their true dwelling; now is crossed by gleam
Of his own image, by a sunbeam now,
And wavering motions sent he knows not whence,
Impediments that make his task more sweet.

(4:256-70)

No longer is nature seen as a place sown with topoi and emblems that are linked to a preestablished decodification. There is no more *tertium comparationis*, or network of analogies whose meaning is known to the cultured reader. Instead of implicit reference to a cultured estate that could decode his work, Wordsworth has as his implied reader anyone who can concretize that scene on the basis of the associative capacity that it activates. Hence the two capacities that the poet will develop in himself as he faces nature: the capacities for observation and for imaginative reflection. (It should be noted that, in the preface to the *Lyrical Ballads* [1815], Wordsworth and Coleridge took observation and description as the first capacity requisite for poetry, adding, in fourth place, imagination and fantasy, the activity of which was defined in the verbs "modify, create, and associate.") That interchange with nature was, then, concomitant with its desacralization, with its character as a secular space wherein the traveler had to create his own destiny. The disillusionment with the Revolution merely led to that emphasis; or, more precisely, it turned the interchange with nature toward poetic ends:

But when that first poetic faculty
Of plain Imagination and severe,
No longer a mute influence of the soul,
Ventured, at some rash Muse's earnest call,
To try her strength among harmonious words;
And to book-notions and the rules of art
Did knowingly conform itself; there came
Among the simple shapes of human life
A wilfulness of fancy and conceit.

(8:365-72)

The fact that the passage comes before the account of disenchantment with the Revolution does not impugn our logic, for the autobiography is not structured around chronologically linear description.

With the abandonment of the concept of a divine level within it, nature becomes the interlocutor of a humankind now located at the center of all things, within which a "vital pulsation" is felt:

> In the midst stood Man,
> Outwardly, inwardly contemplated,
> As, of all visible natures, crown, though born
> Of dust, and kindred to the worm.
> (8:485-88)

Disenchanted, nature is now reenchanted with humankind at its center. And the same difference in cultural context that makes contemporary readers dislike sentimental revolutionary exaltation leads them to look askance at the divinization with which the poet seeks to endow the humankind-nature binomium:

> Thus was man
> Ennobled outwardly before my sight,
> And thus my heart was early introduced
> To an unconscious love and reverence
> Of human nature; hence the human form
> To me became an index of delight,
> Of grace and honour, power and worthiness.
> (8:275-81)

But if one of the primary conditions of an analytical reading consists in not engaging in an anachronistic analysis, then we are obliged to construct a "fusion of horizons," which is impossible unless we attempt—albeit without hope of total success—to reconstruct the expectations to which past works responded. Is it not, then, the romantic *enthusiasm* that separates us from those poets? And how, without romantic enthusiasm, can we understand the concept of poet as *vatis* that they reactivated?

> It shall be my pride
> That I have dared to tread this holy ground,
> Speaking no dream, but things oracular.
> (8:251-53)

As *vatis*, the poet could conceive of himself in the manner of a god, though a purely terrestrial one. If, then, it is correct to speak of the secularization of the world in the postclassical age, it is nonetheless necessary to point out that it was carried out with hold overs from religious experience. Although in different terms, Abrams has emphasized the same point: "The tendency in innovative

Romantic thought (manifested in proportion as the thinker is or is not a Christian theist) is greatly to diminish, and at the extreme to eliminate, the role of God, leaving as the prime agencies man and the world'' (*Natural Supernaturalism*, 91). Therefore, after discovering, atop Mount Snowdon, that his destiny is to be a poet, Wordsworth speaks of his power in the manner of a priestly investiture:

> This spiritual Love acts not nor can exist
> Without Imaginatio, which, in truth,
> Is but another name for absolute power
> And clearest insight, amplitude of mind,
> And Reason in her most exalted mood.
>
> (14:188-92)

* * *

The Prelude, the most elaborate testimony to what the Revolution meant for early romanticism, has presented us with a whole set of questions that cannot be easily shunted aside. We have seen that the self-reflexivity occasioned by nature preceded the moment of disillusionment with the revolutionary process; that that self-reflexivity, or interchange between mind and world, arose as soon as the individual subjectivity, now in effect delivered to itself, came to need an interlocutor that could "teach" it how to speak. To fill that need, the poet had to develop his capacity to observe the other, nature, in order then to discover in himself the metamorphosis of what he had seen, namely, the power of fancy and imagination. Does that trajectory not recall another, already seen here? Just as the role ascribed to observation corresponds to the importance that Diderot assigned to the realistic trace, so is the power of fancy and imagination comparable to the role granted to genius. Thus does Diderot seemingly take on the presence of a broad schema containing all that modern thought would develop with regard to art. In fact, however, another, critical reading would have to be carried out in addition to this one to deal with such matters. The terms genius, imagination, fancy, and even that other term associated with the same paradigm, *vatis*, are still either devoid of operativity or somewhat imprecise. The least opaque of them is *vatis* because of the religious frame of reference that motivates it. Nevertheless, that very anchoring in the area of religious experience seems historically to have been weakened by the notion of the poet as *vatis*, whereas the identification of the poet with genius remains strong, at least in popular conception. And what of imagination? While the concept of observation seems to propose itself as self-evident, at least to unsophisticated minds, the imagination has not acquired more precise definition in the passages heretofore transcribed. In fact, the imagination was raised from that limbo only by a passage from the *Biographia Literaria*. Leaving aside Coleridge's distinction between primary and secondary imaginations, let us concentrate on the following passage. Imagination "dissolves, diffuses, dissipates, in order to recreate; or where this process is rendered impossible, yet still at all events it struggles to idealize and unify. It is essentially *vital*, even as all objects (*as* objects) are essentially fixed and dead. . . . Fancy, on the contrary, has no other counters to play with, but fixities and definites. The Fancy is indeed no other than a mode of Memory emancipated from the order of time and space" (Coleridge, *Biographia Literaria* 1:202). We can now see more clearly why imagination and fancy are connected paradigmatically with the category of genius and why they rise above it. Insofar as observation teaches the artist to *see* in general terms, fancy and imagination arrange themselves in a precise scale, one which breaks with the notion of the object seen. Although fancy, being a manifestation of the memory liberated only from the categories of space and time, does retain a certain fixity in that regard, that mode of existence of the object is done away with completely by the imagination. In summary, the impreciseness attendant upon thought about art in the modern era is overcome only at the moment when it intuits that the art object is greater than the interlocutors that it links, namely nature and the individual. It overcomes them not so much by denying them as by transforming them. Diderot has nothing to say to us about that; his idea of genius now assumes the status of a remote precursor. But, as history rarely recognizes a step forward at the time it is taken, and as Coleridge's formulation had no immediate impact, Diderot's insistence on the "realistic" trace and on genius would continue to have historical gravitation.

* * *

When I began discussing the repercussions that the 1789 Revolution had on early romanticism, I said that it was not my goal to carry on the tradition of the history of ideas. Despite that disclaimer, however, I would be doing exactly that if, in addition to the foregoing, I did not also delve into a parallel source of influence upon the directions of romanticism—this time a source of a socioeconomic order.

Two years after the publication of Diderot's "Essai sur la peinture," a Scottish Enlightenment thinker, Adam Ferguson, published a general reflection on human society, *An Essay on the History of Civil Society* (1767). Much less famous than his French contemporary, Ferguson nonetheless wrote one of the first works about the social impact of nascent industrial capitalism. His contribution cannot be ignored because any study of the modern age would be only partial if it did not take into account the interaction between the material and intellectual realms.

Comparing "the spirit that reigns in a commercial state" to the spirit that dominates societies in which "the tribute of vassalage is paid in blood,"[21] Ferguson evidences the painful discovery of the individual isolation that is characteristic of the former: "It is here indeed, if ever, that man is sometimes found a detached and a solitary being: he has found an object which sets him in competition with his fellow creatures, and he deals with them as he does with his cattle and his soil, for the sake of the profits they bring" (Ferguson, 34).

This does not imply that he assumed an attitude of indignation—either conservative or revolutionary—in the face of the new times. Division of labor, the enabling condition for the commercial state, brings immediate advantages for both the producer and the consumer: "It is evident, that, however urged by a sense of necessity, and a desire of convenience, or favoured by any advantages of situation and policy, a people can make no great progress in cultivating the arts of life, until they have separated, and committed to different persons, the several tasks which require a peculiar skill and attention" (324). But there are disadvantages as well. Division of labor also increases the distance between the members of a society, assigning superintendence of the entire society to some while limiting others to activities that are mechanical and partial: "But if many parts in the practice of every art, and in the detail of every department, require no abilities, or actually tend to contract and to limit the views of the mind, there are others which lead to general reflections, and to the enlargement of thought. Even in manufacture, the genius of the master, perhaps, is cultivated, while that of the inferior workman lies waste" (329). Therefore, even though it does not lead him to oppose the development of the commercial state, Ferguson sees the inevitable problem that accompanies that development: "In every commercial state, notwithstanding any pretension to equal rights, the exaltation of a few must depress the many" (334).

At the very outset of industrial capitalism, Ferguson sees that it will unavoidably produce a class society. Today this is a truism. It is nonetheless important to keep it in mind so that we can better understand the dilemmas that the people of this society in transition had to confront. For example, it is common today to accuse the romantics of assuming attitudes normally seen as conservative. That conclusion, however, is an unequivocal one only if we hold to a teleological conception of history with its outline of phases that are necessary for the creation of ever more advanced syntheses. In such a scheme, capitalism becomes indispensible for the overcoming of its contradictions in the superior stage of socialism, whose *Aufhebung* would—who knows—give us paradise. Conversely, if we think, as Hannah Arendt does, that the ultimate result of the desacralization of history that took place in the modern era lies in conceiving of it as a *process*, and that as such it may not have an end in itself but instead can take any direction whatsoever, and that the technological development of productive forces may allow that process to be *manipulated*, then we must admit that the romantics' indecision, source of the spectrum that reached from reactionarism to opportunism (for instance, in the late Friedrich Schlegel) to revolutionary heroism, was quite understandable.[22] That variation of positions—and not just political ones—

derived from the necessity to conceive a new manner of relating to the world. In the foregoing, I have attempted to show the influence that the intellectual repercussions stemming from the 1789 Revolution had upon that process of conceptualization, and as well the part—to be sure, less developed—played by the advent of industrial capitalism. Let us now concentrate more precisely on the constitution of poetics.

The Theorization of the Poetic

"The great Romantic works were not written at the height of revolutionary hope but out of the experience of partial or total disenchantment with the revolutionary promise" (*Natural Supernaturalism*, 335). Abrams's statement is correct both from the point of view of poetic production and from the point of view of the production of theory. The poems of Novalis and Wordsworth, of Leopardi and Hölderlin, the essays and fragments of Friedrich Schlegel, and Coleridge's *Biographia Literaria* all prove as much. It is important to stipulate both of those areas of production because otherwise we might be deceived into thinking that the exaltation of subjectivity, of the relationship between mind and nature, and of individual liberty amounted to no more than compensatory acts for political frustration and for the rise of the marketplace. Although such conclusions are partly true, they do not tell the whole story. To confuse the theorization of such figures as Schlegel and Coleridge with compensatory expression would be to inhibit its understanding a priori, and that would surely have grave consequences, for what is achieved in their work, especially in Schlegel's, is the first theory of literature constructed on modern foundations, or, to speak in a more radical— and correct—manner, *the* first theory of literature.

It might well be noted at the outset that Friedrich Schlegel's theory of the poetic should not be confused with other formulations also identified with the idea of romanticism. In fact, his emphasis on irony—the mode of activity of which is, for all practical purposes, confused with that of the *Witz*—is in direct contrast to the "experiential poetry" proclaimed by the Sturm und Drang and by Herder, which was based on the affirmation that "poetic language lives upon immediate expression of the soul and of feeling."[23] It is equally at odds, as Strohschneider-Kohrs shows, with the utopian aesthetics that was based on breaking down all dissonances and with the concept, deriving from Schelling, of the poem as an organic whole. It is for such reasons that Schlegel's theory does not fit with what is considered characteristic "romantic" practice in a generic sense. Instead of the expressive immediacy of the events of the author's life, and instead of the conception of the poem as an activity in sublimation of the shocks of life, Schlegel privileges distancing, the fusion of critical examination and poetic expression, the notion that a poem is the theater of an unresolved tension. All that presupposes the conceptualization of the poetic subject as different from the empirical subject, the conception of the poem as different from the expression born of enthusiasm, and, most of all, a conception of the historical positioning of modern times.

Schlegel is acutely aware that the modern age does not form a community with the classical age, that the former's identity should therefore not be sought in combination with models produced by the latter. Fragment 60 of the *Critical Fragments* declares conclusively: "All the classical poetic genres have now become ridiculous in their rigid purity" (*Lucinde and the Fragments*, 150). And fragment 91 adds: "The ancients are not the Jews, Christians, or English of poetry. They are not an arbitrarily chosen artistic people of God; nor do they have the only true saving aesthetic faith; nor do they have a monopoly on poetry" (153).

The basic difference between the two periods consists in the fact that the concord between letter and spirit fundamental to classical art gives way to a discord between the same quantities: "In the ancients we see the perfected letter of all poetry; in the moderns we see its growing spirit" (154). And the author does not limit himself to a statement of that evaluation. He goes on to argue that the reason for the gap between *Buchstab* and *Geist*, between letter and spirit, is to be found in the role that mythology played in classical times. When that function disappeared in modernity, authors were obliged to cultivate history: "Ancient poetry adheres throughout to mythology and avoids the specifically historical themes. Even ancient tragedy is play, and the poet who presented a true event of serious concern for the entire nation was punished. Romantic poetry, on the other hand, is based entirely on a historical foundation, far more than we know and believe."[24]

In this key passage, Schlegel virtually states that modern people are characterized by the historical consciousness that they have had forced upon them. But he does not view this new and uncertain terrain as constitutive of an exile any more than he perceives the gap between himself and the classics as unbearable. Fragment 84 of the *Critical Fragments* treats the production of the classics as a paradigm that the moderns should take as a guide, without subordinating to it the potential available to them for their own production: "From what the moderns aim at, we learn what poetry should become; from what the ancients have done, what it has to be" (Schlegel, *Lucinde and the Fragments*, 153).

The classical paradigm can no longer have an articulating role, for it shines like a far-off star. Between it and the modern author, the quite different constructions of the mythological and the historical intervene. Schlegel does not even present himself as the discoverer of the gulf between the two eras, but rather confesses his debt on that score to Winckelmann:

The systematic Winckelmann who read all the ancients as if they were a single author, who saw everything as a whole and concentrated all his powers on the Greeks, provided the first basis for a material knowledge of the ancients through his perception of the absolute difference between ancient and modern. Only when the perspective and the conditions of the absolute identity of ancient and modern in the past, present, and future have been discovered will one be able to say that at least the contours of classical study have been laid bare and one can now proceed to methodical investigation. (181)

It is a debt that does not even depend on a forced reading, for, as a celebrated contemporary student of the subject corroborates, as long as "we understand Winckelmann's exhortation to imitation of the ancients only as a renewal of the traditional postulate of *imitatio veterum*, his writing will continue to be unintelligible."[25] Supported by Winckelmann, Schlegel not only recognizes the lack of continuity with the canon of *imitatio* but also fights for a new approach to the ancients. In so doing, he takes a course doomed to failure. The same problem that had undermined Winckelmann's position came to weigh upon his project: the new approach to the ancients sought to be a response to "art's loss of social function," a response within which was hidden "a latent escape from contemporaneity, because of which this prescription proved inadequate to give art a new social function" (Weber, 44). It would be within the parameters of this project that Schlegel would praise the novel as a form of "indirect mythology," that is, a temporary mode of reaching the desired rapprochement. If the project was doomed to failure from its very beginning, what could that mean save that the realism proposed by Diderot has accompanied us like an inconvenient ghost during our discussion of Schlegel's ideas?

The basic terms of our discussion are, then, bound up with the following elements: the romantic poet starts from the consciousness of a separation, whereas the ancients, on the other side of the breach, had an integrated view of the world, one formed around mythology, the modern poet has as his material-at-hand only the dispersion offered up by history and by his own life. Mythology is granted that central status because it is considered to be the medium that transcended the merely conscious, that transcended, let us say, the merely descriptive of nature. In this regard, a passage from the "Talk on Mythology," from Schlegel's *Dialogue on Poetry*, represents obligatory reading:

And what else is any wonderful mythology but hieroglyphic expression of surrounding nature in this transfigured form of imagination and love?

Mythology has one great advantage. What usually escapes our consciousness can here be perceived and held fast through the senses and spirit like the soul in the body through which it shines into our eye and speaks to our ear. . . . Mythology is such a work of art created by nature. In its texture the sublime is really formed; everything is relation and metamorphosis, conformed and transformed, and this conformation and transformation is its peculiar process, its inner life and method, if I may say so.

Here I find a great similarity with the marvellous wit [*Witz*] of romantic poetry which does not manifest itself in individual conceptions but in the structure of the whole. . . . Indeed, this artfully ordered confusion, this charming symmetry of contradictions, this wonderfully perennial alternation of enthusiasm and irony which lives even in the smallest parts of the whole, seem to me to be an indirect mythology themselves. The organization is the same, and certainly the arabesque is the oldest and most original form of human imagination. Neither this wit [*Witz*] nor a mythology can exist without something original and inimitable which is absolutely irreducible, and in which after all the transformations its original character and creative energy are still dimly visible, where the naive profundity permits the semblance of the absurd and of madness, of simplicity and foolishness, to shimmer through. For this is the beginning of all poetry, to cancel [*aufheben*] the progression and laws of rationally thinking reason [*vernünftig denkenden Vernunft*], and to transplant us once again into the beautiful confusion of imagination, into the original chaos of human nature, for which I know as yet no more beautiful symbol than the motley throng of the ancient gods.(85-86)

Although our conclusion is that the attempt to reactualize mythology was doomed to failure, we must nonetheless follow its subsequent development, for it is an important theorization.

The long passage transcribed above focuses its praise of mythology on the following points: (1) its relevance for the poet consists in providing a curve that eliminates the analytical, linear character of predictive reason; (2) it thus offers up a magma homologous to the chaos of our nature; (3) our nature is therefore not merely imitated—a premise that would correspond to the theory underlying the poetry grounded in personal experience—but instead embodies the possibility of a dynamic control leading to constant conformation and restructuration; and (4) even though we may not live in a mythic atmosphere, we can still create a provisional substitute for mythology through a game of wits, that is, through a text in poetry or prose that is governed by lightning utterances, penetrating, synthetic, mutable, and dialectical rather than descriptive, sentimental, or analytical of some state or truth. Because a convincing translation of the key term *Witz* is impossible, I shall content myself with drawing out an approximation: it is the role assigned to enrichment through ironic distancing. Schlegel, therefore, organizes his argument in two stages: we should endeavor to approach the classics anew through a procedure of unification, and as long as this is not possible, we should attempt to develop the route of "indirect mythology" using the prismatic *Witz*. But, I confess without rhetorical evasions, that explanation does not give me absolute certainty that I have comprehended the functioning of the verbal regimen that was supposed to hold the "original chaos." Schlegel expressly affirms that the necessary chaos should assume a hieroglyphic form. But how are hieroglyph, arabesque, and "fecund chaos" reconciled with critical control of production? And how may they be distinguished from an irrational phantasmagoria? Although we must here eschew detailed testimonies, the answer seems simple, having been drawn out well in the interpretation of a passage from Schlegel's novel *Lucinde* advanced by Marshall Brown: "What does the expression 'to *complete* the chaos' suggest, if not that the poetic work is limited, circumscribed, and, at least to that extent, disciplined and organized? The work of art achieves a perilous synthesis of chaos and order greater than either of its parts; it fuses the sublime, the beautiful, the objective ('sublime harmonies') and the subjective ('interesting pleasures') into a triumphant totality."[26]

The chaos to which Schlegel attached so many different adjectives is not characterized by babble or confusion but rather by synthetic complexity, in contradistinction to discursive, dismembering, "mechanical" reason. In that sense, his thought approaches Leibniz's monadic principle. Not, of course, that a poem resembles a simple substance. The analogy is established by common opposition in the monad and the poem/chaos to the principle of mechanical explanation. Just as the unity of the monad is not reached through its division into smaller and smaller parts, so a poem is not created by the mechanical juxtaposition of "true" assertions. In other words, the privilege of the organized chaos and the arabesque does not involve giving an impression of the world but turning to creative impressing as a world—that is, the *expression* of the world is given up in favor of a *simulacrum* of the world. Thus, just as chaos is in this case not synonymous with confusion, so the arabesque is not synonymous with capricious ornamentalism. Both embody the purpose of making the poem a complex object in which enthusiasm and irony control each other reciprocally and nurture each other, and in which contradictions exist in symmetrical relationships instead of finding resolution in a harmonic golden key. All these, we know, are the provisional forms of an "indirect mythology." But is there not deposited there an implicit nostalgia for the era in which letter and spirit were interwoven, an era in which we no longer live? Fragment 243 answers in the negative: if, it says, *there was* a Golden Age, it could not have been one of true gold, for then it would not be in the past. The desired encounter with the ancient does not depend on a return—it would then be open to elegiac treatment—but rather lies in the future. But how are we to work toward that future? If Schlegel had an answer, he never gave it. What his practice sets forth, by contrast, leads us to agree with Heinz-Dieter Weber: "The critical self-reflection of art can, at every instance, serve to construct autonomous art as the negation of reality, but it does not, and cannot, through its own power make reality, as criticized and transformed by art, into an object of praxis. Reflection on the potentialities of art in relation to reality remains subordinated to the interest in art's autonomy" (Weber, 216).

Schlegel's theory of the poetic, the proposal for romantic poetry that he formulates has no other objective in mind than the poetic. Autonomy of art here, therefore, means its divestment of everything that is not proper to it. I must, then, reformulate the question. It is not that Schlegel did not know how to fight for a future accord between the ancient and the modern but that for him such an accord did not go beyond the confines of a monadic, self-sufficient art. Thus the identity that he establishes between the fragment, his preferred form, and the work of art: "A fragment, like a miniature work of art, has to be entirely isolated from the surrounding world and be complete in itself like a porcupine" (*Lucinde and the Fragments*, 189).

It is not at all surprising, in the light of that greatly desired plenitude, that the ideas of the early Friedrich Schlegel were much less well received than those of his brother August Wilhelm. Whereas the latter's language is much more accessible, his thought does not contain the complexity that Friedrich's does. The underlying reason for that neglect, however, seems to have been that Friedrich Schlegel's theory of autonomous art conflicted with the "political and intellectual radicalism" that romanticism then maintained despite its disillusionment with revolution. (see Abrams, "Coleridge, Baudelaire, and Modernistic Poetics," 116). For romanticism retained a patina of Christian values, albeit in a secularized version, directing them to the social arena: "Christian millennialism and the cardinal virtues of faith, hope, and above all love, translated into non-theological equivalents, were the ultimate roots of the secular optimism and the belief in the fraternity of equal man which were at the heart both of the political theory of the French Revolution and of the humanism of revolutionary Romanticism" (122-23). Schlegel, in contrast, depoliticizes religion and, much as Mallarmé would later do, makes the artist into a priest who worships his own ideal: "If every infinite individual is God, then there are as many gods as there are ideals. And further, the relation of the true artist and the true human being to his ideals is absolutely religious. The man for whom this inner divine service is the end and occupation of all his life is a priest, and this is how everyone can and should become a priest" (*Lucinde and the Fragments*, 229).

Thus, he did not produce anything like the paradoxical formulation in which Baudelaire combined "counter-Revolutionary and anti-democratic politics and . . . innovative poetics" (Abrams, "Coleridge, Baudelaire, and Modernistic Poetics," 123), Schlegel's approach to the issue of artistic autonomy actually estranged him from his contemporaries, making him much more like the generation subsequent to romanticism and rendering him difficult to comprehend in his own time. If history had spurned the political optimism of the romantics, it would still simultaneously deprecate the self-containedness that Schlegel attempted to impart to art. Romantic optimism would be adapted to forms more sympathetic to the advance of the national state and to the privileging of history, whereas artistic self-sufficiency would have to wait a much longer time, until the end of the nineteenth century, when its pure aestheticization would make it bearable to the bourgeois order.[27]

This project was by no means limited to poetry. One of the most noteworthy of Schlegel's reflections is specifically dedicated to the novel.[28] Deriding the novel "insofar as it wishes to be a specific genre," Schlegel subordinates the novel to all the principles to which poetry in general must be subjected. Moreover, he says that "a philosophy of the novel, the rough outlines of which are contained in Plato's political theory . . . would be . . . the keystone" of a philosophy of poetry in general, and "the novel colors all of modern poetry" (*Lucinde and the Fragments*, 198, 180). Why would Schlegel think that way unless he saw the novel as located close to historical life? Thus at least one window was left open in the monad of art. It was not that our author manifested sympathy for any sort of realism. The breath of air coming from external reality was let in so that it could quicken the forge of irony, of the *Witz*, and of the grotesque, becoming, then, a "fecund chaos." Thus the admiration that Diderot reserved for Richardson was rerouted to Swift, Sterne, and Jean Paul. Moreover, the sentiment that was praised has nothing to do with the "moving and tearful," as they are merely symptoms of its "external letter."[29] And, according to Schlegel, the novel would continue to occupy that unrivaled position as long as, not being itself bound to specific generic contours, it did not develop its own normativeness. Such is the condition for the maintenance of its bipartite contact, with the chemistry of the poetic and the air of life and of history: "The poetics of the novel depends upon the corresponding function of the art with which the novel articulates. Since, however, that function varies according to historical movement, every novel contains its own poetics" (Weber, 206). The key location assigned to the novel thus puts it in the position of mediator between poetic theory and history. It is, then, opportune to note the "fecund chaos" within which Schlegel's own theory is formulated: it proposes an art that is autonomous, unfettered by anything not proper to itself, but, that status notwithstanding, it seeks interrelationship with life: "Romantic poetry . . . tries to . . . make poetry lively and sociable, and life and society poetical" (*Lucinde and the Fragments*, 175).

Because romantic poetry is autonomous but not cloistered, it commits itself to constant metamorphosis: "The romantic kind of poetry is still in the state of becoming; that, in fact, is its real essence: that it should forever be becoming and never be perfected" (175). Such properties could not simply be lent to the formation of any hypothetical romantic school, for fragment 116 ends with a conflation of the romantic modality and the activity of poetry in general. Indeed, we had recourse to that fragment in asserting that Schlegel's theory in fact constituted a general theory of poetry. To justify my present argument, then, I shall invoke yet another passage, from the famous fragment 238, transcribing only its first sentence: "There is a kind of poetry whose essence lies in the relation between ideal and real, and which therefore, by analogy to philosophical jargon, should be called transcendental poetry'' (195).

What exactly might this transcendental poetry be? Let us begin with the interpretation proposed by Heinz-Dieter Weber. For him the meaning is directly linked with Schlegel's denial that aesthetics can function as a philosophical-level prescription for art (see critical fragment 40:147). That break immediately redounds upon criticism, which, then, could presumably not be practiced except through works of poetry: "Poetry can only be criticized by way of poetry. A critical judgement of an artistic production has no civil rights in the realm of art if it isn't itself a work of art, either in its substance, as a representation of a necessary impression in the state of becoming, or in the beauty of its form and open tone, like that of the old Roman satires'' (157). That fragment—*Critical Fragment* 117—which would require detailed treatment[30] if our argument deriving from it were less pointed, seems to deny the right to exercise criticism to all save poets themselves. Schlegel wrote hundreds of fragments and a considerable number of essays, however, and none of them endorse that literal reading, nothing in them suggests subordination of critical reflection to poetic effect. The author returns to the issue in a posthumously published fragment, where it is clarified somewhat: "Critical prose must be fluid and oscillating and must struggle against a fixed terminology, for it would thus take on a liberal aspect, *as though it merely served philosophy''* (Weber, *Friedrich Schlegel's "Tranzendentalpoesie,''* 211; emphasis mine).

The portion of the preceding passage that I have emphasized shows that the requirement that criticism be itself a work of art results from the absolute division that Schlegel made between the fields of art and of aesthetics. Hence the legitimacy of the relationship that Heinz-Dieter Weber draws between that "lack of a center" and the proposal for a "transcendental poetry": "It should be asked if consequences for literary criticism do not ensue from the concept of 'transcendental poetry', consequences deriving from the loss of the grounding within art of aesthetic definitions; the result would be that critical self-reflection within the art object would replace aesthetics, taking over the determination of functionality that aesthetics can no longer accomplish.''[31] In direct terms, Friedrich Schlegel's poetic theory—which does not present romanticism as a school or movement but rather conflates it with poetry in general—originates in a basic estrangement: philosophy of art is not competent to legislate art itself. As a consequence, poetry cannot be a mere compositional practice given over to its own orphanhood; instead it must be "progressive" and "transcendental," that is, simultaneously operative and theoretical. This decentering on its part of an external legislating element is further emphasized when we turn to the question of the poetic subject. It is generally agreed that in romanticism the poet was given the right to express individuality and that the poem derived its value from the quality of that expression.[32] As a consequence of that right of individual expression, the theory of mimesis was ostracized. Beginning with the second half of the eighteenth century in Germany, according to Wolfgang Preisendanz, "poetry is increasingly considered a medium that not only imitates nature but also in itself awakens reflection and nature's creative power."[33] The two propositions contained in that analysis are contradictory. Their conflict would be resolved only by the abandonment of the principle of *imitatio*: "Only in a paradoxical sense is poetry, properly speaking, imitation and reflection: that is, it has those functions with regard to what it contains, with regard to what can begin only with it itself" (Preisendanz, 60). Hence, in turn, there follows a specific concept of the reality contained in the work of poetry: "Wherever poetry does not have merely the value of presentation of forms (*Gestaltungen*), laws, connections, and structures of an antecedent reality, it must be an absolute production, and reality can no longer be its point of origin but merely the result of poetic imagination and of reflection" (61). In summary, a theory of expression by the empirical subject replaces the theory of mimesis (then confused with classical *imitatio*).

That proposition, therefore, still presupposes a center, the individual subject, or, rather, the poet's expressive energy. But in Schlegel even that center is missing. The emphasis on irony, which is the basic feature of his poetics, occupies that position by virtue of its being "the freest of privileges, for through it we surpass even ourselves."[34] The poetic subject is no longer fused with the empirical subject, because, as the subject's activity involves its surpassing of itself, it ceases to be defined by its capacity for expression and becomes a project for construction. As Ingrid Strohschneider-Kohrs writes: "While the artist invents and cultivates ecstasy, he also comes to run the risk of becoming blind to his interest in the object and in his own will to expression. Only when 'he is no longer interested' in the object, only when he no longer 'says everything' and no longer wishes to 'speak' openly, only then will he achieve artistic discernment" (80-81). Therefore, what Schlegel said expressly about romantic poetry is equally valid for the poetic subject: it does not exist, it progressively becomes; it is bound to a futurity without end, for it realizes within itself "a movement that cannot achieve a goal, that never leads to total congruency with the unconditioned, but rather makes evident the limits, the contradiction, the tension between finite and infinite" (82). Poetry becomes a negator of reality, including nature, and it simultaneously rejects the presence of any center for itself, be it one constructed on aesthetic categories or one constructed on the peculiarities of the individual subject. Through its decentering, the poetic achieves heights beyond the horizon of "normal" romanticism. In that romanticism, the tension that pervades Schlegel's theory is frozen in sentimentality, in the liberal optimism of Hugo, in every author's emotive expression. It is through that mitigation that "normal" romanticism continues to have a social function and to accept easily the function that bourgeois society grants to literature: expression of the vicissitudes of history. That function could not be performed by Schlegel's autonomous art, the weakness of which lay precisely in relation to the dimension in which it eschewed any interest, namely the area of the social function of art. Did that weak spot not connect with Schlegel's acceptance, like that of his contemporaries, of an opposition between mimesis and poiesis, and with his confusion of the former with an *imitatio* that he had learned from Winckelmann to see as inadequate to the modern artist? And, even though he does not seem to have thought so, could his theory of the poetic subject, in its refusal to focus on an idolatry of the "I," not provide elements for the reformulation of the concept of mimesis? That hypothesis is reenforced if we reflect on considerations developed by Coleridge.

In an essay probably dating from 1818, "On Poesy or Art," Coleridge, reader that he was of German philosophy, takes up some of the problems we have just seen formulated by Schlegel, such as, the opposition between the ancient and the modern and the role of chaos—which he too describes in positive terms, calling it a "harmonized chaos." Let us, however, pass by those possible paths and concentrate on his hints for the reformulation of mimesis. They arise from the central problem of the brief essay: the relationship between mind and nature. In that connection art emerges as the mediator par excellence between nature and humankind: "Art itself might be defined as . . . the union and reconciliation of that which is nature with that which is exclusively human" (Coleridge, *Biographia Literaria*, 254-55). The condensation of nature into art is still called *imitatio* although Coleridge takes care to distinguish it from the mere copy. The difference between the two is that art mediates between mind and nature, giving predominance to the activity of the former: "And man's mind is the very focus of all the rays of intellect which are scattered throughout the images of nature. . . . To make the external internal, the internal external, to make nature thought, and thought nature,—this is the mystery of genius in the Fine Arts" (257-58). Loyal, then, to the tradition of the eighteenth century, Coleridge persists in attributing decisive importance to genius. That notion is not, however, as imprecisely handled as it was in Diderot. Because of the direct influence of Schelling, the working of genius presupposes the presence of the unconscious, an unconscious that guides the reflection that is achieved: "There is in genius itself an unconscious activity; nay, that is the genius in the man of genius" (258). And it is through that impulsion that the genius transcends the surface of nature and touches its "spirit," its *Natur-geist*. Artistic "imitation" thus contains two ingredients: "These two constituent elements are likeness and unlikeness, or sameness and difference, and in all genuine creations of art there must be a union of these disparates" (256).

The element of "difference" is thus not comprehended by any general faculty of sense but only by that unconscious activity present in the genius: "The artist must imitate that which is within the thing, that which is active through form and figure, and discourses to us by symbols—the *Natur-geist*, or spirit of nature, as we unconsciously imitate those whom we love" (259).

The "difference" is therefore redeemed through the reserve of nature retained by genius in the form of the unconscious. Faithful to Schelling's thought, Coleridge propagates a concept—the concept of the unconscious—whose vicissitudes it would be useful to develop, following the lead of Odo Marquard.[35] That project would lead us away from our purposes here, however, so let me merely emphasize that in Coleridge "imitation" does not have its ultimate grounding in the conceptual framework of realism because of the intervention of the variable of the unconscious, which in turn locates the artist in a superior position with regard to common mortals. Whatever might be the faults of that proposition—its subordination to a religion of nature, to a latent mysticism, to the compensatory elitism of the artist—its further development could have performed a service that Schlegel's better elaborated theorization had rejected: the attempt to (re)unite poiesis and mimesis.[36] Indeed, it is plausible to think that the problems faced by the theory of art in modern times may result from a hasty abandonment of the problematics of mimesis, which was not sufficiently well distinguished from *imitatio*, and that that abandonment led either to fascination with articulation with the everyday (in realism), to search for a hidden dimension in nature (Coleridge), or to simple rejection of mimesis (both in "normal" romantic theory and also in Schlegel's "advanced" theory). But had it been shown that poiesis functions within mimesis, it would have been possible to overcome the conundrum that the postulation of autonomous art has never overcome: the fact that the poietic product has no say about its own circulation and, therefore, about the way its social function is construed. At the margins of Schlegel's and Coleridge's theorization, a path much like that one is hinted at: if the poetic subject is a process of elaboration, if "genius" is marked in a positive sense by the quotient of unconscious that it brings with it, then poiesis is governed by a power of *unconscious figuration* that motivates the imagination of both the producer and the receiver. Now, as chapter 1 illustrated, the power of images was affirmed as early as Augustine. The concept of an "unconscious" has now come into play to reinforce the opening up of that path. But history keeps us from yet declaring it taken. And, because this essay has a clear "archeological" purpose, I shall have to cease this commentary on what, barely suggested at the edges of Schlegel's and Coleridge's thought, was then interrupted and led in another direction.

* * *

In this chapter, I have shown that a new emergence of interest in subjectivity accompanied the collapse of the classical age, with its grounding in a similitude between the human order and the natural order. Subjectivity had, during that age, been limited to preestablished places and activities, whereas nature had served as mediator for the meeting between humankind and God. Now desacralized, disenchanted, nature assumes another aspect: it becomes the second pole in a relationship with the human mind, or the human subjectivity. But, in the field of art theory, that relationship gives rise to a tension. If the focus falls on the mind, the theory and corresponding art either emphasize the expression of the creating empirical subject (the theory and practice of "normal" romanticism) or highlight the poetic subject as a process of endless aestheticizing (Schlegel's theory of autonomous art). In the first case, the category of fiction becomes useless — since the truth and quality of the poem depend on the truth and richness of the "self." That is, subjectivity is self-fulfilling, and if one cannot speak directly of a veto against fictional discourse, one must simply ask why its theoretical investigation has become unnecessary. In the second case, we have the appearance of a fictional subject precisely because the subject of "transcendental poetry" is not explained through the biography of the empirical subject that provides its basis. That is, the latter is not content to remain within its "self" but instead decenters it, transforming it into a means to invention. But, remaining unthematized, the category of fiction itself merely circles around a theorization that, having abolished consideration of the social function of art, favors a poiesis that will be vehemently rejected by its contemporaries. (As is well known, the great autonomous poetry, from Baudelaire on, would be fought against by the literary establishment of the era and would be redeemed only when it came to be seen through the separation of the values of life and of society, that is, through its aestheticization.)[37] The possibility for theoretical development of the category of the fictional appears in an implicitly forbidden area; its later implicit acceptance, through aestheticization, would not lead to any interest in the determination of fiction's status, for that could not be done in the absence of analysis of the relationship between its objects and the world of the nonfictional. Thus, on the two fronts deriving from the primacy of mind over nature, the concept of fiction remained either useless or unnecessary.

Let us now see what happens when the focus falls upon nature (by now, better termed "social reality"). Here we come face to face with realism. Realism would react against "normal" romanticism's infatuation with subjectivity and also against the isolationism of the "autonomous" poet, and would attempt to locate its art close to the everyday and, what is more, close to the directions dominant in its world. It was not by chance, then, that it concentrated on the novel. Because of its narrative form and the personalized conflicts of its characters, the novel is close not only to the prose of everyday life but also to the narrative form privileged since the end of the eighteenth century: the form of history. Therefore, even when it could not veil its origin in plot, the novel sought to ignore its original germ in the fable, making itself like history. Indeed, even before the beginning of history's period of greatest prestige, Fielding senses that it is better for his *Tom Jones* to pass for history:

Hence we are to derive that universal contempt which the world, who always denominate the whole from the majority, have cast on all historical writers who do not draw their materials from records. And it is the apprehension of this contempt that hath made us so cautiously avoid the term romance. . . . Though, as we have good authority for all our characters, no less indeed than the vast authentic doomsday-book of nature, as is elsewhere hinted, our labours have sufficient title to the name of history.[38]

Some years later, Sterne would opt for an ironic and ambiguous solution. Imagining an encounter with a critic of his work, he asks that individual if he has read Locke's *An Essay Concerning Human Understanding*. And, to remove all doubts, he goes on to tell him, in few words, what the philosopher's work consists of: "It is a history. — A history! of who? what? where? when? Don't hurry yourself. — It is a history-book, Sir, (which may possibly recommend it to the world) of what passes in a man's own mind."[39] Under this pretext, Sterne plays with an entire range of ambiguity. To be called the history book of what happens in a human's mind might seem frivolous in application to a philosophical treatise. What it evidences, however, is that *recognition of the rights of subjectivity does not eliminate the veto against fiction*. The extreme irony of the passage lies in its causing that fact to rebound on one of the first people to fight in favor of it. The orientation that the novel will take, being the chosen genre of the realists, illuminates the effort to avoid the stigma of fictionality. Stigmatized instead, as I have previously shown, would be that form of literature that, seeking to make its place on the basis of its own values, implicitly aggressed against the economy of the market in which it was developing: "Alongside the rejection of the Public and of Popularity as standards of worth, increasing complaint was made that literature had become a trade."[40] And it provoked in turn reactions of indifference or hostility. In the same context, although far from professing the concept of autonomous art, Shelley sought to preserve the identification of poet with *vatis*, but — symptomatically — he now speaks of a *vatis* whose pronouncements go unrecognized: "Poets are the unacknowledged legislators of the world."[41]

In contrast, the novel, wishing to locate itself in concert with social consensus and deploying itself to take up even the principles of the biological sciences, becomes a genre in ascent. Accepted to the extent that it remains close to history and science, it overlooks its fictional character, thus in effect endorsing the veto of it.

Between autonomous art and the victorious novel, "normal" romanticism runs its course. And with Hugo, he of the fiery poems and historical novels, it reveals the path to which the times incline. After its desacralization, nature becomes the scenario of a narrative, the narrative of the national state, legitimated by the chosen mode of observation, namely that of science. If the advanced romanticism is characterized by the self-reflection of a subject involved in a process of self-creation, then romanticism seems to die the moment that the two categories reverse ground and the data derived of observation outweigh self-reflexivity. The fates to which nature was subjected are parallel, and homologous, to the constitution of historiography in the period.

History

The Rise of Historical Discourse
and Its Relationship with Literature

Twenty years ago, history, which since the early nineteenth century had consolidated its position as the *scientia princeps*, received the most resounding of attacks. Its author: the French anthropologist Claude Lévi-Strauss. In his now famous "Histoire et dialectique" [History and Dialectic], he accused history of having become the last refuge of "transcendental humanism," which, in the light of dissolution of the mirage of the "I," the "self," located its justification in the collective "we" held up as the unassailable proof of human liberty. Lévi-Strauss could have gone even further. He could have said: throughout the era of its predominance, history has had as its forced companion the optimistic belief in human progress. Along that very line, in 1799, Novalis, who can be considered a historian of sorts, wrote: "Progressive, ever widening evolutions are the material of History."[42]

Linked to the advance of the nation-state, history had become centrally a political history in which the collectivity was replaced by an accounting of facts and by the biography of great personages. To be sure, it would be incorrect to speak of it as the last refuge of humanism at this optimistic moment. In the process of its expansion, bourgeois dominion allied itself with science and with technological development, and it allowed humanity—European humanity—to conceive of itself as a species whose projection was becoming greater and more promising. Historical facts could then be looked on as natural elements, revealing the human species' domination of life.

Lévi-Strauss was in fact writing at a time when that illusion had begun to recede. With the two world wars past, humanistic thought used the tunnel vision of history to assure itself that, despite the atrocities committed and suffered by the various nation-states, its pretensions had not been pure illusion. Despite that refurbishing, the ideology of progress, now in tatters, could no longer fend off the questioning of the "ancient mistress of life": "Historical facts are no more *given* than any other. It is the historian, or the agent of history, who constitutes them by abstraction and as though under the threat of an infinite regress."[43]

The universality of history and its synonymy with the presence of civilized humanity are traded for a cold-blooded scrutiny that begins by comparing the status of history with that of any other branch of knowledge: "What makes history possible is that a sub-set of events is found, for a given period, to have approximately the same significance for a contingent of individuals who have not necessarily experienced the events and may even consider them at an interval of several centuries" (Lévi-Strauss, 257).

The conclusion: "It is therefore far from being the case that the search for intelligibility comes to an end in history as though this were its terminus. Rather, it is history that serves as the point of departure in any quest for intelligibility. As we say of certain careers, history may lead to anything, provided you get out of it" (262).

For us today, the conclusion must merely be modified: history can lead to everything, as long as one gets away from factual history, with its privileging of diachrony and its belief that the chronological ordering of facts and results and/or their explanation as the effects of a single mechanism of history are intellectually sufficient. In other words, if Lévi-Strauss's attack on the popularized ideology of history should be judged impeccable and should prove itself to be fertile ground for the new generations of historians, its weakness would lie in its confusing history, as a specific activity, with current thought about it.

I have begun this section by recalling Lévi-Strauss's remarks to clarify at the outset the purpose of the reconstruction now to be undertaken. I shall work with a relatively small number of sources and concepts because my goal is not an exhaustive survey of the factual and diachronic but rather a demonstration of how those elements correlate with the concept of literature set forth at the same time and with the dilemmas undergone by that literature. In the final analysis, I seek a solider ground for contemporary reflection on literature. I shall therefore take history as a "point of departure" in the "search for the intelligibility" of the very object of study.

* * *

Even though the modern sense of history was created only in the final third of the eighteenth century,[44] for best results we shall direct our analysis to the beginning of that same century—more precisely, to the controversy between Enlightenment thought and what Auerbach has called "aesthetic historicism."

The privileging of reason during the French and English Enlightenment implied taking mathematical accuracy as the ideal of scientific knowledge. Hence the state of inferiority in which historical knowledge necessarily found itself: "Any certitude that does not find mathematical demonstration is a mere probability. Historical certitude is of that sort."[45]

In subordinating historical knowledge to a mathematical paradigm, Voltaire enunciated one of the Illuministes' characteristic positions—one not to be confused with the thought of the German Aufklärers on the subject. P. H. Reill summarizes: "It became increasingly clear to the Aufklärers that each science—be it history, philology, or aesthetics—required its own logic to take cognizance of the point of view from which the science approached its object."[46] German Enlightenment thinkers, however, have until very recently remained unacknowledged and therefore devoid of influence. Voltaire's position could have been successfully combated by those who were thinking of historical knowledge in relation to the model of the biological sciences, which had been acknowledged as early as 1754, in Diderot's *De L'interpretation de la nature*.[47] That struggle was, however, not immediately engaged in, because, as we have already seen, history was at the time still located among the belles-lettres. Thus history could offer only probabilities because it could not lose sight for long of the scenario—albeit a constantly changing one—of the eternal struggle between reason and the passions and prejudices. Ever under siege, not always victorious, reason was ill at ease within history. We can therefore say that the inferior status in which history was held by the bulk of Enlightenment thought resulted from the presence of an ethical standard, sovereign and atemporal, according to which human works were judged. And that ethical standard was confused with reason itself. Moreover, as no gap separated reason from ethics, reason became the judge of all else and left itself open to no judgment in return. Now, the Auerbach of "Vico and Aesthetic Historicism" (1949) was astonished by blatant contradiction between the Enlightenment position and what was developed in the *Scienza Nuova* (1725), as well as by Vico's anticipation of the theses of both Rousseau and Herder:

He saw the original state of mankind as a state of nature, and nature, for him, was liberty: liberty of feeling, of boundless instinct,of inspiration, absence of laws and institutions, in striking contrast to the laws, conventions and rules of rationalized society. . . . Vico, long before Herder and the Romanticists, discovered their most fertile aesthetic concept, the concept of folk genius.[48]

The Neopolitan philosopher answered the Enlightenment thinkers' choice of reason with assignment of superiority to imagination. He responded to the secondary status of history with its dignification and the need to judge human products with an imposition of fixed procedure, his own contextualized one. Auerbach offers no explanation for Vico's singularity. The task of explaining the emergence of the historical horizon that oriented the theses of the *Scienza Nuova* has fallen instead to the historian Allan Megill. According to Megill, Vico's uniqueness derives from the battle between the Ancients and the Moderns that began in the late 1680s and lasted until 1714-16. Megill points to the prominence within that discussion of the studies of Hebrew poetry and music undertaken by the now forgotten Augustin Calmet (1672-1757) and Claude Fleury (1640-1723), in their essays "Dissertation sur la poésie des anciens hébreux" [Dissertation on the Poetry of the Ancient Hebrews] (1708) and "Dissertation sur la musique des anciens et en particulier des hébreux" [Dissertation on the Music of the Ancients and, in Particular, the Hebrews] (1713) by the former and "Discours sur la poésie en général et sur celle des hébreux en particulier" [Discourse on Poetry in General and on that of the Hebrews in Particular] (1713) by the latter. In Megill's words: "Where the neo-classical aestheticians attempted to relate the work of art to a set of cross-temporal and cross-cultural standards, Calmet and Fleury attempt to relate the work of art to the language and way of life out of which the work of art emerges, emphasizing that the critic must cultivate a sympathetic appreciation of languages and cultures different from his own."[49]

Thus, whereas neoclassical aesthetics, in concert with the more popularized areas of Enlightenment thought, professed belief in transhistorical values—namely, both norms to which works should be subjected and reason itself—aesthetic historicism placed greater emphasis on such contextual elements as "climate, education, travels, and especially language" (Megill, 50). Without depreciating Vico's originality, Megill's essay thus builds a bridge between Vico and Herder on the one hand and between Vico and general historicism on the other. Megill, then, draws out two goals for himself: to proffer a new argument contrary to the one advanced by Meinecke, who, in Die Entstehung der Historismus [The Genesis of Historicism] (1936), took historicism to be a typically German movement, born of opposition to the esprit de raison, and to recreate the environment in which Vico's anticipatory position flourished, thus providing bases for the interpretation that Auerbach did not pursue. For my own part, I suggest that those results admit of yet another continuation: demonstration that the internal struggle between the roles played by reason and by imagination underlies the modern concept of history. It is a struggle as yet insufficiently explored, either because aesthetic historicism has seemed to fall to the province of students of the philosophy of art or because the conflict between Enlightenment and historicism has primarily emphasized the conflict between relativization of values and omnipresence of atemporal reason.

But is it correct to hypothesize such a struggle between reason and imagination? Initially, there occur arguments both for and against. As to arguments for, the hypothesis seems plausible, as we see in the words of Fénelon and Gottsched as formulated by Reinhart Koselleck: "History has a 'nakedness so noble and so majestic', wrote Fénelon in 1714, that it needs no poetic adornment. Gottsched states that the historian's task is to 'tell the naked truth', that is, the event that is being related, without bringing in ornamentation" ("Die Herausbildung des modernen Geschichtsbegriffs," 659).

Along similar lines, Voltaire separated history and res fictae, using the Greeks as his example: "The Greeks knew very well how to distinguish fable from history, real facts from Herodotos's stories, so much so that their orators, when speaking of serious matters, never used the discourse of the sophists or the images of the poets'' (507-8).

As to arguments against, however, Koselleck himself sees in the works of eighteenth-century artists and historians a reciprocal osmosis that reveals in its operation neither tension nor rivalry:

> While the art of the novel became compromised with historical reality, history conversely came out well in the face of the poetological pretension to creation of unities capable of laying the foundation for sense. A great descriptive talent was required of history; instead of relating chronologically, it had to inquire into hidden motives and arrange fortuitous events according to an internal order. Thus both genres, through a reciprocal osmosis, led to the discovery of a historical reality won only by reflection. (662)

The truth of the matter is that two positions do not lead to opposing results. It is not by chance that Koselleck's argument is based on the novel and does not even approach treatment of poetry. Now, as we saw in the first section of this chapter, there is a poetic theory that, while recognizing history's importance in the modern era and therefore privileging the novel, attempts to make art autonomous, that is, to give it its own values and principles of composition. In opposition to that theory, the later realistic tradition developed which did indeed deploy itself in osmosis with history. Thus the hypothesis advanced above is confirmed—a tension was created between emphasis on history and the theory of autonomous art. From that tension derives historiography's maintenance, on the one hand, of parallels with literary practice (the novel) and, on the other, of a sharp split with literature's most radical aspirations (autonomous art). It must be noted too that the parallelism and the split are displayed diachronically. Before the split came into being, one can legitimately see a perfect parallel—in Herder's aesthetic historicism, as, for example in the following passage from the *Humanitätsbriefe* [Letters on Humanity] (1796):

> In this gallery of different ways of thinking, aspirations and desires, we certainly come to know periods and nations more deeply than along the deceptive, dreary route of their political and war history. In the latter we seldom see more of a people than how it let itself be governed and killed; in the former we learn how it thought, what it hoped and wished for, how it enjoyed itself, and how it was led by its teachers or its inclinations.[50]

Although the history of poetry is emphasized to the detriment of political and military history, Herder nonetheless thinks in terms of modalities of history, privileging the history that is the history of poetry. But the parallelism vanishes as soon as historicism proper is entered into. Now the inferiority to which Herder had relegated political and military history recedes. History develops precisely through its political sector. And it does so not through an aleatory or arbitrary decision on the historian's part, or as is customary to say today, through the historian's cooptation by the state departments of the nascent states. It was the very rise of the modern state, wedded to the hopes deposited in nationalism, that explains the primacy of political history and the privileged study of that history's great personalities. The poet would still try to compete with the statesperson, endeavoring, in Shelley, to maintain the tradition of the poet-*vatis*. But he himself must confess his power is laughable, for "[it] is seated on the throne of [his] own soul" ("A Defence of Poetry," 138). Similarly, within history itself, the marginalization of those dealing with cultural history was explained as follows: "They were wont to concede that the world of history had been 'delivered over to the political historians', but they took refuge after a fashion in a realm which had not yet been taken over."[51]

History distances itself from all symbolic materials and endeavors to occupy itself with "serious" matters. Questioning the work of the discipline at his time, Droysen, Ranke's contemporary, shows that its methodological basis lies in the concept of source, of "transmission of sources" (*Quellenüberlieferung*), an extremely material and positivistic procedure, with the result that it enabled another historiographic modality: "According to Dönniges' position, criticism must determine the objective facts, which is achieved by strict investigation and comparison of accounts. Criticism must thus authenticate accounts. . . . His presumption seems to be that the production [of an authentic historical account] is accomplished by finding and capturing the idea contained in the facts."[52]

Applied outside political or religious history, Droysen continues, "this method would soon show itself to be unwieldy," for

what are described as objective facts—a battle, a council, an uprising—
are they really such in themselves? Are they not rather evidence of the
innumerable individual elements of an occurrence that only human
representation could summarize as such on the basis of the common
goal or effect or occasion for one of those elements? In truth, they are
evidence of human will; it is the activity and suffering of so many
individuals that resulted in what we designate as the fact of this battle,
of this uprising, as it is compressed in the human imagination. Neither
the battle nor the uprising was objective and real at that moment but
only the thousands who attacked and struck one another and were
confused and noisy.

Droysen's resounding critique was, however, unable to change the course of historiography. Especially when the positivistic belief in the fact, now taking up the model of the biological sciences, imparted to the historian a scientific soberness. The requirement of "scientificity" grew with practically every generation.

Before Ranke, one Chladenius had questioned the existence of general laws for history and had postulated a need for a historical hermeneutics that would start from the central importance of point of view for the understanding of history: "We call 'point of view' those conditions of our mind, of our body, of our entire person that make, or are the cause for, our representing something in one way and not in another."[53]

Therefore, if "histories are narratives of what has happened in the world" (Chladenius, 309:72) by effect of the *position* of their narrator, they will tend to contain differences even when the observers are equally honest: "We merely wish to affirm that, when different people narrate an event according to their correct knowledge, between their true accounts a difference will still be found" (309:72). Thus, "A rebellion is one thing for a loyal subject, another for a rebel, another for a foreigner, another for a member of the court, for a bourgeois, for a peasant, even if they only know of it what conforms to the truth."[54]

The function of point of view diminished drastically in Leopold von Ranke— the most influential figure in modern historiography. In the preface to his first work, *Geschichten der romanischen und germanischen Völker*, Ranke declares in no uncertain terms: "To history has been assigned the office of judging the past, of instructing the present for the benefit of future ages. To such high offices this work does not aspire: It wants only to show what actually happened (*wie es eigentlich gewesen*)."[55]

It now matters not *who* writes history, what his or her position is, or how that position may motivate his or her point of view. The historian is one who, from the observation and investigation of discrete facts, arrives at "a universal view of events . . . a knowledge of the objectively existing relatedness" (Ranke, 59). The historian, in sum, is a scientist because he or she observes and speaks objectively of what happened. A later passage in the same work marks that belief in a quality inscribed in the historical works themselves: "What developed in the past constitutes the connection with what is emerging in the present. But this connection is not something arbitrarily assumed: it existed in a particular way and could be no other. It, too, is a proper object of knowledge. A longer series of concurrent and successive events linked together in such a relationship forms a century, an epoch" (61).

Ranke, however, was not alone, nor was he the first to wrap himself in that belief in the objectivity of facts and the consequent claim of neutrality for the historian. In the beginning of his essay "On the Task of the Historian" (1821), Wilhelm von Humboldt said:

The historian's task is to present what actually happened. The more purely and completely he achieves this the more perfectly has he solved his problem. A simple presentation is at the same time the primary, indispensable condition of his work and the highest achievement he will be able to attain. Regarded in this way, he seems to be merely receptive and reproductive, not himself active and creative.[56]

Belief in fact and in the possibility of simply processing "what happened" then became dogma. One generation later, inquiry into a hermeneutics proper to history is no longer even thought about. With Comte's unified theory of the sciences, the scientific construct comes to be supported by the same requirements already stipulated for history: source criticism, observation of phenomena, and their elevation to the status of necessary objective relationships that are thereby independent of the observer's will. It is but a short step from there to Taine's position: "The productions of the human mind, like those of animated nature, can only be explained by their *milieu.*"[57]

A century after Chladenius, art becomes hemmed in by general laws and causalities similar to those established by physics or by biology. History, in fine, finds its terrain: inscription within science.

How, within that scientific absolutism, can we pretend that the poetic, even if submerged, still has something to do with history? The fact is that it hangs on, like an undesired, clandestine element inherent in the very cult of sources: "As articulations of sense, the sources and documents of the human past are seen in principle as works of art. The historical method is thus, in an extreme formulation, the regularized consummation of the aestheticization of history."[58]

To be sure, it is a perverse consummation, as the word *Ästhetisierung* indicates, for it abandons the inquiry into the willful acts of thousands of agents, which Droysen recommended, for the sober and epic beauty of facts raised to the status of unquestionable objectivity. But Droysen still has something to say about that perverse presence. The passage here reproduced concerns the role of narrative in the creation of an illusion, the illusion that the historian has exhausted his subject:

In the abstract, it is easy to admit the proposition that our knowledge, even our historical knowledge, is incomplete. But the very form of narrative that is predominantly used in historical exposition creates the illusion—intentionally—that we have before us the integral course of history, the chain of events, motives, and ends, complete in itself. The researcher also sets out with the illusion that what has been transmitted to us represents if not everything then at least the essentials, which are all that is necessary to produce an image of completeness. (Droysen, 144)

Here the submerged presence and perverse effect that art has upon that historiography are even more pronounced. Predicting by a century a line of thought taken up anew by Hayden White,[59] Droysen showed that the adaptation of narrative procedures lent history the illusion of being an enclosed whole, objective and exhaustible. It thus freed itself from the worry of being confused with arbitrary, subjective judgments, relegating them to treatment of res fictae through the appropriation, not recognized—much less discussed, of the notion of fable, of the old Aristotelian mythos. Made responsible for describing the acts of recognized legislation, the historian could not but carry out his charge: through his pen facts were systematized that propped up the official history of nations; and objectivities, organized with beginnings, middles, and ends, rendered the totality of a historical period. Rhetoric might be conflated with the search for beauty but not with the seriousness of the historian.

In summary, then, both the animosity nurtured against the res fictae and the importance given poetry by aesthetic historicism lead to the same result: historiography looks on itself as a science, while beneath the self-image lurks the sarcastic and unscrupulous face of art. There submerged, prostrate, art avenges itself, so to speak, through that perverse relationship. Wherever the unwanted double is recognized, it will be so to the detriment of the practitioner. A typical case is that of Michelet, the study of whom, to be carried out systematically in chapter 3, we here anticipate. Michelet "takes to an extreme of dramatic intensity a form of written, literary, poetic history against which all contemporary research, which does not find there the writing of itself, protests."[60]

But does it not seem strange that Michelet pronounced himself the victim of the very history he practiced? Can we forget the praise that Lucien Fevre reserved for him? Can we ignore the doting attention that Le Goff dedicates to him, calling him no less than "the first historian of history's silences"?[61] Would to consider him the victim of a history composed in literary terms not give credence to the vicious critique that the ultraconservative Charles Maurras directed at him? Let us substantiate our suspicion by drawing on the unmistakable praise of Roland Barthes. Many consider the author of Le Peuple, "a bad historian because he writes instead of merely registering."[62] Moreover, he is a writer because he invokes "the excedent of the signifier" (Barthes, 21). That is, lost to history, Michelet will be redeemed by literature. But is that salvation not formulated in equivocal terms? Does Barthes do anything more than perpetuate Maurras's judgment by reversing its polarity? Barthes, to be sure, does not seem concerned with the question. It is as though Gide's narrow door had narrowed still farther, and at the end of the corridor there were light, liberty, and salvation only in the dwelling of écriture. Just as in Barthes the venerable philology comes to be subsumed into its contribution to personal pleasure, so Michelet becomes acceptable because he gives us pleasure: "In sum, in dealing with a text we should use historical reference cynically: reject it if it reduces and diminishes our reading, take it up if, to the contrary, it augments it and makes it more pleasurable" (25).

Michelet's recuperation thus becomes an object of belief revolving around two poles: if everything that is merely registered is relegated to the status of trash, if, conversely, something becomes textually plural and endowed with an excess of signifier when it elicits my pleasure, then I grant literature the status of earthly immortality. But what is accomplished there save perpetuation of the Manichaean division between science and literature, the consequence of which is maintenance of our ignorance of both? Therefore, Barthes's argument can have no force on one seeking rehabilitation of Michelet because of his historiographic practice and not in spite of it. Such is the case with Le Goff, who prizes the historian of the Middle Ages and the French Revolution for his anticipatory insights. He anticipated, for example, later work on the role of the festival in the Middle Ages and also on the function of witches: "The ideal of the festival that Michelet so exalted—especially in *L'Etudiant*—he found nowhere else so well developed as in the Middle Ages. They are 'the long festival of the Middle Ages.' The Middle Ages constitute a festival, foreshadowing of the role—today made clear by sociology and by ethnology—that the festival plays in such a society and civilization as characterized the Middle Ages" (Le Goff, 31).

Michelet's survival in the face of a positivistic, factual historiography comes from his having given us access to what, along with Lévi-Strauss, we might call the *logic of the concrete*. Let us take just one example: "What is astonishing is that witchcraft quickly created a being, with all the attributes of reality. It was seen, heard. Everyone could describe it. Note, to the contrary, the Church's creative impotence. How pallid are its angels, how monochromatic and diaphanous! One looks through them."[63]

Whereas a historian, whether a positivist or not, would find there "facts" to be authenticated or would be limited to "correction" of Michelet, lining up proof of what was said to have been seen through witchcraft but could not be seen through church intervention, Michelet captures the essence of the ambiguity that surrounded the witches, and the essence of their success. If their prestige is documentable, the reasons for it were subconscious, invisible, and therefore approachable only through interpretation. While the church kept its hands clean, so clean indeed that they became diaphanous in the process of legitimating the medieval power structure, the witches gave their attention to the body and effected the rehabilitation of the womb and of the digestive functions. They bravely professed that there is "nothing impure and nothing unclean" (Michelet, 112). Their success and their misfortune have the same explanation: they played politics, without knowing it. Their cohorts of ghosts became real because they were needed by the common folk. How else could their existence be conceived of than as one in relation to the devil, if God was prescribed as existing in a like relationship to castle life? Also, that logic of the concrete bespeaks not only the object of study but also the investigator who pointed it out: Michelet and his repugnance for the hypocritical religious compunctions of the Restoration bourgeoisie. Thus Michelet not only distanced himself from the procedures of factual history but also, in the process, put into question the concept of science as the *founder* of objective relationships. For all those reasons, he becomes for us a precursor—which is not a synonym for "contemporary of the history generally practiced today." For Michelet's history is still linked to the idea of nation and the principle of narration, closely related as they have been: "The exaltation of national power or national consciousness . . . remains one of the great *raisons d'etre* of history-narrative, after having been its undeniable basic impulse" (Furet, 75).

I have moved ahead a bit into the examination of Michelet because he offers an example of historiography from the past century that did not suppress the poetic tradition. That being done, the reader will understand how my purpose lies in substantiating the claim that in the nineteenth century there was a pointed tension in the writing of history between the poetic line and the attempt to find scientific objectivity, and that that tension was resolved through the suppression—suppression, not simple elimination—of the poetic side, which was then transformed into aestheticism (Rüsen) and/or became *naturalized* in the narrative form (Droysen). The prosecution of that model would be carried out in the advance of positivistic history, exact counterpart of the naturalistic novel. The old osmosis operative in the eighteenth century had become, then, a tight model referring to that process of suppression that derived from the scientific "certitude" about a factual and objective political history. Historiography and "narrative" literature now maintained contact precisely because of the dimension most salient in both: the dominant dimension of scientifism and of the service that it provided to the state. The binomium science-state effects the articulation of history with literature through histories of literature, which reached their apogee in the nineteenth century: "History of literature, in our common usage today, did not exist before the nineteenth century."[64]

In truth, that history is less a "literary" one than a peculiar branch of political history, giving a primarily political service to the science-state relationship: "From the beginning of the century to its end, the history of literature remains, secretly or openly, a means of locating the identity and determining the social space of science in post-revolutionary bourgeois culture."[65]

As Jauss both observes and laments: "The new history of national literatures, however, became an ideal counterpart to political history, and claimed to develop, through the context of all literary phenomena, the idea of how national individuality could attain its identity, from quasi-mythical beginnings to the fulfillment of national classicism" (Jauss, 51).

Histories of literature, in effect constituting a branch of the orientation stamped on national history, partake of its central rationale. Furet's study of the adoption of history as a discipline in the French educational curriculum shows as much empirically. The decisive moment for the introduction of history into education occurred under Louis-Philippe. In this modification, introduced in secondary education in 1838, the history of the nation itself stands out most prominently: "The fact that the entire last series was reserved for the history of France underscores the central character of that pedagogy from then on, in contrast to the tradition in the humanities'' (quoted in Furet, 116). Those changes would continue throughout the century. Since our interest here does not lie in recounting them, let it suffice to say that their function consisted in annexing the chapter of the Revolution to the glories of the nation-state: ''The teacher therefore does not have to wound any consciences when he expounds the principles of that Revolution and when he demonstrates how, through the power of our arms and our ideas, absolutist governments everywhere were transformed, as young peoples acquired, in the course of our contemporary history, the right to existence'' (121).

Expurgated of its ''bad'' side, the Revolution is extolled as the first fruit of the eternal French seed, which would grow to its fullness in the modern state. The modern state then became the object of an ''immanent teleology'' (Jauss), displaying itself as an organism that developed thanks to the evolution of moral consciousness. A diffuse Hegelianism and scientifism mix and complement each other in the education of the good citizen, which was to be strengthened by the teaching of both history and the history of literature. That combination was all the stronger in France where there had been no experience of the ''epistemological delimitation of the natural sciences in relation to the spiritual ones, where, to the contrary, the positivistic tradition inhibited the birth of a true hermeneutic tradition, in the sense of Schleiermacher and Dilthey.''[66] This does not mean that nationalist ideology was confined to France alone. In the ''Prinzipien einer deutschen Literaturgeschictsschreibung'' [Principles for Writing a German Literary History] (1833), Gervinus pointed out the secondary status of aesthetic principles for the historian's work and, by contrast, the centrality that nation should have:

> The aesthetic critic shows us the origin of a poem, its growth and completion in itself, its absolute value with respect to the ideal, in sum its relation to the artistic character of the poet. The historian shows us the poem's origin in its time as a result of the era's ideas, aspirations and destiny, its internal relations, of correspondence or contradiction, to them, *its value for the nation*, its repercussion amongst those contemporary or subsequent; he then compares it with the very best that that genre produced at that time, in that nation.[67]

The principle of nationality remained so stable in the immediately succeeding decades that after more than fifty years it reappeared in an even more specific formulation: ''The march of a brilliant and radiant history imposes upon us the duty of giving a general depiction of what we are and what we signify. From this inventory of all our forces, a *doctrine of national values and duties* would be constituted, on the basis of which the fatherland could approach its citizens in an animate form that is both rigorously demanding and lovingly generous.''[68]

Nor was the granting of centrality to the nation limited to Germany. In Italy, even before De Sanctis's classical *Storia della letteratura italiana* [History of Italian Literature] (1870-71), Emiliani Giudicini, in his *Storia delle belle lettere in Italia* [History of Belles-Lettres in Italy] (1844), interpreted the character of the national literature through the presence of two opposing political forces, Guelphism and Ghibellinism.[69]

In synthesis, both in Schlegel's advanced version and in the more popularized one, romanticism exalted history, held it to be the twin of poetry: "The Romantics view formal history on a large scale as an epic in prose, while historical fiction triumphs in all the genres."[70] Their relationship, however, was then deteriorating, to terminate in the creation of a historiographic standard that saw literature's utility for the state in its role as an element in the citizen's education. It should not be surprising, then, that since the time of Baudelaire and Flaubert literature exorcises the grave educator and develops a tradition of negativity. It should be even less surprising that, by the beginning of the twentieth century, a philosopher had set forth the basics of a theory of interpretation that assigned a secondary role to history: "Separate from the cognitive process are of course grammatical and historical study, which, in the face of the past, in the face of the spatially distant or verbally strange, serves only to transport the reader who is oriented toward the comprehension of a given text to the situation of a reader of the author's time and milieu."[71]

It might be thought that Dilthey merely returned to the line of aesthetic historicism in thus endeavoring to reestablish the contact between art and social life. In fact, however, that philosopher effected no return whatsoever. For him, history, in a kind of revenge of the vanquished, became an ancillary discipline that helped illuminate what it is not:

As it is clear that the recollection of the strange and the bygone demonstrates that comprehension depends upon a personally particularized genius and as, however, comprehension constitutes an important and enduring task in its role as the basis of historical science, it then follows that personal genius is transformed into a technique and that technique evolves into the development of historical consciousness. (Dilthey, 216-17)

Recourse to personal genius and the turning of it to interpretive method proclaim the empathetic mode of interpretation that Dilthey would take from Schleiermacher and further develop.[72] Thus, instead of opening the monad of autonomous art to the world, Dilthey's project refines it and links it to the formation of the canon of immanentist analysis, which, from the 1910s to the 1960s, dominated the critical scene unchallenged. Indeed, Dilthey was not the only figure to rebel against the model of literary historiography bequeathed by the nineteenth century. Critical theorists as different as Lukács, Jakobson, and Benjamin, in juvenile essays, respectively "Observations on the Theory of Literary History" (1910),[73] "On Artistic Realism" (1921),[74] and "Literary History and Science of Literature" (1931),[75] reveal the undisguisable crisis in which that branch of history found itself. That consciousness has grown only with time; today, it is much more pronounced. It is not only the history being practiced that is recognized as quite different from its precursors but the fund of questions through which it interrogates its very *raison d'être* and the interests that they awaken which show that the very foundations of modern history have been overturned. That return to inquiry into the bases of the discipline is symptomized in essays by Paul Hernadi[76] and Hans Ulrich Gumbrecht[77] or in such an initiative as editing the journal *History and Theory*.

In summary, historiography's development from the final third of the eighteenth century on is wholly congruent with literature's development, and most especially with its internal bipartition. That congruency makes the veto of fiction even clearer. For what can the calling of poets to sing the glories of the state imply other than the giving of a functionality to them? The novel has adapted well to that environment, deploying itself as a parallel to legitimate history. In the novel, fictionality has an alibi. Poetry, to the contrary, is separated; marginalized as either hermetic or unsound, it drags the fiction that it practices down into the abyss with itself. Shunted off to the margins, the concept of fiction is not redeemed even by those who have rushed to the valorization of the tradition of negativity. For them, a theory of fiction cannot be elaborated without awareness of the relationship between the product of fiction and the reality that it transforms. Thus, the tradition of negativity would take up the very veto that society had ascribed to fiction; poetry must, then, be looked on as a language without a communicative function. The veto of fiction develops with no concern whatsoever for the theory of fiction. Such concern can be possible only when the canon of immanentist criticism comes under fire. But that issue lies outside the scope of this book. For that reason, I shall now go on to consider the transformations that the romantic concepts of nature and history underwent in their voyage to the tropics.

Nature and History in the Tropics

The Influence of Foreign Thought

Of the foreigners who took an interest in Brazilian literature, either by their own volition or by assignment—Bouterwek, Sismondi, Schlichthorst, Garrett, Herculano, Ferdinand Wolf—the legacy of Ferdinand Denis is the most pervasive, and fascinating. From 1817 to 1819, this Parisian, who came to the tropics less from a desire for adventure than for the purpose of saving his family economically, guided by the principles of Mme. de Staël and Chateaubriand, stored up observations and experiences that, after his return, would give rise to an immense output on the country. Among his titles, the *Sc'enes de la nature sous les tropiques* [Scenes of Nature in the Tropics] (1824), *Brésil* (1837), and the "Résumé de l'histoire littéraire du Brésil" [Résumé of Brazilian Literary History] (1837), which had as a companion piece a similar outline of Portuguese literature, are referred to with some frequency by those who study foreign approaches to Brazil and its literature. Thus, while the tropics did not provide him his sought-after fortune, they at least provided a subject matter that lasted him his whole life. Indeed, in 1875, at a quite advanced age, having been born in 1798, he published his *Arte plumaria, les plumes, leur valeur et leur emploi dans les arts au Mexique, au Pérou, au Brésil* [Feather Art, Feathers, Their Value and Use in the Arts of Mexico, Peru, and Brazil].

Denis became a kind of correspondent between the two worlds. Initially his ambitions seem to have been somewhat greater, nothing less than to provide "the new literary school manifesting itself in Paris with yet-unexplored resources: the utilization of tropical nature to renew color and imagery."[78] Because national criticism, as it was presented by Sainte-Beuve's pen, did not react favorably to the general orientation of *Scénes* (see *Premiers Lundis*, fol. of 18 Dec 1824, t. 1), Denis changed course, becoming simultaneously the unveiler of Brazil to France and an aspiring guide of the nascent Brazilian literature. In the latter role, his merit was recognized by Gonçalves de Magalhães, who, in 1836, takes him as one of the precursors of Brazilian literary historiography.[79] And to that evaluation both Varnhagen and Sousândrade added the title of collaborator with Brazilian authors. Nevertheless, his role was in fact even greater. Indeed, Antônio Cândido contends — quite correctly — that Denis was responsible for the "persistent exoticism that has permeated our view of ourselves down to today."[80]

Although the conclusion is a common one, that fact should not deter us from a more detailed examination. Before undertaking it, however, we should give some attention to the discrepancy between the exoticism of Denis's published texts and the marginal musings that he reserved for his letters and diaries from 1816 to 1819. (It is lamentable that there is still not a complete edition of that material.) Immediately upon arriving in Rio, while awaiting passage to Bahia, Denis wrote to his father that it was as if he were "leaving Hell to go to Purgatory" because, although "the Public library is well furnished with books," "there are only four book stores in Rio de Janeiro!"[81] And in Salvador da Bahia, he sent his father a more detailed letter in which he analyzed with a critical eye the Good Friday celebrations. To the twenty-year-old Parisian, the baroque illusionism that the preacher used to illustrate his sermon was "a beautiful demonstration of barbarism":

The priest ascends to the pulpit and begins his sermon, customarily on passion, first censures his listeners for their failings and exhorts them to look into themselves, and then suddenly, pointing to the curtains that hide the chorus, lets out a shout: "Here is our Savior; prostrate yourselves, lowly humans; offer Him the signs of your repentance!" The curtain falls, and we see Jesus crucified, with Mary Magdalen, richly attired, praying at his feet, and the Virgin to the right surrounded by Angels. A Roman soldier, armed from head to toe, mounts guard for a while. Then we see four of Jesus' disciples arrive; they come up and try to approach but are repelled by the soldier, who finally lets them pass after receiving the written permission that they present to him. They fall face down on the ground and worship Him; the sermon proceeds. That is to say, what proceeds is the program of the pantomime. The preacher successively orders the crown of thorns removed, then the nails withdrawn, which are given over to the Virgin and Angels; then the Cross is taken down and Christ's bloody wounds demonstrated. The audience is by now so affected by the noise of the slaps against the body that that noise is exactly repeated by the noise of clapping throughout the theatre. When all this subsides a little, the body is laid on a richly-draped bier, the curtain is drawn, and the farce is presented.[82]

The long passage captures the Parisian youth's shock at coming face to face with the illusionistic practices of the colonial society. The mixture of religious act and what seemed to him mere delight in theatricality scandalized him. Accustomed to neoclassical taste, the prolongation of baroque practices shocked him. He therefore did not take note of one decisive point: in that mixture of theater and religious office, fictionality combined with serious discourse, or serious discourse assumed the trappings of fiction, with the purpose of capturing the minds of the community: "The monks are the directors and often the actors in these mummeries, which to my eyes surpass all ridiculousness. They do not forbear to laugh at them along with the foreigners, but they believe them necessary to the maintenance of their credibility with the people" (Arinos, 652).

The society had eliminated the distinctions between discourses to such a degree that everything had become pretense calculated to instill obedience through terror. Moreover, the wounding of Denis's critical sensibility went beyond the sphere of religion. In speaking of the *entremez* that accompanied the theatrical presentation of *The Sacrifice of Ephigénie*, he says that he found its dances abominable: "There is one that is called the *landou* [*sic*] which is very well executed but whose indecency prohibits description, although the Brazilian public delights in it" (Bourdon, 210).

The discomfiture elicited by that contact with the colonial society only grew when Denis came into contact with the acculturated Indians. The romantic cult of the primitive, especially for a reader of Chateaubriand, was destroyed; the romantic revolt realized that the free space it envisioned had in fact been reduced by the Europeans' arts of devastation: "The history of these peoples would doubt-less offer sad lessons to Europe. One can still see there the happiness of a hun-dred nations in the innocence sacrificed to love of riches and true courage over-come by the dullest of artifices" (179).

But Denis did not content himself with seeing the Indians near the white cen-ters. He ventured into the forest and contacted the Botocudos Indians. Unfortu-nately, he had neither the maturity nor the wherewithal that it would have taken to become a forerunner of Lévi-Strauss's *Tristes tropiques*. Even passion, he noted, was insufficient to animate the savages' countenance, to make them forego their appearance of stolidity and show themselves as *les dominateurs des forêts* (180). Thus a negative pole is constructed: white society, culturally empty, reli-giously farsical. The counterposed pole: the spectacle of the humans of pas-sion—savages who shrank before the European's approach. Only the separation of the latter allowed Denis to feel free and happy. Free of white society, ready to plunge into that black one whose dress recalled "ancient Oriental costumes" (165). Happy especially before grandiose, untouched nature: "Sometimes a vine of blue flowers would crown an elegant palm tree, and vast *copaíbas*, their enor-mous branches intertwining high in the sky, would form what seemed a natural arcade, beneath which a multitude of *colibris* could be seen to show, glittering with the liveliest colors" (177).

These passages suffice to demonstrate how poor the "Résumé de l'histoire littéraire du Brésil" is, that work of Denis's most frequently referred to by the Brazilian romantics. In it, the author's goals at minimum approach exoticizing ones. Exoticism, already steeped throughout the *Scénes* and *Brésil* but counter-acted by the observations reserved for private correspondence, now amplifies itself:

Even if that part of America has adopted a language that our old Europe perfected, it should reject the mythological ideas originating in the Grecian fables. In our long-enduring civilization, they have been put to extreme uses where nations could not comprehend them well and where they must remain ever unknown; they do not harmonize, they are not in sympathy with either the climate or nature or traditions. America, vibrant with youth, should have new, energetic thoughts of its own.
. . . Amidst those beautiful sights, so favored by nature, thought should expand in concert with the spectacle presented to it; majestic thanks to the masterpieces of the past, that thought should remain independent, seeking no other guide than observation. In sum, America should be free both in its poetry and in its government.[83]

The repugnance that the tropical society engendered in him provoked a curi-ous selectivity: nature alone impresses him, it is only to it that he dedicates his enthusiasm, and it is in it that he finds the means of autonomizing literature. I noted that the romantics made nature an object of observation and a stimulus for self-reflection. That is clearly shown in Caspar David Friedrich's painting *Zwei Männer in Betrachtung des Mondes* [Two Men Contemplating the Moon] (1819) or by Wordsworth's "Tintern Abbey":

> The sounding cataract
> Haunted me like a passion: the tall rock,
> The mountain, and the deep and gloomy wood,
> Their colours and their forms, were then to me
> An appetite.
>
> (Wordsworth, 92)

The same program seemingly returns with Ferdinand Denis. In fact, however, such does not occur—it could not—for the conditions under which romanticism was construed among us were quite different. In Europe, both the romanticism that manifested optimism in the progress of human equality and liberty and also the romanticism that soon turned to the ideal of the autonomy of art retained their character of rebellion against established society. Their recourse to nature was, then, a stimulus to a liberating self-reflection. In Brazil, such would have been unimaginable, especially because the first romantic generation, the generation of Gonçalves de Magalhães and Porto-Alegre, was buoyed up by imperial status. In his zeal to civilize the nation that he governed, King Pedro II favored that young generation that was introducing current European culture into the country; he provided them diplomatic posts and help in publication of their works, and even hastened to their defense, as he did in the case of Alencar's attacks on the *Confederação dos tamoios* [The Confederation of the Tamoio Indians]. In the absence of a struggle against established society, the very contact with nature would assume another significance: not stimulus to self-reflection but rather cultivation of ecstasy in the face of its savage marvel. And if a touch of revolt seeps through later romanticism, that of Gonçalves Dias for example, it in fact arises from other motives. As Gilberto Freyre has said:

> Literary Romanticism in Brazil—men's voices groaning and lamenting
> at times to the point of seeming women's—was never the same as other
> Romanticisms, as that "revolt of the Individual" against everything—
> society, era, species—that the French critic speaks of. In some cases it
> seems to have been less the expression of individuals in revolt than the
> expression of men of mixed race feeling, like those of mixed sexuality,
> the social, and perhaps psychic, distance between them and the
> definitely white, or pure, race, or the definitely masculine and dominant
> sex.[84]

Moreover, in a nation lacking even the rudiments of an intellectual system, that sense of unhappiness was not pushed to assume other proportions deriving from reading and/or criticism undertaken by lucid amateurs or by professional thinkers. Incapable of benefiting from the intellectual exchange that so favored German romanticism, and, albeit in lesser proportions, English romanticism as well, the sense of unhappiness distilled into a simple sentimentalism. Thus was nature either sung because of its exuberance or made the backdrop for the plaints of a wounded soul. In either case, Europe was implicitly alluded to. In the first case, either because the foreigners who concerned themselves with Brazilian letters criticized that literature for not exploiting more fully the uniqueness of tropical nature or because, since the introduction of romanticism coincided with the perceived threat of a "re-Europeanization" of the country (Freyre, 309), zeal in observation of nature became a defense of autonomy. And Europe was paid heed to in the second case as well:

> Even while feeling themselves differentiated from the Europe or the metropole where they had studied, and wishing for an independent and republican Brazil, [the Brazilian authors had had] that European education remove their taste for the raw, hot nature of the tropics and replace it with a lukewarm, merely literary naturalism located in the shade of planted mango trees amid monkeys that had been tamed by black domestics and parrots that repeated, instead of Tupi words, Latin and French phrases learned from these new gentlemen. (576)

The cult of sadness and yearning [*saudade*] and the frequent use of the theme of exile coordinated a symbiosis within the young poets, between the melancholy of one who was far from Europe and the melancholy of another who felt himself inferior or unrecognized in his own country. Thus, even the sentimentalism common to both Brazilian romantics and "normal" romanticism sprang from different motives. And that divergence only increases if we add to the equation the already observed factor that with us the cult of observation was not the springboard to self-reflection and thence to approach of the question of imagination. Indeed, self-reflection was simply replaced by sentimental nostalgia. In short, the dialectic between observation and self-reflection gave way to an intimate tie between observation and sentimentality. While society seemed small and insignificant, a parody of real civilization, at least nature could enchant us with its variety of forms and colors. In Europe, the negative dialectic with the present gave the self-reflection resulting from contact with nature the character of an exploration of the imaginary. Present albeit negated, the contemporary world required that romantic imagination not be merely self-compensatory, self-gratifying, that it not simply revolve about its own navel. With us, to the contrary, the depreciation occasioned by parodistic civilization—which was the current evaluation of *our* contemporary scene—kept self-reflection from being anything more than the fanciful staging of a poet's lamentations. We see, then, the basis for accord between Denis's proposal and its Brazilian reception: our only possible originality would have lain in the contemplative observation of nature. The individual "I" does not seek to unfold itself to, for example, Turner's storm of phantasmagoria or to Hölderlin's poetic-philosophical soundings. It can content itself with the fantasy of its exile. Thus "Oh, what yearnings" becomes the paradigmatic utterance of our romantics. How, then, was nature to be conceived so that it might underwrite our so-called "originality"? Denis's writings provided this suggestion:

> What a spectacle, and how can one not admire it! At the sea's edge, on the deep bays where weak waves die upon the beach, the cocoanut palms almost always sway gently, the pink periwinkle or the morning glory cover the bare sands, mango-groves form green labyrinths; and if one turns his eyes to some distant island, to the panorama of those shining-green forests . . . the imagination collaborates with the idea of the tranquil retreat, of the solitude that no one would appear to break. (Denis, 39)

With the shunting aside of society, the very element whose presence had led to reflection about the imagination in *La Nouvelle Héloïse* the sought after, sweet refuge was converted into a scene for the chastening of style until the yearning for one thing or enthusiasm for another cried out on the page. Thus nature lost its character of stimulator to reflexivity and took on an openness to annotation and, with the use of a dictionary, minute observation as well. To Denis's European eyes, exoticism could carry the day only if such observation were extended to include attention to customs:

> For literature, and even more for the sciences, the creation of a weekly newspaper would be very useful, one in which accounts sent from the provinces could be printed, along with oral traditions that might be collected daily. Through this means not only would the products of nature become better known and commerce be enriched, but there would also be added the advantage of gathering accounts of great interest about the savage peoples who still inhabit that vast portion of South America. (78)

And let us persist a bit further: if, for European romanticism, observation of legends and customs formed part of the negative dialectic with the present, for us such observation served as the stimulus to the exoticism of that "superior" being, the poet, who evidenced difference and originality in being able to observe, to reveal, and to point out. It is thus easier to understand how we passed from romanticism to realism without great struggle. Since nature was not the battleground of the tension between observation and reflection, the realist had merely to overthrow infatuation with sentiment to be able to give himself or herself over to observation of the coarse and ugly. Our exoticism, then, combined a wish to demonstrate our uniqueness and an internalization of European evaluation of our cultural processes. Moreover, for reasons just dealt with, the language advanced about Brazil by other Europeans only strengthened that same canon.

In the same year Denis's "Résumé" appeared, Almeida Garrett published his essay "Histéria abreviada da léngua e da poesia portuguesa" [Short History of Portuguese Language and Poetry]. Garrett lacked the Lusophilia of a Gama e Castro—who simply denied any possible autonomy for Brazilian literature because "literature does not take the name of the country, it takes the name of the language"[85]—he did not hesitate to assign a place to Brazilian (neoclassical) poets, lamenting, however, that their European education had extinguished "the national spirit" in them: "The new and majestic scenes of the nature in that vast region must of course have given its poets more originality . . . ; European education has extinguished the national spirit in them: they seem to fear showing themselves to be Americans."[86]

Albeit lacking the complexity of a Ferdinand Denis, Garrett exalts nature as physical element, considering it capable, in and of itself, of occasioning "different images, expressions, and style."

The stress placed on observation is still more explicit in the passage in which the German Schlichthorst explains the "learned Brazilian's" predilection for The Lusiads: "Any man who has made long sea voyages will find this poem fascinating; the descriptions that the chivalric poet creates of distant countries and customs are surprisingly accurate and at the same time so ingenuous and picturesque that we seem actually to be seeing what he tries to set forth in his beautiful verse."[87]

Even Alexandre Herculano subtly reiterates this ongoing, implicit project assigned to the Brazilian poet. Although praising Gonçalves Dias, he censures him for not disentangling himself enough from Europe, for not listening to the call of the jungle: "That New World that gave such poetry to Saint-Pierre and Chateaubriand is rich enough to inspire and nourish the poets that have grown up in the shade of its primitive jungles."[88]

And, finally, even the Austrian Ferdinand Wolf, whose Le Brésil littéraire—histoire de la littérature brésilienne [Literary Brazil: History of Brazilian Literature] was published (Vienna, 1963) at the expense of the Brazilian emperor Pedro II, emphasizes the power of nature to create national literary autonomy. Wolf actually went so far as to suggest that nature is not merely a differentiating element but, indeed, a determining one for the form of expression. Thus, to explain why the novella had had lesser success in Brazil than the novel, he proclaims: "So precise and highly realistic a form could not fit a people living in a tropical nature that made them love material abundance, exuberant imagination, sensual development, and the enchantment of the fantastic."[89]

Actual development in fact went in the opposite direction. In Wolf's terms, the novella was much more frequent among us than the novel, especially during romanticism. Wolf's mistake is, however, quite understandable if we look through the European prism: if we had retained the observation-reflection dialectic, the "novel" would probably have predominated. Nevertheless, as the late Heron de Alencar observed some years ago: "In the case of Brazil, that type of novel [the regional novel] was also born of the Romantic aesthetic—not, however, as a reaction against exaggerated subjectivism, which we never experienced to any great degree. The Realistic tendency . . . was always predominant in our Romantic novel; it lent dimension to the historical novel and even gave substance to our sentimental novel."[90]

In fact, instead of an "exaggerated subjectivism," what characterized us was a weak, facile, self-satisfied, and rhetorically inflated sentimentalism. Perhaps the very adjective "exaggerated" has been a comfortable one for us, permitting our avoidance of a more careful analysis of what our romanticism was, and why. Hence the innovative nature of the rereading that Haroldo de Campos proposes: "Its most coherent freedom of movement came along the line of least ideological resistance, the line that best allowed it to exercise its novelistic activity (so productive in number of works, so slight in effectively lasting creations): ethnographic retreat to the pre-history of the bourgeois novel, to just this side of epic, to the ritual matrix of myth and legend, the folkloric pre-history of the novelistic, the *Ur-Epos*."[91]

Instead of perpetuating the half-truth that our Indianism constituted the Brazilian romantic response to our lack of a Middle Ages, Campos capsules the formal novelty of Indianist novels such as José de Alencar's. That novelty consisted in the domestication of the epic form used by both the neoclassicists and Gonçalves Dias, the taking of Tupi as an Adamic language, and the refusal to establish undeniable "beginnings," creating instead the same fictional basis for them as for Tupi, which was invented as an "aesthetic device."

By retroactive movement within the literary canon, the Alencar of *Iracema* was able to neutralize the exoticizing of nature and the realism of its trace. That a solution could be found outside the canon as well is attested to, during the same time period, in the more advanced passages in Sousândrade's *Guesa*. *Iracema* was published in 1865; the first version of the episode of *Guesa*, the initial stanzas of which are reproduced here, in 1867:

(*The historical* Muxurana:)
The first ones made
Slave women of us;
They stole our daughters
Took advantage,
Then sold them afterward.

(Tecuna, *swinging in a hammock and wishing for her independence*:)
They stamped the cheeks
Embossed in flower,
High, fleshy breasts,

Coming to a point
Where love naps lie.

(Mura, *a slave bought for eleven coppers*:)
For gentle young women,
A good legal measure.
Or a pretty skirt
Of calico
The King would give *pro-rata*.[92]

The scene involves a diverse group of Indians who, belonging to different nations, have only their acculturation in common. Their disconnected speeches bespeak their uprootedness. The tropics prefigure Hell. There are no lyrical lamentations or warrior consciousnesses; each Indian acts in the way that he or she can, although they all know perfectly well who has sold them, has parceled them out in sale, and to whom they must look for either destruction or orgy.

In regard to their regressive and progressive forces respectively within the literary canon, the Alencar of *Iracema* and the Sousândrade of "Tatuturema" had to be either "normalized" within the interpretation of romanticism or else excluded from canonized literature. In truth, they can have no other fates until we reinterpret our romanticism. And such an undertaking seems quite remote even today. As Haroldo de Campos points out, the two contemporary models for Brazilian literary historiography, those of Antônio Cândido and Afrânio Coutinho, despite their deep differences, see Brazilian literature in the image of a seed that breaks open, grows, and matures in the manner of "a process of genealogical construction."[93] Although the moment of reexamination seems distant, we can at least look to the pieces that will have to be dealt with. They take shape with the initial repercussions of the essays by Denis, Garrett, Herculano, and Wolf.

National Acceptance of Romantic Thought

Let us now concentrate on some texts—dating from the publication of the review *Niterói* in 1836 to 1888, when Sílvio Romero published the first systematic history of Brazilian literature—that consolidate the concept of literature developed in our country.

It may seem strange that romanticism in Brazil bore an official stamp and, at the same time, was a movement of considerable popular dimension. Examination of these texts, however, shows that there is no mystery to it. The authors learned to impart to their texts a vague and grandiloquent tone that would upset no one save the actual enemies of national independence. Even so, it is still strange to find in Gonçalves de Magalhães the simultaneous defense of religion and praise of the French Revolution, "which tore down all the thrones of Europe and shared royal purple and the sceptre of kings with men" (Magalhães, 260).

What had happened was that romantic libertarian principles found a handy enemy: Portuguese dominion. The reason why the nation had not yet produced its best fruits was explained, why its authors had not really differentiated themselves from foreign figures was argued, and the need for the poet figure was advanced, all in relation to the image of the Portuguese yoke. Moreover, it was to that end that literature was politicized in a way that would be agreeable to the ears of governors and prospective readers as well. The very opening of Magalhães's essay is symptomatic: "A people's literature is the development of the most sublime of the ideas that it has produced, the most philosophical of the thoughts, the most heroic of the aspects of its morality, the most beautiful of the nature; it is the living picture of its virtues and its passions, the awakener of its glory, and the progressive reflex of its intelligence" (241).

In short, it was necessary for literature to justify itself as a chapter in the history of the nation. In that sense, Magalhães's essay does not differ from the writings of his contemporary Gervinus—with the comparative advantage to the Brazilian that Gervinus's Germany was still disunited while the poet from Rio de Janeiro could praise his monarch and emphasize service owed to country at the same time: "At the beginning of the present century, with the changes and reforms that Brazil has been undergoing, its literature presents a new aspect. A single idea absorbs all thought, an idea all but unknown before that time; it is the idea of country. It dominates all else, and all is done in service to it or in its name" (263).

In linking the destiny of literature to the celebration of nationality, Magalhães could leave established society aside and look directly to nature. It had in effect been betrayed during the centuries of civilization: "Brazilian poetry is not a civilized native; it is a Greek dressed in French and Portuguese style and acclimated in Brazil. Beguiled . . . by this beautiful foreigner, Brazilian poets have let themselves be led on by her songs and have forgotten the simple images that a virgin nature offers them with such profusion" (256-57).

Thus is created an opposition between a nature that had been painted over by a servile political spirit and an authentic nature awaiting its singer. That such was not merely an individual position is shown by similar assertions from Pereira da Silva:

> In Brazil, however, that poetic revolution has unfortunately still not been fully felt, our bards reject their country, they give off singing the beauty of the palm trees, the charming banks of the Amazon and the Plate, the virgin forests, the superstitions and thoughts of our countrymen, their habits, customs, and religion to celebrate instead the gods of Greek polytheism . . . and thus become nothing more than mere imitators, and repeaters of others' ideas and thoughts.[94]

Those passages bespeak the different role that nature assumed in Brazilian

THE FATES OF SUBJECTIVITY □ 113

romanticism. It became symptomatic of the battle against Portugal and of the struggle for national identity. Thence immediately derived the function assigned to literature: to demonstrate the victory of spirit and morality, for "however much the taste for, and independence of, literature spreads in a nation, to that degree does it prosper and flourish. The truth of experience is that spiritual culture has great influence on our qualities and that the practice of the moral virtues necessary to societies encounters more or less resistance in a people according to the degree of its illumination" (Silva, 214).

But what kind of morality was being invoked? The Brazilian writer quickly learned the use of noble words, words so unquestionably noble that they could count on public allegiance a priori. That process of abstraction, however, had to have a limit and to be able to suggest to the more attentive reader the political party being advocated: "In contrast to the subjects of despotic governments, condemned to hide their virtues, men in a free government, forced to hide their vices, giving themselves to the study of letters, elevate their characters and strengthen them against the seduction of the passions, which aim them along a thousand different paths, like contrary winds on a tossing sea" (216).

The allusion to "despotic governments" was directed against the old continentals, whereas the "free government" — that is, the established Brazilian monarchy — could count on those dedicated to letters, for they would aid against countryfolk seduced by the passions. The phrase might seem strange coming from a romantic mentality, but it is quite explainable from the elite that Brazilian state patronage had fomented. Thus was the poet taken as the faithful subject and the spokesperson of the people: "Thus too the man of letters, who does not serve as an interpreter, who does not enter into the superstitions and secret thoughts of the people, who wishes to dissect it with his scalpel, is an anachronism" (216).

The poet hastens to carry out this mission of charismatic auxiliary. For the exercise of that task, it seems necessary for the poet's words to be capable of convening, of creating enthusiasm, while at the same time remaining abstract and generic — that is, taking care that there not be too great an expenditure of mental energy for comprehension and that there not be too close an examination of the arguments.

That schematic analysis seems embodied in, for example, the passage in which Santiago Nunes Ribeiro defends popular religiosity:

In all Brazil that divine sentiment was manifest (and happily it is still in some areas). Popular poetry revealed it everywhere. . . . Go into the backlands, go to the oratories on the estates, the churches in the villages and hamlets, and you will see there the tenderness and devotion with which the Brazilians sing the psalms, the hymns, the pious orations composed in this nation in honor of God, of the Holy Virgin, and of the heroes of Christianity.[95]

The examination of concrete issues was unimportant—especially if it added dimensions that did not further the text's rhetorical idyll. Bracketing off reflection, then, had a precise function: to justify, with an economy of effort, the "right side," which the writer advocated. It is, however, obvious that that abstractness is often pushed toward declaration of the writer's party allegiance. Ribeiro does precisely that, making Gregório de Matos his target: "Gregório de Matos is celebrated as a satirist; but it must be confessed that Brazil has not yet had a poet in that genre to compare with the Portuguese satirists, and especially with the original Nicolau Tolentino. This, however, does not bother us, since *satire is not one of the genres in which ideality ennobles art*" (Ribeiro, 22; emphasis mine).

That critic's choice of poet comes on the score of his handling of language, for it had to be precisely controlled to sublime ends. Therefore, Gregório de Matos is again attacked, this time by the historian and diplomat Varnhagen: "If in his descriptions of festivals or hunts, which in general are overly prolix, he pleases and entertains us, we must continually lament that in the personal satires the poet goes beyond the bounds of decency and at times ceases being a gentleman."[96]

As a result, for the poet—or, by extension, the intellectual—to become celebrated, he had to discipline the privileged song of nature. Thus their failure to open out into self-reflection had much to do with the political situation in which the members of the young intelligentsia found themselves. Self-reflection would not only make access to their work difficult for the already reduced number of readers but also reduce the control that Varnhagen demands:

America, in its different states, ought to have a poetry, basically a descriptive one, only offspring of the contemplation of a new and virgin nature; but he would be mistaken who would conclude that to be an original poet one must go back to the abc's of the art. . . . *The opposite could be compared to one who, to look for originality, spurns all the elements of civilization, all the precepts of religion, that our forefathers have transmitted to us.* (Varnhagen, 73; emphasis mine)

It is true that a passage from Alencar, in which the poet's first concern is language, leads in the opposite direction:

But when man instead of an idea writes a poem, when the life of the individual is raised to the life of a people, when, simultaneously historian of the past and prophet of the future, he reconstructs upon nothingness a generation that has disappeared from the face of the earth and shows it to posterity, he has to have sufficient confidence, not only in his genius and his imagination but also in the word that must make that new and unknown world appear.[97]

Even though the rationale remains abstract, in Alencar a differential criterion of the poetic is hinted at. Instead of a political ethic, dominant in Varnhagen, "genius," "imagination," and revelatory language are stressed. Contemporaries of the exchange see the issues that are drawn, as the response by an Alencar defender shows: "The critic does not see in Mr. Magalhães' poem either an attack upon religion or tendencies to debase the word of Ipiranga. The doctrines of morality and of nationality remain coordinate with the overall proportions of that artistic whole and harmonize with the development of action in the antagonism between savage and civilized man."[98]

Two forms of argumentation thus exist in opposition: one by a thematic criterion—following the dogmas of religion and the political order—the other by a formal criterion. The former, in remaining abstract and generic, has the advantage of being able to concretize what interested it, whereas the latter lacked development of a capacity to reflect on the specificity of poetry, which our romanticism had not learned to do. Thus Alencar's praise of the word was soon transformed into an almost purely grammatical—and, later, stylistic—criterion. Unfortunately for Brazilian letters, Alencar—as he himself recognized—had no critical expertise. A comparison between Alencar and Magalhães shows his efficacy in disagreement with the thematic criterion but inability to ground his own position. He knows, however, that mere contact with nature is not enough, that one must develop as well an adequate position: "If one day I were a poet and wished to sing the praises of my country and its beauties, if I wished to compose a national poem, I would ask God to make me forget for a while the ideas that I have as a civilized man."[99]

An indirect proof that he was eventually able to find such a position is to be found in his opting for *Iracema* as a result of dissatisfaction with his own poetry (see the letter to the first edition of *Iracema*, 1865). But the felicity of that novel seems to have been an occasional one. The author's nationalistic concerns led him to locate his activity where it could cultivate a national theme. Therefore, he practiced the urban novel as well as the regional novel and gravitated from the figure of the Indian to the backlander and even to the gaucho. Belief in the word had been transformed into belief in ability to capture the national. Thus Alencar, in his writing, came to reinforce the purely thematic criterion that as a critic he had opposed. Against the backdrop of the Brazilian mentality of the era, such a passage over to the Indianist vogue was not his alone:

Cultivation of the backlands was, therefore, born of Indianism. The false nativist illusion of independence had set our literature in search of a new spirit, of themes provided by the land and developing in the local milieu. In the Indian, in the autochthonous race that had been devastated by the invaders, a race whose persecution and whose indomitable character inflamed novelistic taste in the era, we thought we saw the typical representative of the nation. . . . With the illusion of the jungles dissipated, we still continued to feel the need to find a local originality and turned to the backlands, inhabited by that race, now nationalized and incorporated to the body of the nation: the mestizo backlander. Thence derived "backlandism" [*sertanismo*].[100]

That trajectory has double importance for the thesis defended here: it demonstrates that the primacy of "observation" among us made the antithesis between romanticism and realism less marked, and it shows that that *primacy did not imply so much the development of a taste for field research, for a search for facts, as it did a defense of "local originality."*

* * *

With service to his country consolidated by attention to Brazilian nature and respect for the dogmas of progress, religion, and the nation-state, the Brazilian romantic poet saves himself from the absence of a public for the written word by becoming a public servant. At his side is the literary historian who, also deprived of a reflective function, sought to advance the project that the nation had confided to him. In those circumstances, what question could seem key to those who wrote about literature other than the question of nationality? It seemed the inevitable starting point for the postulates of nature and of country. Symptomatic of that preoccupation and of the vagueness with which it was formulated is Santiago Nunes Ribeiro's essay "Da nacionalidade da literatura brasileira" [On the Nationalism of Brazilian Literature]. In that essay we can understand the threat that the poor writings of Gama e Castro represented. How, in the final analysis, can we explain a literature like ours? To inquire into the mission of literature, the direction that initially absorbs Ribeiro would constitute the easiest route: "To neutralize the effects of the harmful instruction that those books [of sensualist philosophy] have impressed upon us, then to elevate moral sensation to the height of its divine essence constitute without a doubt the mission of the contemporary literature of the great peoples" (Ribeiro, 7).

But the thorniest question merely remains: do we have, or not, a "properly national literature"? To approach that question, Ribeiro sought to arm himself with the principle of differentiation:

It is not an unquestionable principle that the division of literatures must invariably be made according to the languages to which they are consigned. Another, perhaps more philosophical division would be one that attends to the animating spirit, the presiding idea of the intellectual works of a people, that is, of a system, of a center, of a focus of social life. That literary and artistic principle is the result of the influences, of the sentiment, of the beliefs, of the customs and habits peculiar to a certain number of men who are in specific, determined relations which can be very different within some peoples even when they speak the same language. The social conditions and the climate of the New World must necessarily modify the works written within them in this or that language of old Europe. (9)

A literature, in summary, could become national through the combined action of an external conditioning factor, the climate, and a cultural conditioning factor, society. The term climate seems to be nothing more than a scientifically digni- fied name for nature—so much so that the author cites Buffon and Montesquieu. Furthermore, in developing his argument, Ribeiro had recourse precisely to jus- tification through landscape: "Yes, phenomenal beauty is to be seen with greater pomp on this fortunate soil; and not few foreign and Brazilian artists have drunk the purest inspiration from it, inspiration creative of excellent works, bedecked with lively colors, with elegant forms idealized in the harmonies of the musical and poetic art" (10).

But what does our author have to say about social conditioning? Although he has the merit of defending the poets of the eighteenth century from the often advanced charge of having been mere followers of European patterns, Ribeiro in fact has little to offer in that regard! Indirectly, he confirms what we have said about the passage of romantic thought to Brazil: nature either becomes the pre- text for expression of emotionality or becomes transformed into a testimony to nationhood. Let us not forget, however, that the author has the merit of having said as much long before us: "If we pass from the descriptive to the sentimental part, who can deny that some Brazilian poems exude a tender melancholy quite distinct from the somber sadness of many Romantic ballades, ballads, and ele- gies?"[101]

During the era under consideration here, the question of nationality remained the war-horse. As late as 1873, Machado de Assis's precious article "Instinto de nacionalidade" [The Instinct of Nationality] proves as much. It could have put a wet blanket on the problem, with his impeccable formulation: "What should be required of the writer above all else is a certain intimate feeling that makes him a man of his own time and country, even when he deals with matters distant in time and space."[102]

National sentiment had ceased to be seen as a *substance* capable of being described, of being weighed, and had come to be viewed as a *form*, to be sure, as a form of self-perception and attitude in relation to one's own time and coun- try. As form, it is variable, adjustable to the position of the speaker, not to be confused with a constant way of being arising from eternal roots. But to capture in a literary work what it meant to be a person of your time and country would require a subtlety of appreciation unknown to our criticism. As a result, the ques- tion of nationality persisted, coming to receive the more "scientific" support of the so-called Generation of 1870.

Within that nationalistic paradigm there arose some brief reflections on pecu- liarities of ours. I have noted the one by Santiago Nunes Ribeiro. A more interesting example was printed in the *Ostensor Brasileiro*, accompanied by the signature "Gz" (with "translated by M" in parentheses). It is a sort of fictional fantasy in which the author intends to follow a woman who is an allegory of the continent itself: "Before hearing her speak I had already known that she was a daughter of America, because of the smallness of her foot and particularly because of the color of her eyes and hair, black like the shiny *jacarandá*."

The piece is a curious potpourri of observations about the land and notes about ruins. Entitled "The Monuments in Ruin," it seems above all else a pretext for pointing out the diverse significations that our ruins could assume. I transcribe the decisive passage:

> With the future, American cities will come to mock European grandeur
> with the grandeur of their own palaces, of their own temples. As for
> now, time has wrought in America the most impious work that could be
> carried out on the happy virginity of its soil: it has strewn it with ruins.
> They are, however, unlike the ruins of the Asiatic grandeur or the ruins
> of the Greek splendor, which are ruins forevermore, cursed ruins that
> bare time destroys more and more, ruins that nature itself attacks,
> covering them with its sands or lashing them with the sea. No,
> American ruins are a transformation, they constitute the larva of an
> incomplete thought that will rise from its death of a few years upon the
> wings of grace and perfection. Time helps nature in America. Time
> locates its ruins within nature, so that there may be grave and
> melancholy places that give the spirit rest, at the height of the pleasant
> impressions that beguile us beneath the Tropic.[103]

In the New World, ruins should not elicit the serious reflection that they might in Europe. The topos is adapted to relaxation of the mind. Nowhere is it clearer than in this forgotten text how romanticism in the tropics became a justification for antireflexivity. The tropical Eden saved us from the effort of conceiving of time and its devastation. The ruins are there merely for our diversion: nature takes it upon herself to further optimistic thought. Reflexivity could even be taken as proof of a lack of Brazilianness. (Let us not forget that Sílvio Romero accused Machado de Assis of using features—humor and pessimism—that would not be Brazilian "features.") And, as regards literature, would that imagining reflexivity not be confounded with useless, empty daydreaming? It should not surprise us, then, that for all the critics here touched on, the observation of nature, the apprehension of its local color, are the prominent features. Indeed, I find only one critic in the entire era who casts doubt on the primacy of observation. In his article of 1861, while commenting on the poetry of Gonçalves Dias, Macedo Soares reiterates the lament that we still do not have "a national poetry in all its integrity." In contrast to all others, however, he then adds: "Perhaps we do not know where to go to look for the source of inspiration."[104]

The subsequent passage indicates that the sentence was not a merely rhetorical one, that it indeed pointed toward rethinking of the critical canon: [Gonçalves Dias] "prefers sentiment to description, and that says it all. Description denotes great talent in observation, fineness in view, delicacy and correctness of brush stroke, knowledge of perspective. The poet, however, does none of those things, they are the attributes of the painter; and poetry is as superior to painting as the word is superior to line and to color for the expression of idea and feeling" (Soares, 1:294).

The step forward is quite small, it is true. In any case, the focus on feeling permits Soares to approach more closely the problem of the poetic word: "Sound can never compete to advantage with the word for the individual expression of every sensible phenomenon. The realm of music is the vague, the undefined. . . . It can express, in general terms, happiness, sadness, anger, abandon, but its power does not extend to discrimination of the thousand varied forms that those mental states can take on" (1:297).

Although a step forward, however small, was taken, Macedo Soares did not create a school and romantic criticism did not advance beyond that stage. Unable to develop a concept of poetry, it appeared, to its realistic, scientific, and positivistic adversaries, to be interested only in defending the flights of a miniscule fancy and in the poets' privilege to say that they had seen what others could not. In 1878, Urbano Duarte de Oliveira would write: "The poet, the artist, in the whole meaning of the term, an unconscious, predestined microcosm, senses and sings; he is the butterfly of a light that we cannot see—we, ideal-less bourgeois."[105]

It is a defense as ridiculous as the one that Pedro Ivo offered in the same review: "We do not intend this modest article to throw down the gauntlet before the followers of the Realist school . . . they can remain there, with their geometric outlook, for I still believe in the great speculations of the human spirit."[106]

Against that defensive poetics grounded in taste, intuition, inspiration, and fantasy that nonetheless do not point beyond the "I" itself, the positivist Dantas Barreto would counterpose an optimistic and doctrinaire articulation of truth: "The positivist philosophy, that great beacon that arose with the extraordinary genius of Auguste Comte, goal of all evolutions of the human spirit from the remotest era on, must, inevitably,influence the arts just as all branches of human knowledge."[107]

The romantics are thus poor, miserable beings given over to an "unlimited subjectivity" that produces nothing "useful and pleasant," whereas "modern poet[s]" represent their opposite (Barreto, 58-59). That optimism develops to epidemic proportions when, as Licínio Cardoso emphatically declares, "the fine arts and industry march with hands interlocked."[108]

Quite apart from the insignificance of these texts, how can we say, in the light of them, that romanticism and realism did not stage a combat of some intensity in Brazil? There is to be sure an inescapable opposition: the realist generation starts from a cult of science that no romantic would tolerate. Therein, however, we forget that both movements partake of the same primacy accorded to observation of nature. The realists alone add that such observation would be of little use without the collaboration of science. Such are not quite the words of Dantas Barreto, but one needs only translate "for nature to be sung" as "for one to apply himself or herself to its observation," and "prior knowledge of [its] various secrets" as "science" to create a perfect version of that equation: "How can nature be sung without prior knowledge of the many secrets involved within it, how can society be studied without our having the least notion of the history of humanity?" (Barreto, 60).

By adding, then, consideration of the role that science should play for the artist, the realist generation believed that it had overcome the fear of an empty literature. But at what price? That of propagating the veto of fiction without ever even risking theorization of it. We must find an author endowed with the pure naïveté of Salomé Queiroga to hear the emphatic confession:

> *Maricota e o Padre Chico* is not mere imaginative writing; *it is a historical fact* authenticated by a verse legend that the boatmen of the São Francisco River still sing today. If it were mere fancy perhaps it would please the reader more, because then the subject matter could, with no obstacle to thought, activate the imagination to produce brilliant scenes decked out with the cloth of fable. Unfortunately, however, the fact is real; would that it might not repeat itself even yet today in our midst. Fancy, however, seldom enters this ever-linear narrative.[109]

That reinforcement of factuality was not carried out through mere repudiation of romanticism: indeed, from it onward, literature would be conflated either with the cult of melancholy or with the fixing of local characters and their local color. And let us not assume that his is a phase that has been surpassed: today, among those who write literature, that veto of the imaginary remains in place—and this is not to speak specifically of literary critics and literary historians. Many have concretized their thinking so thoroughly around the principle of nationality that some little time ago one of them managed to proffer this precious bit of wisdom: "What is curious—and inevitable—is that these stories stray from *Brazilian* literature to the very extent to which they have made their goal the search for *literature* itself."[110]

For such figures, how could the practice and study of literature be justified in the absence of the primordial figure of the nation? And why would literary historiography need another basis? Nationality was—and is—the means of justifying the veto of fictionality by giving it a "usefulness."

Chapter 3
What Are the Building Blocks of History?

The professor confessed that he had now lost his bearings when it came to history.

"It is changing every day. The kings of Rome and the journeys of Pythagoras are disputed. There are attacks against Belisarius, William Tell and even the Cid, who thanks to the latest discoveries has become a mere bandit. Let us hope there will be no more discoveries, and the Institute even ought to draw up some sort of canon to prescribe what is to be believed!"

Gustave Flaubert, *Bouvard and Pécuchet*

Direction and a Hypothesis

The way in which the writing of language develops exercises a specific force on its outcome, the text: itself necessarily linear, it linearizes it. And what can be formulated by that process is arrived at through the overcoming of two limiting conditions that stand in opposition to each other. The first of them we might call the margin of chaos. Because of the writer's lack of ability, because of his or her inadequacy in the face of the verbal code, or because of difficiencies of expression within that code itself, the linearity does not flow, the phrases seem jumbled, their transitions confused or equivocal; as in a canvas by a bad painter, the stroke is first too thick, then too thin. But whatever success is achieved in the face of that condition in turn leads us to the other. In it, the writer, be he or she a writer of literature or not, proves to be so much the master of fluency and verbal precision that his or her fabric seems seduced by the attraction of that transparency itself. Narrative efficacy is achieved, but at the price of an exclusive linearity, at the effacement of the dimensionality contained in the utterance. The phrase then becomes melodic precisely because it contains but one simple tune.

All writing is written between those two limiting situations—chaos and absolute transparency, a jumbled condition and excessive lightness. Given the impossibility of a technique like that of counterpoint, or of the orchestral organization of blocks of sound, the writing of language ever bears the mark of linearity. Whereas that fate makes the worker with words aware of the dangers that the two limits represent, it also makes it necessary for him or her to organize material according to what Hayden White has called *emplotment*, the posing of a plot by means of which the parts of the account will link together and motivate each other progressively. But such concatenation encounters a material limit. Let us say that the elaboration of a theme *A* has enabled the emergence of *B*, *C*, and so forth. Nevertheless, for the *emplotment* to avoid a narrow linearity or the character of a report, each of the nuclei *A*, *B*, *C*, *ad infinitum* must contain within itself internally differentiated and articulated zones. The risk is then run that those segments, A^1, A^2, and so on, might develop to such a degree as to compromise the architectural equilibrium of the *emplotment* itself.

It is the case, of course, that in writing, no one has total control over this process—except if we consider the mere recopying of what has already been written. Only hard practice or an intuitive eye to the competency expected of the projected reader will tell when the development threatens to overturn expository harmony, thus necessitating a new *emplotment*. (Obviously, I have in mind a case in which the writer, *in the very process of writing*, realizes that a certain development is necessary but is then impossible.)

The sense that chapter 2 was marked by many such shifts became clear to me when I reread its typed pages. Chapter 3 deals with one of the continuations that could not be explored to its full potential in that format. This very statement, however, may lead to the false impression that what follows is made up of leftovers from the prior *emplotment*. Although in the strictest of senses that is true, it is hardly the whole truth. When a previously subordinate segment becomes the orienting focus of a new plot, it ceases being a part of the already constituted *horizon* and rises to the status of *theme*, it reaches the foreground of the stage. Thus the greater space that is allowed it both permits, and simultaneously imposes, an organization that, maintaining ties with the previously completed development, also extricates itself from it, relatively speaking, for an expansion to areas that either were not present before or could not be directly treated. That metamorphosis is the necessary condition for us to pass on to work with a new *emplotment* and not a mere appendix to what has already been done.

The issue that was relegated to a subordinate segment and excluded from the development of chapter 2 as a consequence of its linear constraints concerns Michelet's observations on historiography. Furthermore, if this amplification of that issue exceeds the scope of an appendix, it does so for two reasons: because, in this broader format, consideration of Michelet will permit us to reconsider history's relations with verbal fiction (literature) on a level more theoretical than historiographic, and because, above all else, my analysis will allow us, albeit in what will then amount to a subordinate segment, to approach the issue of mimesis. In the course of this study, I shall endeavor to link more firmly these reasons.

Compositional Planes in the Historiography of Jules Michelet

In chapter 2, my interest in the work of the French historian was articulated around demonstration of the relationship between history and poetry during romanticism. But a reading of that chapter could elicit the following question: What, in the final analysis, was the goal of that examination? Was it presentation of a vast panorama whose intent was to test the comparison between European romanticism and Brazilian romanticism and reveal the latter's poverty and distortion of fundamental romantic principles? If such was the reader's conclusion, I should declare right here that I have failed. Beyond the fact that the problematic to which nature was subjected and the hidden struggle involving the relationship between history and literature in romanticism are sufficiently important to merit monographic attention, those issues come imbedded in an even greater one: since the Renaissance, the theory of the fictional — never presented as such, but as a form of eloquence — has endeavored to secure for its object a legitimate place among intellectual activities while at the same time denying that it was a locus of truth, thus reserving for it an inferior position in the hierarchy of discourses. In that sense, the effort on the part of the early writers of treatises on poetry, principally the Italians, was to justify the right of the fictional to exist by subordinating it to the discourse of truth. Hence the currency of the term by which it was referred to: *imitatio*. As a consequence, the modern era has, since its beginnings, been unable to deal with the question of mimesis without either locating it in an inferior space or, as it would from the nineteenth century on, rejecting it outright. I suggest that problem here to establish links between its origins and the text we are about to read. Thus the inquiry now to be carried out should allow me to demonstrate as well the presence of something that lurks within Michelet's text, the ghost of mimesis.

It should not be surprising that that ghost is so obscure that its name is hardly ever heard, that its presence can never be unequivocally affirmed, that we must content ourselves with inferring it through reasoned examination. Without ever questioning it, Michelet overwhelmingly concerned himself with a duty to serve his country through the recording, in a series of volumes, of its real past, in which the strength and vigor of one principal agent, the people, would shine through. In clear dissymmetry with historiography contemporary to his time, Michelet does not deal with individual personages without also taking into account the ground from which they derived their animation. As he notes in his *Journal*, on 22-23 February 1845:

> The last hero to appear was not, as is usually said, Napoleon; it was the Revolution. And its greatness consisted precisely in that there was no great man to absorb the fecundity of the movement itself into the phantasmagoria of a new mysticism. It [the Revolution] offered this great new spectacle, of an idea that had become abstracted from great men, from heroes, from false gods, from idols. It, much more than Kant, was the critique of pure reason.[1]

It could be alleged against that *Journal* passage that chapter after chapter, even entire volumes of Michelet's work, assign no particular place to the people. If we consider, for example, the second volume of the *Histoire du XIX siécle* [History of the Nineteenth Century] (1872), we find the historian concerned with the following developments: with Royalists on one side and on the other the alliance from the old Commune, represented by Babeuf, along with the remaining Jacobins, the directorate found itself in a precarious position. It therefore sought its stability through Bonaparte, then famous because of his victories in Italy. At the same time, however, the members of the directorate feared that the young general's power might end up delivering the Revolution over to a military dictatorship. For that reason, according to the testimony of Carnot, they sought to rid themselves of him.[2] Bonaparte, for his part, vacillated between respect for the directorate, which he still needed, and the Royalist party, for which he was attempting to show sympathy and had indirectly favored when he prevented the Italian revolution from growing by both refusing to allow the sale of church possessions and allowing the continuation of the Austrian throne.

Although such is an extremely schematic résumé, its further elaboration would not change what is obvious in it, that is, treatment of the intricate underpinnings for political decisions. Where do the people figure in them? They do not appear at all, of course, because they were kept far from such palace intrigue. It is because of the very absence of the people that, for Michelet, the Revolution failed. At the historical moment that we have highlighted, then, the principal motive force of the Revolution was silent. To find it, we must march back in time to the instant before "the resolute hatred with which the clergy and the English persecuted it all over the earth."[3] That prior instant is the beginning of the revolutionary process itself. The "Préface de 1847" (Michelet's foreword to the 1847 edition) declares as much in comparing the model of glory with that of incipient decline: "A thing to be told to everybody, and which is but too easy to prove, is that the humane and benevolent period of our Revolution had for its actors the very people, the whole people—everybody. And the period of violence, the period of sanguinary deeds, into which danger afterwards thrust it, had for actors but an inconsiderable, an extremely small number of men."[4]

In the light of that statement, it is only natural that the pinnacle of glory was seen in an act of greater symbolic import than actual effect, namely the taking of the Bastille. A reading of Michelet's description of that event is important, for there he is seen at the height of his enthusiasm. The creator comes face to face with his creation, recognizes it, caresses it with words, identifies with it, and finally finds in it justification for his own labor. Let us look to only the most symbolic scene:

> The keys too were carried,—those monstrous, vile, ignoble keys, worn out by centuries and the sufferings of men. Chance or Providence directed that they should be intrusted to a man who knew them but too well,—a former prisoner. The National Assembly placed them in its Archives; the old machine of tyrants thus lying beside the laws that had destroyed them. We still keep possession of those keys, in the iron safe of the Archives of France. Oh! would that the same iron-chest might contain the keys of all the Bastilles in the world! (Michelet, *History of the French Revolution*, 176)

Our suspicion of obvious rhetorical ploys could lead us to take umbrage at the final sentence. If we were to do so, however, we would misunderstand Michelet entirely. His rhetoric embodies his bitterness toward the time in which he is writing. For in 1847 the popular revolutionary clamor had been stifled by another force, a more subtle and calculating one which still in all had not escaped an observation that was as condemnatory as it was disenchanted: "Who would say, quiet as we are today, that we used to be such a noisy people? The ear becomes gradually accustomed to quiet, and so does the voice. The diapason has changed. Many a man thinks he is shouting, but he is only squeaking. The only real noise comes from the stock exchange."[5]

It was a transformation that had not occurred in isolation, for it was parallel to penury itself. Whereas during the Revolution, a worthy penury was common, it had now retreated from the centers of activity and taken refuge in "the poor quarters of our cities, those vast dens of death where women are wretchedly fecund and give birth only to weep" (Michelet, *The People*, 126).

Once that basis is established, individual portraits are presented. The portrait of the unfortunate Hoche, who, in the *Histoire du XIX siécle*, was killed by those who were fighting for the return of *l' ancien régime*. That of Marie Antoinette, who, wrapped in the spirit of the Austrian court, half-devout, half-enlightened by the *philosophes* did not even have the king's confidence at the beginning of their marriage and who nonetheless would be considered one of those responsible for the fate of the royal family. And the picture of Robespierre, the most powerful of all: "It is hardly surprising, that that eminently retrograde province [Artois] should have sent to the Estates-General a rigid partisan of the new ideas, that that man, unfamiliar with the indirect, knowing only the straight and narrow, should have brought to the Revolution a kind of geometrical spirit—the square, the compass, and the level" (Michelet, Les Fédérations, 258).

Those portraits become all the more effective when they imagistically subsume the specific social group with which their individual subject correlates. Thus the picture of Robespierre is in harmony with the ambience of Jacobinism: "The Jacobins, in their esprit de corps, which continued to grow, in their dry, burning faith, in their harsh inquisitorial curiosity, had something of the priest about them" (274). Nor does Michelet's technique of manipulating planes of characterization end there. According to what we have seen thus far, the "painter" describes three such planes: a general one, occupied by the people; an intermediate one, populated by the specific social group in question; and an individualized one, which is reserved for those personages seen in isolation. His narrative technique could, however, accommodate other refinements as well, such as the contrasting of one specific group with another on the basis of their corresponding physical milieus. Thus, treatment of the ideological difference between the Jacobins and the cordeliers is begun with the fixing of the environment in which the latter meet: "Almost across from the School of Medicine, look, at the back of a patio, that chapel of strong and sober style. It is the sibylline lair of the Revolution, the club of the Cordeliers. There it had its frenzy, its tripod, its oracle. Low and therefore supported by massive buttresses, such a vault seems eternal: it has heard, without collapse, the voice of Danton" (276).

As the description proceeds, the contrast with the Jacobins is foreshadowed by the emphasis on Danton, even though the ideological differences between the Jacobins and the cordeliers has not yet been spoken of. Michelet, however, master of this balancing of developmental planes, does not rush to establish his narrative center in that figure. He instead delays, narrating the episode of the assembly, in which workers, students, priests, monks, and men of letters all crowd together. Only afterward does he concentrate on the presiding figure: "But who is it who presides there? My God, it is terror itself. . . . A terrifying figure, that Danton! A cyclops? A god come down to earth? . . . That face terribly small-pox-scarred, with its small, dark eyes, has the air about it of a deep volcano. . . . No, what is there is not a man, it is the very element of turmoil; inebriation and giddiness circle thereabout—and fatality. . . . Dark genius, you make me fear! are you to save, lose France?" (286).

As soon as he or she perceives that interweaving of planes, the reader, on coming across an isolated figure, understands how to insert that figure into his or her milieu and thus visualize the entire scene. Michelet would have had difficulty accepting the notion that he had adopted a pictorial mode of composition.

It is important, however, for us not even to ask about his degree of awareness of it but instead to note the frequency with which the pages of especially the *Journal* betray his immense interest in painting. As a result of his trips to Italy, Germany, and England and his visits to French palaces and museums, he has frequent recourse to descriptions of canvases by Rembrandt, Rubens, Van Eick, Memling, Titian, Raphael, Michelangelo, Tintoretto, Veronese, Albrecht Dürer, Holbein, Van Dyke, Géricault, Masaccio, and Murillo. Nor in fact does he limit himself to mere admiration for them; to the contrary, the fashioning of his impressions of contemporary life is carried out, directly or indirectly, through modulations of such pictorial representations. I record merely a few examples:

> In Lecco, fair. . . . Here we are in a Celtic region. Enchanting physiognomic indecision: Lombard grace in the children and young girls. . . . There is in these beautiful Lombard villages of the North-East an admirable rhythmic progression. (Michelet, *Journal de Jules Michelet*, 263)

> After having dinner, visit the Armenians in the Lido. Beautiful and original situation for the convent, which is a small oriental one, with gardens of pink laurel. On the inside of the cells, Rembrandt-style heads. (270)

> On the journey my coach crossed briefly with M. Rothschild's, so quickly that I was not even able to greet him; his wise-monkey profile struck me as a Rembrandt sketch, a pencil line that says everything. (458)

The issue's implications reach far beyond merely proving Michelet's admiration for certain painters. For now, however, I will merely relate it to an annotation from 19 May 1846: "The novel interests as an individual destiny; we say to ourselves: *'That could happen to me'*. But the people are not satisfied with that; they want the true. . . . History, not collective but biographical, would have a great effect upon them" (642).

That is to say, the historian sees that he or she can emulate the novel through adaptation of its technique of individuation, with the added advantage of being able to count, as a result, on the reader's prior acceptance of the principle that real personages are being dealt with. And if the novel is the narrative genre to be rivaled, painting is the medium for effecting that competition. Through it the *emplotment* that the historian establishes is able to coordinate a vision of collective masses with a focus on figures that are only seemingly autonomous individualities and through whom the recognition and interest of the reader are guaranteed. Moreover, that articulation of planes, learned from the painting that Michelet admired—not from a Goya, for example, to whom he refers only in passing, and not from a Cranach, whom he accuses of coldness—renders unnecessary any conceptual effort on the author's part. Does a painter define terms, or does their import not derive instead from the composition of the painting? The cultivation of painting in fact serves as Michelet's compensatory justification for his own conceptual poverty. As a consequence, too, any verbal technique can be found legitimate as long as it functions to embody the force of the overall composition. Thus is nature made over into an allegory for human commerce. If, for example, agriculture had become progressively weaker economically during the eighteenth century, why not proclaim that a consequence of the lack of liberty? "How can we be surprised that the crops should fail with such half-starved husbandmen, or that the land should suffer and refuse to yield? The yearly produce no longer suffices for the year. As we approach 1789, Nature yields less and less. Like a beast over-fatigued, unwilling to move one step further, and preferring to lie down and die, she waits, and produces no more. Liberty is not only the life of man, but also that of nature" (Michelet, *History of the French Revolution*, 49).

And if the king cavils at opening the Estates General, even after the deputies have been elected, why not locate among the voices of protest the voice of nature itself? "A perilous delay! To so many voices then arising another was added, alas! one often heard in the eighteenth century, — the voice of the earth — the desolate, sterile earth refusing food to man! The winter had been terrible; the summer was dry and gave nothing: and famine began" (88-89).

It cannot be doubted that in such passages we are far from observance of the statement of purpose with which Ranke defined the role of the historian: description of the past *wie es eigentlich gewesen ist*, that is, "as it really happened" (see p. 95). That difference seems to suggest less a difference between individual personalities than one between the education of the intellectual in Germany as opposed to France. Whereas the German intellectual had no political — or even public — influence, being restricted only to contact with students at the secondary schools and universities, the French intellectual remained in the model of the *philosophes*, which envisaged the formation of public opinion through cultivation of a language tailored more to persuasion than to strict demonstration or speculation. To avoid detailed argumentation on the matter, which in this context would lead us into side issues, I will merely relay Voltaire's remarks about the man of letters of his time, in the article "Gens de lettres" [People of Letters] in the *Encyclopédie*: "The spirit of the century has made them, for the most part, equally fitted for the world and for the study; in this sense they are much superior to men of prior centuries. Up to the time of Balzac and of Voiture, they were separate from society; since then they have become a necessary part of it."[6]

That polemicist is so accurate in taking the man of letters (in the French language) not only as the denizen of the private reading room but also as a figure vital to the world, that is, to society, that Robert Darnton has recently interpreted, in convincing fashion, the cutthroat competition among editors to bring out the different editions of the *Encyclopédie* as proof that "the interest in enlightened ideas had spread very widely throughout France—to a grand public if not a mass audience."[7]

That eye to the general reader explains not only the allegories of nature and the adaptation of the painterly model in Michelet's *emplotment* but also his failure to define whence came the strength of the people. In Michelet's little book of 1846, *Le Peuple*, he examines the working conditions and the economic insecurity, if not penury, of various segments of society. According to his observations—which are often very fertile for the modern historian, pointing to the importance of factors not generic but rather particular and concrete, such as climatic conditions, state of the food supply, or unhealthy conditions in work places—it would be impossible to say who faced the worst conditions, the peasant, the urban worker, the small businessman, the low-level public servant, or the schoolmaster. That pessimistic evaluation would grow still more acute in treatment of the private pressure exerted by the family on the *paterfamilias*, a pressure that would force him to practice certain small connivances to achieve some measure of financial tranquility: "It is a sad and cruel thing to say, but it must be said: a man today is not corrupted by the world he understands all too well, or by his friends . . . for who has friends? No, most frequently he is corrupted by his own family. An excellent wife, worried about her children, is capable of anything to advance her husband and will even push him to base and cowardly acts" (Michelet, *The People*, 80).

What did Michelet oppose to that characterization? Nothing less than faith in the virtues of the French people: "There is an invincible repugnance for whatever is false and base in this noble country. The mass of men is good; do not judge it by the floating scum" (80).

To be sure, that hope had the merit of satisfying public opinion without upsetting the authorities. But, now complicated by the need to deal with that particular French virtue, the question in fact remains: whence did the people obtain their indomitable energy? Perhaps the question form itself makes response difficult. The fact is that Michelet himself never endeavored to formulate the question, let alone the answer to it. The most that we can glean from him on the subject is the notion of an articulation between the timeless people and the spirit of the country. It appears in the passage in which he describes his method:

(1) Sympathy for these diverse nationalities, while condemning an incurable discord.

(2) Sympathy for solitary labor, for the weaver, consoled in his darkness by God. . . . But after solitary labor, labor for the family, labor for the guild completed the harmony and, above all the guilds, sounded the carillon, the great voice of public peace that harmonized all. . . . Everyone, unaware of the others, prayed together.

(3) Finally, sympathy for the true, the great nation which has come to replace the commune, for true centralization, for France. (Michelet, *Journal de Jules Michelet*, 358-59)

That is to say, diachronically the medieval guilds proclaimed the presence of the people, which in turn was constituted in synchrony with the centralizing power of the nation-state. That set of interrelationships is, to be sure, a poor substitute for a conceptual framework. Does the painterly model substitute adequately for it? Or is Michelet's place to be defined by his "anticipations," as is commonly held by French historians today? The fact is that neither answer is sufficient. No other positive formulation is practicable, however. Let us attempt, then, through a purely analytical mode, to develop the question.

It should be noted to begin with, as Hayden White has remarked, that the lack of attention to theory was by no means a procedure restricted to Michelet alone. Although history's transformation into a legitimate academic discipline culminated, at the end of the last century, with the publication of the classical reviews of historical studies, that development was still not parallel to the "sort of conceptual revolution that has accompanied such transformations of other fields, such as physics, chemistry, and biology. Instruction in the 'historical method' consisted essentially of an injunction to use the most refined philological techniques for the criticism of historical documents, combined with a set of statements about what the historian ought *not* to attempt on the basis of the documents thus criticized."[8] Included in what the historian ought not to attempt was participation in current controversy or partisan undertakings—all in the name of objectivity. Such instructions in effect represented an endorsement of the politics of the hegemonic sectors of society in the post-1789 era and substantiated the triumph of an impoverished and naive empiricism:

The "historical method"—as the classic historiographers of the nineteenth century understood the term—consisted of a willingness to go to the archives without any preconceptions whatsoever, to study the documents found there, and then to write a story about their events attested by the documents in such a way as to make the story itself the explanation of "what had happened" in the past. The idea was to let the explanation emerge naturally from the documents themselves, and then to figure its meaning in story form. (White, *Metahistory*, 141)

It is of course paradoxical that the same observations apply to Michelet as well since his cult of the people was not well accepted by the *restaurateurs*, who definitively removed him from the Collége de France in 1852, and his historiography did not rest on empiricistic premises. To be cogent, however, Michelet would have had to have explicitly grounded his practice in other bases, and he was by no means prepared to do so. The critiques directed against his work in his lifetime regularly point to his literary qualities while censuring his antifactualistic enthusiasm, as the notes appended by Paul Viallaneix to his edition of the *Journal* make clear. To the academic community of the era Michelet had debased himself by refusing to arrogate olympian status to himself, refusing to see himself as an archeologist who could remain neutral with regard to the stones that he collected. The problems are similar with reference to today's academic community as well—because Michelet did not fashion a critique of historiographical knowledge, as did Droysen, or search for a theory of history, as did Marx. Trapped between those two fires, Michelet is either afforded the way out represented by the literary salvation that Barthes represents or receives the ambiguous praise of those who take him as a precursor. Is there, then, really not even the skeleton of theorization in his work? The fact is that there is, and the first person to point it out, albeit in a reticent and ironic manner, was Heine, in an article of 15 July 1843. I reproduce only the key passage:

> Is he a great historian? . . . Is it the historian's task, beyond his research and meditations, to place before our eyes our ancestors and their customs, to evoke from out of the tomb, with the magical power of the word, the past that sleeps beneath its shroud? If it is, then we must admit that Michelet has known how to carry it out. My illustrious teacher, Hegel, told me once: "If the dreams that men had during a given period had been written down, the reading of that collection of dreams would give the most accurate idea of the spirit of that period." Michelet's *Histoire de France* is just such a book of dreams.[9]

The German poet captures the very spirit that motivates the historian: his obsession with providing a survival for those dead to history. Apparently, there would be no difference between that notion and the dominant concept of establishing the facts as they occurred. In fact, however, the difference between the two is crucial. The establishing of facts presupposes the neutrality of the person who unravels them. No matter what his or her own inclinations might be, the task of the historian is to register the facts and submissively discover their ordering and concordance. Even though Michelet never entertained the audacity of Droysen, much less evidenced sympathy for the speculations of Hegel in *Lessons on the Philosophy of History*, he did hold himself in high enough esteem, as professorial *causeur* and as writer, to accept that implicit effacement of "himself." Thus, even though Michelet did not try to thematize it formally, the relationship between the historian's individuality and his or her object of study became problematic for him. How could he deal with the issue? It is in this key connection that he unconsciously approaches, and appropriates, the example of painting. Just as the painter does not paint *himself or herself in* the painting but instead *sets himself or herself forth* through the painting, so too Michelet sees in the practice of historiography the possibility of quitting his cloistered "self" for the survival that he himself provides to the past. As he declares in the invaluable note of 18 June 1841: "History: a violent moral chemistry, in which my individual passions turn into generalities, in which my generalities become passions, in which my people become me, in which my 'I' animates the people in turn" (Michelet, *Journal de Jules Michelet*, 362).

His opposition to a history conceived as faithful to the facts becomes more explicit in consequence of that "chemistry." History is, as he declares in another location, the practice of resurrection: "Thierry called it [i.e., history's object] *narration*, and Mr. Guizot [called it] *analysis*. I have named it *resurrection*, and this name will last" (Michelet, *The People*, 19).

And that declaration takes up almost literally the meditation recorded in his diary on 21 March 1844: "the philosophy of history as resurrection, the art of reviving the people of Antiquity and of the Middle Ages" (Michelet, *Journal de Jules Michelet*, 549).

Those passages authorize me to go beyond what I have stated about the underlying difference between history as faithful narration and history as resurrection. The two are not in opposition only to the extent that the former abolishes the writer's "self" while the latter effects its transformation into a "violent moral chemistry." For what can such a metamorphosis imply save a mimetic transmigration, a reaching out to what is different, an understanding of the other's difference on the basis of empathy, that is, on the basis of the discovery of a similarity with oneself? It is not my conclusion that Michelet tried to make historiography into an art form. To his mind, nothing was more arbitrary than the so-called historical novel. And we have already noted the passage from his *Journal* in which, in comparing what he does with what is characteristic of the novel—"the novel is of interest in relation to personal destinies"—he adds that such does not satisfy the people (read, in this case, "the public") because "it needs the truth" that "not collective, but biographical" history can provide to it. Furthermore, it is important to this question for us to remind ourselves that in the era in which Michelet was writing mimesis had lost its prestige and that Michelet's practice of it had little to do with the normativeness that had characterized its exercise from the Renaissance through neoclassicism. My point is as follows: in his struggle, ever an indirect one, with the concept of history in the nineteenth century, Michelet was forced to envision a form of theorization that did not exist in his time. So that I do not repeat what has already been said in chapter 1, I shall limit my present endeavors to emphasizing some issues necessary for comprehension of the problem.

The traditional concept of mimesis, against which the romantics rebelled, was developed at the same time as classical science. For the latter, truth resided in the object, and the subject, albeit the bearer of values, had to remain silent. That subject became, then, either a scrupulous registerer of phenomena, according to the empiricistic position, or, according to the Kantian position, a translator of how phenomena are codified on the basis of the a priori categories of the human understanding. In parallel fashion, in the traditional theory of mimesis, the subject (i.e., the artist) had to obey the universal legislation of the beautiful, following the rules exemplified by the paradigmatic (classical) works of art and/or established by consecrated theoreticians. Emphasizing faithfulness in the reconstruction of the past, nineteenth-century historiography followed the pattern of classical science. In attempting to overturn that pattern, Michelet transgressed against its norms and, without knowing it, engaged in that practice which here becomes comprehensible to us through reelaboration of the theory of mimesis. This reelaboration presupposes that the relationship between subject and object is not an exclusive one in which either the subject imposes itself on the object, leaving it no room in which to manifest its autonomy, or the object "guides" the hand of the human subject, enabling that subject to reveal its truth. That exclusivistic viewpoint has presided over a drastic separation between fiction and science—for the case in question, between novel and history. It is a separation that became increasingly obligatory the more "science has emerged as a kind of religion, an ultimate frame of reference for determining what is real and true."[10] Michelet did not dare break with that religion. He "only"—if that restrictive can be valid here—excavated it. He did so by unknowingly engaging in a mimetic act: one in which the agent—that is, the writer—is not the same as the character, but the character would not be as he or she is if the agent were not as he or she is. In concrete terms, mimesis is a strategy directed against the indissolubility of the presence of the "self."

It should not surprise us, then, that, during times of individualistic societies, mimesis has been taken as useless trash. Nevertheless, from the moment when the originally Nietzschean and later Freudian critique of the doctrine grounded in *cogito ergo sum* was disseminated, so that mimesis became incorporated into the spectrum of contemporary knowledge, the conditions were created under which precisely what mimesis implies could be rethought. This not being the proper forum for that project, let me merely say: it is the practice through which we approach what we are not, what we do not internalize as our own "self." It is thus a practice that allows us to present ourselves as though we were an other—on the basis, however, of the difference from what we are. Note the similarity between that statement and the following: "History only accomplishes its unifying function therefore if some unifying element interferes in its disorder and forces it to give birth to truth. Its unifying power depends on the existence of some 'subject who is supposed to know,' and who exercises that power in its own name. This subject of historical knowledge is of course the knowing narrator, the totalizing narrator."[11]

To be sure, that passage does not deal with the concept of mimesis, nor is it my intent, as the rest of this chapter will show, to argue that that concept is in itself sufficient to characterize the work of the historian. The proximity results from the fact that both mimesis and the historian's work imply the breakdown of the classical conception of knowledge which, bracketing off the knowing subject, enabled the radical difference between science and fiction. While I am not suggesting that the salvation of the human sciences lies in its taking refuge beneath the protective cloak of mimesis, I am affirming, precisely and only, that Michelet's tacit rebellion against the historiographic standards of his time brought him near to a mode of theorization that was not considered in his time but which begins to emerge today. I have, however, not provided all the passages that justify that analysis. I still must, for example, establish the relationship between his approach to theoretical innovation in his time and the problems involved in his sanctification of the people. It is necessary, as regards the first of those elements, to examine more closely Michelet's concept of history as resurrection and also the kind of mimesis that would be involved therein.

In an entry from January 1839, Michelet wrote: "'Harsh fate, the historian's: to love, to lose so many things, to begin over again all the loves, all the griefs of humanity. I have just read some of Petrarch's sonnets. But how many sonnets and *canzoni* would I need to lament all the many unhappy loves that my heart has gone through, century after century. . . . To love the dead is an immortality" (Michelet, *Journal de Jules Michelet*, 289).

The same sentiment reappears in a passage from the following year: "'Camões, exiled in Macau, had the small office of 'Official Inspector of the Deceased'. . . . Small office? But it is the true duty of the historian and of the epic singer'" (226).

It is his declared love for the dead—certain dead, that is—that enables the migration of the "self," the moral chemistry that transforms passions into generalities and generalities into passions. What is centrally characteristic of Michelet, then, is that he operates between the limit-lines of the "self" and of alterity, between the limit-lines of emotion and knowledge. It is regularly said—implicitly—that at the core of his work—that is, in his historiographical efforts—there is no pure objectivity, precisely because his subjectivity has broken out of its cocoon, abandoned its cloister, becoming copresent with the passions and values that particularize that work. Similar statements could be adduced from the confessions of a poet or a novelist. Why, then, do I maintain so great a reserve in saying that a program like Michelet's realizes *a kind of* mimesis, instead of identifying it with mimesis pure and simple? For two reasons: because historiographic discourse possesses its own specific features that differentiate it from a poetic genre, and because, his "anticipations" notwithstanding, Michelet, to identify and present himself as a historian, continued to think in terms of the traditional mimesis.

Leaving substantiation of the former argument for my next item of business, I shall first focus on the latter. In the private journal entry (p. 127) from 19 May 1846, Michelet explains the high degree of interest that the novel elicits by suggesting that the reader senses that the destinies of the individual characters have to do with his or her own destiny so that it seems *probable* to that reader that what befalls the fictitious character could befall him or her as well. That sense of a similarity does not result from some mysterious property possessed by the novel as genre. To the contrary, it stems from a specific historical conjuncture: "If narratives are accounts of agents whose character or destiny unfolds through actions and events in time, then such narratives presupposed a social order of meaning, a political economy and collective psychology, in which public action by moral agents was possible, in which a sense of lived connection between personal character and public conduct prevailed. Such a presupposition is no longer valid in advanced industrial societies" (Brown, 545).

In other words, the novel's success in the eighteenth and nineteenth centuries depended on the maintenance of a network of homogeneous representations that enabled the reader to find and recognize himself in the actions of the fictitious individual. While the historical conjuncture elicited that interest, however, the knowledge that governed decoding placed the genre in a position of secondary importance: novels did not embody truth, a function that was reserved for the sciences. Michelet simply juxtaposes the two expectations: as historian, he will satisfy the "religious" need for presentation of the truth of the past, but he will carefully appropriate to his use what he considers the reason for the novel's success. Thus a historical narrative is punctuated with individualized characters. Now, from the point of view of mimesis as I have just revealed it in operation, that procedure presupposed the existence of a model of reality to which the historian's writing would conform—for the character, being historical, would be portrayed *wie es eigentlich gewesen ist*. The historian's passions, his or her subjective focus, would merely be awakened, stimulated; they would not, however, interfere in the veracity of characterization. They would surround it, so to speak, being present in the portrait's rhetorical configuration. Rhetoric would constitute the frame, leaving the nucleus of reality intact; it would aid in the passage without adhering to the passenger. *That set-up conformed to the one to be found in the traditional model of mimesis in that it presupposed the presence of a prototype, or source, to be faithfully transposed, regardless of idiosyncrasies on the part of the artist or the choice of rhetoric to be used in the portrait.* Rhetoric would be restricted to the area of beauty, to the creation of an aura of delight that would facilitate communication of the true.

This entire interpretation seems strange, however, because it suffers from a root anachronism. Could Michelet, contemporary of the romantics, described, justly, as a romantic historian, have regressed and adopted a concept of mimesis that had already run its course? Let me answer by means of another question: how could a historian who accepted the premise of factual objectivity adopt *tout court* the romantic principle of expressivity? According to that principle:

A work of art is essentially the internal made external, resulting from a creative process operating under the impulse of feeling, and embodying the combined product of the poet's perceptions, thoughts, and feelings. The primary source and subject matter of a poem, therefore, are the attributes and actions of the poet's own mind; or if aspects of the external world, then these only as they are converted from fact to poetry by the feelings and operations of the poet's mind.[12]

The result of that definition was that poetry was taken as the antipode of science and of the reliability of facts: "The essence and end of poetry is simply the poet's expression of feeling; hence poetry is independent, in its component sentences, from any judgement of truth to fact" (Abrams, 323).

Michelet's romantic bases manifest themselves in the right that he grants his own "I" to exteriorize itself, to attempt—with its vital flame—the resurrection of loves lost for ages and centuries. But that self-extension, through the mind and hence through the writing process as well, had to respect the contours of the science that it had never intended to stop practicing. In the light of the absence of both a reflection specifically on the theory of knowledge and a critique of the concept of "fact," Michelet could only weld romantic expressivity onto the base provided by the classical doctrine of mimesis. While in this respect his solution may also anticipate a certain contemporary theoretical practice, I can see no other route that he could have adopted. In synthesis, then, in outlining the problematic of mimesis in regard to Michelet's historiography, we must take care not to make it over, illegitimately, into a glorious and ingenious example of what we who do the analyzing are ourselves. Such would indeed be to practice anachronism, as well as to imply the inversion of the theory of knowledge that underlay the historiography of the period—that is, truth would cease to be conflated with the facts and come to be identified with what we think of the facts. Consequently, to be a romantic and, at the same time, a historian, Michelet really had access only to a compromise solution: the historian's "self" does indeed express itself, and its object is motivated according to the values of that "self"—country, the people—but to maintain his identity with the parameters of history, he has to believe that he is resurrecting the dead *just as they had been in life*. The process of writing, selection of the material to be incorporated into that process, and the modality of *emplotment* resulting therefrom are not seen as interfering in any way with the objectivity of the material itself. The object is given the status of transparency and security. The opposite of this would be to have Michelet declare that "the historian works with forceps. Meaning comes forth only at the price of an artifice in writing" (Gaillard, 149). Now, for Michelet that would be an absurd statement, as it would for the vast majority of historians then and now. This is not, however, a reason to deny Michelet's importance for anyone today who reflects upon the theory of knowledge that grounds the practice of historiography and its relations with the fictional.

With the foregoing in mind, let us return for the last time to the capstone of Michelet's work, namely the people. We have seen that he advances no concept in definition of the people and at best derives its virtues from dependency on country. We should, then, ask ourselves explicitly: how do his painterly model and practical adoption of a specific view of mimesis relate to that failure? The answer initially seems easy: we have already seen, with Hayden White, that the historiography of the nineteenth century did not operate with an installed theory as such. And if such was the case for a purely documentary historian, why should it not be the case as well for one who believed that his emotions, in coming into contact with the memory of past facts, could bring them to life anew? In other words, belief in empathy as illuminator of knowledge and stimulus to the "violent moral chemistry" of history made Michelet believe as well in the inoperability of concepts. They were thus simply unnecessary. The heart had a capability for empathy that no concept could supplement. A curious phenomenon takes place as a result: the actual material chosen, that is, the people, seems to rebel; at key moments it seems not to correspond to the fervid and beatific image that its cultivator wishes to impart to it. I cannot omit transcription of a few examples to the point, although they are long. The first comes from the description of the massacre that took place in Paris on 2 September 1792:

> The Assembly had sent various of its most popular members: the good, old Dusaulx, whose noble military figure and beautiful white hair could evoke from the people their time of heroic purity, the taking of the Bastille; the orator of the war, Isnard, as well, with his flaming speech. To them was added a popular hero, violent, obscene, fitted to respond to evil passions, perhaps to mitigate by participating in them; I speak of Chabot, the Capuchin.
> All that was of no use. The crowd was deaf and dumb; it drank more and more and understood less and less. Night came; the somber patios of the Abbaye became more somber. The torches that were lit made what they did not illuminate with their ominous glow seem all the darker. The deputies, in the midst of that frightful tumult, were completely insecure.[13]

Could it be that the historian explained such an irrational thirst for blood on the grounds that the people had become a mass, a mob no longer oriented by national values? The author himself does not hazard an explanation. Or could it be that the people take on the appearance of a god, marvelous even when arbitrary or animallike, marvelous precisely because it encarnates human emotionality in action? Or, as a third hypothesis, it might be that emphasis on the people is not, as is assumed in the previous alternative, illustrative of any value at all. Given over to itself alone, stolid and blind, the people body history forth in a pure and savage state, in which unreason, countersense, savagery emerge in contiguity with irruptions of tenderness, justice, and self-sacrifice, in an entertwining that has no other justifying value than that of manifesting naked human energy. The people, then, are worshipped a priori because they encarnate human physiognomy prior to its shackling in the "social contract." How else can we interpret the unrestricted cult of the people that we see in passages such as the following?

> The massacrers . . . were made up of diverse groups which, indistinct and intermixed on the first day, gradually divided up; the worst imposing themselves as leaders. There were paid agents; there were drunkards and fanatics; there were brigands. These came little by little to the fore.
> Save for the fifty-some bourgeois who had killed at the Abbaye, most of whom doubtless stayed close to it, the others (two or three hundred in all) went from prison to prison, getting drunk, progressively smearing themselves with filth and blood, covering in three days a long course of perversity. The massacre which, on the second day, was for many an effort, became, on the third, a pleasure. Little by little pillage was added in.
> The beginning was modest. On the second night, that is the night between the second and third days, various of those who had killed at the Abbaye, having neither stockings nor shoes, looked greedily upon the artistocrats' footware. They did not want to take them without authorization; they went to ward headquarters, the office of which was in fact in the Abbaye, and asked permission to take the corpses' footware. As that request was readily allowed, their appetite grew, and they asked for more: vouchers for wine to be taken from the merchants, to sustain the workers and animate them in their labor. (Michelet, *La Gironde et la Montagne*, 156)

Here again the historian makes no effort to separate the people and criminal activity. If at least it were justified as defense of the Revolution, it might be said that the wonted objectivity should cease its bothersome protests. But Michelet himself would not have agreed with that justification. In fact, according to his own interpretation, those events formed the prelude to the "reign of terror," which in turn led to the final betrayal of the Revolution. What then? Perhaps the best course would be to say, in relation to the third hypothesis, that senselessness is proper to the people because history too is senseless. And let us give little credence to the tranquilizing declaration by Michelet himself. Instead, the continuation of his description of the massacre catches him returning, so to speak, to the comfortable, banal course indicated by the first hypothesis: "It was a shameful thing to see some fifty men, by no means supported by the people, speaking in the name of the people and making their true representatives, the members of the Commune, give way" (159). In the same vein, he deals with the measures taken against massacres: "The true voice of the people was at last heard" (193).

But why reserve the notion of the true voice of the people only for demonstrations ruled by good sense? Doubtless because, to maintain his fervor, Michelet retreats and establishes distinctions that seem at the very least arbitrary, fearing to involve himself in the kind of virulence that he has just described. At a juncture where the "neutral," "objective" historian would descry no obstacle whatsoever—as was the case with Ranke, whose *History of the Popes* angered not only the Catholics but also the Protestants, who should have seen themselves represented by it—Michelet must in effect either *say* more than he had written or establish distinctions between the "true voice of the people" and the crazed actions of anonymous groups, distinctions which he would never ground.

We are thus led to suppose that Michelet, at cross-purposes with himself, is forced to declare that history contains a strong dose of chance and senselessness. To a certain degree, that position would still be acceptable to him because it would oppose the concept of a purely causal determination of history. And in favor of that conjecture, we might recall his portrait of Robespierre as someone who did not understand indirectness, who comprehended only straight lines and thus introduced "a kind of geometric spirit" into the Revolution. Now, at no time does the historian manifest any sympathy for the Jacobin tribune. Conversely, I shall compare that description with the aforementioned description of the taking of the Bastille. Developing an allegory around possession of the keys to the fortress, he declares that "either chance or Providence had chosen that they be given" to someone who knew them well—a former prisoner. "Chance or Providence" is surely a nucleus in opposition to the geometry of the "reign of terror." An unexpected route for our interpretation of what Michelet's language itself does not state in so many words is, then, to be found in analysis of his metaphors. Michelet seems to find his greatest pleasure, so to speak, before a scene in which the historian can only order in narrative form a multiplicity of events and facts that at every turn give a new profile to the nature of the historical phenomenon, without the historian's being able to have recourse to a logic that would link those elements definitively together according to some law of compass and measure. In sum, history, in Michelet's conception, has a motive core, namely the people, whose activity is stimulated for specific reasons—in this case, hatred for the symbol of *l' ancien régime's* dominion—and, simultaneously, through its emotionality. That mixture is so intricate that—like Bergson's butterfly, which had to be caught for its movement to be explained—the logic of events can be postulated only a posteriori. Over against a consciously elaborated model of the historian, then, we shall here advance a daring hypothesis: that, lacking pretty words of justification, Michelet found in a focus on the people his substantiation of history itself, at its most savage core. History laughs uproariously at the ratio of historians. The true pure reason, as Michelet said, was not Kant's pure reason but rather the reason encarnated by popular movements. He refused, however, to see that true pure reason has nothing to do with the cult of man's natural goodness. To allow that would be to condemn oneself to an abyss that French *clarté* would not admit.

Finally, I must insist on one last detail. Is to declare history motivated by chance in that manner still to propose a *realistic* vision of it, maintaining that it *is* one thing and not another? No, that is not the case. Whereas that supposition may be plausible in the instance of Michelet, because in withdrawing explanation through causality from the heart of his historiography, he all the while continued to ascribe objective status to facts, it is to my mind insufficient. The characterization of history's various comings and goings as relatively senseless is conditioned by the filter that guides its very proposition—the filter that was Michelet himself. Through a wholly different line of thought, Hayden White came to a conclusion that I can present only schematically in this forum. It basically states that, according to Michelet, the Revolution was sacred because it "resulted in a dissolution of all differences among men, between men and women, young and old, rich and poor, which finally transformed the nation into a people" (White, 157). Its unfolding, however, led to new differentiations, a new class hierarchy, which had already been consolidated by the time when Michelet was writing his *Histoire*. He therefore considered the Revolution to have been betrayed. Hence White's final conclusion: "Although Michelet thought of himself as a Liberal, and wrote history in such a way as to serve the Liberal cause as he understood it, in reality the ideological implications of his conception of history are Anarchist" (161-62). His indiscriminate praise of the people and failure to judge it according to a conceptual standard result, then, from an anarchistic optic. The importance of that conclusion does not reside in our assigning some specific value, or lack thereof, to anarchism but instead in the removal of any hint of substantialism that might linger in our interpretation of Michelet. That is to say, the implicit admission, in his historiography, of the presence of the aleatory within the eddies of history derived from the anarchistic nucleus that structured that history.

The Example of Michelet in the Light of Contemporary Thought

The previous section was basically dedicated to an analytical description of Michelet's historiography. The theoretical reflection introduced in the process merely comprised enclaves destined to further that examination. The order of elements will now be reversed: I shall take the described material as the basis for a primarily theoretical continuation of our discussion. In it we shall begin by concentrating on what the historian considered to be real. In fact, if one does not specifically focus on differences in methodology, in school, or in individual talent, the differences among historiographical modalities result from how each construes the real and, hence, how it conceives of its object, namely the real of history. On that score, two basic concepts exist in opposition to each other, though in cross-fertilization as well, as Michel de Certeau has shown: "On the one hand, the real is the *result* of analysis and, on the other hand, it is its *postulate*." The first concept "asks about what is *thinkable* and about the conditions of comprehension; the other endeavors to encounter the *lived*, exhumed through a knowledge of the past." To those two conceptions there correspond antagonistic expository modalities: whereas the one privileges the narrative presentational mode, the other, "much less descriptive, instead confronts the series that produce different types of methods."[14]

To be sure, Michelet's history intended to revive the past, having as its postulate the recovery of the real, which it sought to resuscitate through the narrative process. It thus presupposed that the real remained self-identical, transparent, and unaffected by the chemistry performed on it. Now, despite the differences that Michelet nurtured with regard to his professional colleagues, their historiographies conformed to a single design: "A hundred years ago, it represented a society as regards the mode of a (re)collection of all its becoming. It is true that history had been fragmented into a plurality of histories (biological, economic, linguistic, and so on). But among those diverse positive elements, as among the differentiated cycles that characterized each, historical knowledge restored a *sameness* through the relation that each maintained to an *evolution*" (de Certeau, 98).

And what other name could that *sameness* have, permanently appointed, inscribed, and reproduced by the various partial histories, save the name reality—a reality retained in the registers of the past? And how could it have been so generically conceived of unless science was the discourse assigned to unveil the real, thereby taking on a truly religious function? Therefore, if our concept of history is undergoing change today, it is not merely because its methods are being refined, archives being expanded, and computers being put into service. Its fundamental change in fact results from a change in our concept of reality. Again according to de Certeau: "History no longer occupies, as it did in the nineteenth century, that *central* place organized by an epistemology which, having lost reality as an ontological substance, sought to find it again as a historical force, *Zeit-geist*, and hidden becoming within the body of society. It no longer has the totalizing function that consisted in the replacing of philosophy in its role of giving the meaning [of experience]" (93). It was as a result of that premise that Michelet worked with a version of classical mimesis. Mimesis had become a strategy for the recuperation of what was already there—what, having once been present, had marked the human world so indelibly that time itself could not change it: the reality of the historical event. The refractoriness of the real served, then, as an epistemological guarantee for the historian's achieving of accuracy. It is not surprising, then, that such a historiography did not present, except in rare cases, a theoretical construct per se. Theories are imposed only when we become insecure in the face of our own accumulated knowledge. And the historian had no reason to doubt his or her knowledge systematically because his or her more prestigious cousins, the exact sciences, conceived of reality in parallel terms: "Science, in its beginnings, successfully posed questions that involved a dead and passive nature; seventeenth-century man was able to communicate with nature only to reveal the horrifying stupidity of his interlocutor."[15]

Nature, that dumb, voiceless object, could be captured in its whole, atemporal truth, independently of the investigator's position: "Galileo and his successors conceived of science as able to reveal the *global* truth of nature. Not only is nature written in a mathematical language decipherable through experimentation but that language is unique; the world is homogeneous, local experimentation reveals a general truth" (Prigogine and Stengers, 51-52). It is true, as scholars point out, that Kant's thought has made it clear that that concept of science cannot be thought of as *realist* (see p. 140). The difference, nonetheless, is unimportant in practical terms: whether it derives from the universality of laws emanating from the atemporal presence of the object or from the transcendental a priori categories through which humans determine those laws, the fact is that, in practical terms, the object of scientific investigation stands as self-identical. Hence the inefficacy of Droysen's criticism of the historiography of his time, which he viewed as mired in a circle comprising three illusions—that it was possessed of a full totality, that historical periods had a definite beginning and end, and that it could mount an objective look back into the past.[16] The appropriateness of that critique would be recognized only when it found echoes in similar analyses coming from other areas of endeavor.

Only a specialist in the history of science will be able to show how the destruction of the premise upon which that branch of history was based came about. I shall merely point to a few testimonies to that change. In the theory of physics what Heisenberg writes is symptomatic:

It has become clear that the desired objective reality of the elementary particles is too crude an oversimplification of what really happens. . . . While, in observing everyday objects, the physical process involved in making the observation plays a subsidiary role only, in the case of the smallest building particles of matter, every process of observation produces a large disturbance. *We can no longer speak of the behaviour of the particle independently of the process of observation.*[17]

And: "The scientific method of analysing, explaining, and classifying has become conscious of its limitations, which arise out of the fact that *by its intervention science alters and refashions the object of investigation. In other words, the method and the object can no longer be separated*" (Heisenberg, 29; emphasis mine).

Whereas there need not have been a direct influence of the epistemology of the exact sciences on the theory of history—in this regard, it is important to note the impact of Lévi-Strauss's critique in "Histoire et ethnologie" [History and Ethnology]—cognizance should be taken of the correspondence between the passages from Heisenberg and the analysis by de Certeau: History "is a *narrative* that in fact functions as a *discourse* organized by the *place* of the 'interlocutors' and grounded in the place that the 'author' claims in relation to his readers. It is the place from which it is produced that gives the text authority, and, above all else, the recourse to chronology confesses as much" (de Certeau, 106).

We are not dealing here, however, with a chance coincidence. Prigogine replicates the change in the conception of the relationship between scientific investigator and his or her object from the point of view of the theory of chemistry:

The physicist does not reveal an already-given truth that the system has hidden; instead he must choose a language, that is, a set of macroscopic concepts, in terms of which the system will respond. . . . Bohr used to say that he could not think of the meaning of quantum mechanics without becoming dizzy; and in effect it is a dizzying wrench away from the habits of good sense to contemplate that all macroscopic properties are inseparable from the "illumination" that we choose to project upon reality and that that reality is too rich and its contours too complex for a single projector to be able to illuminate it in its totality. (Prigogine and Stengers, 232-33)

The reader, however, may well wonder about the purpose of all these citations and about my delving into such areas as physics and chemistry, about which I obviously have no in-depth knowledge. It is because these different arguments force us to thematize the disturbance that we now witness in the normal conception of the relations between scientific undertakings and the activity of fictionality. Until now, everyday wisdom has taken them to be antithetical procedures. Continuing the old Platonic dichotomy, it has been believed that poetry beautifies what it does not know, whereas science, after having dethroned philosophy, extracts the truth from the inward nature of things. But if there is no longer a truth to be wholly and fully recuperated, if science comes to be conceived of as an ongoing dialogue between the properties of the object and a *language*—which in turn presupposes the occupying of a *position*—which formulates and interrelates certain of the object's aspects, then what validity can be said to remain in the old dichotomy and the hierarchy on which science rested? From the viewpoint of science, Prigogine replies: "Within a rich and diverse population of cognitive practices, our science occupies the singular position of poetic ear to nature—in the etymological sense in which the poet is a fabricator—active, manipulative, calculating exploration but after that able to respect the nature that it makes speak" (281).

The *poietic* becomes, then, an all-encompassing category that breaks down the boundaries of the "reservation" to which the poets had been relegated as though they were primitives, a category designed for a specific branch of "anthropology" to be carried out by critics, aesthetes, and literary historians. But what does that all-encompassing character imply? Could it be complete eradication of the boundaries? If such were the case, would both history and novel be literary genres? Or, as Barthes postulates, keeping the old dichotomy but reversing the weighting, would the difference be between writers and notaries, the former surpassing the latter by the plethora of signifiers with which they operate? With the death of some gods, the birth of others always follows. To the death of the god "reality," who had the scientist as his preacher, there has corresponded the appearance of the sect of *écriture*, which has the *écrivain* as its high priest. I shall not go on to speak of its "theologians," for to do so would keep me from my proposed goal. Because their names are known, I shall let them pass in favor of reflection on some of their—perhaps involuntary—"fellow travelers." A discussion of their ideas has an additional value: that of preventing confusion of their contributions with the church of *écriture*.

I do not doubt that I know but a few of these "fellow travelers." In any case, a complete list would be unnecessary. Allow me to limit myself to four names: Robert Nisbet, Richard H. Brown, Hayden White, and Hans Robert Jauss.

Nisbet's book *Sociology as an Art Form* has as its basic goal to show descriptively that the logic of discovery is not to be confused with the logic of demonstration. Confusion of the two has resulted in the arbitrary identification of scientific practice and demonstrative practice. Conflation of the two would be valid, according to Thomas Kuhn, only if we did not distinguish between revolutionary scientific theory and the practice of "normal" science. As demonstration is not a constituent part of the field of literature (and the arts), the logic of discovery unifies rather than separates sociology and literature: "I cannot help thinking that the renewal or reinvigoration of idea and theory we so badly need in sociology in the present age, indeed in all the social sciences, would be greatly accelerated if sufficient awareness of the unity of art and science, especially with respect to the sources of imagination in each area, were present at all levels of teaching and research."[18] And he adds, somewhat later: "Except in style and format, there is little difference to be found between a Dickens and a Marx, a Zola and a Proudhon" (Nisbet, 58).

That sociologist's small volume is thus a pointed attack on the maintenance of the old separation, which ends up being more harmful to the scientist than to the fictionist because it at least leaves the latter free from the straightjacket it has ready for the former. We must, then, give their due to the author's usefulness, not to mention his courage, for let us not forget that Nisbet wrote from within a scientific community in which the power exerted by neopositivism remains quite strong. Nevertheless, we must also not forbear to point out that Nisbet's contribution may be somewhat dimmed in that it does not concern itself with treatment of an issue that today grows more unavoidable: if there is "little difference" between a Dickens and a Marx, it is absolutely necessary to examine what difference there is. Now a reading of *Sociology as an Art Form* not only frustrates the expectation of any such examination but also could lead to the conclusion that the difference is in fact so insignificant that such an examination would not be worth the bother. What could we say, as a result, about—to stay with questions already touched on—the equally predominant function of narrative in the novel and in historiography during the past century? And, if we accept the above analysis of mimesis in Michelet's history, how can we separate it from mimesis in the work of, say, Balzac? Perhaps in trying not merely to transpose from his own area of speciality, Nisbet has reduced his contribution.

A similar occurrence prevails in *A Poetic for Sociology*, by Richard Harvey Brown, even though it is epistemologically a considerably more sophisticated work. A part of the author's plan is to deconstruct the classical concept of reality that underlies the paradigm in which science and fiction appear as antipodes. In contradiction of the notion that reality is something autonomous and self-identical, Brown incisively writes: "Seeking correspondence between measures and reality is fruitless, because 'reality' is knowable only through some set of measures. What we can achieve, however, is correspondence between two sets of concepts—that is, between our nominal and our operational definitions."[19] What he seeks to do in thus swimming against the current is to call attention to both the presence and the fertility of the use of poetic processes—point of view and modes of metaphor and irony—in the practice of sociology. Indeed, in his analysis he brings sociological praxis and poetics in so close a conjunction that he begins to take the former as constitutive of a "structured mimesis":

> In contrast to this approach [one which sees knowledge as independent
> of subjectivity] we have argued that knowledge is possible only through
> the interpretive processes which the knower enacts in his encounter with
> the subjects in question. In this view, objectivity is not
> depersonalization, but a mastery of passion. Through such an attitude,
> the inquirer is presumed to be able to "accept the other's illusions as
> real money," and then ask how such "illusions" are possible. . . . The
> various voices do not cancel each other out, nor is truth limited to those
> points on which they agree; instead, much as characters in a play, each
> voice enriches the others, each contributes to the dialectical construction
> of more and more comprehensive *meta*-perspectives. These
> metaperspectives are not objective in that they have eliminated bias but
> in that they organize the "biases" of various actors into astructured
> mimesis of the domain of experience to be explained. (Brown, 69-70)

Long ago rejected by poetology, mimesis thus returns to the scene via specialists in other areas, who seem to want to recuperate what romantic expressivity cast among the rubble. I have argued that point in a prior essay on Goffman and the great fecundity that his concept of *keying* holds for the study of fiction.[20]

Despite being thus provocative, Brown's thought either contents itself with showing that in the social sciences "reality" has about it the character of a construct or—as, for example, in his analysis of daily drama and the theater as communicating compartments (see Brown, 153ff.)—suggests that the difference between day-to-day fictions and fictions recognized as such is a transitory one. While I certainly agree with the notion of an easy transitivity that carries pragmatic, day-to-day affairs over into a fictional frame, and vice versa, I insist on a need to investigate with greater care the moving boundary therein involved.

Hayden White's "Historical Text as Literary Artifact" also fails to assay that task. Perhaps that phenomenon takes place because the authors whom I cite present themselves so much as trailblazers, as defenders of positions that by no means directly threaten the primacy of objectivism and factualism in sociology and history, that they take care not to expose themselves to counterattack any more than necessary. No matter whether that explanation is plausible or not, the fact is that White's reasoning leads to an epistemology of history that is analogous to the one we find in those of his sociological colleagues whom I have just mentioned. He merely formulates that position more directly: "*How* a given historical situation is to be configured depends on the historian's subtlety in matching up a specific plot structure with the set of historical events that he wishes to endow with a meaning of a particular kind. This is essentially a literary, that is to say fiction-making, operation."[21] It is true that in the last paragraph of his essay White explains that his purpose is not to abolish the line between historiography and fiction but rather, by comparing them anew, to reestablish an alliance that has been destroyed by scientism, and thereby to contribute to an authentic theory of history:

> In my view, history as a discipline is in bad shape today because it has lost sight of its origins in the literary imagination. In the interest of *appearing* scientific and objective, it has repressed and denied to itself its own greatest source of strength and renewal. By drawing historiography back once more to an intimate connection with its literary basis . . . we should be by way of arriving at that "theory" of history without which it cannot pass for a "discipline" at all. (White, 99)

By now it is hardly necessary to emphasize that that effort is extremely important in our time. I, however, presenting myself as neither historian nor sociologist, wish to push it to yet another front. Hence the frustration that I experience with regard to a recent essay by Hans Robert Jauss.

In dealing with the era that runs between Richardson and Balzac as the time when "there was an effort made to interpret and understand, through the medium of fiction, History as day-to-day reality and as social totality,'' Jauss takes that process as one in which ''the Classical division between *res fictae*, as the realm of poetry and *res factae* as the object of History was broken down so that poetic fiction was raised to the horizon of reality and historical reality to the horizon of poetry.''[22] In that reciprocal relationship, the presence of the fictional within history—despite what the historians of the last century might have said—ceased to be spurious, for ''*fictionalization* is ever present in historical experience, for the episodic *essence* of an historical event is always conditioned by the perspectivistic '*when*' of its observation or reconstruction as well as by the '*how*' of its presentation and explanation'' (Jauss, 416). That infiltration of the fictional into history would, in its turn, be legitimated by the category of verisimilitude, which ''forms the terrain common to poetry and historiography'' (418). We are thus led to conclude that for Jauss the illusions of which Droysen accused the historiography of his time should instead be considered *hallmarks of the fictional*, the error having all along been that those who practiced history before simply did not recognize them as such. Jauss's inversion of the factors is, however, unconvincing—for the very force of the term ''fictional'' *as it exists in history, or in literature generally*, depends on the maintenance of a substantialistic concept of reality. Let us look further into the matter. The historian would behave *as if* his or her work dealt with all of a period, *as if* in fact he or she had begun work with a given moment, x, and ended it with another such moment, y. The historian would know that his or her description was not *in fact* identical to the order of reality. He or she would, however, retain the idea that the real is self-identical, as an artifice, an initial ploy enabling the historian to pull together his or her procedure. If I understand Jauss's position correctly, the concept of fictionality, then, merely moves to substantiation on the basis of an axiomatic fiction. But, if that argument were valid, why restrict the area of fiction's activity to history and literature? To accept the concept of an axiomatic fiction would be to make all human products fictional! And the absolute extension of the term would make it absolutely useless. Because such is not my intention, I shall try another route.

I find a possible avenue in Alfred Schütz's essay ''On Multiple Realities.'' I outline only what is essential for present purposes.

The a priori factor that is irreducible to experience in the world is not the mere statement that something locates itself before me—that is, that I perceive something. To the contrary, in fact, the object of perception becomes *visible* to me to the extent that I give it meaning. Meaning converts the perceivable into the objective. The illusion that the *objects of perception* are the base terms in any process of knowing derives from the fact that most acts of knowing are carried out so automatically that we do not realize that process. That automatization will be both more powerful and more ingrained where interpretation, whence derives meaning, is more habitual. Thus, only through reflection can we correct our understanding of the cognitive process: ''Meaning . . . is not a quality inherent in certain experiences emerging within our stream of consciousness but the result of an interpretation of a past experience looked at from the present Now with a reflective attitude."[23] The concept of reality stems from the articulation of those interpretations received as meanings. Thus, to our naïveté, reality seems to tell us what the generic name is that is attached to the set of things that, in being *given meaning* by us, seem to us *to be* what we say they are, and that it can itself only be single and self-identical. The reason for the first error has already been elucidated—that is, as the interpretations we make *consolidate* into meanings, we come to take those meanings as *natural*, as properties of the things to which we give meaning. The second error also requires explanation, but it ends up being rather simple. As Lacan has posited, our place in the world is conditioned by the way we see others see us, and then by the way we come to see them. That is, our place is conditioned by a community of agents who act according to common expectations and standards of conduct. While it is obvious that the content of those standards is socially variable, that diversity of contents does not alter the *orientation* of the standard. That orientation implies that, for all members involved in the field that it governs, *reality* appears to be identical because it is constituted by identical principles: "It is characteristic of the natural attitude that it takes the world and its objects for granted until counterproof imposes itself" (Schütz, 228). It is hardly remarkable, then, that the world seems to be *naturally* as it is, when all that is natural is that it should seem that way given the premises that constitute it. Those premises, then, compose the features of a *cognitive style*. The features are as follows, in summary form: (1) a specific attentiveness on the part of the consciousness that results in an alert attitude toward life; (2) a specific suspension of doubt—we suspend all doubt about what we take as naturally real until an incongruency overturns it; (3) a dominant form of spontaneity—working—that is, activity in the external world on the basis of a planned project; (4) a specific way of experiencing ourselves—the working self, taken as the total self; (5) a specific form of sociability, grounded in the everyday intersubjective world; and (6) a specific temporal perspective—one governed by a "standard time," the time common to all those governed by that same cognitive style (see Schütz, 230-31). In other words, *we come to master the basic experiencing of the world by internalizing the rules of conduct specific to everyday experience*. These features have to do with that basic sphere. The world of everyday life, of work in common, thus constitutes the nucleus of our place in the world. It, then, at least as long as the suspension of doubt remains in force, seems to be *the* reality. Nevertheless, as Schütz notes with great incisiveness, this sphere covers only a *finite province of meaning*. It is only *a* reality. Other provinces lie lateral to it, ones that impose other cognitive styles: "All these worlds—the world of dreams, of imageries and phantasms, especially the world of art, the world of religious experience, the world of scientific contemplation, the play world of the child, and the world of the insane—are finite provinces of meaning'' (232). Thus, instead of a single reality we have a multiplicity of realities, each one located by the rules that socialize the conduct of those who act within it.

Those clarifications seem to me a decisive point of departure for investigation of the problem of the relations between history—and the social sciences in general—and fiction. The former might be called the *discourse of reality*, simply because its object is located in the sphere that we ingenuously believe to be the reality. And there can be no doubt that its investigation is poietic, requiring a *faber*, an inventor. As discourse of reality—the latter term no longer being taken to be a substance in itself—historiography, as Lévi-Strauss has stated, is as much governed by an operative code as is any other science or any other human activity. Its code is constituted by chronology: "All historiography supposes a time of things as the counterpoint of a discursive time (the discourse 'advances' more or less rapidly, slows, or rushes on)" (de Certeau, 104). In this sense, and only in this sense, can we say that the narration that it employs *coincides* with a beginning and an end of what it describes and interprets. That coincidence is postulated by the chronological code that orients it. It has nothing to do with the presence of a fictionality always in action within it, as Jauss argues. We might add that, according to White, the narrative principle imposes itself both on fully realized history and on the popular narrative and the novel, for they all sense the pressure of "law, legality, legitimacy, or, more generally, *authority*." The principle of authority, therefore, converts narrative into an "anthropological constant" (Hans Ullrich Gumbrecht, personal communication).

We cannot equate all narratives without considering the *finite province* in which each one acts. Now, the province of fiction is that of the subuniverse of art. It is not that it does not thematize the world of everyday experience or that such utterances as the famous "the Marquise left at 5:00" are irrelevant to it. It is only that that thematization is passed through another filter. According to Wolfgang Iser, it does not intend direct action upon the world, to interfere in it and manipulate it. It does intend to elicit in the reader the double sensation of familiarity and estrangement. Familiar conditions become estranged because, in the specific space of fiction, they do not call for the response that we would give within the sphere of everyday pragmatic life. That is, the fictional thematization of reality in modern times contemplates putting into question the habitual norms of conduct itself.[24] Iser, in advancing that formulation, does not present himself as an enlightenment-type figure because he does not take that questioning as a means of proposing another reality. That is to say, the power of fictionality's questioning of habitual norms does not presume the presence of any sort of revolutionary program "illustrated" by the text. How the reader is to cope with day-to-day existence on the basis of that questioning is a problem that does not concern the theory of the fictional in itself. To be sure, it can be linked to a political position of interference in the established order, but that will take place because the theoretician of fictionality is also, hopefully, a person of political convictions.

On the basis of the feature just formulated, there appears a second one that more fully clarifies why the questioning provoked by the fictional is not directed by a program in articulation with "reality" (i.e., with the sphere of standard time and everyday life). Whereas the utterances made in the world of the day-to-day have a semantic ground as their essential characteristic—that is, it is supposed a priori that what is said in fact means what it says because its formulator is subject to the criterion "Is it true or false that . . .?"—fictional utterances do not have an ultimate semantic dimension that would translate interpretively as "This means that . . .". Instead of having the semantic as its ultimate dimension, fiction, to the contrary, has its basis in the imaginary:

> The imaginary is not semantic in nature, since, in relation to its object, it has a diffuse character, while sense [Sinn] becomes sense through its degree of preciseness. The diffuseness of the imaginary is, however, the condition by means of which it is capable of assuming diverse configurations, which is always required if one tries to adapt the imaginary for use. Fiction is the configuration appropriate to the use of the imaginary.[25]

The fictional utterance utilizes the semantic as a set of orientations to be properly semanticized by the reader. As, however, it is not my intent to comment on Iser's theory in its entirety or to use it as a springboard for another argument, I shall limit myself to stating that it is not to be deduced from what has been proffered here that every receiver of a fictional text may semanticize it as he or she wishes. The German theoretician is quite explicit: if the fictional utterance contains empty areas to be semanticized in the reader's interpretation, that supplementary activity on the reader's part is not arbitrary, for cues within the fictional text form a structure (see Iser, The Act of Reading). The relationship between those empty areas and the structure, though, is not one of mere translatability and the "reading" of the spaces is not correct through mere "recapturing" of the structure. Such is the case because, if we compare Iser's work of 1976 with the line of thought assayed in his 1979 essay, we see that the structure of the fictional work is governed by the diffusion of the imaginary (wherein, incidentally, lies the great difference between Iser's concept of structure and Lévi-Strauss's).

The inversion of the substantialist view of fictionality—which view is seen at work in those who seek a supposed literariness—therefore does not lead to a position that valorizes everything indiscriminately. If, then, a social-scientific work opens up the possibility of many varied interpretations, such does not occur because it contains empty areas analogous to those in a fictional work. Using the passage by Richard Harvey Brown (p. 145), we can say that the variety of interpretations of a social-scientific text results from the fact that *the correspondence between nominal and operational definitions* can be approached in different ways because of authorial lapse, changes—undeclared or unrecognized—in his or her positions, or the diversity of stances from which the work can be read. That diversity of stances can itself give either different weighting or different sense to the nominal definitions or merely invoke alternative definitions. The reading of a fictional text, on the other hand, is always dependent on the *stance* from which it is carried out.

Even though I am aware that this question could be developed to a greater extent, I shall end here by touching on one last problem: that of the presence of mimesis in the work of the social scientist. Does pointing out its activity there accuse the author of fictionality—or, inversely, praise him or her for it? Absolutely not. Mimesis has a legitimate role in the social sciences, just as it has in our everyday existence. It is simply the case that in the hands of the social scientist it is limited to the status of an analytical strategy rather than being the key concept that it is in fiction.

The reader will have by now surmised that the full development of these last questions would require another *emplotment*. I only hope that, seen here as *subordinate segments*, the immediately foregoing brief observations will be taken as parts of the central theme of this chapter, in which analysis of Michelet's historiography has provided the basis for examination of the relations between history and fiction without repudiation of the substantialist conception of reality leading to adoption of, or even sympathy with, the notion of a general, totalizing fictionality.

Chapter 4
In the Backlands of Hidden Mimesis

Because Brazil is a kind of museum of retrospective sociology,
or social history.

Oliveira Vianna, *Instituições Políticas Brasileiras*

Cunha among His Contemporaries

Euclides da Cunha was a dislocated person, as his biographers have emphasized—
marked by the early loss of his mother, by his father's financial limitations, by his
aloof character, by his stormy rebelliousness, by his emotional sterility, and by his
severe morality. Not only that, but, seen retrospectively, he also takes on a similar
dislocation with regard to the turn-of-the-century intelligentsia—his contemporaries. Where, in effect, does he fit amid the intellectual figures of the now distant
1900s? Among them we can enumerate those academically recognized—at their
head, Machado de Assis and Coelho Neto, the former for his ironic purity, the latter
for his florid verbosity—those legitimated by world opinion—among whom the poet
Olavo Bilac stands at the front of the Parnassians and the glib lecturers—the aristocratic stars, noteworthy in politics and/or diplomacy, formers of a true constellation—Rui Barbosa, Joaquim Nabuco, Rio Branco, Taunay, Oliveira Lima.

Although a member of the academy and a friend of Coelho Neto—perhaps
influenced by the latter in his cultivation of arcane vocabulary—and although,
too, a collaborator with, and prótegé of, the influential Rio Branco, in truth Cunha
was not at ease in any of the above categories. (Nor would he have been in one
formed around Lima Barreto, who was also marginalized, it is true, but because

of an economic penury, which Cunha did not experience.) Can we imagine Cunha rising with "aristocratic distinction" to receive a visitor, "all dressed in white linen, a white shirt with cuff links and starched collar," at eight in the morning, in the way that Bilac hastened to receive his interviewer João do Rio?[1] His engineering barracks near the bridge at São José do Rio Pardo (São Paulo) would not even permit us the comparison. Or could we picture him, like Rio Branco, organizing dinners for such foreign intellectuals as Anatole France or, like Oliveira Lima, spending his diplomatic holidays consulting rare book dealers and European museums? Considering himself a mixture of Celt, Greek, and Tapuia Indian, Cunha, although born in the state of Rio de Janeiro, seemed instead a kind of provincial who had got lost among the stuffed shirts of the south of Brazil. Because he lived at a time when "we [had] no university life and all our thinking [was] focussed on the presidential succession,"[2] the most appropriate place for Cunha—and one he himself endeavored to occupy—was alongside such men as Sílvio Romero and José Veríssimo, high school teachers and periodic contributors to newspapers. Who knows, however, if he would have adapted to the sedentary life, to the contact with adolescents, to the inevitable group meetings? The fact is that he remained within his role as wandering, ill-paid, "public-service" engineer. In that role, however, he had at least the partial advantage of avoiding such fates as the legalistic bent of a Rui Barbosa—who, after the Canudos campaign was over, lamented the fact that he had not filed a writ of habeas corpus on behalf of the *jagunços* (backlanders), now his constituents—or the idealistic political and diplomatic posturing of a Joaquim Nabuco. It was, to be sure, only a partial advantage, for it was not strong enough to disengage him from the patterns of tremulant rhetoric, of taste for "high-sounding speech," of involvement of the written word in the pomp and prestige of public oration. It is with good reason that Afrânio Peixoto says of him that "he possessed the natural defects of his qualities" and that therefore "the word had to be sonorous and obscure; the image was to be rejected unless it crackled with flame or flashed with illumination; thought itself, serene gift of those who meditate without pressure or care, seemed spurious to him if a stance of arrogant emphasis did not have it arch its back."[3] It is an observation that develops the criticism with which José Veríssimo opens his article about *Os Sertões* [Rebellion in the Backlands], in which he laments the presence of a certain "tone of Gongorism, of artificiality" in Cunha's work.[4] But Peixoto does more than just develop Veríssimo's censure—a censure with which his friend Cunha would never make peace. Peixoto in fact carries that criticism in another direction by considering Cunha's style the incarnation of the national spirit, since "Brazilians remain pompous, high-sounding, empty, and enfatuated in just this way, expressing strange ideas in unlikely and difficult terms. . . . Euclides did not abandon his people" (Peixoto, 36).

Peixoto, little read today, nonetheless provided the seed for Gilberto Freyre's explanation of the success that Cunha's masterpiece has enjoyed with foreigners: it is that "the Brazilian author did not fear offending the European reader with his tropicalism or irritating him with his Brazilianness. To the contrary, he flaunted them."[5]

What in Afrânio Peixoto was still clothed in a touch of reticence and irony appears in Freyre as decided praise: the mark of Brazilianness is the requirement that its writer be a little barbarous, without the fineness of a Machado de Assis or the delicate turns of an Alphonsus Guimarães; Gongoristic, arbitrary, and impetuous. The merit of having been the initiator of a systematically culturological vision of Brazil does not keep Freyre from continuing to require of Brazilian writers the exhibition of a certain hallmark, the expression of a certain *substance*, just as first the romantics and then the partisans of biological interpretation had done before. I shall touch on the long history condensed into that cliché, which, while by no means avoiding praise of Machado de Assis, cannot but manifest some reserve before his supposed English characteristics. Thus Cunha's marginality may have enabled him to be the quintessence of the nation. Our search for respect for the substance of our nation imposed servitude to grandiloquence. Nevertheless, it was not in that regard that Cunha was a marginal writer. His taste for technical terms and expressions came from his familiarity with engineering manuals, but he also fell easily into step with the pleasure of hollow and empty language—testimony both to his reading of dictionaries and to his sterility in regard to ideas. In that sense, Cunha is hardly a monument to the nationality but instead its most expressive (and lamentable) document. His jumbled writing has nothing to do with the position of engineer, about which the poet Cabral de Mello would say:

> Pencil, t-square, paper;
> sketch, project, number:
> the engineer thinks a straight world,
> a world that no veil covers.[6]

The daily practice of engineering in fact involved close attention to the cultural reality of the area with which it had to deal, whether it was the *sertão* (backlands) of Bahia or the world of the Amazon. It was that attention that made Cunha the precursor of what Oliveira Vianna would call "state culturology," that is, an understanding of the nation less in legal-juridical terms than as a function of the diversity of the customs and values of its different regions. In still more direct terms: Cunha's marginality stemmed not from his maintenance of a style made for ears easily impressed by dictionary erudition but from his precise investigation of a whole nation in the interior of the country that had yet to be recognized. In his language, he, among his contemporaries, remained closer to Rui Barbosa and Coelho Neto. In his marginalization, however, he blazed the trail to our understanding of the dissimilarities that constitute us. But that is not the only differentiating point to consider in studying him. In opposition to his liking

for simple oppositions—the man of the coast versus the backlander, the backlander versus the gaucho, and so on—Cunha also requires of us a much finer
differentiation of proximities and separations. Such an approach will, however,
in its turn produce only half-truths if one does not find an ultimate confluence
that brings together at a convergence point all the divergent elements that we have
laid out: the turn of phrase aimed to aural consumption, Cunha's marginalization, consideration of cultural diversities. That common point of convergence,
in fact, would bespeak an "origin"—which is to be found in those early romantic essayists studied in chapter 2, for whom tropical nature elicited not movement to self-reflexivity but rather descriptive annotation aimed at demonstration
of that nature's originality to the eyes of the Old World. Nevertheless, before
exploring that linkage, I shall attempt to capture a sense of the climate in which
Cunha's masterpiece *Os Sertões* was composed and look at the kind of interpretive tradition to which it gave rise. In regard to the first of those issues, I have
heretofore referred only to his position vis-à-vis his intellectual peers. Even there,
however, one additional distinction is vital: the marginalization of the man did
not wholly correspond to a marginality for the writer as well, for Cunha's eru-
dite style contained little that was not common to his time and place. To turn
from consideration of intellectual climate to examination of the interpretive tradition that has accompanied his work, thence to link up to the cult of observation carried out among us since the beginning of the nineteenth century, I shall,
however, have to rely on a series of condensed statements.

Euclides da Cunha's generation was formed in the scientific tradition, of
which Comte, Haeckel, and Spencer were the high priests. A student of military
engineering who was then little given to the discipline of the military, whose
ranks he would soon abandon, Cunha received the influences of positivism and,
albeit more gradually, of evolutionism as well. Those were, in effect, the two
currents that separated the youth in the military from those in civil society at the
time:

> In the youth of the military, especially in the Rio School where
> Benjamin Constant taught, it was the philosophy of Comte with its
> mathematical underpinning, its primary conception of moral facts, its
> anti-mysticism, its strong dogmatic and disciplinary bent that had the
> greatest doctrinal influence. If liberty and equality were the highest
> ideals for the rationalists and evolutionists of the Academy, for these
> positivists disciplining authority predominated instead. Liberty and
> equality fit either in republics like Switzerland or the United States or in
> Scandinavian- or English-style monarchies. The moralistic authority of
> Comteanism held the dictatorial republic up as the perfect form of the
> State.[7]

Because both currents professed evolution as the law of history, however, it would not have been surprising for an evolutionist to be protected by a positivist, even if the latter were in the service of the monarchy. Medeiros e Albuquerque relates that, when he was a young primary school teacher, he indoctrinated the children in a most scandalous manner, looking for "the best ways, the simplest and most eloquent examples to make them understand the main problems of evolutionism."[8] Although that activity was reported by an inspector of schools, it did not lead to negative consequences. On the contrary, he received "extraordinary praise" from the authorities. The fact, he adds, is that they were positivists. Thus conflated, evolutionism and positivism were the intellectual currents characteristic of the end of the empire and the beginning of the republic:

In that group of republican ideologues and of high-sounding orators, there stood out a small contingent for which belief in the republican ideal had a solid philosophical basis. They were the positivists. —The positivists were republicans but after their own fashion, their highly original fashion. . . . They were suspicious of the majority parties of the parliament; they did everything possible to avoid the working of democracy in the functioning of the government. . . . The government of their dreams, the ideal government, the perfect government was the dictatorial republic of Comte and not the democratic republic of Ledru-Rollin.[9]

Cunha's years in the military school gave him an initial exposure to positivist teachings and to the passionate republican dream that would cause him to fling his cadet sabre to the ground in front of the Minister of War, an act that resulted in his discharge. To be sure, according to Cunha himself, he would soon reject positivism and deny that it had had the impact commonly attributed to it: "Because in truth what was taking place was the transfiguration of a society that was feeling for the first time the energizing force of contemporary philosophy. And we are certainly not going to find such philosophy in that ill-fated and ill-understood positivism that sits there, without the influence that is attributed to it, immobile, crystallized in the profoundly religious and incorruptible soul of Teixeira Mendes."[10]

Comtean positivism had been only one of several currents that had swept the country into favor of "the great liberal conquests of our century" (Cunha, 376). In fact, the Comtean political program had little to do with the liberalism that Cunha so praises, and it was not accidental that it took root among members of the military during the first two republican governments. No matter the force of the difference, the fact is that the republican form seemed to all shades of evolutionists a more advanced mode of government. For Cunha, return to monarchy is so absurd and demoralizing a possibility that he does not even feel the need to substantiate its repugnance. "That is all that we would need," he says in a correspondence with his father-in-law on 10 January 1895, "to complete our demoralization in the eyes of the world." That must have been the belief of the "philosophical cadets," of the barracks philosophers, and of the majority of the politically active intellectuals. As a result, during the outcry elicited by the failure of the military expeditions against Canudos, Artur Azevedo, giving voice to current opinion, which saw restorationist political connotations in Antônio Conselheiro's resistance, could write:

> It's backlandish, that empty babble
> That doesn't want the nation to progress,
> And, without a thought in its head,
> Preaches ideas of restoration.[11]

Moreover, the powerful example of the United States, which Nabuco called "the magnet of the continent," must have strengthened the attractiveness of evolutionary doctrine, but among the monarchists, on the other hand, whether it was because of the emperor's temperament or impairment of the regime's alliance with the rural proprietors, there seemed little oppositionist will. The truth is that, despite the small number of their adherents, evolutionist currents played a decisive role not only in the character of intellectuality at the end of the nineteenth century and beginning of the twentieth but also in the very fall of the monarchy. Incapable of such a feat in and of themselves, the evolutionists—in this case, the military positivists—pushed the military question to great proportions, and that question, linked to the religious question and to the way in which abolition had been handled, were, according to Oliveira Vianna, the causes that brought down the throne. Cunha, an inveterate republican, was famous, despite his age, for participation in the events of Praia Vermelha, but he neither would nor could have taken advantage of Floriano Peixoto's offer of a position. The relevant document is of his own authorship:

> I have in hand an invitation that I have received with indifference and read today with sadness. "January 29, 1893. Euclides—the Marshall needs to talk to you today. Pinto Peixoto." . . . The great giver of positions, alluding to my recent graduation and to my enthusiasm for the Republic, has declared to me that *since I have the right* to choose a position for myself, *he does not judge himself* competent to indicate one. . . . What an outlook! It would be best to tell him that state governmental leadership has simply collapsed.[12]

Moreover, Cunha became disenchanted with the republic itself: "Cultivating, as he would for his whole life, that ideal of high morality which, along with a love of order, characterized positivism's influence, Euclides could by now no longer have entertained illusions about the possibility of having doctrinal influence from within the government."[13]

Nevertheless, in contrast to Oliveira Lima, who, after giving noteworthy service to the newly established regime, converted to monarchism and had his diplomatic career damaged as a result, Cunha never abandoned his loyalty to the republic. To do so would have been to abandon evolutionism, which had served as his compass. That compass, however, was also responsible for the impasse in which we see him at the end of *Os Sertões*. Although it fell short of the desired form, the republic was still a more advanced political arrangement. Whether that conviction was his alone or shared with his peers, it could always be rethought. The key event of his life, the episode of Canudos, had, however, been presented in press accounts in Rio and São Paulo as the first movement toward monarchical restoration. Newspaper coverage of the event generally transmits a very clear idea of how the "rebellion" had been managed. At the origin of the view of Canudos as a monarchist stronghold were the very political vicissitudes of the moment. Floriano Peixoto had recently died, and his successor, the civilian Prudente de Morais, lived under the threat of being deposed. In a letter to Bernardino de Campos, the president remarked: "I know that the jacobins hate me and become more arrogant every day—to the exact extent that they are being urged on by Chiefs-of-Staff Quintino and Glicério—and as soon as they feel strong enough to replace me with some *general* who will carry out the Marshall's politics, they won't delay for a single day."[14]

Born under military tutelage, the republic, on the appearance of its first civilian president, began suffering the instability that it carries with it to the present time. The followers of the dead marshal made Antônio Conselheiro's backlands community one more instrument of struggle against civilian presidency:

> The jacobins, who wore the red vest of "Floriano's time"—peasants
> and military men for whom the Iron Marshall and the Republic were
> one and the same flesh—did not let the opportunity escape: they made
> Canudos into a stronghold of monarchical restorationists. A menace to
> republican institutions, which the tolerance, or even connivance, of
> Prudente de Morais' civilian government had allowed to grow with
> impunity. (Rabelo, 73)

And the press, whether for like reasons or in purely sensationalistic exploitation, was primarily responsible for propagating the interpretation of Canudos as monarchistic, both by creating imaginary comparisons and by proclaiming, through its war correspondents, the immanent discovery of definitive proof of the backlander's alliance with restoration supporters. In regard to the conspiracy theories, Walnice Nogueira Galvâo observes:

> More interesting and even more unimaginable—though equally
> fantastic—are the conspiracies created by the newspapers, with all
> possible journalistic coverage buttressed by reporters doing investigative
> work, with sources of unimpeachable though secret information; the

readers are kept in suspense for several days or weeks and finally never learn what the truth is, even when they have called for the discovery and punishment of the guilty as an example.[15]

Regarding the proofs of a monarchist plot, we must limit ourselves to transcription of a few brief passages. In a letter to the newspaper *Republic*, General Artur Oscar, leader of the fourth expedition against Canudos, writes: "I do not actually possess any dispatch regarding munitions shipments from the capital of that State to the bandits, nor do I know of any. — But I look forward to the city's complete occupation so that we can find in its archives eloquent proof of the restoration plans which, under the label of *New Christians*, lodged in a church, which is the wall that protects them . . . " (quoted in Galvão, 69).

And, on 29 August 1897, the *Gazeta de Notícias's* correspondent pronounces: "A Mauser carbine has been found, with the mark . . . Buenos Aires" (quoted in Galvão, 156).

It is true that an officer in the fourth expedition, from the very scene of the battle, stated in no uncertain terms that there was no link whatsoever between the backlanders and any external forces: "Like many others, I too believed in the existence of such outside aid of monarchistic intent, but after my march through the backlands of Sergipe and Bahia and my arrival in Canudos I became convinced that all of that is no more than fantasy" (quoted in Galvão, 88).

It is true too that, in Salvador, voices were raised against the conspiracy theory (quoted in Galvão, 93), but they were minority expressions, not listened to in the capitol. More powerful political interests suffocated them, for the "jacobins" were irritated at the death of the third expedition's commander, Moreira César—a death that had robbed them of a possible military savior—if not alarmed by the inability of well-armed troops to take an unprepared, ill-armed settlement. Following those very lines, Cunha, before arriving at Canudos, partook of the general opinion, writing in an article for the *Estado de São Paulo*: "Just as was the case in Vendée, the religious fanaticism that predominates in their simple and ingenuous souls is artfully taken advantage of by the propagandists of the Empire."[16]

And in Bahia, as correspondent for that same newspaper, his belief remained unchanged: "We shall soon tread on the soil upon which the Republic will surely administer the final blow to those who vex it" (Cunha, 2:495). In that same correspondence, carrying further the comparison with the Vendée of the *chouans*, he undauntedly adds: "Would that our Vendée would hide itself under a large, shadowy cover of clouds and take the shape of the shade of an ambuscade amid the blinding light of the great tropical day that warms us. . . . The Republic is immortal!" (2:496).

Shortly, of course, the journalist's outlook would change. He would stop speaking of a defiance of the institutional form represented by the republic and undertake a biologically based explanation. António Conselheiro would become a "bizarre kind of great man in reverse," "a noteworthy example of atavistic retroactivity" (correspondence of 15 August 1897; Cunha, 2:506). The notion of monarchist conspiracy would give way to sociological transformism. And although it no longer appears in explicit, literal form, the metaphor of Vendée would continue being a guiding element. The republic, an advanced form of social organization, had been attacked by an atavistic incarnation of the past. That explanation, as Sílvio Romero demonstrates in his important but little-known essay "O Haeckelianismo em Sociologia" [Haeckelianism in Sociology], was very common in the era. In the superimposing of biology on sociology, it was held to be a law that "whenever civilization moves from one region to another and the civilized group comes into contact and fusion with peoples still living in inferior cultural periods, history turns back to centuries before and *repeats in summary form past phases of human history.*"[17] Without actually rejecting it, Romero attacks the notion of an ethnic basis as explanation of the differential conduct of peoples, labeling it an arbitrary generalization and allowing it only "a small dose of truth in the special and unique case of the comparison of colonial peoples with the people who gave rise to them" (Romero, 23). Cunha does not make even that differentiation; the ideas of an atavism characterizing Conselheiro and of his community's regression to an earlier, inferior form of society are continually proclaimed in *Os Sertões.* The Vendée metaphor becomes his Verdun. But the movement from political interpretation to interpretation of an evolutionistic nature was not made in a single leap. The political alternative still figures in his correspondence of 9 and 10 September: "We are not lacking in men ready to die, pierced by musketballs, for the Republic" (Cunha, 2:94). And, on 26 September, he ruminates on the number and quality of the adversary's arms: "How can we explain the enormous abundance that the backlanders enjoy?—Let us not deceive ourselves. There is to this entire struggle a mysterious character that must be uncovered" (2:555). Some of the musketballs "are made of steel, like those of the Mannlichers, some others, however, are completely unknown. They are undeniably the projectiles of modern balls that we do not possess" (2:557). Two days later, however, he begins to ascribe another character to the backlanders' resistance: "The strange monotony of the siege continues on. Three days ago, though, I believed that our opponents could not last another three hours, that they would be crushed in a quick breakthrough. . . . Such instances of heroism are all but incomprehensible" (2:558). Finally, at the end of the *Diary,* an admission of heroism stifles language about supposed political purposes: "Let us be honest—there is something great and solemn in that stoical and indefatigable courage, in the sovereign and strong heroism of our coarse, misguided countrymen. More and more I believe that the most beautiful victory, the real conquest would lie in incorporating them, tomorrow, soon, once and for all, into our political existence" (2:565).

From this point on, we can assume that Cunha was convinced that crushing the settlement would be a crime, and that, instead, the causes for the conflict should be subjected to detailed examination. He would in fact dedicate himself to just such an examination, from the time of his return to São Paulo to 1901, when the manuscript of *Os Sertões* was sent to the editor. At that point it assumed the status of the work that would vindicate the nationality. That effort on Cunha's part was clearly unparalleled. While such figures as Bilac, the toast of the nation, remarked with pleasure in 1908 that we were governed by the fashion of Paris and that, because of it, we had even "begun to write socialist books" (Rio, 7), Cunha, buried in the interior of São Paulo, was using his barracks full of books to try to understand the tragedy he had witnessed. Did he arrive at an understanding? The answer is at best an ambivalent one. On the one hand, there seems to be success, for the process leads to the wish to comprehend the land, to comprehend the "most legitimately Brazilian people," as Afrânio Peixoto would write. On the other hand, it is clear today that there was not total success: the Vendée metaphor supports an evolutionistic explanation, with unmistakable biological underpinnings, which runs throughout the book. And on that basis, a clumsy and erroneous explanation of the phenomenon of Conselheiro and his followers would be propounded, one that would contaminate explanation of the country in general. Moreover, even my distinction between success and failure is oversimplified. If, because of the ethnic bases ascribed to it, evolutionism predominates — negatively — the issue of intermixing with the "inferior" races and the anthropologically based observations, also abundant in the book although subordinated to its biological framework, can and should be disentangled from that framework. That effort, however, must be carried out in opposition to Cunha himself, for he never abandons the notion that biology is the *scientia princeps* of sociological interpretation. And whereas it may be incorrect to suppose that that interpretive closing was imposed by the horizon of Cunha's time, we must nonetheless remember, as an extenuating element, that the ethnicity factor had considerable weight in the early stages of the development of Brazilian social science. Even if we do not highlight the role that the contributions of Nina Rodrigues and Artur Ramos played, we can still recall Sílvio Romero's analysis in an essay previously noted. Despite his attack on the law of regression in history, in his chapter "Immigration and the Future of the Brazilian People," Romero saw the nation's future imperiled unless it put an adequate immigration policy in place: "The way to form a strong nation in Brazil is to attract foreign colonization by a method entirely different from the one that has been practiced up to now" (Romero, 227). For the location of European immigrants in the South would only lead to two simultaneous evils: the future of the Portuguese race and of its language and culture would be adulterated within that favored region, while "in the north [those factors and their future] would wither, would die of atrophy, denatured and crushed by the overpowering infusion of the blood of the inferior races" (222). For Cunha, the problem would have been an even weightier one because unlike Sílvio, he had not abandoned the thesis of regression: the people, he concludes, are incapable of understanding the abstractions either of constitutional-monarchical government or of republicanism; they are, then, unadapted "to the higher legislation of the newly-inaugurated political regime."[18] Hence the pinpointing of an originary tragedy:

> After having lived for four hundred years on a vast stretch of seaboard, where we enjoyed the reflections of civilized life, we suddenly came into an unlooked-for inheritance in the form of the Republic. Caught up in the sweep of modern ideas, we abruptly mounted the ladder, leaving behind us in their centuries-old semidarkness a third of our people in the heart of our country. Deluded by a civilization which came to us second hand; rejecting, blind copyists that we were, all that was best in the organic codes of other nations, and shunning, in our revolutionary zeal, the slightest compromise with the exigencies of our own national interests, we merely succeeded in deepening the contrast between our mode of life and that of our rude native sons, who were more alien to us in this land of ours than were the immigrants who came from Europe. (Cunha, *Rebellion in the Backlands*, 161)

His evolutionism is, then, complicated by his maintaining of the thesis from which the view of Conselheiro as a synthesis of atavistic errors and regressions derived. Thus what was for Sílvio Romero a minor problem resolvable through the measured infusion of white blood, becomes for Cunha the prelude to an impasse that we shall see arise in *Os Sertões*. Thus, rather than being a difficult book, *Os Sertões* is difficult to evaluate only in its entirety, so great is the number of quantities that must be given their individual weighting. Nevertheless, it is in the confronting of such inequalities that we may expect a less mechanical approach to the book. To that end, it must be understood at the outset that the author's debts lie not only with the scientism of the era, as is customarily held; that scientism had already found fertile ground in which to take root, especially in the tradition that, in chapter 2, we saw constitute itself from the time of our independence on. In the same chapter, in fact, we endeavored to demonstrate the change in function that reflection in relation to nature underwent in our country. Whereas in European romanticism nature provided a stimulus to self-reflection, functioning like a kind of book comprising merely suggested lines whose filling out could be achieved only within the meditative consciousness, with us nature offered itself up to pleasurable observation and description, with the appreciator of nature pausing before its exuberance, its barbarous plenitude so much in contrast with the garden landscapes of civilized Europe. Observation did not find its ground, so to speak, in a subject who would convert nature into a means of stimulating and ordering the reading of himself or herself; its ground resided instead in the object observed, in the land that was to be replaced on the written page.

Now that tendency, even while diluting the difference between romanticism and realism, would be added to anew by the promotion of evolutionism, by Tobias Barreto and the Recife school, and of positivism, both orthodox and heterodox. If the primacy of observation of tropical exuberance sought to give our writer his function—to imitate (now in the realistic sense) our specificity, thus bearing true witness to it—the primacy of biology within sociology reinforced that function, defining it more closely: the writer, the intellectual in general, was one who, invested with scientific objectivity, could propagate knowledge within a public that was not only ignorant but also stigmatized by the inferior blood that ran through its veins. But, it might also be asked, why was that intellectual not taken as a leader, supported by cultural privilege, disdainful of inferiors? Why, to the contrary, was he led to wander along the path of an idealism that failed to benefit the very people it sought to aid, through ignorance of the very conditions of their existence? Perhaps because the monarchy was unable to create a privileged hereditary caste or did not wish to do so—titles of nobility were not hereditary with us—thus not endowing the intellectual with a set of distinctive values to defend. Hence the combination of cult of nature with cult of the man of the people, and depreciation of fine folk—to be seen in, for example, the mediocre verses of another war correspondent assigned to Canudos, one Fávila Nunes. If nothing were known of the author—ex-officer, public functionary, and businessman (see Galvão, 111)—one might picture an "advanced" thinker:

> Let others adore their noblewomen
> Opulent baronesses
> Rich daughters of marquises—
> Rich young ladies of salons.
>
> My tastes are much humbler:
> I adore the pretty planter's daughter,
> Light butterfly,
> Queen of my backlands!
>
> Let them adore the rich ladies
> Their waved hair
> And white breasts palpitating
> Tired from the waltz:
> I love the sacred reticence
> Of the backlands girl's breast
> And its palpitation
> Tired from working!
>
> I want the life of the forest
> To feel the waterfall's roar

And hear when the storm
Breaks over the backlands! . . .
To be free by nature,
Enjoying nature in my soul,
And in the midst of poverty
To have my soul happy.[19]

My schematic explanation here is, to be sure, merely provisional. In this format, it is important merely to emphasize the fact that the scientifism of the Generation of 1870 prolonged and intensified the role that had been assigned to observation since Gonçalves de Magalhães's "Discurso sobre a História da Literatura do Brasil" [Discourse on the History of Brazilian Literature] (1836). That role was intensified, it must be understood, in that it was given a more precise function: the person carrying it out had to apply "scientific" principles to the study of society to aid in its improvement. To be sure, as we now know, the supposed correlation between the prominence of that role and its relationship to science was a mistaken one. For the era—and for common opinion even today—observation stands independent of a theoretical framework, for the latter is seen as abstract and distant from operational conditions. In this regard, as substantiation of his lack of appreciation for Benjamin Constant, Medeiros e Albuquerque writes: "The grand science of the mathematician has never inspired my respect, for I know well the extent to which it really is a science and where it begins to be fantasy. The extraordinary constructions and hypotheses that mathematicians build only prove that their own ratiocinations are coherent *and not, therefore, that the things upon which such ratiocinations are performed are so precise*" (Medeiros e Albuquerque, 165; emphasis mine).

What that memorialist says about mathematics can be extended to thought about scientific theories in general, for they are classically constructed on the ideal of mathematizable quantification. Beyond that point, however, mathematics does not venture. The other sciences are redeemed from depreciation through the role that observation plays in them. And Euclides da Cunha did not hide the similar nature of his position on that score. Indeed, lamenting his deficient knowledge of botany, he declared: "I have never decried so much the lack of a practical and solid education and never recognized so much the uselessness of the theoretical marvels with which we delude ourselves in our school years" (Cunha, 2:531).

That line of thought would reappear in an article in *Contrastes e Confrontos* [Contrasts and Comparisons] in which, praising Marx and scientific socialism, he could write, curiously enough:

No idealizations: facts; and unassailable inductions deriving from a
rigorous analysis of objective materials; and experience and observation,
organized through a lucid apprenticeship in the lesser sciences; and the

inflexible logic of the events; and that terrible ground-to-ground argumentation without tortuous syllogisms, without the transcendental idiocy of the old dialectic, but all made up of axioms, of real truisms, in such a way as not to require of the minds the least effort to understand it, for it is it that will comprehend them independently of their will, and will dominate them and carry them along with the strength of its very simplicity. (2:194)

It is difficult to imagine the Marxian text in which our author found so great a simplification, such "ground-to-ground argumentation," such independence on the part of facts. The only imaginable text is the *Communist Manifesto*. But what is of greatest importance here are the terms in which that praise is cast: facts versus idealizations, inductions made from the observation of objective materials, experience, and observation itself. What Cunha understood of Marxism is of little interest—save that it should be noted that his praise of it did not lead him to renounce evolutionism, for, among those to whom he points as providing concrete measures for the realization of socialism, he reserves his agreement for Ferri and Caloganni, "correctly evolutionists" (195). What is important is that he considers Marxism's correctness to depend on its privileging of fact, observation, experience, and induction. In fact, in his privileging of those operations and lack of attention to theory, which was for him no more than an idealization running contrary to the truth of facts, one sees the most enduring mistake about what the construct of science consists of. Cunha implicitly declares that facts speak for themselves; it is sufficient that we merely be capable of precise observation of them. Behind that error we see project itself the Brazilian romantic ideal, according to which for us to constitute a genuine national literature we have only to use our eyesight. With the advent of the scientifistic currents propagated from the end of the empire on, that principle leaves the course of literature proper and sets itself up at the door of science. There, allied to the premise of qualitative racial difference, it takes imagination as a trace that is both negative and peculiar to the inferior races. That connection is found even in a figure like Oliveira Vianna, author of perhaps our greatest work of sociology: "What gave so much intensity to the ideal of abolitionism and contributed to its reaching the climax of exaltation that it did, was the pressure of the foreign example *acting upon an imaginative race* extremely susceptible to idealism and richly endowed for enthusiasm" (Vianna, 63; emphasis mine).

Thus the use of the imagination becomes the legacy of inferior peoples. If not ethnically inferior peoples—since such are not quite Vianna's terms—at least people who behave in an inferior manner in relation to the severe lines of science. It is clear, then, that the paradigm based on observation is important not only for the reinterpretation of the concept of literature in Brazil but also for the very conception of science that we have internalized and for the alliance that it forged with the messianic function assigned to the intelligentsia. As a result of the extension of that paradigm into the area of science, in defending himself from attacks on his style by José Veríssimo, Cunha writes to him: "I am convinced that the true artistic impression requires, fundamentally, the scientific notion of the incident that awakens it—and that, in that case, the measured intervention of a technography proper is obligatorily required—and it is acceptable as long as it is not exaggerated to the point of giving the book being written the aspect of a compendium" (Cunha, 2:621).

Without the weight of experiencing facts, without the exercise of observation, art would be gratuitous fantasy, dangerously close to the "animism" of peoples incapable of achieving higher abstraction. Hence Cunha's remark in the same letter: "Nothing justifies the systematic depreciation that men of letters direct to them [e. g., technical terms]—especially if we consider that the marriage of science and art, under any of their aspects, is today the most elevated tendency of human thought" (621).

This letter, moreover, is important in showing us that it was Cunha's conscious purpose to establish a higher accord between scientific basis and artistic embellishment. That purpose did not escape the attention of his early critics, José Veríssimo, Araripe Júnior, and Afrânio Peixoto. The first of the three states in his opening paragraph:

> Mr. Euclides da Cunha's book, noteworthy on so many fronts, is, all at the same time, the book of a man of science—a geographer, a geologist, an ethnographer—the book of a man of reflection—a philosopher, a sociologist, a historian—and the book of a man of sentiment—a poet, a novelist, an artist who knows how to see and how to describe, who senses and feels both aspects of nature and also the contact of man, touched to the depths of his soul, moved to tears in the face of human pain, whether it comes from the fateful conditions of the physical world, the "droughts" that scourge the backlands of northern Brazil or whether it comes from human stupidity or evil, as in the Canudos campaign. (Veríssimo, 45)

Cunha was, then, a poet in his ability to sense, to feel, to be touched in the depths of his soul, to be moved to tears. The opposite qualities—to experience, to observe, to calculate—are left for the scientific side of his nature. And how could his sensitivity and force of sentiment manifest themselves other than through his use of language? Thus, logically, Veríssimo's criticism of his style wound Cunha's literary pretensions and occasion his defense in the letter of 12 March 1902.

The second great critical consecration of *Os Sertões* was written by Araripe Júnior. Much longer and more sympathetic than Veríssimo's review, Araripe's work carefully describes and comments on the principal parts of *Os Sertões*. His examination of Antônio Conselheiro perpetuates the error in interpretation that would finally be undone only with Ataliba Nogueira's publication, in 1974, of the backlands leader's "Prédicas e Discursos" [Sermons and Speeches].[20] But that is not a detail of great concern here. In comparing Cunha to Walter Scott, Araripe does not even see fit to state that the genres in which they work are different: "We are fully in novel à la Walter Scott; and only thus can we understand how that Scots writer was able to gather, with little effort, true facts about the highlands battles and embellish them with his poetic fictions."[21]

To take that comparison literally would in fact amount to declaring that *Os Sertões* too was decorated with "poetic fictions," which, in relation to the book's own purposes and the concepts of the time, would amount to censure. Where, however, does the logic of that statement reside? The critic answers that question implicitly in the last part of his essay. It is the style that makes the artist: "From the pages of this book come piercing shrieks, war cries, explosions, roars of caged beasts, sighs of the dying, noises of every sort, grindings of teeth, distant echoes of the backlands, trumpet calls. And the style holds it all, molding itself to all the modulations of the spirit" (Araripe Júnior, 123).

The last part of the last sentence, in its turn, will act as a touchstone from which, in a later article about Cunha's *Contrastes e Confrontos*, Araripe will compare the styles of Rui Barbosa and Euclides da Cunha, giving the latter the nod because his resonance is superior to the monochordic tone employed by the Bahian publicist: "Precisely opposite to what we see in the style of Counsellor Rui Barbosa, the style of Euclides da Cunha has nothing blockish about it. Emotionality moves just below the surface of the ground that he treads."[22]

Taking for granted familiarity on the reader's part with Afrânio Peixotos's criticism of Cunha, we can conclude that for his principal commentators Cunha was the poet by dint of the quality of his language and that such was affirmed on the basis of his ability to sense and to move, to touch the harp strings of emotionality. Let us reiterate that conclusion: that is the power that distinguishes the poet from the scientist, master of coldly transmitted observation. We underscore that conclusion because it clearly shows how the cult of observation reached into the generation of scientifism and acclimated itself there. Only now the tree has grown: capacity for correct observation is reserved for scientific understanding, and the artist is asked to mobilize the reader's emotionality in correlation to that understanding. It is on the basis of precisely that type of reflection that the concept of Cunha as a combination of sociologist and writer, of scientist and man of letters, has been grounded. The bases of that evaluation—it does not hurt to repeat—presuppose a radical difference between science and art, with the former cultivating the cerebral faculties, the latter the heartstrings. That cliché has become so firmly entrenched that it still guides the thinking of a recent publication by Gilberto Freyre:

Only the writer who is also a poet, in the German sense of the word, reveals the most inward nature of the characters, countrysides, and societies that his art either revives or surprises still in motion. . . . Only the great writer, never the scientist only as scientist, writes clearly and correctly; nor does the specialist who is incapable of transcending his speciality, not to invade other specialities but rather to come to dominate the matters that he treats of as interrelated wholes. (Freyre, 27)

For the scientist not to be only a scientist, he must leave his field and become a poet as well. If in that statement it is understood that he must also be a *faber*— the *Schöpfer* of German—the gesture does not go beyond the status of a hackneyed commonplace. The scientist only as scientist would correspond to what Thomas Kuhn has called "normal science"—that is, the science that merely extends the already accepted paradigms to yet unexplored areas.[23] But if, in its status as a truism, that sort of statement is wholly dispensable, it is nonetheless of importance here because it shows that, to be acceptable, the granting of a poetic dimension to *Os Sertões* required broader justification. And it is also important because it reveals that as a first step, from Veríssimo to Gilberto Freyre, *the poeticity of Cunha's work is affirmed on the basis of the primacy of observation*, which, entrenched at the beginning of the past century and expanded through the currents of evolutionism, remains unchallenged even today. In chapters 2 and 3, I noted that the differential characterizations of the poetic and the scientific were established in the eighteenth century, deriving from theorization about the discourse of history. But ours was not merely a late, simplified adaptation of that arrangement. Since romanticism, observation has, for us, made self-reflexivity disfunctional, conflating compensatory fantasy—incarnated in the paradigmatic phrase "Oh, what longings have I"—with exercise of the imagination and setting literature to service of the land and of authorial melancholy. With the arrival of scientifism and the European model of science, the distinction was established between "neutral," impersonal, merely analytical observation, taken as scientific, and emotional, personalized, concretizing observation, taken as poetic. Because Cunha embraced both, a powerful alibi was facilitated in his case: if the science on which he based himself is no longer accepted, the gates of literature swing wide open to accept him. The previous example of Michelet shows that to make "literature" the port of salvation for writers in danger of losing their place in eternity is not a privilege that falls to us. To be sure, I do not argue that Cunha does not have the right to be looked at literarily. I merely state that, if he is so considered, it must be for reasons other than those that dominate in works heretofore written along that line. It is to that end that the following pages are directed, and for that reason that they must necessarily delve into Cunha's masterpiece itself.

Sociological Transformism in *Os Sertões*

In October 1897, after Canudos's resistance had ended, Cunha, correspondent for the *Estado de São Paulo*, went back to Salvador and then returned to the South. After a period of rest at his father's estate, he returned to the capital of São Paulo and, in January 1898, was named engineer of public works. The next year found him in São José do Rio Pardo, where he would remain until 1901. That, as his biographers would recognize, would be the most productive period in the nomadic writer's life. In São José, during moments of surcease in the construction of bridges, amid his bank of works, Cunha would study and resume writing his book. In a select few friends — among whom was the legendary Francisco Escobar, who lent Cunha rare books and translated Latin texts for him — he found a team of disinterested collaborators, who even today revere his name and work. It was through them, as the scrupulous Olímpio de Sousa Andrade tells us ("História e Interpretação," chaps. 11-13), that Cunha, to overcome one of the lacunae in his background, was encouraged to frequent Portuguese classics, reading Vieira, Bernardes, Herculano, and Camilo. The manuscript was finished in 1900. But it was not until December of the next year that the trepidations of the editors in the house of Laemnert were finally assuaged; the book was published in December 1902. Unknown to intellectual circles in the nation's capital, Cunha mainly feared the army's reaction. That reaction, however, was manifested in articles by only two officers, José da Penha (*Gazeta de Notícias*, 14 and 18 December 1902) and Moreira Guimarães (*Correio da Manhã*, 1903).[24] This slight military reaction was eclipsed both by the laudatory publications of José Veríssimo (*Correio da Manhã*, 3 December 1902) and Araripe Júnior (*Jornal do Comércio*, 27 February 1903) and by the unexpected commercial success. In two-and-a-half months, the thousand printed copies had been sold; the second edition appeared in July 1903. "It was," says Sílvio Rabelo, "an unprecedented case in the country's book market" (Rabelo, 215).

Although Canudos had long since ceased to be a topic for press treatment, Cunha's book revived the subject, not as current journalism but rather under the heading of how little Brazil really knew about itself. Moreover, because of the book's very character as a revelation of an unknown backlands, the public of the era, accepting the notion that it had literary value, could not likewise accept the proposition that it was a work of fiction in general, much less that it was a historical novel. Cunha thus escaped the scandal that might have ensued if Siqueira de Menezes, one of the army officers whom he most praises, had published the statements that he made in the oral interview he gave to Gilberto Amado. Amado declares in his memoirs that, in late 1911, he went to the government palace in Aracaju [the capital of the state of Sergipe] to visit the president of Sergipe, the recently promoted general Siqueira de Menezes. Intending to flatter him, he mentioned the author of *Os Sertões*. To his astonishment, the ensuing dialogue took place:

"It's a lie! Don't talk to me about that (word that I have a hard time reproducing about Euclides da Cunha). He never saw me. It's all a lie. He was never there! I never saw him there. Nobody did!"
I recall that before shaking hands with him to take my leave, I once again stammered: "But General, the details . . . minute details . . . Euclides shows you riding, drawing up outlines, crossing grottoes, studying, contemplating, leading . . . "
Looking at me sternly, he replied: "It's a lie. He saw nothing of it. None of what he says is true."[25]

And Gilberto Amado comments:

The conclusion is inevitable: Euclides poeticized his characters. . . .
The knowledge, the courage, the contemplation, the depth of soul of the expeditionaries to the backlands or of the sun-blonded backlanders are procedural aggrandizements deriving from one original deformation, from the same sublimizing grandiloquence that led Castilhos to call water in Ovid "lymph" and Coelho Neto to call the knife or machete that the black sugar plantation slave uses "dagger." (Amado, 181-82)

It is impossible to say if that conclusion is correct or not, or what the reasons might have been for the ex-combatant's outburst.[26] His very indignation, however, shows why ascription of literary character to the book could not have recourse to a grounding in the perilous epithet "work of fiction," why it had to remain in the realm of "stylistic features." While our intellectuals were parading through the Rua do Ouvidor, chatting at the door to Garnier's, giving high-sounding lectures on trivial subjects,[27] punching the clock at some office, and awaiting the novelties from Paris, Cunha was opening out to the nation's "profound heart" and giving birth to "Brazilian nationalism."[28] His book, then, elicited a kind of empathy from his readers, which was deepened by the nature of the culminating tragedy that befell him in August 1909 [he was shot and killed by his wife's lover]. Nevertheless, with the fiftieth anniversary of the publication of *Os Sertões* well past, that climate of exaltation has seemingly given way to more analytical work on the book. Walnice Nogueira Galvão's collection of articles on Canudos from the newspaper press of the day and Antônio Conselheiro's published manuscripts are outstanding in that vein. Those manuscripts, having once belonged to Cunha himself as a gift from Afrânio Peixoto, would seem not to have been consulted by him (see Ataliba Nogueira, *Antônio Conselheiro e Canudos*, 23.) Let us now turn to the work itself.

Its preliminary note presents us with a Cunha totally convinced of the truth of evolutionism: because the passage of time would not permit him to set forth a simple listing of the campaign's events and because the subraces therein involved would surely soon disappear, he intends to "sketch in . . . for the eyes of future historians, the most significant present-day characteristics of the subraces to be found in the backlands of Brazil" (Cunha, *Rebellion in the Backlands*, xxxi). That foreseeable extinction—in accordance with the doctrine stipulating disappearance of inferior races that come in contact with stronger ones—was seen as tragic, for it signified that time was running against us and would not permit the slow fusion necessary for the constitution of a great race. If, as Afrânio Peixoto says, "Brazilian nationalism" begins with *Os Sertões*, its appearance is accompanied by a pessimistic view of the national destiny. (Racial stigma would, thirty years later, be replaced by the stigma of underdevelopment, basis for the future Northeast novel.) But in *Os Sertões*, the drama bequeathed by our formation would be much more serious than these initial reflections suggest. In truth, that drama takes shape in "The Land," the first of the book's three large divisions. The geological study of the region included in the São Francisco basin suggests mistakes that foreigners may fall into: "First, there are the powerful gneiss-granite masses which, starting in the extreme south, curve around in a huge amphitheater, rearing those admirable landscapes which so enchant and at the same time prove such an illusion to the unaccustomed gaze of strangers" (Cunha, *Rebellion in the Backlands*, 3-4).

They would be deceived not because the surrounding countryside was not beautiful but because that first impression did not betray its true nature. When one quits the coast and penetrates into the São Francisco basin, its true aspect is revealed: "The last fragments of buried rock, disclosing in them the form of ridges which in height are scarcely reminiscent of the 'Brazilian Himalayas' of the long ago, now crumbled in a constant ages-old disintegration" (6).

Unexperienced outsiders would be deceived, ultimately because that interior desert holds the image of death, of extinction, of water that has been dissipated: "And however inexpert the observer may be, upon leaving behind him the majestic perspectives which unfold to the south and exchanging them here for the moving sight of Nature in torment, he cannot but have the persisting impression of treading the newly upraised bed of a sea long extinct, which still preserves, stereotyped in its rigid folds, the agitation of the waves and the stormy deeps" (15).

From before one enters the backlands, nature is "more depressed and rugged in appearance" (8). The image of death implanted in the land is anticipated by the image of disequilibrium—one of Cunha's favorite words: "The fact of the matter is, the stupendous drop with which the eroded slopes of the plateau fall to the sea, or to the Paulo Afonso backwater, afford no point of equilibrium for a normal hydrographic network; and the torrential rains, together with the chaotic drainage system, accordingly give to this corner of Bahia an exceptionally wild appearance" (15).

The countryside, then, assumes a phantasmagorical character; it is a "strange region," avoided by the pioneers, "absolutely forgotten throughout the four hundred years of our history" (9). Thus the geological description, grounded, as Sílvio Rabelo and Sousa Andrade have said, in the teachings and annotations of Teodoro Sampaio and Orville Derby, parallels the construction of a monstrous amphitheater made of ruins and of climatic and rainfall deficiencies. A disequilibrium and aridity that seem consonant only with the aggressive, cactus-filled solitude. The geological and climatic description serves as the basis for the author's goal of objective observation (only someone technically trained in those areas could speak to its accuracy). At the same time, an anthropomorphia of nature is constructed, working beneath a strongly expressionistic process. The very density of the sentence, precious and tortuous, a centaur armed with science, lends itself to this double function:

> The torrential rainfalls characteristic of such a climate of alternating
> flood and drought, coming of a sudden after protracted dry periods and
> beating down upon these slopes, carrying away all the loose rock
> mantle, have left largely exposed the older geologic series of these last
> mountain spurs: all the crystalline varieties, and the rough quartzites,
> and the phyllades and calcites, alternating or interlacing with one
> another and reappearing crudely at every step, barely covered with a
> stunted flora, and forming pictures which give the landscape here its
> impinging and tormented aspect. (13)

But the interpreter would be in error were he to conclude that the anthropomorphizing of nature is guided by an intent to embellish the sentence or carry it beyond the status of annotation by "a scientist only as scientist." That proposition presupposes that neutral observation is possible, with the agent functioning as mere registerer of the phenomenon. And that may have been Cunha's belief (cf. his letter to Veríssimo transcribed on p. 166). In fact, however, a description does not cease being scientific by being selective, no matter whether it is well or poorly formulated. The point that must be discussed is the *degree* of selective subjectivity, whether it is capable or not of *transgressing* its nature as a *discourse of reality* and, if it is, of then *converting it* into fictional discourse. But apprehension of the backlands' phantasmal character is not exhausted by what we have seen thus far. If that character often results from mention of old cataclysms, in other cases it depends on a series of succeeding mirages. Cataclysm, ruin, and mirage now combine in a single serpentine sentence: "The same gneiss hillocks, capriciously rent into almost geometric planes, which resemble square blocks, and which may be seen rising at various points, giving one the illusion at times of suddenly finding himself amid the lonely and deserted ruins of a majestic castle" (14). And again they separate, with emphasis falling on this or that aspect. As the vision of a deserted and catastrophic land is much more salient,

I give here only the example of the mirage: "Viewing these proud peaks from afar, practically on a horizon level, this observer had the pleasant impression of standing upon an elevated plateau, a desert extraordinary resting on the mountaintops" (20).

We are now near the scene of the battle, at the top of Mount Favela, and the portentous illusion just developed has lent itself to the belief within the backlanders' "naive imagination" that "this was Heaven" (20). To the "outsider" Cunha, the mirage would be colored with other tones; instead of Heaven, it was formed by a rapid succession of hallucinatory images:

Severely wounded and floundering, it had slid down the steep side of the hill and, halfway down, had become wedged in between the rocks. Struggling to retain its footing, it had planted its front feet firmly on a stone ledge. And there it had remained, like some fantastic animal, hanging perpendicularly over the hill and fairly prancing as it seemed, in the last forward bound of the steed and its paralyzed rider. There it was, still, with all the appearance of life, especially when a rude gust of wind from the northeast came to ruffle its long wavy mane. (24)

It is a hallucination that, in the context of the cited chapter, becomes all the more intense because its formulation is preceded by the location of the remains of one of the victims of a prior expedition: "At the storming of the Canudos encampment, one of the horses had stood out impressively, above all the others. This was the one ridden by the valiant Sublieutenant Wanderley, who had fallen in death with his mount" (24).

Aside from the expressionistic touch, which is not to be found in Tolstoy, such passages explain why readers find similarities to *War and Peace* in Cunha's work. But let us not forget: all this anthropomorphizing is a texture not autonomous or superimposed but rather parallel to the purpose of description of the geological conditions within which the battle unfolds. To be sure, it would have been purged from the work of an analyst less desirous of personalizing his or her analysis. Doubtless too that expurgation would have made the work into something akin to a report, by now rendered obsolete by others more detailed and accurate. But is that parallel anthropomorphizing sufficient to locate Cunha within the field of literature? For the time being, I shall reiterate one of the conclusions extracted from chapter 3: contrary to the belief in absolute objectivity characteristic of the historiography and theory of science in the past century, we now know that the scientist's work does not imply the bracketing off of his or her social position or way of reacting to the field being studied. The observer's position, even his or her physical position, has an impact on the nature of his observation.

For our purposes, the above annotations suffice: the first part of *Os Sertões* seeks to set forth the physical environment of Canudos. As has been demonstrated, however, that environment is not a mere neutral envelope but instead an amphitheater that anticipates the fate of its inhabitants, whom it seems to contaminate or by whom it will be contaminated. In Cunha's presentation of the backlands, then, humans are a factor before they are dealt with. And Cunha begins "Man," the part dedicated to those inhabitants, by making their biological sociology even more obvious. First, he emphasizes the Portuguese, "the aristocratic factor of our own *gens*" (51). To this he adds the brutishness of the Indian, whose "mental state" had led to the failure of the Jesuit's attempt to get the Indian to attain "the abstractions of monotheism" (70). The same inferiority is assigned to the African, who, despite the efforts of the best teachers had not been able "to approximate at least the intellectual average of the Indo-European" (86). The brand of the inferior race had descended upon the mestizo, of whom the backlander is a variant. That provenience left the backlander in a "phase of evolution in which the only rule he can conceive is that of a priestly or a warrior chieftain" (161).[29] Cunha thus complicates the notion set forth at the beginning of the book: because we have no racial unity, are condemned to civilization, and "our biological evolution demands the guaranty of social evolution" (54). Moreover, to achieve that racial stability in regions of hostile climate, it would be indispensable for the white man to cross with, and thus take on the resistance of, the inferior races. Otherwise, the country would end up experiencing what the Cunha of that time felt was happening in the Amazon and other regions of necessary racial contact: "Like the Englishman in Barbados, in Tasmania, or in Australia, the Portuguese in the Amazon region may flee miscegenation, but after a few generations his physical and moral characteristics will be profoundly altered, from his complexion, turned copper colored by the tropic suns and the incomplete elimination of carbon dioxide, to his temperament, which is weakened by having been deprived of its original qualities" (61).

Therefore, although he maintains the premise of white racial superiority, Cunha can moderate absolute affirmation: miscegenation would continue to be a stigma for him; nonetheless, in the immediate situation it would be a lesser evil, capable of avoiding the total collapse of the superior race. In the South, by contrast, the early colonizer was aided by favorable mesological conditions. Whereas in the North and Northeast, he was forced to regress in order to adapt, in the opposite area he could continue traveling the path of civilization. That contrastive view, linked to the principles of evolutionism that underlay it, contained everything necessary to lead Cunha's sociological interpretation along the road to failure. Nevertheless, the intelligence that he demonstrates in "explaining" the need for miscegenation in an aggressive environment now produces a simply brilliant result: the notion that the sociocultural isolation imposed on the backlander by mesological conditions has impeded his ethnic disintegration, allowing him to be "an ethnic subcategory that has already been formed" (84). Cunha must have been aware of the criticisms from the evolutionists to which he thus exposed himself. So much so, in fact, that he opens a parenthesis to reiterate the canonical position: "The mestizo—a hyphen between the races, a brief individual existence into which are compressed age-old forces—is almost always an unbalanced type" (85). Only after that reiteration does he openly express his thesis: the backlander "is a retrograde, not a degenerate, type" (88), for the abandonment in which he had existed had had a beneficial effect, the effect of freeing him "from a highly painful adaptation to a superior social state" (87). That must have been the greatest transgression allowable within the boundaries of biological sociology. All theorization is selective and thus possessed of limits. In its European version, transformism could not explain the backlander's ability to resist the much better prepared expeditions. In that sense, explanations based on monarchist plots, even on Canudos receiving aid from officials of foreign countries, had their acceptance facilitated by the scientifism of the elites in the capital. When Cunha, however, while still a correspondent, abandoned the hypothesis of political causation, he came face to face with an enigma: how could an ethnically corrupted people resist the onslaught of military troops and modern armaments? Pushed by those considerations, he elaborated an alternative line of argument not found in the treatises of his masters, namely one to the effect that the backlands society, because of its isolation, had been able to arrest the path of inevitable degeneration. Let us not, however, grant our author more than his due. The isolation that he proposes as an explanation, while possessing cultural elements, is basically governed by biological factors. His central concept is not the *isolat* of contemporary sociology, for that implies retention of cultural features lost in the surrounding environment. The caveat is decisive for our understanding of how Cunha could categorize the missionaries' efforts as failed. They were frustrated because: "It is not strange if, in troubled times, the lofty ideology of a Catholicism which is beyond the comprehension of these backwoodsmen breaks down, while the crude religious practices of the latter reveal all the stigmata of their undeveloped mentality" (112). It is the very thesis of regression that we have seen Sílvio Romero reject. As was common in the era, Cunha saw the lines of biology and sociology as parallel and as developing in an ever-ascending direction. If, therefore, a people has had its biological stock retarded, its social institutions must perforce remain in a corresponding state. Western ethnocentrism may never have achieved more coherent expression.

To see the total force of that expression, let us take note of the following with regard to the case in point. I have praised Sílvio Romero's essay "O Haeckelianismo em Sociologia" for its correction of a general thesis from which Euclides never withdrew. In the case under consideration, however, the two authors did not disagree, for Sílvio Romero emphasized that the law of regressivism held some truth only in the situation of "comparison of colonial peoples with the people who gave rise to them" (Romero, 23). And it could do so because "*all colonies reproduce the political, economic, religious, etc. structure of the mother country at the time when the colonization took place*" (40). Now, is such not precisely what came to pass with the backlanders, as an effect of the isolation through which they came to be protected and which made them the contemporaries of the values of Portugal at the moment of the discovery? As though foreseeing our question, Cunha responds: "Nor is there lacking [to the backlands society], by way of rounding out the comparison, the political mysticism of *Sebastianism*. Extinct in Portugal, it persists unimpaired today, under a singularly impressive form, in our northern backcountry" (Cunha, *Rebellion in the Backlands*, 112).

Thus, even as it was being rectified by Brazilian thinkers, evolutionism still revealed its metropolitan shadings. By remaining within the evolutionist circle, then, Cunha, no matter how much he may have sympathized with the people he sought to vindicate, necessarily remained an outsider to them—a prejudiced outsider. Thus his view of Antônio Conselheiro runs along virtually inevitable lines. Comporting himself in the manner of Simão Bacamarte, Machado de Assis's famous alienist,[30] specialist in the cataloging of forms of insanity, Cunha, guided by Nina Rodrigues's "A Loucura Epidêmica de Canudos" [The Epidemic Madness of Canudos] (1897), takes pleasure in reciting the supposed "companions" of the backlands leader. They were: "hysterical doctors," "repugnant cases of insanity," unbalanced and maniacal. Conselheiro himself is a "striking example of atavism," in which "all the naive beliefs from a barbarous fetishism to the aberrations of Catholicism, all the impulsive tendencies of lower races given free outlet in the undisciplined life of the backlands, were condensed in his fierce and extravagant mysticism" (118). If, then, Cunha succeeded in dispensing with the notion of monarchist conspiracy, he was nonetheless unable to see that the punitive expedition's crime had much wider implications. It may be argued that this criticism on my part is unjust because it relies on a reading of Conselheiro's manuscripts, which Cunha himself never consulted. I doubt, however, that such a reading would have significantly modified his conclusions because his interpretation of Conselheiro, who is taken as "an extraordinary case of intellectual degeneration" attacked by a "hereditary flaw," results from the entire arsenal of evolutionism, reinforced by readings of such figures as Lombroso and Maudsley. Moreover, in the condemnation of the backlander there weighed heavily the antireligious sentiment that Cunha shared with the progressive intellectuals of his time. Involved neither in hostility toward religion nor in the Bacamarte complex, Ataliba Nogueira gives us today a very different Conselheiro: "He does no miracles nor do his admiring followers ascribe the practice of miracles to him. He does not take over priestly functions, or medical ones, or pharmaceutical ones. He is not a witch doctor. He is not referred to as 'Good Jesus'. He does not present himself as God's messenger. He is not a prophet. He merely preaches the doctrines of the scriptures and of the Roman Catholic Church" (Nogueira, 8).

Only, "placing himself on the side of the poor and needy people, the despoiled and oppressed, Antônio Conselheiro calls down upon himself certain civil and religious authorities" (8-9). These are, to be sure, pieces of information of which Cunha was not unaware. He himself calls attention to the spite of the priests who felt themselves in competition with that figure. Commenting on the 1897 article by Nina Rodrigues, Sílvio Rabelo notes that there was, "in that negative outlook on Conselheiro's part toward the republican reforms, a reflex of the campaign that the Catholic clergy had directed, in and outside of the churches, against the regime in its incipient stages within the country" (Rabelo, 68-69). A casual acquaintance with his "sermons and speeches" would confirm that he was anything but unbalanced. His texts, directed to devotion and spiritual reflection, are surprising not only for use of a language that is almost always highly correct but also — and especially — for a conciseness that contrasts with the stylistic pyrotechnics emanating from the capital city. The morality that Conselheiro professed is as sober as his language. Let us look, for example, at what he wrote about adultery: "And thus let all women who wish to keep themselves virtuous in relation to God and at peace with their husbands not only flee from falling in so horrible a sin but also not give their husbands the slightest reason for doubt, for they often dissimulate with patience what they later carry out in passion, with reason" (in Nogueira, 139).

How can we presume that such words led to the "promiscuity [of an] unbridled hetaeraism" (Cunha, *Rebellion in the Backlands*, 150) that is denounced in *Os Sertões*? If, however, we peruse Conselheiro's sermons and pick at random a passage on which to concentrate — "If Mary was poor of goods of the earth while she lived in Judea, she returned to Egypt poorer yet: adding that the exile and deprivations were such that they gave an even greater test to the virtues of that most blessed soul" (Nogueira, 69) — how can we reconcile it with the notion of "sermons [that] were barbarous and terrifying," that led to a ludicrous and fearful impression, and that were delivered by a "buffoon maddened with a vision of the Apocalypse" (Cunha, *Rebellion in the Backlands*, 133)? Moreover, it was not the religious factor alone that was involved in Cunha's disdainful lack of comprehension. Collective use of land and goods seemed to him another form of regressive barbarism:

> They asked nothing of this life; and, for that reason, property with them took on the exaggerated form of the tribal collectivism of the Bedouins. Personal property was limited to movable objects and their individual huts; there was an absolute community of land, pastures, flocks, and herds, and the few cultivated products, the landlords receiving merely their quota, while the rest went to the "society." . . . Carried far enough, this self-enforced destitution led to the loss of those high moral qualities which for so long had been distilled in them by the patriarchal life of the backlands. (149-50)

In the final analysis, evolutionism was for Euclides da Cunha less a theory than a sort of solid barricade against whatever was repugnant to his ethnocentrism. There can be nothing strange about that conclusion, for I have noted that the cult of fact and of observation led Cunha and his contemporaries to misunderstand the very function of a theoretical framework. To conclude that observation renders the truth of an object to us makes us into mere objects of the working of our prejudices. Theory has ethical as well as other dimensions: it organizes abstractly the elements selected for observation, it creates limit conditions against the overflowing of common sense. Evolutionism took root so easily with us, however, for precisely the opposite reason. Beginning from a concept of qualitative differences among the human races, ones favoring the white race, it melded perfectly with two of our major preconceptions: that the white race is socially superior and that theory is merely the elegant accumulation of propositions that reveal themselves to be either narrow or foolish in practice. (This is our irrational and unconscious pragmatism.) Evolutionism was easily propagated because it kept us from having to think and act differently from how we had previously thought and acted. And the intellectuals were thus "whitened," even if they were Tapuia Indians, for their greater intellectual capacity gave them superiority over the others.

For all these reasons, even though Canudos was an object of revolt and pity for Cunha, it could never, in turn, have elicited any sympathy from him. Its leader was on a "mission of perversion"; his sermons were said to incorporate "a daring resort to Latin quotations"; family disorganization embodied "the promiscuity of an unbridled hetaeraism," collective land use represented a regression to "the exaggerated form of the tribal collectivism of the Bedouins," the settlement itself was a "monstrous *urbs*," an "aggregation of clay huts [which] was a good indication of the sinister *civitas* of the erring ones who built it," for "the houses were a gross parody of the ancient Roman dwelling" (144). Could these by any chance have been elements of fiction, as they did not represent the fruits of scientific observation?! Ethnocentrism occupies a vast intermediate area between Cunha's science and his literature, making the task of panegyrics quite difficult. Thus, whereas in the first part, description of the land permitted Cunha to sympathize with the humans of the region—a reaction underlying the expressionistic anthropomorphizing that we have pointed out—in the second part, "Man," the ethnocentric view originating from the civilization of coastal Brazilian society is presented. To the good fortune of Brazilian culture, ethnocentrism shrinks when Cunha looks about him and describes his own "white race." To begin with, the soldiers of the federal forces are also mestizos, who, on the third expedition when faced with the death of their commander-in-chief, actually allowed themselves to be invaded by the same fear attributed to the products of "regression":

But this very night the backlands conflict had begun to take on that mysterious aspect which it was to preserve until the end. The majority of the soldiers were mestizos, of the same racial stock as the backwoodsmen; and in their concern over the inexplicable defeat which they had suffered and the loss of their commander who had been reputed to be invincible, they readily fell victim to the power of suggestion and, seeing in it all an element of the marvelous and the supernatural, were filled with an unreasoning terror—a terror that was further increased by the extravagant stories that were going around. (269)

After this, the institutions of the legal nation become nothing more than a facade, the illusions of a "borrowed civilization." Cunha denounces the distance at which the national elite keeps itself, copying codes out of step with the state of the nation. That position would serve as the conduit for criticism of the military campaign, both the expeditions that ended in defeat and the ultimately victorious one, all described as using strategy and tactics inappropriate to the situation. If we consider the general lines of the critique, we can say that the inappropriateness of national institutions constitutes the second basic axis on which *Os Sertões* turns, the first being the Vendée metaphor. Being an explicit verbalization, that metaphor has a much wider use. The implicit metaphor of inappropriateness would be fed by the impasse into which the evolutionist explanation would progressively place itself.

Since the third part of the book, "The Rebellion," would thematize the collision of those two axes, let me formulate synthetically the interpretation carried out until now: that the Canudos rebellion made obvious the presence of two Brazils—one a coastal Brazil, apparently civilized, developing on the basis of a reflection of the cultured nations; the other, living in the interior, strong though tied to regressive forms of social life. In the light of those two antagonistic elements, pretended national unity was no more than a legalistic myth. When the southern press had interpreted Conselheiro's base as built on a monarchistic nucleus, it was merely endeavoring to establish a meaning that would make him comprehensible to the coastal people. It was, however, an arbitrary meaning. Euclides da Cunha's effort consists of replacing that meaning with another more adequate one that would also be assimilated by his contemporaries: that the backlanders were heroic, capable of a resistance that would end only with the literal death of the last of the combatants, for they had isolated themselves from the pernicious effects of miscegenation. But if their success implied a regressivistic disposition to forms of socialization unacceptable to those aware of higher forms, how could one go about forming a single nation? That question finds evolutionism in a state of perplexity. As the coast is not "white," that consideration cannot be made into a factor for the building of civilization. As the backlanders' isolation had been of value only to paralyze the federal troops but not to raise the backlanders themselves to the status of civilized citizens, to emphasize it would likewise not represent a solution. In the recounting of the struggle in the third and most exciting part of the book, two narrative levels recur: the first deals with the military undertaking proper; the second, more tragic, will end without answer, it being the search for a route to solution of the national dilemma. Through the following-out of the former, I shall explore facets of the latter.

Arriving in Canudos only at the end of the final expedition, Cunha nonetheless does not refrain from analyzing the preceding expeditions. For him, their failure resulted from underestimating the adversary and using battle tactics correct only for classical warfare fought on European terrain. In the case of Canudos, to the contrary, such tactics ran afoul of the mobility and great knowledge of the terrain that the backlanders possessed. The immediate solution would be, then, to adopt the very tactics of the enemy: "This is a formula which we ourselves should have followed under similar conditions. It was, without a doubt, a throwback to primitive warfare" (190).

It is an explanation that seems to put in peril the biological axiom on which the interpretation itself depends. If the form of "primitive war" employed by the backlanders correlated with the isolation through which they had preserved themselves from mestizo degeneration and also with environmental conditions, would its adoption by the biologically superior group not in effect serve to quash the very notion of that alleged superiority? In the final analysis, what good would advanced biological stock be if, to conquer, one had to retreat from it? The biological basis recedes from the front of the stage and gives primacy to mesological conditions. If he had been aware of that shift, or had admitted it, Cunha could have located himself much closer to the cultural definition of *isolat* and admit that it might be necessary to "imitate" the enemy's combat disposition because it possessed a culturally based superiority as regards the form of fighting. It was a culturally based counterbalancing factor that permitted Conselheiro's followers to compensate for their weakness in firepower, astonishing and decimating the invaders:

> On the heights, at a distance, along the back of the mountains the sertanejos now reappeared. There seemed to be two kinds of fighters in their ranks: those who ran swiftly up and down the roads, bobbing up and dropping out of sight from moment to moment, and those who remained stationed in their positions high up on the mountain. Taking advantage of these positions, they had an ingenious method of making up for the shortage of weapons and the time that it took to load the few they did possess. Forming groups of three or four about a single marksman, they sat in the bottom of the trench and, without being seen, passed the loaded weapons up to him. In this manner, if the marksman fell, one of the others was ready to take his place, and the attacking soldiers would see the same torso, apparently, rising up again

immediately, before the smoke had cleared away, and once more aiming a musket at them. (213)

But, like the generals who insisted on maintaining the deployment stipulated in manuals on tactics, Cunha resists changing his interpretive scheme. Of one of Conselheiro's lieutenants, he does not forbear to write:

They were commanded now by an unusually fierce mestizo whose bravery was unexcelled, Pajehú by name. A full-blooded cafuso, he was endowed with an impulsive temperament which combined the tendencies of the lower races from which he sprang. He was the full-blown type of primitive fighter, fierce, fearless, and naive, at once simple-minded and evil, brutal and infantile, valiant by instinct, a hero without being aware of the fact—in brief, a fine example of regressive atavism, with the retrograde form of a grim troglodyte, stalking upright here with the same intrepidity with which, ages ago, he had brandished a stone hatchet at the entrance to his cave. (220-21)

Thus, although the backlanders were not cut down by government barrages, they would be by the writer's verbal artillery. In fact, the composition of the federal troops helped to keep Cunha's biological sociology intact: the ill-fated Moreira César too had stopped at an evolutionary stage, he was epileptic and unbalanced (see 230). And, among the soldiers, he can point to the "backlanders batallion" of the Bahian police:

What these men were exhibiting was the primitive temperament of a race which, in the isolation of the uplands, had been unaffected by outside influences, and which now of a sudden was making its appearance with its original characteristics intact. Here was an interesting admixture of illogical attributes, with a charming ingenuousness, a loyalty carried to the point of sacrifice, and a heroism that could readily become barbarism, all inextricably intermingled. (297)

On both sides, therefore, lack of balance on the part of leaders and primitivism in the masses are ascendant. It is on the basis of that consideration that Cunha can recommend return to primitive war without feeling any necessity to review his biological premises. Even so, he does not pretend to pronounce the victory of its orienting thesis. When he speaks of it, as the many passages here transcribed amply testify, it is to ratify its correctness. But doubt persists, bespoken in particular by a heroism that Cunha cannot successfully explain. If, after all, the mestizos in the federal expeditions had "regressed" to primitive war and their superior firepower thus became even more advantageous, how could the backlander still hold out?

What did it matter that they had six thousand rifles and six thousand sabers; of what avail were the blows from twelve thousand arms, the tread of twenty thousand military boots, their six thousand revolvers and twenty cannon, their thousands upon thousands of grenades and shrapnel shells; of what avail were the executions and the conflagrations, the hunger and the thirst which they had inflicted upon the enemy; what they had achieved by ten months of fighting and one hundred days of incessant cannonading; of what profit to them those heaps of ruins, that picture no pen could portray of the demolished churches, or, finally, that clutter of broken images, fallen altars, shattered saints—and all this beneath a bright and tranquil sky which seemingly was quite unconcerned with it all, as they pursued their flaming ideal of religious belief of absolutely extinguishing a form of religious belief that was deeply rooted. (464)

And how was one to comprehend the fact that, at the end of the siege, there were no spoils of value found and not a single prisoner to take? "Canudos did not surrender. The only case of its kind in history, it held out to the last man. . . . It fell on October 5, toward dusk—when its last defenders fell, dying, every man of them" (475).

The evolutionist explanation still had some applicability to the question of the federal troops' ferocity, for, in an instance of semidefeat, the "single soldier's" inability to understand abstractions coming from their leadership allowed them to be galvanized by the "concrete" leaders who pushed them on by example. Among the backlanders, however, Conselheiro had already died, as had his bravest captains. The heroism on that side, then, was incomprehensible. Transformism had no means to explain it, for now not even familiarity with the environment would suffice as an answer. The besieged backlanders could be seen only as heroic, for they had nothing else to defend but their form of life, their social, political, economic, and domestic organization. Cunha, however, could not conceive of that. The most that he admits amounts to the aestheticizing of the old evolutionist line: "The legitimate pardo type predominated, a mixture of Kafir, Portuguese, and Tapuia Indian—bronzed faces, stiff and straight or curly hair, unshapely torsos. Here and there would be a profile with perfectly correct lines, pointing to the admixture of a higher racial element" (473).

Or, alternatively, he reaffirms it through rearticulation of the entire thesis, as in referring to one of the prisoners: "This lad was, of course, tremendously depraved; but he was a lesson to those who guard him, all the same. Here was a finished bandit, cast up by this backlands conflict, with a formidable legacy of errors resting upon his boyish shoulders" (408).

Or even, as in the passage in which he sets forth his vehement protest against the expedition:

As one came down the slopes and caught sight of the enormous bandit's den that was huddled there, he might well imagine that some obscure and bloody drama of the Stone Age was here taking place. The setting was sufficiently suggestive. The actors, on one side and the other, Negroes, caboclos, white and yellow skinned, bore on their countenances the indelible imprint of many races—races which could be united only upon the common plane of their lower and evil instincts. (444)

Because of their racial mixture, both sides were therefore destined to incite the rekindling of the basest instincts. Even though they were strangers to each other, the coastal people and the backlanders partook of the same stigma. Neither side understood the abstract form of government that directed it. Those who governed, in turn, copied what was organic for civilized peoples and thus distanced themselves from their own society. It was a thesis according to which the "authoritarian democracy" of the 1930s' New State would be legitimated (see Vianna, *O Idealismo na Constituição* [Idealism in the Constitution]). Without his recognition, admission, or confession, in Cunha national evolutionism reached a state of complete impasse. The people did not participate—indeed, could not—because it had not reached the level hypothesized by the legal structure. Cunha thus obliged the following generation to set out in search of another mode of interpretation of the nation. Even when its members discarded biological sociology, buried its Haeckels and Spencers, they would still start from a common factor: the proposition that national politics is a farce because the people do not understand its function except in the "primitive" modality of loyalty to local political bosses. Hence the *authoritarian* tradition according to which our political thought is constituted, both on the right and on the left (impulses which are to be distinguished only by their tendencies toward messianic or populistic authoritarianism, respectively). But we have now reached a circuit of inquiry that goes beyond our purposes. Let us, then, merely thematize the dramatic impasse with which *Rebellion* ends.

Os Sertões: Work of Literature?

It should hardly surprise us that, despite their sundry approaches, the most diverse critics of *Os Sertões* have referred to its content as "tragic." Indeed, such was the conclusion of Araripe Júnior's 1903 article. And Cunha touched similar chords in his later recollections of the geological formation of the region in question, from which he removes the imagery of paradise, to leave a calcinated land: "Even today, when in mid-summer one contemplates the strange nature of the North, especially in places where there suddenly start to be tablelands intermittently ringed with steep, sharp mountains, one is unsure whether he is treading upon the recently-emerged floor of some tertiary sea or upon an ancient jutting-up of the earth brutally scored by the elements" (Cunha, *Obras* 2:136).

Among more recent commentators, Olímpio de Sousa Andrade and Cavalcanti Proença reiterate that same categorization. The latter in fact goes so far as to compare the book to a Greek tragedy: "The hero is going to be wounded while in a state of innocence, there is no evil in the rebellion but rather only lack of comprehension. And that innocence increases the plot's tragic sense, for the forces of chance converge to crush the hero."[31]

In fact, along with admiration both for Cunha's language—with the expectable reservations always attached—and for his ability to see beyond what other "mere scientists" were able to see, this has been the primary gesture in consideration of *Os Sertões* as a work of literature. We should, then, ask "why does the force of language characterize literature?" Is it the case that verbal power, capacity to go beyond descriptive appearance, and discovery of condensing metaphors mark the province of literature? If we were to accept that proposition, we would have to say that Gibbon, Freud, Bergson, and other such figures are literary and, in the final analysis, agree with Searle that it is impossible "to give an analysis of literature" because "whether or not a work is literature is for the readers to decide."[32] Such would be the outcome because a stylistic criterion is a mere reiteration of the rhetorical characterization of belles-lettres, which, as I noted in chapter 1, sprang from the need to ground a conception of the poetic after validity had been denied to fictional discourse. Although the realm of the fictional is larger than the boundaries of literature—aside from film and comic strips, there is a day-to-day fictionality that is not to be confused with literature—there is not literature, in the strict sense of the term, where there is not fictionality. And, as we have already concluded in chapter 1, fiction is the result of a process in which mimesis is dominant. Now, this route allows us to arrive at a conclusion that is not arbitrary. In 1911, in the speech inaugurating Euclides da Cunha into the Brazilian Academy of Letters, Afrânio Peixoto stated that *Os Sertões* "is not a work of history, tactics, or geography, it is simply the book that tells of the *backlands' effect* on the soul of Euclides da Cunha" (*Poeira da Estrada*, 33).

That passage, cited in various conjunctures down to the present, leads us, however, to a point that has so far in this text remained obscure. We have seen from the foregoing analysis that that effect gives rise both to expressionistic anthropomorphism and to expression of civic prejudice fortified by the "theory" of evolutionism. The effect of something upon someone, however, has nothing directly to do with mimesis. That sort of effect has the much simpler name of "impression." To avoid repetition of what I have written both elsewhere and in chapter 1, let me observe simply that a set of impressions that are more than merely passive tends to precipitate a mimetic figure when it is organized around a specific and precise principle of selection. The child imitates superheroes when he or she organizes his or her impressions through the principle of superpower and then pushes himself or herself to eat more or to leap from dangerous heights. It must be added, however, that for mimesis to "grow up"—that is, for it to become expressively productive—the mimetizing object must elicit not only the indispensable element of the mimetized agent's identification but also that agent's own recognition—not necessarily a conscious recognition—of the *resistance* that is being presented to it: recognition of the mimetizing source's *difference*. If such does not take place, the product is a mere *reproduction*, a copy. We therefore can no longer speak only of a principle of mimetic selection in "The Man," for in that section of Cunha's work we often see the *reproduction* of ethnocentric prejudices in the confrontation with an other so different that the mimetizable agent—the author—rejects it and takes it as unorganized, unbalanced, and retrograde. Conditions propitious for mimetic organization are, then, concentrated in "The Land" and in "The Rebellion." In dealing with the former, we have emphasized the images of ruin and tragedy by means of which observation is *produced*. Decisive recognition of the role played by that mode of organization belongs to Antônio Cândido. In an article of some years ago, unfortunately no longer in print, the great critic explains:

> There is in it a "tragic" vision, so to speak, of social movements and of the relation between personality and environment—both physical and social. *"Tragic," in the Classical sense of agonistic vision in which human destiny seems directed from above.* . . . Such a vision is not to be confused with the mechanicism of many determinists of Euclides' time or previous to him. In Ratzel, or in Buckle, there is no tragedy: what there is is almost mechanical interplay between man and environment.[33]

That is, it is the tragic, agonistic sense of the land, by extrapolation from humankind—with the exclusion of the ethnocentric evaluations that give rise to both tragedy and impasse—that functions as the principle of selection for Cunha's mimesis. In that sense, it is legitimate to see a literary level in *Os Sertões*. *But it is a subordinate presence, for another form of tragedy, one having nothing to do with mimesis outweighs it.* It is to the tragedy of the impasse itself that explanation, unconfessedly, always reduces. Since the tragic-agonistic shares power with the tragic-of-impasse, or, better, since the former results from the organizing principle of the work whereas the latter derives from the fact that a given theoretical schema cannot adequately account for its object without in the process leading to another schema, it becomes improper to speak of *Os Sertões* as a work of fiction. As we have already remarked, mimesis is a process the final result of which is the fictional product. The presence of that product forces us to turn our attention to another of the "finite provinces" of the thematization of reality (Schütz). A work, then, cannot contain the double structure of discourse of reality and discourse of fiction. The boundaries between the two are, to be sure, sliding ones. And, to be sure as well, the reader can privilege one or the other the dominant or the subordinate. Did Borges not say, in jest, that metaphysics is no more than a branch of fantasy literature? He who accepts Borges's premise may not, however, simultaneously take metaphysical discourse as the interpreter of the essence of reality.

As a discourse of reality, *Os Sertões* is predominantly a sociological work. Those who fear that its place in history may be being lost with the eclipse of its guiding theory attempt to open the gates of literariness to it. But, if we consider them seriously, those gates are just as narrow as any others. Only fictional bodies can pass through. If, for Cunha's contemporaries and the subsequent generation, calling it a work of fiction amounted to an insult, for us to call it such today is synonymous with bad or displaced reading. Moreover, the very fear of the book's eclipse seems precipitous. What work of Brazilian sociology could be more contemporary than this one sharing the analyst's perplexity in confrontation with the task of interpreting his country? Perplexity is never comfortable, for it requires of those undergoing it that they not content themselves with set patterns. Moreover, all this does not suggest that the specialist in literature has no role in relation to *Os Sertões*. Very much to the contrary, in addition to enabling one to consider how the book's mimesis became dominated through an inverting of its own position—an exercise recently accomplished by Vargas Llosa in *La guerra del fin del mundo* [The War at the End of the World] (1981)[34]—it also allows it to be seen as the most radical product of a direction that we have seen begin its activity in the first decades of the nineteenth century. That fecundity seems to be compromised only if we insist on calling *Os Sertões* a work of literature or of fiction without setting out to attempt understanding of what in fact we mean when we use such language.

Chapter 5
Machado de Assis
and the Veto's Inversion

Machado de Assis is remarkably well known for a Portuguese-language writer. The translations of his work into English, German, French, and Spanish ensure him of a modest international renown, with no concessions being made to what is normally expected of a writer from the tropics. His second to last novel, *Esaú e Jacó* [Esau and Jacob] (1904), however, has not figured in that renown. Even in Brazil it is less celebrated than *Memórias Póstumas de Bras Cubas* (1881) [translated as *The Epitaph of a Small Winner*] and *Dom Casmurro* (1900). As this chapter will deal exclusively with that 1904 novel, it will be useful to recall something of its plot.

With the close of his career as a diplomat, the character Aires returns to Rio de Janeiro to enjoy his remaining years in an unhurried, worry-free manner, using the income from his former position. He is a childless widower, has played no great roles during his diplomatic life, and is destined for no great activity during his retirement either. Indeed, he would live the rest of his life in polite society, and, upon his death, as the author tells us in his preliminary "Advertência" [preface], a souvenir scrapbook and the narrative of the novel *Esaú e Jacó* were found among his effects.

In addition to our master of ceremonies, there are three salient characters in the novel: Flora and the twins Peter and Paul. Physically similar, equally educated and loved, the twins nonetheless quarrel from childhood on. When Aires is consulted on the matter, he gives evasive answers—which are, by the way, typical of him. When the twins go to secondary school, their differences take on a political character. While one of them is a monarchist and favors order, the other is a republican and a proponent of change. They agree on only one point: they court the same woman, Flora, who encourages both of them with seeming ingenuousness. Flora in fact does not comprehend the antagonism that the twins persist in manifesting and, when she is with one, mentally completes his image with the image of the other. Moreover, she recapitulates that lack of selectivity in her own person: she cultivates both painting and the piano, without definitively opting for either. Death, in fact, finds her in that situation: her life ends without her having ever made emotional or professional commitments. After Flora's death, the twins intensify their strife. As legislative deputies, they are bitter adversaries. The fall of the monarchy and advent of the republic does not change the situation. They simply change positions symmetrically: the republican becomes a monarchist and the ex-monarchist becomes the defender of republican order. For our purposes here, it is not important to see Aires as anything more than the neutral and impassive narrator of a minidrama that initially appears to reside at the level of the family. It will, however, be of interest to us to take Flora as our point of departure and to explore the relationship between her affective and professional indecisiveness and the character of sociopolitical institutions in Brazil in the second half of the nineteenth century. On the basis of that optic, we shall see how Machado dealt with the then loudly proclaimed paean to Brazilian nationality, the cult of observation, and the veto of fictionality.

To that end, I shall now discuss one of the instances of Flora's dual indecisiveness to illustrate their common motivation. I shall then link them to the political situation on which Machado was ironically and sinuously reflecting.

Flora and Affective Indecision

The dilemma within *Esaú and Jacó* about selection in a love relationship does not represent the first time in Machado's fiction that a female character faces that problem. It is in fact a recurring theme in prior stories. Let us note two: "A Parasita Azul" [The Blue Parasite] and "A Desejada das Gentes" [The People's Choice]. The first, from 1872, republished the following year in *Histórias da Meia-Noite* [Midnight Stories], is from before Machado's mature phase. The story is in itself of little importance for our purposes, but its relating of indecision in a love relationship to political concerns and also the kind of denouement it presents are central to this discussion.

The son of a Brazilian planter has exhausted the time of his stay in Paris and, with no other alternative left to him, has to return to his parental lands. He, a doctor, returns to his country, then, as though going into an exile, one indeed further accentuated by the fact that his memories of Paris will in no way be mitigated by the provincial city that was the Rio de Janeiro of that time. The uncomfortable trip on donkey-back, the tales of misfortune in love that his traveling companion tells, the silence of the stark land, and the birds' songs only increase his suffering and despair. As soon as he arrives home, however, the landscape is transformed: there appears a beautiful, if coy, woman, the daughter of another local farmer. She, however, flees from his every advance, as though knowing some indecipherable secret. The story is thence elaborated, at great length and some tedium, through appearances by a mysterious character, a premonitory dream, and a suicide attempt.

At one brief moment, however, another narrative possibility presents itself; Machado, however, is not yet able to avail himself of it. As though predicting the ambition that will characterize future female figures in Machado's work, the village priest explains to the doctor the probable reason for the young woman's evasiveness: "I suspect she's very ambitious; she has rejected Soares' advances. Let's see if she doesn't arrange some marriage that will open the door to political grandeur for her."[1]

As the subsequent development of the story shows, that hypothesis is substantially correct. In fact, the young woman is saving herself for an impossible love that she has retained for a young man who, years before, had acceded to her girlish caprices by risking his life to satisfy her request. That young man is Camilo himself, formerly of Paris, now a doctor, whom she nonetheless continually rejects because "immensely proud, she had resolved to marry neither him nor his rival" (Machado, 2:186). The young woman, whose name is Isabel, thus locates herself at a crossroads: she can be the "origin" either of such later characters as Sofia, Virgília, and Capitu, Machado's ambitious and deceitful female figures, or of the enigmatic Flora. The two passages have the value of showing how both themes are predicted in this early tale. Moreover, because Camilo's father has political ambitions for his doctor-son, there is the logical possibility of this story's being directed either toward the novel of dissimulated ambition or toward the novel of impossible choice. The solution on the part of the early, romantic Machado avoids both routes. Camilo renounces his political career — in favor of his rival to Isabel's hand — and she, hearing that the doctor almost committed suicide, relents in her pride and agrees to marry him.

Happiness does not seem to represent highly acceptable material for modern narrative. Machado, however, had not yet learned that fact. Camilo and Isabel's idyll proposes the surpassing of Paris's charm and the overcoming of the malice of Camilo's father. The narrative subordinates those quantities to that integration with the land that Brazilian romantics sought. The solution in favor of domesticity was, then, the first step in the search for national identity. The nostalgia for a society that was, if not merely imaginary, then at least conflated with an aristocratic Middle Ages, took root in Brazil as a longing for the nation and an attempt to rediscover it. Domestic happiness constituted a microcosm representative of a greater identification with the land. An abstract country was thus concretized through the description of its nature and of the emotions that it awakened; together they justified the absence of a thematization of the society itself.

Camilo's renunciation shows that complex well: the hearth is opposed to politics and ambition, and it saves the characters from the folly of dreaming of another land or of an impossible love. Machado may have been rescued from this line of thought, clearly formulated in "A Parasita Azul," by his incapacity for fluency and eloquence. His "stuttering style," as Sílvio Romero maliciously characterized it, kept him from remaining content with bucolic idylls of ex-Parisian doctors and beautiful farmers' daughters.

Despite being thus nondescript, the story contains the markers of the game that the later, mature Machado de Assis would construct for himself. The game itself, however, did not yet exist. Between Flaubert and Feydeau, so to speak, between *Madame Bovary* and *Fanny*, Machado, who made reference to both at the time, still resided in the Feydeau camp.

Our second story has a different function in this context. By the time he wrote "A Desejada das Gentes," Machado was indeed an accomplished writer. And the story's republication as a part of *Várias Historías* [Various Stories] (1896), puts it at a date comparable to that of the creation of Flora. Despite the temporal contiguity, however, the characters' similar problems result in divergent solutions. Just as had Isabel years before, Quintília had a considerable renown among young men for both her beauty and her inaccessibility. Because the story is narrated after Quintília's death, the narrator can construe himself as simultaneously the happiest and the most unfortunate of her pretenders. His long courtship of her would have ended in another total failure if Quintília herself, aware of the approach of her own death, had not accepted him *in extremis* as her husband. The tale, then, possesses all the features necessary for elaboration within a "normal" romantic form. But such is not the outcome. The explanation that the widower gives for his wife's conduct in fact explains very little: "I do not know what her physiology implies. My own, which is that of a profane being, senses that that young woman had a purely physical aversion to marriage" (511).

I shall not transcribe that explanation but undertake another one instead. I refer to "A Desejada das Gentes" only to indicate that there is in Machado a constant problem of impossible love, a problem that is not self-explanatory. In "A Parasita Azul," the treatment given to the narrative surrounds and resolves that problem by means of what René Girard calls a *mensonge romantique* [romantic lie]. In "A Desejada das Gentes," the problem may perhaps be understandable in terms of female hysteria. Because, in the tropical Victorian society in question, woman has no function other than to dress up the home, she either feigns domestication and becomes an adroit dissimulator—as is the case with Machado's gallery of great female characters—or she pretends to spurn men. In fact, however, she hopes to be convinced to return to the role of slave—as in Alencar's *Senhora*—or she reverses roles and becomes violent and arbitrary with men, reducing her husband to the status of "adornment of the home"—as in Oliveira Paiva's *D. Guidinha do Poço* [Dona Guidinha of Poço]—or, finally, she becomes evasive and seductive—as does Quintília. Flora is not to be identified with this last solution only because, in *Esau and Jacob*, Machado combines it with two other themes: the theme of the lack of a political alternative and the theme of the absence, in this society, of space for the "professional" practice of fictional material.

I am not sure, in fact, if the hysteria thesis is arguable with regard to Quintília. I mention it here only to point out that the interpretive solution we shall explore in relation to Flora becomes a viable one because in *Esau and Jacob* the theme of the female with a phobia about erotic-matrimonial relations has combined with other themes. In Machado, in other words, female hysteria corresponds to the "navel" that Freud attributed to all dreams:

> There is often a passage in even the most thoroughly interpreted dream which has to be left obscure; this is because we become aware during the work of interpretation that at that point there is a tangle of dream-thoughts which cannot be unravelled and which moreover adds nothing to our knowledge of the content of the dream. This is the dream's navel, the spot where it reaches down into the unknown [*Dies ist dann der Nabel des Traums, die Stelle, an der er dem Unerkannten aufsitzt*].[2]

I shall now examine the elements with which Flora's affective indecision combines—which is to say, I shall determine along what lines we should let ourselves be led to keep in touch with the "navel" without surpassing it.

The False Distinction between the Twins

It is not my purpose to ask what politics meant for Machado de Assis. The question, however, is indispensable as the guiding horizon for interpretation of the twins Pedro and Paulo. Faced with the question, I can do no more than reduce it to dimensions usable here. My task is made easier by the fact that research into Machado's fiction provides univocal data, so univocal in fact that I can limit myself to reference to a very few passages.

In "Miss Dollar," one of the *Contos Fluminenses* [Rio Stories] (1870), one character, finding his friend pouring over books, "asked him if he was studying to be a deputy. Jorge really thought that he was studying to be a deputy!" (Machado, 2:39). It does not take great attention to understand the exclamation's irony: Machado's deputies do in fact consult written works—less, however, to study them than to extract thunderous quotes.

In a different story, we find another character, Menezes of "A Mulher de Preto" [The Woman in Black] (1868). Asked why he had become a deputy, he replies: "I both am a politician and am not one. I didn't go into public life by vocation; I went in much as one enters a tomb: to sleep better" (2:78).

Machado's politicians are not usually driven by any serious commitment whatsoever. Nevertheless, despite Menezes's weariness, a position in the legislature is something that sharpens ambitions. Let us look to the reactions of a former provincial president: "As they were speaking of a Minister's wife, it occurred to Sophia to be pleasant to the ex-President, so she told him that he too should marry since he would soon be in the Ministry. Viçoso gave a shiver of pleasure at the remark, smiled, and protested that that would not happen; then, with his eyes on Mariana, he remarked that he would probably never marry" (2:408).

Politics is an activity that signifies a worthy occupation, as the father of our aforementioned Camilo well understood: "One who has lived in those lands which are said to be so pretty and animated cannot be wholly happy here. It is necessary to have some occupation for him . . . politics, for example" (2:171).

And it is an activity abandoned only when the deputy finds that he will not go far in it—like Luís Tinoco of "Aurora Sem Día" [Dawn without a Day]—or when his career is intercepted by an inheritance, as in "Pílades e Orestes" [Pylades and Orestes]: "Quintanilha, rather than pursuing a legal or judiciary career, became involved in politics. Yet after serving his term as a member of the Chamber of Deputies, he abandoned his career, for he had inherited an uncle's estate, which brought him nearly thirty thousand dollars."[3]

In short, for Machado, politics is an activity as important as it is ornamental. From any point of view, however, the politician does not see himself as the representative of actual social interests. That statement—absolutely redundant though it may be for anyone aware of Brazilian political history—is important in that it casts light on Flora's dilemma. She in fact does not distinguish between the twins because they are indistinguishable from each other. They quarrel about everything and nothing because their society requires them to trade their great similarity for a difference that will mark them as individuals.[4] In quarreling, in taking up opposite positions, they convince themselves of their "difference" (in the dual sense of the word) and convince everyone else as well—except Flora. Aires, faithful to his position as "unreliable narrator" (Wayne Booth), weighs us down with evasions. Or rather, if Quintília was hysterical and gave in to marriage only at the approach of certain death, Flora's problematic takes on another dimension, for her problem in choosing is now explained by there being no real choice to make. The second part of this chapter will show that the analysis of political institutions under the empire emphasizes the accuracy of Machado's observation. Our undertaking will, however, not end there. The character's affective indecision is reduplicated in another sphere: Flora is also unable to opt for only one of the art forms that attract her. Does that pattern describe a mere element of plot or, inversely, the node of a reflection that we should explore? To enter into the problematic, we must also enlist the evidence of the variants that bear upon the issue.

Flora's Indecision with Respect to the Arts

Just as has happened in the two areas examined above, Flora's indecision is better illustrated if we look at the prior varieties of the question in Machado's work. In all three cases—Flora's affective indecision, the lack of differentiation between the twins, and Flora's professional indecisiveness—the investigator must establish the *corpus* of variants that will permit him or her to formulate, to rectify, and, in sum, to control his or her hypotheses. In the present case, the primary variants are well known: "Cantiga de Esponsais" [Betrothal Song], originally published in 1883 and included in the following year in *Histórias Sem Data* [Stories without Date] and "Um Homem Célebre" [A Celebrity], later included in *Varías Histórias*. The stories' main characters, Mestre Romão and Pestana, have in common the fact that they are frustrated musicians. Thus what the first narrative tells us of Pestana would be true of Romão as well: "He had an intimate vocation for music; he carried around inside him many operas and masses, a world of new and original harmonies, which he was never able to express and put down on paper" (Machado, 2:387).

As the story shows, his sterility seems to have no cause other than cruel nature itself, which, in his case, being greedy with regard to the very notes that he would like to put together, nonetheless delivers them up to the effortless voice of his young wife:

> Desperate, he left the clavichord, grabbed the paper, and tore it up. At that moment, the young lady, caught up in her husband's stare, began to hum randomly, unconsciously, a melody never before sung or even heard, in which one "la" brought with it an entire beautiful musical phrase of just the sort that Mestre Romão had been seeking for years with no result whatsoever. He listened to her sadly, shook his head, and that night expired. (2:389-90)

The story would not seem to be a variant of Flora's indecisiveness if we could not group it with "A Celebrity." Pestana suffers from the same problem as does Mestre Romão. Nevertheless, his is a specific kind of sterility: from his pen come only polkas, popular pieces that make him famous for a music that falls short of his own ambitions: "She slept to the tune of the polka, which she knew by heart, while its author was thinking of neither the polka nor the girl but of the old classical works. He questioned the heavens and the night, begging the angels and the devil himself. Why couldn't he compose just one such immortal page?" (Machado, *The Devil's Church and Other Stories*, 109).

Mere nature cannot be blamed for *this* failure. Another element is involved: the society that nourishes Pestana is satisfied with the service that he gives it. It is only he who judges that service to be inferior. Despite the change of gender in our characters, then, the problem of the impossible reappears. What was an impossible love for a woman becomes for a man the impossibility of a path to a "marriage" that is desired but not realized: the marriage of his name with an unrivaled composition. It should be noted too that Pestana's musical sterility is linked to a political allusion. Since his very clever editor has had the task of giving his polkas names that allude to momentous events, Pestana, near death, gives that editor two new polkas, one dedicated to each of the two political parties that have been alternating in power: " 'Look','' said Pestana, 'since it's quite likely that I'm going to die any day now, I'll make you two polkas right away — the other can be used when the liberals come to power again''' (115).

It is as though the composer had said: "Since this party is the same as that one, my same style can celebrate them both," perhaps adding: "Since society uses me only to keep the seats filled, a polka for the conservatives is just the same as one for the liberals." What, then, is missing in Mestre Romão and Pestana? The equivalent of a Grub Street which, employing artists and writers in eighteenth-century London, made it necessary that they come up with a varied production, one capable of reaching the most varied of tastes:

> By the beginning of the eighteenth century, the booksellers, especially
> those in London, had achieved a financial standing, a social
> prominence, and a literary importance considerably greater than that of
> either their forebears or of their counterparts abroad. . . . Together with
> some of the printers they owned or controlled all the main channels of
> opinion, newspapers, magazines and critical reviews, and were thus
> well placed to secure advertising and favourable reviewing for their
> wares.[5]

With the market established, competition would attract varied talents which, at the same time, would mold their productions to the various interests that they served. Thus the rise of the novel, favored over the other genres because of "the amount of attention it habitually accords both to the individualisation of its characters and to the detailed presentation of their environment" (Watt, 18). Of the many who depended on the booksellers, few would become famous like a Richardson or a Defoe. But the basic structure within which to seek such fame was laid down. To be sure, it did not correct nature, giving talent to people who did not possess it, but it did increase the number of players, increasing as well the possibility of felicitous combinations. Now, Romão and Pestana would know no equivalent to the market situation, even though the story of the latter shows him linked not to a patron but to an editor. In what conditions did they find themselves? They could count on a small public that was content to consume facile pieces and works written in a flowing language, productions bathed in rhetoric and nativism:

Writer and public defined each other here around two characteristics that were decisive for the general configuration of literature: rhetoric and nativism, joined within the Romantic movement after a prior development. . . . Even today, *local color*, exhibition of emotion, descriptive picturesqueness, and eloquence are more or less pressing requirements, showing that the man of letters has been accepted as a citizen disposed to *speak* to the groups.[6]

Literature, and art in general, was as ornamental from the point of view of the real public as politics was unrepresentative of the interests of social groups. Hence the absence of a reading public and the absence of a public opinion were failings to be found at the core of the problem both of artistic sterility and of the unrepresentativeness of the imperial political elite. That homology seeks only to point out that the problem underlying the lineage of Romão-Pestana-Flora is not grounded in a fantastic and idiosyncratic aspiration but, to the contrary, comes as a response to a sociomaterial lack. With that point made, we can join the foregoing three partial developments and direct them to the elucidation of Flora's dilemma.

* * *

It is now all but redundant to write that in the novel *Esau and Jacob*, which has deceived its interpreters to the extent that one of them has praised it by calling it an "entertainment" (Barreto Filho), Machado condenses in the figure of Flora two decisive issues: the impossibility of choice between the existing parties—and it should be noted that it is not the classical parties of the empire that are being dealt with but rather what the empire defended and what a new regime proposed—and the absence of employment for the artistic creator. It should be reiterated, however, that that linking does not exhaust the problematic that Flora represents. Quintília is the point of excedence. Through Flora and the thematization of emotional choice linked to politics, Machado profiles the question of female hysteria and deploys it in a textual schema open to interpretation.

I will now turn to the findings of some sociological studies of Brazilian society and see how much they clarify and reiterate what analysis of the novel itself has provided.

* * *

Since the publication of Raymundo Faoro's *Os Donos do Poder* [The Owners of Power] (first edition, 1957),[7] it has been claimed that it is not the concept of class but rather the concepts of estate and of patrimoniality that are decisive for an understanding of the character of the Brazilian state and of Brazilian political organization. More recent studies have, however, partially rectified that conclusion.[8] Instead of a purely class or a purely estate state, those studies indicate a mixed one: decidedly not one representative of a dominant class but likewise not one formed by a pure estate grouping. The latter analysis seems impossible to those who have carried out that recent work because the state could not forego the income from the only substantial economic activity of the era: export agriculture. As a result, the mechanism of cooptation of the rural landowners was used, which, in the absence of a market, gave rise to a clientelistic politics: "Whatever may have been the degree of government centralization in all those periods, at no time was the state capable of effective governance without establishing agreements with private groups so that it could count on their cooperation. The central government was acutely conscious of the fragile limits of its authority and of the legal order that it had been able to institute" (Uricoechea, 112).

To that observation let us add one by another investigator: "The problem of the excess of college graduates generated the phenomenon, frequently mentioned in the era, of the desperate search for public employment for those graduates without occupations, which reinforced the clientelistic character of the imperial bureaucracy" (Carvalho, 71).

That state mechanism, favoring graduates as a group, came to favor the man of letters as well, among whom, of course, was Machado de Assis. Thus, in dealing with the "republic of letters" in the period from 1870 to 1930, Machado Neto found, for a set of sixty intellectuals, forty-eight cases of writers who were public functionaries: "Public functionarism, including the bulk of those who went into teaching, was responsible for the subsistence of our intellectuals."[9]

Thus do we see confirmed a factor fundamental to the nature of Brazilian literature: it circulates in a state served by politically unrepresentative elites, and this state also serves as the patron of writers. In both regards, unrepresentativeness and patronage, the same absence is projected: the absence of a participating public. From this very point derive the lack of editions of works and the lack of stimulus to the constitution of an authentic intellectual system. On the first issue, Olavo Bilac's observation is indicative:

> In the statement by the manager of the house of Garnier to the author of the article we can see that, of all of the books—and there were many— edited by that house, only *two* had *an edition* sold out *in a little more than a year*: a novel and a book of poems. For one who knows that Garnier always ran between 2,000 and 2,200 copies and that their books were not sold exclusively in Rio de Janeiro but rather throughout Brazil—eighteen million inhabitants—that statement . . . can only . . . justify the apprehensions of those who, like I, live pointing to illiteracy as the principal—perhaps only—cause of our backwardness. (In A. L. Machado Neto, 120)

Hence the paradoxical fact bitterly noted by José Veríssimo: "In books I think that there is in Brazil the freedom for us to say what we want, because books, seldom read, have no effects in our milieu."[10]

Once again, what is good for the writer is also good for the state. In his classical work, *Instituições Políticas Brasileiras* [Brazilian Political Institutions], Oliveira Vianna has written: "The State is conceived of as a structure foreign to society, fitted to it, coming from above as though by divine right, and not emanating from it, partaking of its material and spiritual conditions, living the life of its 'culture', and feeling the influence of its transformations."[11]

This gap between the state and the nation was replicated between the writer and the public. In an aesthetic conception of literature, such a correlation would be laughable. And in the final analysis, it did not hinder Machado de Assis, Euclides da Cunha, and Manuel Antônio de Almeida from writing, just as in the first half of this century it did not prevent writer-functionaries from achieving greatness—Carlos Drummond de Andrade, João Cabral de Melo Neto, and João Guimarães Rosa. But such is the tributary outlook of the hypernationalist who justifies the losses as a function of the exceptional names, which are then enlisted for perpetuation as originary myths. What is important is to insist that the very social conditions that prevented the separation between public and private and the formation of a state run according to modern rationality—bourgeois in origin—has also impeded the formation of an intellectual system and that that statement is not countered by a few exceptional names. The previously cited Machado de Assis passage on politics is not to be explained only by a pessimism that he learned to cultivate by a reading of Montaigne and Pascal. The farmer-parents want to give their illustrious offspring an equally illustrious occupation, ambitious graduates want to have paths open to them, or at least to rest their boredom in a respectable situation. For all of them, the solution is election to a deputyship. That is, as Habermas would say, there is no *public space* to be filled by representatives of social class and group interests. Hence the occupying of a public space does not imply its separation from private space. As Uricoechea writes with respect to the nineteenth century:

The institutionalization of a legal order bureaucratically administered by the State was made even more difficult by the weak differentiation between public and private. The notion that the society as body politic could be subjected to an objective system of norms different from those that coordinate and guide the actions of its individual members in the private sphere was certainly retarded by the patrimonial representation of the political community. . . . The abstract rational notion that the political rights of the society as institutional order arise from the private rights of its individual parts while not being identical to them was a representation repulsive for the dominant patrimonial normativity. (Uricoechea, 274)

Even today, matters do not seem modally different.[12] The lack of distinction between public and private sectors does, however, relate to the character of the political parties during the empire. We have seen in *Esau and Jacob* that Flora was unable to choose between Pedro and Paulo because she found no essential difference between the two inimical brothers. Was that novelistic element articulated with regard to a real basis? We cannot review here the long bibliography on the programs of the imperial political parties. Let us accept the judgment of Murilo de Carvalho that they were not mere markers without difference:

> The landowners who were linked to the Conservative Party tended to belong to the areas of agricultural production geared to exportation and to the areas of oldest settlement, such as Pernambuco, Bahia, and, principally, Rio de Janeiro. These groups had the most interests in national politics and in the stability of the system. They were thus more easily disposed to support of measures favorable to the strengthening of central power. The landowners linked to the Liberal Party came more frequently from areas like Minas Gerais, São Paulo, and Rio Grande do Sul, with fewer interests in centralization and in order at the national level. (Carvalho, 165-66)

Although there were, then, differences of interest in the two parties' composition, they had in common their formation by persons linked to the agricultural export sector of society. Their conflicts derived, then, from "fissures within the elite" that did not involve the possibility of radical disruption: "By the very fact that the elite was linked to the State and by the fact that it came primarily from sectors of the dominant class, the conflicts to which divergences gave rise were of a limited nature" (179).

To be sure, it should not be inferred from the foregoing that the state in question is a static one, refractory to all change and attentive only to guarding against the murmurings of masses that might suddenly assault it. Neither the stasis nor the possibility of assault were the actual case. Of the latter hypothesis, Carvalho has stated:

> The fulcrum of stability in the imperial system . . . implied, on the one hand, a basic conservatism, in that the price of legitimacy was a guaranteeing of the basic interests of the large landholders and a reduction of the sphere of legitimate political participation. But, on the other hand, it permitted a dynamics of political coalitions capable of implementing reforms that would have been inviable in a situation in which there was total domination by rural landholders. (39)

Flora's love-relation dilemma, then, rested on a social base prior to the text itself. She did not find the twins indistinguishable because of a personal inability to discriminate; the social base functioned as a *contextual sensitizer* that "oriented" her response. The same can be said of her professional indecision and consequent artistic sterility. It should be emphasized, however, that the form of interpretation proposed here has no tie whatsoever to a reflection theory. Machado intuits that his society prohibits the exercise of serious fiction—that is, fiction far removed from what would be constituted by a perceptual or documentary basis. The conditioning caused by the absence of a public and the presence of a necessarily clientelistic state, in addition to the cult of observation and documentarism that, as we have seen, has marked our tradition from romanticism on, led to a fiction that either was light and superficial or sought to occult its fictional nature. Because of the lack of a better evaluation of the problem, our culture still distills a strong veto of fiction today. Hence the vogue of novels about customs, poetry that locates its justification in eloquence—in fluid sentimentality, in indignation based on genuine feelings—and, more recently, novels of reportage. The writer remains riveted to the external reality of facts or to the internal reality of sentiments, to hide the stigma of fiction. (This observation could generally be extended to our cinema as well.)

I shall now limit the scope to consolidation of this concept in consideration of Machado de Assis's relations with realism. I stated that the romantic Machado opted for Feydeau over Flaubert. That choice, later reversed, is a key one in understanding what I have called the production of fiction.

* * *

In the years following the publication of *Madame Bovary* (1857) and *Fanny* (1858), criticism linked them to the same literary school. Thus, commenting on the success of the two novels' sales in England, the long-forgotten Neulsort ironically remarked: "Oh purity of spring mornings, oh candor of British virtue, what tempest in your country, in your hearts must these two offensive boreal figures named Flaubert and Feydeau unleash."[13]

Nevertheless, in his celebrated review of *Fanny*, Émile Montégut not only captures that novel's weakness but also differentiates its technique from Flaubert's: "What they—i.e., Roger and Fanny—take as passions are very real vices, very positive concupiscences dressed in Romantic tinsel, in poetic rags, in remnants carried along in all literature for the past fifty years. *Open a modern novel and there you will always find this useless effort to poetize vice, taken seriously, as in* Fanny, *or parodied, as in* Madame Bovary."[14]

The opposition between seriousness and parody in the poetization of vice is all the more relevant because Montégut shows no greater sympathy for Flaubert. The critic's analysis serves us as point of departure from which to see the key terms in which Flaubert's novel was received in its time. Even before its publication, Duranty had accused *Madame Bovary* of being "an application of the calculation of probabilities," a defect made all the more inexcusable because "a great deal of study still does not replace the spontaneity that comes from sentiment'' (quoted in Dumesnil, cxlviii).

On 25 April 1857, Sainte-Beuve, in a letter to Flaubert, after the expectable formulaic praise, observed: ''I would also have liked, while not knowing how it might have entered into your composition, to see some figure with sentiments that were gentle, pure, deep, and contained, while true. That would have calmed me. That would have proclaimed that there is good will, even in the realm of the evil and the animal'' (quoted in Dumesnil, clv). Curiously, Sainte-Beuve's terms are very similar to those in Veríssimo's wish about *Dom Casmurro*: ''If criticism has the right to formulate a desire, I would like it if, even if it meant not completing the trilogy with *Brás Cubas* and *Quincas Borba* that many expect, the writer finished that evolution—which this last work may perhaps imply— with a more compassionate, if not more human, way of conceiving of life and gave us, as he did with those two admirable books, an entirely new work'' (Veríssimo, 36).

The strength of the reader's irritation at that lack of idealism is obvious in the ferocious criticism by Tony Révillon: This book ''is a pamphlet against humanity written by a skeptic who makes virtue a matter of temperament'' (quoted in Dumesnil, clxxvi).

Moral indignation combines in turn with a criticism of coldness in Dumesnil's article of 3 May 1857: ''One in fact senses, in the manner of Mr. Flaubert, the surgeon beneath the critic; that is betrayed in the care given in the details and in the uncompensated crudeness of certain pictures'' (clx).

The argument returns under other authorship. In that of Sainte-Beuve—''Son and brother of distinguished physicians, Mr. Gustave Flaubert uses his pen like a scalpel'' (quoted in Dumesnil, clx); in that of León Aubinet: ''Art ceases the moment it is invaded by filth. What is treated is the story of a woman who falls from the noble and sacred state of marriage, which she has embarrassed through a sentiment that the author, in medical style, defines as 'an irritation caused by the presence of the man who sought her hand', into the lowest shame of wantonness'' (quoted in Dumesnil, clxx). The moral argument, however, remains offstage when J. Habans, on 28 July 1857, dissects Flaubert's style: ''The book's weakness lies in the fact that Mr. Flaubert is not a writer. The style is sometimes uncertain, incorrect, and vulgar; his school would represent the invasion of language by the daguerreotype under the pretext of naturalness and preciseness'' (quoted in Dumesnil, clxxii).

I leave it to the reader's initiative to recall the details of Sílvio Romero's and José Veríssimo's remarks on Machado's style. The former enlists stylistic virtues that are not Machado's own: ''Imagination either fantastic or representative or descriptive; emotion profound, spontaneous, original; form facile and natural.''[15] Veríssimo is even more direct: ''To be perfect, his language lacks only

polish, eloquence, color, albeit only the showy, which so pleases our still unrefined taste."[16]

It is clear from such attestations that, in the very year of *Madame Bovary's*
publication, the critics loudly attributed failings to it under two categories: attack
on morality and attack on art. The only exception that I know of comes from
Barbey d'Aurevilly, who employs an industrial metaphor to speak of the innovative character of the title he is reviewing: "If, in Birmingham or Manchester,
there were forged, from good English steel, narrating machines that would run
by themselves or through unknown dynamic procedures, they would work just
like Mr. Flaubert" (quoted in Dumesnil, clxxiii-clxxxiv).

Aside from the moral argument, which would condemn both writers, the comparison between Flaubert and Feydeau rests on the reception of style. If we take
into account the popularity that *Fanny* enjoyed at the time, despite not having
the advantage of the trial that aided its rival, we can conclude that that popularity resulted from exactly what Flaubert rejected: the "mediocre ragout of sentimentality," the "romanesque tinsel," the "poetic scraps" that Montégut remarked on so precisely. Is it mere coincidence that the terms of Machado's
reception are so similar? That coincidence is even more curious because Machado
never stirred up the clamor that Flaubert did with the story of Emma Bovary.
There is, however, no gainsaying the similarity in the reactions. By the standards of modernity, a work, to be recognized as fictional, besides being composed of quasi statements—that is, utterances the truth or falsity of which cannot
be determined—must have those utterances clash with, even irritate, the receiver's expectations. (That requirement is, of course, conditioned in turn by the very
posture of modern art with respect to established values.) Because Machado de
Assis lived in a provincial environment under a clientelistic state, he had to
develop a technique of which Flaubert would have had no need, a technique that
I have called narrative in palimpsest—a narrative formed of two levels, one
apparently consistent but hiding with visible ink the critical virulence deposited
in the other, hidden level. Thus recourse to sociopolitical institutions in interpretation of Machado's novel has not led us to a reflexological explanation. Fictional production locates itself between the institutions of reality and fictional
realization. Moreover, lest I seem to speak of it in the abstract, there is a route
to concretization: the examination of how that production was received by its
readers. That examination, however, should not be made absolute so that we do
not limit ourselves to a sociology of readership. As I do not propose such an
approach here, the reader's reaction must lead us back to the text and permit us
to see more clearly its similarities and differences with regard to other texts. Such
has been my procedure in relation to Machado and Flaubert, in which I simultaneously showed the mark of modernity that they have in common and the difference that surrounds Machado's specific modernity, which is translated into the
necessity of the palimpsest.

In summary, I have endeavored to show that Flora's dilemma has its roots in the sociopolitical institutions of the Brazil of the era; that nonetheless that articulation does not authorize a view of that dilemma as a reflexion of social reality, for it is not a document of that reality but instead is elucidated precisely in the moving of that reality toward the fictional. Moreover, I have shown that, in terms of modernity, that process is characterized by the breaking of the reader's "horizons of expectation" (Mannheim). I, then, emphasize the temporal dimension of that fictionality: because it developed in harmony with the reader's expectations, it could be accepted as the beautiful falsehood that Renaissance thinkers spoke of (see chap. 1). By the middle of the nineteenth century, however, such is no longer possible. Through critics, when not through tribunals, society protests attacks against its moral and aesthetic codes. To call a style "medical," to accuse a writer of proceeding with the procedure of calculation and the scalpel, is to insist that he or she does not correspond to the quest for lyricism, emotion, and color. Machado, astutely, found an escape, although he was thus seen as cold, cerebral, and nonnational. But did he really escape, or has he simply been misunderstood? No matter which is the correct answer, the fact is that by depositing his caustic fiction on the undersurface of the palimpsest, he inverted the terms in which fiction was related to history in his time: instead of making the former subject to the path of the latter, he made historicopolitical material the source of fiction's unfolding and radicalization.

Afterword: Can the Imagination be Mimetic under Conditions of Modernity?

Jochen Schulte-Sasse

I

When one writes about the role of the imagination in the history of ideas, it is surely important to consult the rich history of that concept since Plato and Aristotle.[1] At first glance, the tradition of the concept seems to be rather uniform and coherent. Nevertheless, radical social and material changes in the history of the Western world profoundly changed the conception of the imagination and, presumably, the imagination itself. There can be no doubt that concerns about the status of the imagination in human culture have gained a new urgency since the eighteenth century and that theoreticians from Addison and Bodmer to Duff, Gerard, Kant, Schlegel, and Coleridge began to rethink the conception of the imagination at a time when the status of the human imagination within the broader context of socio-cultural formations began to change. As I will argue in more detail, there exists a simple reason for this development: The eighteenth century was characterized by an intense reaction toward the process of modernization and its manifold forms of social differentiation, psychological splitting, and divisions of labor.

A dominant feature of this reaction is that more often than not the imagination is seen as a redemptive counterforce vis-à-vis modern civilization. Ever since the late eighteenth century, the imagination has been hailed as a savior from the perils of modern civilization. In the historical avant-garde of the 1920s, it was considered the only human power that "can in no sense be domesticated."[2] But not only artists have tried to valorize the imagination as a critical and redemptive force; numerous philosophers and sociologists have placed a rethinking of the imagination at the center of their rethinking of the dialectic of enlightenment.[3] In many ways, Luiz Costa Lima's book belongs to this tradition. Costa Lima joins forces with those who want to liberate the imagination from restrictions that have been imposed upon it since the beginning of modern civilization. His declared intent is to turn a rethinking of the control that historically took hold of the imagination into a liberating reflective force that might allow us to reappropriate the imagination's critical potential. However, when Costa Lima claims that, "from the beginning of modern times, fictional texts have been subjected to either explicit or hidden forms of taming or control" (p. vii), he postulates a taming of the imagination that took control long before the turning point of the eighteenth century. According to Costa Lima, the Aristotelian tradition of a mimetic (rather than imitative) imagination was suppressed ever since the Renaissance, if not earlier.

Is the question whether the turning point took place in the Renaissance or the eighteenth century a superficial one—one that concerns (always questionable) methods of periodization alone? I do not think so—at least not if historical change has had any effect on the constitution of human subjectivity. If the constitution of subjectivity changes under conditions of modernity, then this change must necessarily affect the human imagination. Costa Lima does not directly address the question of how historical changes have affected the constitution of subjectivity. Implicitly, however, he asserts that a self-constitution of subjectivity is still possible under conditions of modernity. This becomes clear when he connects the issue of imagination under conditions of modernity with the issue of mimesis, and when he contends that the imagination is an indispensable mimetic faculty. However, if one holds that the imagination, by mimeticly appropriating reality, mediates between a subject and his or her environment, one must simultaneously hold that the possibility of a self-constitution of subjectivity remains possible even under conditions of modernity. Only on the basis of such a premise can Costa Lima argue that a mimetic imagination, as an innovative and independent force vis-à-vis the conditioning powers of civilization, is able to create artistic figurations that serve as testing grounds for cognitive appropriations of reality. The historical and the theoretical question thus prove to be two sides of the same coin. If one can indeed convincingly argue that historical changes in the process of civilization did not effect the possibility of a mimetic function of the arts, it is much easier to argue in favor of such a function under current conditions.

Costa Lima's defense of the fundamentally mimetic nature of art comes at a time when the conditions for the possibility of resistance, of agency, of subjectivity have been subjected to intense theoretical scrutiny. The two issues are intimately connected. Only if art, as an autonomous institution, can resist the conditioning powers of civilization, only if subjects are able to constitute themselves as historical agents and only if individuals, as historical agents, can appropriate the arts as a medium of resistance does it make sense to claim that the arts are fundamentally mimetic. Costa Lima's book might be considered important and timely simply because it reflects anew upon the possibility and (the supposedly repressed) history of an imaginative mimesis as an autonomous aesthetic realm of simulation. Yet the single most important question after reading this very learned book is still: Is it true that the aesthetic realm continues to offer a medium for working through our experiences and for testing the impact of norms and values within a fictional configuration of human behavior?

Following the critical tradition of fore-and afterwords in this series, I will not elaborate upon the many strengths of Costa Lima's study. They should be obvious. I will instead concentrate on the two aspects of his study that, in my view, are in the greatest need of critical scrutiny: his attempt to downplay the radically different nature of a control of the imagination in premodern and in modern times—an argumentative strategy that effects the author's assessment of imagination's potential in the present—and his notion of a *mimetic* imagination. If the question whether contemporary art still can and should be perceived as mimetic can be answered at all, it is only on the basis of a sociohistorical analysis of the diverse interests that sustain the manifold forms of a control of the fictional throughout history.

II

The two questions that I have directed against Costa Lima's book could be countered with two questions concerning my initial contention: is it really correct to perceive the eighteenth century as a turning point in the history of the imagination? And can we correctly separate a premodern from a modern conception of the imagination, again using the eighteenth century as a turning point? Historical changes take place slowly. In the long-standing debate regarding the origins and starting point of the process of modernization, numerous "causes" of this process have been suggested—from the settlement of craftsmen and merchants around castles, which led to the founding of cities and to the accumulation of capital, to the replacement of tithing by taxes as motivated by the refined needs of the feudal classes, which could be satisfied only within a money system. All of these (and many more) factors contributed to the gradual growth of a capitalistic system. Nevertheless, in the 'material' history of social and industrial developments, the first *radical* changes that deserve such a label might very well be the two surges of industrialization in the nineteenth century. If this is correct, why should the eighteenth century be a turning point in the history of modern consciousness? There may not be a convincing answer. The fact remains that, if we look at the process of modernization from the perspective of the human mind's reaction toward this process, the eighteenth century is *the* century of a more or less conscious reaction against the process of modernization. As if actual developments, no matter how insignificant, had been sufficient for reaching a critical mass, and thus lifting modernization to a qualitatively new level, eighteenth-century thinkers react massively and more intensely than ever before to the process of modernization. They react affirmatively by discussing and institutionalizing new forms of social organization (e.g., codified law in Prussia and France; the introduction of vocational high schools and technological institutions; the establishment of state-owned banks to finance industrial developments; "enlightened" philosophies that legitimize the centralization of societies), and they react negatively by bemoaning the effects of centralization and differentiation of society (e.g., Rousseau's attack on civilization and its effect on virtually every major thinker of the second half of the century; the young Goethe's and Herder's valorization of premodern times and figures; early romanticism's discussions of society as an increasingly totalized and totalizing entity). Within this context, one can observe among intellectuals an increasing anxiety caused by what was seen as the deadening effect of the instrumentalization of human thinking. Some of the questions raised by intellectuals who felt such an anxiety were: Will a space for "free," innovative, noninstrumentalized thinking be left, once the human mind is "logified"? What does one have to do to make sure that the human spirit will not atrophy in the process of modernization?

The concept of imagination plays an ambiguous role in this process. Numerous thinkers fear the disruptive potential of the imagination more than its demise. Thus Alexander Gerard writes: "Imagination is a faculty so wild in its own nature, that it must be accustomed to the discipline of reason before it can become tame and manageable enough for a correct production."[4] The fundamental mistrust of the imagination expressed by Gerard can also be found in Kant, probably the most systematic and seminal thinker of modernity: "Unbridled fantasy can always be bent. . . . But lawless fantasy comes close to madness. Here fantasy makes the man its mere plaything and the poor fellow has no control at all over the course of his ideas."[5] For other thinkers, however, the imagination or fancy provides an instance of resistance vis-à-vis the conditioning forces of society. Witness Friedrich Schlegel and Coleridge, for instance. Schlegel writes: "For it is the task of all poetry to dissolve the course and the law of rationalistically-thinking reason, and to cast us back into the beautiful confusion of fantasy, into the original chaos of human nature, and I know of no more beautiful symbol of the process than the motley crew of ancient gods."[6] Coleridge promotes essentially the same cultural function of the imagination when he states that the latter "dissolves, diffuses, dissipates, in order to re-create. . . . It is essentially *vital*, even as all objects (*as* objects) are essentially fixed and dead."[7]

Of these two reactions, the anxiety that the process of modernization might atrophy noninstrumental thinking is the more common one; it is more widespread than a narrow concern with the debates surrounding the concept of the imagination can reveal. It is an anxiety shared by many theoreticians of modernity who, without participating in the debate on the imagination, nevertheless play a major role in the emerging critique of modern civilization. To a certain extent, even Kant shares this anxiety. For from another perspective that transcends the narrow focus on the imagination, the difference between Kant and authors like Friedrich Schlegel and Coleridge disappears. Kant holds the sublime to be the most important realm in which a mode of thinking untouched by the efforts of instrumentalization does survive and continues to be productive. He defines the sublime as a "state of mind produced by a certain representation with which the reflective [i.e., noninstrumental] judgment is occupied."[8] In a sublime state of mind, we experience our independence from nature and from the laws of theoretical or instrumental cognition. Kant locates the mental force that is resistant to instrumentalization in the speculative realm of theoretical and practical reason. Even when he deals with the ideas of reason in their nonaesthetic purity, as a force of resistance his notion of ideas remains largely aesthetic. Within the history of Western philosophy—and here especially within the development from German Idealism to the aesthetic theory of the Frankfurt School—the notion of reflexive reason was increasingly turned into a reflexive-aesthetic counterforce to the developmental tendencies of modern civilization. Already, Novalis no longer sees a contradiction between a reflective, practical use of reason and the creative imagination: "active reason is productive imagination."[9] In a famous document known as the "Oldest Systematic Program of German Idealism," probably authored by Hegel,[10] the same thought finds its most direct and succinct expression: "I am now convinced that the highest act of reason, which—because it comprises all ideas—is an aesthetic act, and that truth and the good are only united in beauty—The philosopher must possess just as much aesthetic strength as the poet. Those people without aesthetic sense are our alphabet-philosophers [*BuchstabenPhilosophen*]. The philosophy of the spirit is an aesthetic philosophy. One cannot be clever in anything, even in regard to history, one cannot reason cleverly—without aesthetic sense."[11] Significantly, these thoughts are developed after a critique of the modern state as "something mechanic." Whereas before the eighteenth century the imagination was seen as a useful, if unreliable and inferior, cognitive faculty that remained dependent upon the corrective intervention of the rational and superior faculties, from now on the imagination (in some cases reflexive-aesthetic reason) was increasingly perceived as an indispensable counterforce to rationality.

Both the broader theoretical context of the very possibility of a resistant force and the particular historical constellation within the process of modernization, in which the search for such a resistant force gained momentum, should be kept in mind when reading Luiz Costa Lima's historical account of a *Control of the Imagination*. Even if we assume, for the time being, that there exists a long-standing tradition in controlling the human imagination, imagination's relation to rationality must have an effect on the mode of that control. Costa Lima tends to downplay or disregard the radical difference between the control of art and the creative imagination before and since the redefinition of imagination's relation to rationality and the accompanying emergence of a conscious reaction to the process of modernization. For the moment, I will leave the issue of how cultural agents reacted toward modernity and will look at one element of the cultural-political struggle that established a turning point in the history of the control of the imagination. This will permit me to separate a premodern from a modern mode of control.

III

Around 1700, an intense battle took place in Europe between church functionaries and secular intellectuals over who should have the right to educate and socialize the public, and regarding the discursive means best employed in the moral improvement of society. Theologians defending the educational monopoly of the church launched broad attacks against fictive narratives in general. Secular intellectuals, arguing the superiority of fictive narration as a means of moral socialization, accused the religious discourse of being repressive; they tried to institutionalize narratives as a less repressive means of engineering consent—as a liberal mode of influencing the population and establishing a moral society, a mode that refrains from imposing moral standards in the form of forthright rules and provisions.

Out of this conflict grew the project of a modern narratology that aimed at psychological identification with narrative configurations. According to this project, the narrative configuration of literature is more suitable than anything offered by the church to mediate norms and values in a way that is not experienced as externally imposed. Not only did the new project change the *formal* mode of socialization, but the normative content was increasingly based on the necessities of a secular, especially commercial, mode of interaction. With its static perspective of this life versus the life to come, devotional literature, which was until that time a medium of normative self-understanding (that is, a medium for the social reproduction of patterns for meaning and value), could perform this function only under certain conditions. In the case of the eighteenth century this meant that devotional literature performed its traditional cultural function only where hierarchical structures had survived, i.e., in regions that had not yet considered those customs and norms that, together, regulate a large-scale public association. It was the practice of the father of the family to read devotional literature aloud in the family circle, thus providing for a binding experience of community, which in principle did not extend beyond the confines of the house. With the crossing of these boundaries, as necessitated by economic change, and with the development of the bourgeois public realm and of public interaction, a need arose for a medium that could develop norms and could regulate interaction within the social realm. In addition to the fact that the churches were too authoritarian and lacked the flexibility to be able to fully satisfy these needs, they were ultimately unable to respond to the new bourgeois public realm. Despite the unquestionable moral authority of the churches as a nonbourgeois institution and—not only in Protestant Europe—as an institution connected with the power of the state, the churches did not seem to be the appropriate institution for setting the standards for a bourgeois practice of living.

It is understandable that the churches fought this process, which was going to divest them of an important monopoly, with all the means at their disposal. Thus the profusion of theological polemic writings in the early eighteenth century against profane narratives, in which the reproach is made that such literature is amoral, because it tells fictive, that is, untrue, purely fabricated stories. Let us take an example to illustrate the process. The Swiss theologian Gotthard Heidegger laments the mounting flood of profane narratives in his *Mythoscopia Romantica* of 1698 as follows: "Many a person does not lack a book case full of novels, but to be sure lacks Bible and prayer book. Men and women sit on them, as if on eggs, by day and into the night. Some don't do anything else: one even thrusts them into the hands of youth at an early age. This novellistic foolishness is supposed to be the artificial source [*Kunst-Quelle*] of all pleasantry, civility and gallantry."[12] Heidegger argues against profane literature in general (and not only against novels, as becomes apparent in many parts of the text), which he correctly sees as a secular competitor to "Bible and prayer book," and which he also correctly identifies as the artificial source of social behavior patterns, namely of "pleasantry, civility and gallantry."

Let us examine the arguments of the reformed theologian Heidegger more closely (the reformed theologians were the most impassioned watchdogs of fictionality). Heidegger's *Mythoscopia* is an account of a discussion group, where the pro and contra of worldly literature were weighed out against each other. The contra positions that are represented in the group, and which are rejected by Heidegger, already contain arguments that will gain common acceptance in the high Enlightenment: that fictional texts project possible situations, and that their readers can work through any series of fictive situations and in this way practice modes of behavior. The Swiss poetician Breitinger will later coin the term of *einspielen* (playing into) for this nonrational process of mediating values, thus specifying in a precise manner the new element in the moral effect of belletristic literature. The imagination could be perceived as mimetic only after the bourgeois-enlightened project of establishing a playful and probing mode of socialization had emerged. This is to say, attempts to valorize the human imagination in any meaningful and substantial sense as mimetic and to institutionalize a cultural practice corresponding with a newly defined notion of a mimetic imagina-

tion presuppose fundamental changes in the prevailing mode of cultural reproduction—changes which usually are discussed under terms like "modern,"
"bourgeois," or "bourgeois-enlightened."

The church fought with all its might against new modes of cultural reproduction. In his opposition to the more playful effect of worldly narratives, Heidegger advances, for the most part, two arguments: the first follows from the rational, antisensual position of reformed theology, which places it philosophically
in the neighborhood of Descartes. Heidegger proceeds from a statement of the
French philosopher and theologian Pierre Daniel Huet, who in 1670 in his *Essai
sur l'origine des romans* submitted one of the earliest and most noteworthy bou-
geois-enlightened attempts at the vindication of novels (and of fiction in general). Here Huet describes readers of novels as people who "follow affects more
than reason . . . and are more capable in imagining than in understanding
things." Heidegger's dissenting commentary on this quote: "If one only would
pay attention to it, [this argument] is an excellent reason for taking all respect
away from novels."[13] Indeed, here Huet voices an argument that was soon to
play a central role in the theories of Gottsched, Bodmer, Breitinger, Prévost and
others, namely the possibility of influencing the "masses" (*"den grossen
Haufen"*) (as less amenable to rational thought) through morally upright belletristic literature. For Heidegger, who holds the traditional disdain for the lower
faculties of the human mind, of human sensuality, to be unrestrictedly justified,
such an argument can be supported under no conditions. Morality results from
the suppression of the affects; to wish to enlist the latter in the service of moral
cultivation is in itself amoral. Morality can only be mediated through commandments and prohibitions. It therefore requires a medium of directly denominating
language, the sermon: "Now it has long been known that, while reading, one
should watch his own disposition, whether it has, in reading, become quietened
of bad passions, not unlike how one, upon leaving the barber's, stands before
the mirror, or feels with one's hands, whether hair and beard have been cut
properly."[14] This kind of thinking is still far removed from a "playing into"
(*Einspielen*) of modes of behavior; reading should function to rid the reader of
passions and should place the reader in an unclouded frame of mind.

To be sure, only a repressive morality can be mediated by commandments and
prohibitions; the verbal gesture of the "thou shalt not. . ." allows neither for
differentiation nor for that kind of mobility that, in the eyes of Enlightenment
thinkers, was held to be desirable for "tasteful" social interaction. This difference between the repressive morality of the church and the moral aspirations of
the Enlightenment can be seen even more clearly in Heidegger's second argument against the reading of belletristic literature; it issues from an evocation of a
letter of St. Paul that is stereotypical for the early eighteenth century: "If it is
true (as it cannot fail to be) that St. Paul commands the Christians that all whore-
ing and all uncleanliness should not be named among them, because this way,

and no other, is worthy of the saints, and that the Lord God did forbid the remembrance of the names of other gods, and forbid that they be heard out of the mouths [of men] . . . : thus it is far from the truth that novels are permitted since they are mostly nothing other than the well-spoken naming of illicit matters of courting and lechery and the reestablishment of pagan idols.''[15]

At first glance, this reads like a polemic against immoral novels, if not against pornography, as it could still be expressed today by ecclesiastical critics. Heidegger, however, means something different; he means that narrative texts must in general generate counterpositions, that narrative texts allow their action to develop out of the interplay between good and bad, virtue and vice, and that it is in principle reprehensible—even in fictional texts—to name the wicked counterpart. Nowhere is the one-dimensional thinking of the church's conceptions of morality more obvious than in its reformed variants; nowhere does it become more apparent, to what an extent thinking in narrative positions meant an increase in freedom (at least at first glance). The playful moment in the narrative mediation of morality had to rouse suspicion in people with an ecclesiastical (and fundamentally repressive) prohibitionary mentality.

For the moment, let us remain on the modern side of this conflict. With the help of narratives, and in a by-passing of rational discourse, authors such as Prévost and Gottsched wanted to work directly upon the ''masses'' and through this *direct* effect, to educate them and to develop their powers of critical reasoning. Gottsched and Prévost[16] repeatedly discuss the direct efficacy of narrative and its social function. Gottsched, for example, writes with respect to tragedy and comedy: ''One seeks, through examples of virtues and vices, to instruct the spectators. The excitement of affects is here still much more lively than in the latter [the epos], because the visual presentation of the characters [on the stage] touches in a much more affective manner than the best description. Through this, however, one seeks to purge the passions of the spectator.''[17] The high estimation of the immediate effect of drama, the accentuation of the excitement of affects and emotions could seem surprising in a rationalist like Gottsched. This notion, however, lies within the course laid out by the early Enlightenment, namely not only to influence by means of a rationally presented argument, but also to affect the public in the preconceptual and nonconceptual presentation of actions that can claim to be exemplary. Gottsched sticks to the priority of rational cognition; he grants narratives a complete validity as a medium of cognition only in the case of the ''masses,'' who are incapable of rational cognition. ''The understanding of the masses is not penetrating enough to see a truth which cannot be seen with our senses.''[18] In order to convey truth to the masses, according to Gottsched, narratives are culturally and pedagogically absolutely necessary; if all people were capable of rational cognition, one could dispense with narratives— at least this is the conclusion implied in his deliberations.

I have devoted considerable space to the project of an early modern narratology because I will contend that Costa Lima's arguments in favor of a mimetic imagination rely ultimately upon premises first advanced in and closely connected with this project (the same can be said about related arguments used within the Constance School of literary criticism, and here especially by Jauss and Iser, to which Costa Lima feels a certain affinity). These very premises will motivate Costa Lima to defuse the radical otherness of the romantic project by partially identifying it with the bourgeois-enlightened project.

IV

So far I have emphasized the *difference* between the cultural political project of church functionaries and secular critics. Again, from a different perspective, these differences disappear. For if we disregard the institutional difference between the church and a secular community of critics, between religious and secular norms and values, and between the discursive modes of socialization, quite a few epistemological, philosophical, and cultural presuppositions of the two projects are identical. This becomes obvious when we look at an argument by the Renaissance poetician Castelvetro—quoted by Costa Lima—that, although three centuries older, shares several premises with Gottsched's stance: "Poetry was invented only to delight and to entertain, by which I mean to delight and entertain the souls of the rude multitude and the common people, who understand neither the reasonings nor the distinctions nor the arguments, subtle and far from the talk of the stupid, used by philosophers in investigating the truth of things and by artists in organizing the arts. Since they do not understand them, it is only natural that when others use them they feel annoyances and displeasure, for it is bothersome beyond all measure when others speak in a way that we cannot comprehend." Not surprisingly, Castelvetro calls poetry from the point of view of truth "a superfluous and empty thing to be laughed at" (see p. 24 above).

Up to the first half of the eighteenth century, poetry enjoys less freedom and less prestige than other realms of cultural activity like history, philosophy, and science because the arts address our senses whereas the access to "truth," to the transcendent anchor both of knowledge and of the social body, is a rationality that supposedly can sidestep the senses. As a cognitive faculty that synthisizes and reorganizes the impressions of our senses, the imagination was necessarily perceived as inferior as well. The reason for this is obvious when one looks at the social structure of these societies and at the discourse of legitimation engaged in culturally reproducing these societies.

Premodern European societies were stratified societies. In order to clarify the status of the arts in premodern societies in relation to the unquestioned validity and the political and cultural function of transcendent anchors such as "God" or

"Reason," I will introduce Niklas Luhmann's definition of such societies. Stratified societies are hierarchically organized societies. As a principle of structuration, stratification "differentiates society into *unequal* subsystems. It aligns the asymmetry of system/environment with that of equality/inequality" in the sense that people are equal only within a given (sub)system of such a society; equality does not exist among people belonging to different strata of such a society. "Equality thus becomes a norm regulating internal communication and inequality becomes a norm regulating communication with the environment," i.e., among subsystems:

> The Greek term *isonomia* . . . referred to the equality of citizens located within one stratum of society. These citizens successfully claimed to be (or to represent) the whole system. But *isonomia* presupposed inequality with respect to other strata of society. In other words, the class of citizens defined the internal environment of their society by means of 'inequality'. The citizenry depended on this category for their own identity and self-understanding. Stratification, of course, requires an unequal distribution of wealth and power—or, to put it more generally, an unequal distribution of communication chances. . . . The *structural* problem of stratified societies is that the *identification of subsystems requires a hierarchical definition of their environment in terms of rank order or equality/inequality*. Subsystems can maintain their identity and their boundaries only by defining the character of other subsystems. In this sense, the upper classes have to fuse their own identity with a hierarchical conception of the whole society. . . . The structural problem of stratiform differentiation is that it limits the complexity of society. It can be institutionalized only if higher complexity cannot be attained for other reasons. As a result, an increase in aggregate wealth has a tendency to revolutionize stratified societies.[19]

Such societies have a tendency to legitimize themselves by positing a transcendent anchor that 'anchors' the hierarchy, i.e. the privileges of the dominant classes, in a transcendent entity and that reappears within the discourses of such societies as an organizing semantic center. As a given, such a center is always considered to be universal and "rational" in the sense that its discursive defense has to claim that it is independent from the idiosyncratic materiality of the world.

In an excellent and monumental study, Panajotis Kondylis[20] has shown how and why Occidental history from the Middle Ages to the Enlightenment (and beyond) can be described as the constant displacement and ultimate disintegration of a transcendent anchoring of discourses of legitimation. Since the urgency with which cultures search for a transcendent anchor of their linguistic or ideological and social order is determined more by psychological and social concerns than by religious ones, it should not be surprising that the transcendent anchor "God" could be secularized and replaced by "worldly" anchors such as the sovereignty of an absolute ruler (Hobbes), reason (early Enlightenment), nature (Hume), or, in the many enlightened philosophies of history, by a golden age projected into the future. Secularization basically means a displacement of a transcendent anchor from metaphysical transcendence into a form of world-immanent, physical transcendence. In a secularized context, the valorization of order over chaos, stability over change is achieved on the basis of an *immanent* structuring of the world; however, the secularized substitutes of the former metaphysical anchor do not lose their basic function to anchor dominant discourses and our psychosocial existence in a transcendent entity. In the eighteenth century, the anchoring of cognition, language, truth, norms, values, and being in the eternal speech of "God" is replaced by an anchoring in a moralized (and equally eternal) "Nature," supported by the idea that an uncorrupted, graphic, and intuitive language (art) may restore the lost unity of language, being, value, and truth.

To summarize: the mode of cultural reproduction of stratified societies depends upon the existence of a global and universal transcendent anchor; their hierarchical structure is mirrored in a legitimizing discourse that anchors the existing hierarchy within a universal entity. Structurally, the displacement of such an anchor from "God" to an absolute ruler, to nature, and so on, does not change anything. Structurally, "Nature" or "Reason" still serves as a metaphysical entity that legitimizes societies and their discursive practices.

To return to the church functionaries, Castelvetro, Prévost, and Gottsched: their positions all depend upon the premise of a universal transcendent entity that anchors "truth." As a matter of fact, even when the arts, in the wake of the valorization of sensuality, supposedly had been "valorized" around 1750, i.e., freed from the dominance of reason, the premise remained the same. The valorization of sensuality occurred on the basis of a moralization of nature. As *the* representation of moralized nature, art (and a mimetic imagination) now could be considered, for a very short time, to be an untamed, uncontrolled mode of human expression and, simultaneously, a unique mode of cognition (see the terms *anschauende Erkenntnis* and intuitive cognition). What I treated above as the first modern form of literature, and what is often labeled a bourgeois-enlightened institutionalization of art, mirrors—in this perspective—a secularized discursive practice that remains structurally dependent on stratified societies, replicating their mode of cultural reproduction. Here the control of the imaginary follows from the premise that human society and human discourses are anchored in an entity transcending the contingency of history. The imagination as a human faculty that appropriates and prepares material phenomena for the human mind could never claim to discover a "truth" not anchored in a universal entity.

V

This form of cultural reproduction changes with the disintegration of stratified societies. In the seventeenth and eighteenth centuries stratified societies were gradually transformed into functionally differentiated societies. I again follow Luhmann's definiton:

Functional differentiation organizes communication processes around special functions to be fulfilled at the level of society. Since all necessary functions have to be fulfilled and are interdependent, society cannot concede absolute primacy to any one of them. . . . Functional differentiation requires sufficient capacity at the level of subsystems to differentiate and reintegrate function, performance, and self-reflection. This is the only way subsystems can attain operative autonomy as systems-in-their-environment. . . . Any form of differentiation presupposes boundaries or 'lines of demarcation.' Boundaries delimit society's internal environment and establish selective relations between internal and external environments.[21]

The transformation of European society from a stratified into a functionally differentiated society was initiated during the seventeenth and eighteenth centuries. During this period, the strata of a hierarchically organized society were replaced by a system of functionally interdependent subsystems: "functional differentiation leads to a condition in which the *genesis of* problems and the *solution to* problems fall asunder. Problems can no longer be solved by the system that produces them. They have to be transferred to the system that is best equipped and specialized to solve them."[22] With regard to art, this means that the needs it satisfies, particularly the need for emotional and decentering experiences, originate in other realms such as the realm of industrial production with its requirements of agonistic and rational behavior. In this context, Luhmann employs a useful distinction between autonomy and autarchy which is able to clarify the many misunderstandings about the autonomy of modern art: There is, he says, "on the level of subsystem, less autarchy and self-sufficiency but higher autonomy in applying specific rules and procedures to special problems."[23] Autonomy does not exclude interdependencies. Art develops its own strategies to satisfy needs that originate in other realms of social interaction.

In premodern times, the imagination and imaginary experiences did not play an essential role within the discursive practices that legitimized the make-up of stratified societies: the concept of imagination and imaginative practices remained outside the system of discursive legitimation. In functionally differentiated societies, imaginary experiences assume an essential function as compensatory experiences. They compensate for the lack of emotional and decentering experiences outside the aesthetic by responding to these needs. eighteenth-century writers were amazingly aware of these changes. There exist hundreds of statements similar to the ones I offer here. In his essay on the imagination, Addison writes:

> There are indeed but very few who know how to be idle and innocent, or have a relish of any pleasures that are not criminal; every diversion they take is at the expense of some one virtue or another, and their very first step out of business is into vice or folly. A man should endeavour, therefore, to make the sphere of his innocent pleasures as wide as possible, that he may retire into them with safety, and find in them such a satisfaction as a wise man would not blush to take. Of this nature are those of the imagination, which do not require such a bent of thought as is necessary to our more serious employments, nor, at the same time, suffer the mind to sink into that negligence and remissness, which are apt to accompany our more sensual delights, but like a gentle exercise to the faculties awaken them from sloth and idleness, without putting them upon any labour or difficulty. We might here add, that the pleasures of the fancy are more conducive to health, than those of the understanding, which are worked out by dint of thinking, and attended with too violent a labour of the brain. Delightful scenes, whether in nature, painting. or poetry, have a kindly influence on the body, as well as the mind; and not only serve to clear and brighten the imagination, but are able to disperse grief and melancholy, and to set the animal spirits in pleasing and agreeable motions.[24]

The second example is taken from a book by Adam Bergk, a German philosopher who was strongly influenced by Kant and whose *The Art of Reading Books* (*Die Kunst, Bücher zu lesen*) helped establish a modern reading culture for the educated classes. Bergk sees reading clearly as a compensatory activity that remains functionally related to other realms of human activity: "We require a diversion that is at the same time recreation and instruction; where else could we seek it than in our books, which divert ill humor, chase away cares, soothe pain, elevate the spirit, and strengthen the heart."[25] The poet "puts the imagination into play, and work itself becomes a pastime and we forget the real misfortune that weighs upon us, as he conjures us into another world."[26] Elsewhere, Bergk claims that aesthetic pleasure is able to counteract the pressure toward homogenization in "large cities."

> How often the real world disgusts us, and we flee into the world of the imagination in order to chase away this discontent, and to ward off uniformity. The imagination therefore requires culture, which we can primarily acquire through the reading of works of the fine arts. If we place the development of the same at the end of our priorities or even look down upon it, then we will become everyday people [*Alltagsmenschen*], especially when we avoid the pleasures of free nature and bury ourselves in large cities, where people seem to all be

cut out of one cloth, since fashion and the unnatural life style have
blunted all original particularities of the spirit, and have smothered all
natural germen. . . . The poet gives to nature—who is mute in respect
to us, we who are worn down by the day's business—a language,
which sets all of the strings of our heart into motion, and excites the
feelings of friendship, of love, of sympathy, of noble-mindedness. . . .
Whoever does not take part in the magic, the enchantments of
imagination, does not live a human life, but merely the life of a plant.
He is a play of blind mechanism, and is no free man, who makes
himself the master of fate.[27]

Imaginative reading is able to overcome the fragmentation of modern life. Bergk
therefore complains:

It is only too often the case, that one finds people who are educated
only one-sidedly, and who therefore disdain everything that is not
pertinent to their science or art or business. No one is more intolerant in
his judgements than he who has perfected *one* strength of his intellect
[*Geist*] at the cost of all others.[28]

Such quotes are precipitates of broader changes in the mode of social organization; as insights, they remain insufficiently aware of the actual changes. Once
functional differentiation was established as the prevailing mode of social organization, art's content was unable to refer "freely" to other realms of everyday
life. An ideological or social functionalization of the arts that was not always
already defused by an autonomous and functionally differentiated institutionalization of the arts seemed possible only as long as a nonaesthetic, all-encompassing other, i.e., a transcendent anchor, guaranteed such a functionalization;
which is to say, first, that a social functionalization of artistic content was only
possible as a nonconstitutive, nonessential functionalization within stratified
societies and, second, that autonomous art, having assumed a specialized function within differentiated societies, cannot simultaneously assume a social function unrestricted by its mode of institutionalization, at least not in regard to the
normative configurations of *individual* works.

A social functionalization of autonomous art under conditions of modernity
would presuppose a "shortcircuiting" of the contents of the arts with the contents of other social subsystems. Arguing against the aesthetic concept of sympathy and the possibility of a moral effect of a sentimental theater, Rousseau was
one of the first to recognize the improbability, if not impossibility, of such a
"shortcircuiting" of art and reality, imaginary and actual behavior:

The heart of man is always right concerning that which has no personal
relation to himself. In the quarrels at which we are purely spectators,
we immediately take the side of justice, and there is no act of
viciousness which does not give us a lively sentiment of indignation so

long as we receive no profit from it. But when our interest is involved, our sentiments are soon corrupted. And it is only then that we prefer the evil which is useful to us to the good that nature makes us love. . . . If . . . the heart is more readily touched by feigned ills than real ones, if theatrical imitations draw forth more tears than would the presence of the objects imitated, it is less because the emotions are feebler and do not reach the level of pain, as the Abbé du Bos believes, than because they are pure and without mixture of anxiety for ourselves. In giving our tears to these fictions, we have satisfied all the rights of humanity without having to give anything more of ourselves. . . . In the final accounting, when a man has gone to admire fine actions in stories and to cry for imaginary miseries, what more can be asked of him? Is he not satisfied with himself? Does he not applaud his fine soul? Has he not acquitted himself of all that he owes to virtue by the homage which he has just rendered? What more could one want of him? That he practice it himself? He has no role to play; he is no actor.[29]

Shortly thereafter Rousseau specifies the functional separation of art and reality very clearly: "The theatre has rules, principles, and a morality apart, just as it has a language and a style of dress that is its own."[30]

It is an essential aspect of the paradoxical nature of modernity that social differentiation has never generated difference but has instead brought about homogenization. Functional differentiation implies a general subjection of society as a whole to a unifying and all-encompassing principle of organization. That principle unfolds itself in the form of functions. For art, this established what has been called its implosive narcissism: "The implosive narcissism of art forms the context, within which we might better understand an enigmatic social event: the modern isolation of the individual which recently has been in danger to degenerate under the weight of civilization forced upon it."[31] The implosive narcissism of the arts is attached to a displacement of human needs to the imaginary; the social system of modernity tends to privilege imaginary satisfactions.

VI

Costa Lima alludes to this historical constellation quite often, as when he states that Romanticism "saw itself as characterized by a reflection carried out on the basis of the *hic et nunc* and no longer as a function of a verisimilitude with the permanently and universally present. . . . Therefore, the concept of *imitatio* would be replaced by the notion of *expression* by an individual. Subjectivity seemed to be rending the veil that had covered it over, and reason, identified with mean truth, that is, common sense, to be losing its position as guardian of the temple" (p. 44 above). He fails, however, to thematize reasons that could explain these changes. In my opinion, this not only obscures his historical

d by Walter Benjamin, was intended "to elevate thought above all social
s to such a degree" that the possibility of a self-constitution of subjec-
ens up "magically out of the insight into the falseness of strictures."[35]
whole is the *medium* of reflection through which self-constitution of sub-
can be attempted.[36] This is a very different notion of infinity than
For the latter, the "infinity of reflection" could only exist as endless
gumentation, as a set of logical steps from identical content to identical
However, for the early Romantics, as Walter Benjamin has shown, what
nt is "not the infinity of process but the infinity of correlation. . . .
eflection means reflection within the absolute Thesis [i.e. within the
the other, which for the individual has always already taken place], it
n that is supposed to remain within the Thesis, and is not intended to
eaning outside it, because there it would lead nowhere."[37] The early
wanted to rescue the ego's capacity for self-limitation or self-consti-
, its capacity to transgress the realm of the always already posited;
ed for rhetorical strategies that could transgress those limitations
ichte predate the ego.

sta Lima does not see the linguistic and deconstructive aspect of the
ion of *poiesis*, he tends to erase the difference between *poiesis* and
herefore should not come as a surprise when Costa Lima, toward
is study, joins forces with the so-called Constance School, espe-
olfgang Iser. Iser and Jauss have always been fond of seeing liter-
d of testing ground or *Simulationsraum*. Costa Lima fully adopts
en he writes that art intends "to elicit in the reader the double sen-
iarity and estrangement [in relation to everyday life]. Familiar con-
e estranged because, in the specific space of fiction, they do not
onse that we would give within the sphere of everyday pragmatic
e fictional thematization of reality in modern times contemplates
estion the habitual norms of conduct itself" (see p. 149). Here
asing of the problem evades the problematic stated above. How
norms of conduct be put—in a nonaffirmative sense—into ques-
ting, first and foremost, the structural appropriation of language
hed orders into question, i.e., by submitting language to rhetor-
at reorient its very use?

VII

roach to fictional thematization of reality disregards the two
such a thematization problematic under conditions of moder-
al separation of art and the question of representation. As Fou-
The Order of Things," until the end of the sixteenth century
seen as a medium, as a means of cognition, but as the lan-

account but, more importantly, causes him to promote a notion of literature that
is fundamentally a bourgeois-enlightened one. The transition from imitation to
expression, Costa Lima correctly asserts, is only possible after a functionally differentiated society has been established. Ultimately, the new organizational mode
undermines a possible mimetic function of the artistic imagination. In functionally differentiated societies, art is no longer directly integrated into a thematization of the world and a legitimation of domination, since such a society does not
need a guardian of the temple to the same extent a stratified society needed one.
In a functionally differentiated society, an organizational principle rather than a
principle of reason tends to serve as a guardian of the temple. The increasing
complexity of the structural organization of social and psychological systems will
gradually undermine the identification of reason and subjectivity, the self-assess-
ment of subjects as historical agents and the unquestioned linkage of reality and
its linguistic representation.

Romanticism and its valorization of expression is a thoroughly modern phenomenon that is wholly dependent upon the new role the arts took over. With
reference to this function, Luhmann emphasizes that, in nonaesthetic subsystems, there exists "a widespread deficiency with respect to self-reflection. . . .
Subsystems, therefore, differ in their tendency to use either function or performance as a substitute for self-reflection. And there is at least one subsystem (art)
which tends to use self-reflection as a substitute for function and performance."[32] The self-reflection Luhmann speaks of is an internal self-reflection
that leads to an emphasis on expressive means, not a self-conscious reflection
upon the specialized function of art within a differentiated society. Despite eventual partial insights into the social function of the arts in modern societies, such
societies tend to be incapable of insights into their own mode of organization.

In my view, Costa Lima shares this blind spot. His theoretical project requires
him to argue (see pp. 64-65), first, that romanticism and nineteenth-century realism were not that far apart and, second, that a balance or mediation between realism and romanticism, mimesis and imagination is culturally desirable. "The
question of romanticism and that of the later realism sprang from the same soil:
the necessity of offering art a new legitimation after the collapse of the classical
order"(p. 65). Art finds its legitimation supposedly in accepting its mimetic task.
But how can one claim that art is mimetic if its compensatory function in modern
societies is not thematized simultaneously? "Mimesis" presupposes that art still
can successfully refer to "reality" and that the "reading"of art's semantic configurations still has an effect on other realms of life. If modern art is indeed insti-
tutionalized in such a way that our commerce with it is—on the level of its institutionalization already—compensatory in nature, then any effect a socially
relevant, i.e., mimetic, content might have will a priori be defused by its mode
of institutionalization.

At one point, Costa Lima himself reflects upon the possibility that aesthetic experience might be fundamentally compensatory. However, it is interesting to see in which context the term occurs: Quoting Abrams's statement that the "great Romantic works were not written at the height of revolutionary hope but out of the experience of partial or total disenchantment with the revolutionary promise," he asserts that to "confuse the theorization of such figures as Schlegel and Coleridge with compensatory expression would be to inhibit its understanding *a priori*." Such a misunderstanding "would surely have grave consequences, for what is achieved in their work, especially in Schlegel's, is the first theory of literature constructed on modern foundations" (see p. 76). Costa Lima is right in rejecting a kind of contingent, accidental compensatory motivation for romantic writing. Such a compensatory motivation is not at issue here. For if "compensatory" is at all used in a rigorous analytical sense, it cannot mean a passing "disenchantment." Rather, it means a compensatory function of the *institution* of art, a function dependent on the *mode of organization* of modern societies. Art's compensatory effect cannot be sublated or eliminated without rupturing the very function of the arts in modernity and, thus, the very mode of organization of modern societies. This is precisely what informs avant-gardistic projects from early romanticism to French surrealism.[33]

Because Costa Lima does not discuss this more fundamental meaning of a compensatory function of the arts, he does not grasp the radical stance of the romantics when they assert an "opposition between *mimesis* and *poiesis*" (p. 85). Shortly thereafter, in a sweeping statement, he asserts that "it is plausible to think that the problems faced by the theory of art in modern times may result from a hasty abandonment of the problematics of *mimesis* " (see p. 86). Does *poiesis* really function *within mimesis*, as Costa Lima asserts on the same page? Such a statement relies on problematic epistemological and historical premises regarding the possibility of representing reality in art; these premises would have to be thematized and supported by arguments rather than tacitly assumed. From the perspective of Schlegel, poiesis has to be "governed by a power of unconscious figuration" precisely because such figuration opens the only chance to escape the atrophy of thinking by the conditioning force of instrumental reason. If the artistic imagination is defined as a (deconstructive) force of renewal vis-à-vis established representational orders, it can no longer be perceived as mimetic in the sense of an artistic appropriation of reality.

In another context, Costa Lima quotes Coleridge without doing justice to the latter's distinction between the imagination and fancy. For that quote indicates why, in the eyes of the romantics, imagination and *poiesis* had to be merged and separated from the mimetic. Imagination, says Coleridge, "dissolves, diffuses, dissipates, in order to re-create; or where this process is rendered impossible, yet still at all events it struggles to idealize and to unify. It is essentially *vital*, even as all objects (*as* objects) are essentially fixed and dead. Fancy, on the con-

trary, has no other counters to play with, but fixities indeed no other than a mode of Memory emancipate space; and blended with, and modified by that empi which we express by the word choice. But equally must receive all its materials ready made from th imagination is the creative faculty precisely becau vis a reality and a mode of thinking dominated (the adjectives turn this into a tautological phras

The mimetic would only be possible on th fancy. What does this mean? The philosophic thought was Fichte's *Wissenschaftslehre*. Here scious nature of the act of positing the non-e precedes all *individual* thought and provides means concretely that the division between cannot be eliminated or sublated, and that the already filled up with perceptions. As soon nally and "logify" our thinking, we encoun conditions under which innovation is poss be possible *within* a rationally ordered who posed to move from identity to identity al and rules of rational associations. If meth mine human thinking, we are turned into only compare differing perceptions or i one over the other according to always ically assess qualitatively innovative pe nected with established orders; as a ma vative perceptions or identities withou orders. For a theory of literary criticis favor, or reject norms and values po cussion, but that our conclusions are

To a limited degree, the rom "enlightened" approach to literatur of social totality on the ego (and it thought as the only possible thou romantic thought to dislodge "p expression from Novalis. The rom a form of critical practice viewin nite reflection. The infinitude of progressing from one particular infinitude established by the c whole. "Infinitude" is a ling *poiesis* that revives and renew

analyze
stricture
tivity o
Art as a
jectivity
Fichte's.
human a
content.
is import
Fichtean
positing o
is reflectio
have any
Romantics
tution, i.e.
they search
which for F
Since Co
romantic no
mimesis. It
the end of
cially with W
ature as a ki
this stance w
sation of fami
ditions becom
call for the res
life. That is, t
putting into qu
already the phr
can the habitua
tion without pu
by or as establi
ical strategies th

Costa Lima's ap
issues that make
nity: the institutio
cault argued in "
language was not

guage of being itself. God had inscribed the same laws into language as he had written into nature; the decoding of the laws of language encompassed as much science as the contemplation of nature itself. Both nature and writing held within them a communication from God that was fully equivalent, and whose discovery must lead to identical conclusions. Signs, be they linguistic signs or signs of nature, existed in complete independence of humankind; signs "did not need to be known in order to exist: even if they remained silent, even if no one were to perceive them, they were just as much *there*. It was not knowledge that gave them their signifying function, but the very language of things."[38] This is obvious in Castelvetro when he states: "Since truth is naturally prior to verisimilitude and the thing represented naturally prior to the representation, and verisimilitude therefore refers to, and depends entirely upon, the thing represented . . . it is more necessary to have first of all a thorough and rational knowledge of the truth and of the thing represented than of verisimilitude and the representation" (see p. 24).

Foucault has shown that, from the seventeenth century onward, the question would be asked, "how a sign could be linked to what it signified."[39] Here the connection between being and writing is dissolved, and language is analyzed as a means of the representation of something that lies outside of it, where there is no longer a relationship of equivalence. "Things and words were to be separated from one another."[40] Thus begins the analysis of language as a medium of cognition, which will be interposed like a prism between the cognizing subject and the object of cognition. It is only an analysis of language as representation, as a medium, that opens the possibility of distinguishing qualitatively different, but equal, modes of representation. And only from this point is it possible to think the difference between two modes of cognition, the intuitive or aesthetic and the rational, as was common from the mid-eighteenth century on.

Nevertheless, the historical moment in which it became common to distinguish between these two modes of representation as well as cognition was in a rather paradoxical sense a transitional one. On the one hand, the distinction was still dependent on old premises; on the other hand, it reflected the disintegration of these premises. Particularly the artistic and "natural" mode of cognition still carried old semiotic and epistemological premises. In the eighteenth century, one of the most urgent issues confronting philosophy and literature was the comprehension of how an "ability of the representations that mediate all human cognition" could be obtained "to deliver some knowledge of ultimate, unmediated, extralinguistic reality."[41] Even after the belief that this was possible had begun to disintegrate, art was commonly named as the one mode of representation in which signifier and signified, reality and representation were still united. Thus, at the core of the enlightened conception of art lay a quest for unmediated presence in the mediation of signs. Lessing, for instance, stated in a letter to Nicolai (May 26, 1769): "Poetic works must attempt to elevate their arbitrary signs [*willkührliche Zeichen*] to natural signs." The arts and a "natural" language exemplify the sacral, revelatory, transcendental function of a sign that overcomes the gap between language and reality. For a long time, it was a widely shared belief that the graphic and symbolic mode of representation that the arts display overcomes alienation, distance, mediation.

The notion of art as revelatory sign is still dependent on the notion of "nature" as a transcendent anchor. In this sense, the two variants of an enlightened notion of art—art as cognitive vehicle for the masses and art as revelatory sign—are dependent both on a transcendent anchoring of cultural reproduction and, ultimately, on the mode of social organization typical of stratified societies. One of the premises of such a notion of art is the effacement of the materiality and arbitrariness of language. Only when art shifts from a grounding in verisimilitude to a grounding in expressiveness can the materiality of art be foregrounded. Only after such a shift has taken place can linguistic chance events be perceived as a positive force. The materiality of language can become the focus of attention only after "transcendent anchors" have lost their function within discursive strategies of legitimation; the aesthetic realm can be emancipated from subjugation to a transcendent anchor only after those anchors have lost their constitutive role for all of society. Ironically, the potential of the fictional to thematize reality (which otherwise might have been a consequence of the arts' liberation from the metaphysical) was defused by the differentiation of society at precisely the same time this "liberation" took place. The "revaluation" of the sensual and of art (which includes the imagination as a mimetic faculty) was a phenomenon of transition between stratified and functionally differentiated societies. Moreover, it was a project that was from the beginning destined to fail, since it was based upon an understanding of nature as moral, disregarding the unconscious and the production of human desires. In addition, can one really speak of the imagination as being tamed or "controlled" prior to its "revaluation" in the eighteenth century? I do not think so. Despite the attacks against the imagination during the Middle Ages, the Renaissance, and the Baroque, in each case it was a matter of a theoretical, not practical exclusion of the imagination from discourses that were designed to legitimize the existing social order. An untamed imagination could be found at work in the carnivalesque, to name one example. But imaginative cultural practices did not affect the official discourse of legitimation. It is only in such instances, when the discursive reproduction of "society" is no longer dependent upon a transcendent anchor, that the concept of imagination can be revalorized within the official discourse of legitimation. However, such a valorization was from the beginning restricted to the realm of the aesthetic. As a human faculty contained within an appropriate field of activity, the imagination was considered to be free. Where an untamed fancy was attacked, as in Gerard or Kant, the foe was not the aesthetic imagination but the infringement of fancy upon other realms of human life. Ever since, the question has remained whether the arts might be able to overcome their own institutionalization and regain a nonaffirmative social function. From romanticism to the historical avant-garde of this century, artistic movements have searched for an answer to this question. The mere insistance on *mimesis* will not be able to change the institutional integration of the arts into modern societies. As a matter of fact, the insistence on mimesis indicates an affirmation of modernity's mode of social organization. *Within* the (unchallenged) organizational framework of modernity, the individual work of art can very well appear mimetic without the institution of art actually being a mimetic medium. The individual work thus turns into a testing ground without effect. This is possible because we tend to organize our "habitual norms of conduct" along the lines of institutional demarcations; we defuse the impact of art's mimetic elements by differentiating our habitual norms of conduct parallel to the functional differentiation of society and never permit our aesthetic norms of conduct to penetrate other realms of our life.

Notes

Preface

1. Ingemar Düring, *Aristoteles Darstellung und Interpretation seines Denkens* (Heidelberg: Carl Winter—Universitätsverlag, 1966), 165.

2. Alasdair G. MacIntyre, *After Virtue: A Study in Moral Theory* (Notre Dame, Ind: University of Notre Dame Press, 1981).

3. David Émile Durkheim and Marcel Mauss, "De Quelques formes primitives de classification: contribution à l'étude des représentacions collectives," *Année Sociologique* 6 (Paris, 1903): 1-72.

4. Jean-Paul Sartre, *L'Imaginaire* (Paris: Gallimard, 1940).

5. Wolfgang Iser, "Akte des Fingierens. Oder: Was ist das Fiktive im fiktionalen Text?" *Funktionen des Fiktiven*, ed. D. Heinrich and W. Iser, *Poetik und Hermeneutik* X (München, 1983), 121-51.

"Introductory Note"

1. André Breton, *Position politique du surréalisme* (Paris: éditions du Sagittaire, 1935), 147.

2. Northrop Frye, ?.

3. Paul Zumthor, *Essai de poétique médiévale* (Paris: éditions du Seuil, 1972), 115.

Chapter 1. Controlling the Imaginary

1. Johan Huizinga, *The Waning of the Middle Ages* (Garden City: Doubleday & Company, 1954), 27.

2. R. Howard Bloch, *Medieval French Literature and the Law* (Berkeley: University of California Press, 1977), 130.

3. Jacques Le Goff, *La Naissance du purgatoire* (Paris: Gallimard, 1981), 229.

230 □ NOTES

4. Paul Zumthor, *Langue, texte, énigme* (Paris: Éditions du Seuil, 1975), 168.

5. Jacqueline Cerquiglini, "Le Clerc et l'écriture: le *voir dit* de Guillaume de Machaut et la définition du dit," *Literatur in der Gesellschaft des Spätmittelalters* (Heidelberg), 1:167.

6. Elizabeth L. Eisenstein, *The Printing Press as an Agent of Change* (Cambridge: Cambridge University Press, 1979), 270.

7. Ramón Menéndez Pidal, *Poesía juglaresca y juglares* (Madrid: Espasa-Calpe, 1956), 246.

8. Cerquiglini, "Le Nouveau lyrisme (xive-xve siécles)," *Précis de littérature francaise du moyen âge*, ed. D. Poirion (Paris: Presses Universitaires de France, 1983).

9. Fernão Lopes, *Crónica de D. Pedro*, ed. G. Macchi (Roma: Edizioni dell' Ateneo, 1966), 215.

10. Lopes, *Crónica de D. Fernando*, ed. G. Macchi (Lisboa: Imprensa Nacional-Casa da Moeda, 1975), 157.

11. Lopes, *Crónica de D. João*, 2 vols. (Lisboa: Livraria Civilização Editora, 1945), 1:1.

12. Hans Robert Jauss, "Zur historischen Genese der Scheidung von Fiktion und Realität," *Poetik und Hermeneutik* 10 (1983): 429.

13. Concetta Carestia Greenfield, *Humanist and Scholastic Poetics, 1250-1500* (Lewisberg: Bucknell University Press, 1981), 71.

14. Marc Fumaroli, *L'Age de l'eloquence. Rhétorique et "res literaria" de la renaissance au seuil de l'epoque classique* (Genève: Librairie Droz, 1980), 85.

15. Franscesco Petrarca, *Opere di Petrarca*, ed. Giovanni Ponte (Milano: Mursia, 1968), 816-17.

16. Paul Oskar Kristeller, *Renaissance Thought II* (New York: Harper & Row Publishers, 1965), 26.

17. Erwin Panofsky, *Renaissance and Renascences in Western Art* (Stockholm: Almquist & Wiksell, 1965), 100.

18. Walter Ullmann, *Medieval Foundations of Renaissance Humanism* (London: Paul Elek, 1977), 66.

19. Bernard Weinberg, *A History of Literary Criticism in the Italian Renaissance*, 2 vols. (Chicago: University of Chicago Press, 1961), I:60.

20. Weinberg, *Critical Prefaces of the French Renaissance* (Evanston: Northwestern University Press, 1950), 35.

21. O. B. Hardison, Jr., *English Literary Criticism. The Renaissance* (New York: Meredith Publishing Company, 1963), 61.

22. Lodovico Castelvetro, *Poetica d'Aristotele vulgarizzata et sposta* (reprint; Munich: Wilhelm Fink Verlag, 1967), 61.

23. Francis Bacon, *The Advancement of Learning* (reprint; London: Oxford University Press, 1974), 97.

24. Rosamond Tuve, *Elizabethan and Metaphysical Imagery* (Chicago: University of Chicago Press, 1961), 222-23.

25. Martin Fontius, "Das Ende einer Denkform. Zur Ablösung des Nachahmungsprinzips im 18. Jahrhundert," *Literarische Wiederspiegehung Geschichtliche und theoretische Dimensionen eines Problem* (Berlin: Aufbau Verlag, 1981), 208.

26. Luiz Costa Lima, *Mimesis e Modernidade. Formas das Sombras* (Rio de Janeiro: Graal, 1980), chap. 2.

27. Keith Thomas, *Religion and the Decline of Magic* (London: Weidenfeld and Nicolson, 1971), 69.

28. René Bray, *La Formation de la doctrine classique en France* (Paris: Librairie Hachette, 1927), 94.

29. Erich Auerbach, *Scenes from the Drama of European Literature* (Minneapolis: University of Minnesota Press, 1984), 158.

30. Jeremy Bentham, *Theory of Fictions* (London: Kegan Paul, Trench, Trubner & Company, 1932), 7.

31. François-René de Chateaubriand, *Essai sur la littérature anglaise et considérations sur le génie des temps, des hommes et des révolutions* (Paris: Furne, Jouvet et Cie·, éditeurs, 1867), 123.

32. M. Augur, "Discours sur le Romantisme," in Augur et. al., *Recueil Factice de Manifestes pro et antiromantiques* (1824; reprint, Genève: Slatkine Reprints, 1974), 24.

33. Stendahl, *Racine and Shakespeare*, trans. Guy Daniels, forward André Maurois (New York: The Crowell-Collier Press, 1962), 133.

34. This understanding on our part does not mean that its course is now completely run. Two clear issues seem to have considerable import: the appearance, between romanticism and contemporary immanentism, of the scientifistic and impressionistic critical modes launched in the second half of the nineteenth century, the latter continuing, albeit with an increasing marginalized status, into the present century; and the development of Marxist thought about art, which, although it should have been able to counter the immanentism begun in German stylistics, after showing promise in the first decades of this century, rigidified under the Stalinist model and remains today weighed down by reflectionist doctrine.

35. Saint Augustine, "De Cura gerenda pro mortuis," *Oeuvres de Saint-Augustin* 1re Série, Opuscules 2, Problèmes Moraux, trans. (from Latin into French) Gustave Combès (Paris: Desclée de Brouwer et Cie., 1948), 12.

36. For further clarification, see Wolfgang Iser, "Akte des Fingierens. Oder: Was ist das Fiktive im fiktionalen Text?" *Poetik und Hermenuetik* 10 (1983): 121-51.

37. This is Iser's position in "Akte des Fingierens."

38. See Costa Lima, *Mimesis e Modernidade*, 128-33.

39. Allan Janik and Stephen Toulmin, *Wittgenstein's Vienna* (New York: Simon and Schuster, 1973), 223.

40. Sigmund Freud, *Group Psychology and the Analysis of the Ego*, Standard Edition of the Complete Works of Sigmund Freud 18 (London: The Hogarth Press, 1955), 105.

41. Sérgio Paulo Rouanet, *Édipo e o Anjo. Itinerários Freudianos em Walter Benjamin* (Rio de Janeiro: Tempo Brasileiro, 1981), 146. Some years ago too, Jean-Luc Donnet and André Green, in a simple footnote, referred to the "primary identification without objective bond" as "mimesis" (within quotation marks). See their *L'Enfant de ça. Psychanalyse d'un entretien: La psychose blanche* (Paris: Minuit, 1973), 79.

42. Freud, *Jokes and Their Relation to the Unconscious*, Standard Edition of the Complete Works of Sigmund Freud 8 (London: The Hogarth Press, 1960), 191-92.

43. Freud, *Beyond the Pleasure Principle*, Standard Edition of the Complete Works of Sigmund Freud 18 (London: The Hogarth Press), 14-17.

44. Regarding those two thematizations, see Jean-Paul Sartre, *L'Imaginaire* (Paris: Gallimard, 1940).

45. Quoted in Herbert Dieckmann, "Die Wandlung der Nachahmungsbegriffes in der französischen Asthetik des 18. Jahrhunderts," *Poetik und Hermeneutik* 1 (1969): 43.

46. Hans Ulrich Gumbrecht, "Erzählen in der Literatur/Erzählen im Alltag," *Erzählen im Alltag*, ed. K. Ehlich (Frankfurt: Suhrkamp Verlag, 1980), 414.

47. E. H. Gombrich, *Art and Illusion* (Princeton: Princeton University Press, 1972), 274-75.

48. For a more detailed exposition of this issue, see Costa Lima, "Social Representation and Mimesis," *New Literary History* (Spring 1985), 447-66.

49. See Iser, *Der Akt des Lesens. Theorie ästhetischer Wirkung* (Munich: Wilhelm Fink Verlag, 1976), esp. chap. 4. The English translation is *The Act of Reading: A Theory of Aesthetic Response* (Baltimore: Johns Hopkins University Press, 1978).

Chapter 2. The Fates of Subjectivity: History and Nature in Romanticism

1. Jean-Bernard-Léon Foucault, *Les Mots et les choses; une archéologie des sciences*

humaines (Paris: Gallimard, 1966). The English translation is *The Order of Things; An Archaeology of the Human Sciences* (London: Tavistock, 1970).

2. Nicolas Boileau-Despréaux, *Oeuvres complètes*[2] (Paris: Philippe Libraries, 1837), 110.

3. Gottfried Wilhelm von Leibniz, *The Monadology of Leibniz*, with an introduction and commentary by Herbert Wildon Carr, trans. R. Latta and G. M. Duncan (Los Angeles: University of Southern California Press, 1930), 38-39. [References are to proposition and page.]

4. Ernst Cassirer, *Rousseau, Kant, Goethe* (Princeton: Princeton University Press, 1945), 51.

5. François Furet, *L'Atelièr de l'histoire* (Paris: Flammarion, 1982), 148, 152.

6. M. E. Montaigne, *The Essays of Michel de Montaigne* 2, trans. and ed. Jacob Zeitlin (New York: Alfred A. Knopf, 1935), 78-79.

7. Denis Diderot, *Oeuvres*, texte établi et annoté par André Billy, Biblioteque de la pléiade (Paris: Gallimard, 1951), 1118.

8. Wolfgang Preisendanz, "Voraussetzungen des poetischen Realismus in der deurschen Erzähikunst des 19. Jahrhundert." Reprinted in *Begriffsbestimmung des literarischen Realismus*, ed. R. Brinkmann (Darmstadt: Wissenschaftliche Buchgesselschaft, 1974), 472.

9. For a detailed analysis of the socioeconomic conditioning factors that led to this passage, see Martin Fontius, "Produktivkraftentfaltung und Autonomie der Kunst zur Ablösung ständischer Voraussetzungen in der Literaturtheorie," *Literatur im Epochenumbruch*, ed. G. Klotz, W. Schröder, and P. Weber (Berlin: Aufbau-Verlag, 1977), 409-529. Although I recognize its merit, I differ with it because, grounded in reflection theory as it is, it cannot admit that German "idealist" theory in fact has validity and not mere explanatory power.

10. Johan Huizinga, *Homo Ludens. A Study of the Play-Element in Culture*, trans. R. F. C. Hull (London: Routledge & Kegan Paul, 1949), 189.

11. Quoted in Kurt Böttcher, *Romantik. Erläuterungen zur deutschen Literatur* (Berlin: Volkseigener Verlag, 1977), 36.

12. Meyer H. Abrams, "Coleridge, Baudelaire, and Modernist Poetics," *Poetik und Hermeneutik* 2 (1966): 115.

13. Friedrich Schlegel, *Lucinde and the Fragments*, trans. and intro. Peter Firchow (Minneapolis: University of Minnesota Press, 1971), 233.

14. Samuel Taylor Coleridge, *Collected Letters of Samuel Taylor Coleridge* 1, ed. E. L. Griggs (Oxford: Clarendon Press, 1956), 527.

15. Coleridge, *Biographia Literaria*, ed. J. Showcross (London: Oxford University Press, 1962), 123.

16. Coleridge, "France: An Ode," *The Complete Poetical Works of Samuel Taylor Coleridge*, 2 vols., ed. Ernest Hartley Coleridge (Oxford: Clarendon Press, 1912), 1:243-47.

17. Friedrich Hölderlin, *Hyperion*, trans. Willard R. Trask (New York: Signet, 1965), 131.

18. Percy Bysshe Shelley, *Letters of Percy Bysshe Shelley*, 2 vols., ed. Frederick L. Jones (Oxford: Clarendon Press, 1964), I:504.

19. Abrams, *Natural Supernaturalism; Tradition and Revolution in Romantic Culture* (New York: Norton & Company, 1971), 95.

20. William Wordsworth, *The Prelude*, in *The Poetical Works of Wordsworth* (Boston: Houghlin Mifflin Company, 1982), 124-222. [References to *The Prelude* are to section and verse.]

21. Adam Ferguson, *An Essay on the History of Civil Society* (Philadelphia: A. Finley, 1819), 34.

22. "What the concept of process implies is that the concrete and the general, the single thing or event and the universal meaning have parted company. The process, which alone makes meaningful whatever it happens to carry along, has thus acquired a monopoly of universality and significance": Hannah Arendt, *Between Past and Present: Eight Essays in Political Thought*, expanded ed. (Harmondsworth: Penguin Books, 1968), 64.

23. Ingrid Strohschneider-Kohrs, "Zur Poetik der deutschen Romantik II: Die romantische Ironie," *Die deutsche Romantik*, ed. H. Steffen (Göttingen: Vandenhoeck und Ruprecht, 1967), 87.

For a more detailed treatment of the role of irony, see the same author's *Die romantische Ironie in Theorie und Gestaltung*, rev. and expanded ed. (Tübingen: Max Niemeyer Verlag, 1977).

24. Schlegel, *Dialogue on Poetry and Literary Aphorisms* trans., intro., and annot. Ernst Behler and Roman Strue (University Park: Pennsylvania State University Press, 1968), 100.

25. Heinz-Dieter Weber, *Friedrich Schlegels "Tranzendentalpoesie"* (Munich: W. Fink Verlag, 1973), 41.

26. Marshall Brown, *The Shape of German Romanticism* (Ithaca: Cornell University Press, 1979), 87.

27. See Luiz Costa Lima, *Mimesis e Modernidade. Formas das Sombras* (Rio de Janeiro: Graal, 1980), esp. 1 28-32.

28. [The Portuguese version of this study contained two appendixes consisting of athenaeum fragment 116 (Appendix I) and a portion of Schlegel's 1800 "Letter about the Novel" (Appendix II), in Portuguese translation. This passage alludes to the latter text. It can be found in English translation in *Dialogue on Poetry and Literary Aphorisms*, pp. 94-105.]

29. [Again, the reference is to the "Letter about the Novel" (Appendix II). The allusion is to material found on p. 99 of the English translation cited in note 28, although translation tactics differ.]

30. For a wide-ranging treatment of the problem of criticism in romantic times, see the still classical Walter Benjamin, *Der Bergriff der Kunst Kritik in der deutschen Romantik* (Bern: A. Francke, 1920).

31. Weber, *Uber eine Theorie der Literaturkritik* (Munich: W. Fink Verlag, 1971), 33-34.

32. Abrams, *The Mirror and the Lamp. Romantic Theory and Critical Tradition* (New York: Oxford University Press, 1953).

33. Preisendanz, "Zur Poetik der deutschen Romantik I: Die Abkehr von Grundsatz der Naturahmung," *Die deutsche Romantik*, ed. H. Steffen (Göttingen: Vandenhoech und Ruprecht, 1967).

34. Schlegel, as quoted in Strohschneider-Kohrs, "Zur Poetik der deutschen Romantik II," 80.

35. Odo Marquard, "Zur Bedeutung der Theorie des Unbewussten für eine Theorie der nicht mehr schönen Kunst," *Poetik und Hermeneutik* 3:375-92.

36. Readers of the last portion of chapter 1 and of my prior essays as well will note the wide implications that I attempt to impart to the terms "similarity" and "difference."

37. See Erich Auerbach, "Baudelaires *Fleurs du mal* und da Erhabene," *Gesammelte Aufsätze zur romanische Philologie* (Bern-Munich: Francke Verlag, 1967), 275-90. On the reaction of Baudelaire's contemporaries to *Les Fleurs du mal*, see W. T. Bandy and C. Pichois, *Baudelaire devant ses contemporains* (Monaco: Éditions du Rocher, 1957), and A. E. Carter, *Baudelaire et la critique française (1868-1917)* (Columbia: University of South Carolina Press, 1963). This aestheticizing is decidedly not to be confused with Schlegel's autonomist project, for, as we shall especially see in the valorization of the novel, the latter leaves a window open for contact with social values.

38. Henry Fielding, *The History of Tom Jones, a Foundling* (New York: Dodd, Mead & Company, 1967), 334.

39. Laurence Sterne, *The Life and Opinions of Tristam Shandy, Gentleman* (New York: Liveright Publishing Corporation, 1942), 65.

40. Raymond Williams, *Culture and Society, 1780-1950* (New York: Doubleday & Company, 1960), 38.

41. Shelley, "A Defence of Poetry," in *Essays, Letters from Abroad, Translations and Fragments*, 2 vols., ed. [Mary Wollstonecraft] Shelley (London: Edward Moxon, 1860), I:57.

42. [Friedrich Leopold von Hardenberg] Novalis, "Die Christenheit oder Europa" (1799). Reprinted in *Werke, Tagebücher und Briefe*, ed. H.-J. Mähl and R. Samuel (Munich: Carl Hanser Verlag, 1978), 2:735.

43. Claude Lévi-Strauss, *The Savage Mind* (Chicago: University of Chicago Press, 1968), 257.

44. Reinhart Koselleck, "Die Herausbildung des modernen Geschichtsbegriffs," *Geschichtliche Grundbegriffe. Historisches Lexikon zur politisch-sozialen Sprache in Deutschland*, ed. O. Brunner, W. Conze, R. Koselleck (Stuttgart: Klett-Cotta, 1975), 2:469: "When one speaks today of

'history', it must be recalled that the beginnings of the sense and force of the term were achieved only in the last third of the eighteenth century.''

45. [François-Marie Arouet] Voltaire, "Histoire," in his "Dictionnaire Philosophique," *Oeuvres Complètes de Voltaire* 31 (Paris: Perronneau, 1819), 517.

46. Hans Peter Reill, *The German Enlightenment and the Rise of Historicism* (Berkeley: University of California Press, 1975), 41.

47. See Cassirer, *Die Philosophie der Aufklärung* (Tübingen: J. C. B. Mohr, 1932), cited from the Spanish translation, *Filosofía de la ilustración* (México-Buenos Aires: Fondo de Cultura Económica, 1950), 93.

48. Auerbach, "Vico and Aesthetic Historism," *Gesammelte Aufsätze zur romanischen Philologie* (Bern-Munich: Francke Verlag, 1967), 272.

49. Allan Megill, "Aesthetic Theory and Historical Consciousness in the Eighteenth Century," *History and Theory* 17, no. 1: 43.

50. Hans Robert Jauss, *Toward an Aesthetic of Reception*, trans. T. Bahti, intro. P. de Man (Minneapolis: University of Minnesota Press, 1982), 50.

51. Cassirer, *The Problem of Knowledge; Philosophy, Science, and History Since Hegel*, trans. William H. Woglom and Charles W. Hendel (New Haven: Yale University Press, 1950), 268.

52. Johann Gustav Droysen, *Historik; Vorlesungen über Enzyklopädie und Methodologie der Geschichte*, ed. R. Hübner (Darmstadt: Wissenschaftliche Buchgesellschaft, 1971), 95-96.

53. Johann Martin Chladenius, *Einleitung zur richtigen Auslegung vernünftiger Reden und Schriften* (1742). Reprinted in *Seminar: Philosophische Hermeneutik*, ed. H. G. Gadamer and G. Boehm (Frankfurt: Suhrkamp Verlag, 1979), 309:72. [References are to proposition and page.]

54. For a systematic exposition of Chladenius and his position within the German Enlightenment, see Reill, *The German Enlightenment*.

55. Ranke, as quoted in *The Varieties of History; from Voltaire to the Present*, ed. Fritz Stern (New York: Meridian Books, 1957), 57; emphasis mine.

56. Wilhelm von Humboldt, "Über die Aufgabe des Geschichtsschreibers" (1821), in *Werke in fünf Bänden*, ed. A Flitner and K. Giel (Darmstadt: Wissenschaftliche Buchgesellschaft, 1960), 1:585.

57. Hyppolite Taine, *Lectures on Art*, 2 vols., trans. John Durand (New York: Henry Holt and Co., 1875), 1:34.

58. Jörn Rüsen, "Ästhetik und Geschichte," *Geschichtstheoretische Untersuchungen zum Begründszusammenhang von Kunst, Gesellschaft und Wissenschaft* (Stuttgart: J. B. Metzler, 1976), 89; emphasis mine.

59. Hayden White, *Metahistory: The Historical Imagination in the Nineteenth Century* (Baltimore: The Johns Hopkins University Press, 1973), 1-42, and "The Value of Narrativity in the Representation of Reality," *Critical Inquiry* 7, no. 1 (Autumn 1980): 5-27.

60. Pierre Nora, "Le Troisième homme?" *L'Arc* 52 (1973; special issue on Michelet): 55.

61. Jacques le Goff, "Le Moyen âge de Michelet," *Pour un autre Moyen âge* (Paris: Gallimard, 1977), 44.

62. Roland Barthes, "Aujourd'hui, Michelet" *L'Arc* 52 (1973; special issue on Michelet): 21.

63. Jules Michelet, *La Sorcière* (Paris: Garnier-Flammarion, 1966), 37.

64. Manfred Fuhrmann, "Die Geschichte der Literaturschreibung von den Anfängen bis zum 19. Jahrhundert," *Der Diskurs der Literatur und Sprachhistorie*, ed. B. Cerquiglini and H. U. Gumbrecht (Frankfurt: Suhrkamp Verlag, 1983), 271.

65. Friedrich Wolfzettel, *Einführung in die französische Literaturgeschichtsschreibung* (Darmstadt: Wissenschaftliche Buchgesellschaft, 1982), 91.

66. Ibid., 99; for a contrasting view of the epistemological bases of philology in France and in Germany, see Erika Hülterschmidt, "Tendenzen und Entwicklungen der Sprachwissenschaft um 1800: ein Vergleich zwischen Frankreich und Deutschland," in *Der Diskurs der Literatur- und Sprachhistorie*, ed. B. Cerquiglini and H. U. Gumbrecht (Frankfurt: Suhrkamp Verlag, 1983),

135-66, and Hans Ulrich Gumbrecht, " 'Un Souffle d'Alemagne ayant passé'. Friedrich Diez, Gaston Paris und die Genese der Nationalphilologie," unpublished.

67. Georg Gottfried Gervinus, "Principien einer deutscher Literaturwissenschaft" (1833), in *Literaturwissenschaft und Literaturgeschichte*, ed. T. Cramer and H. Wenzel (Munich: W. Fink Verlag, 1975), 21-22; emphasis mine.

68. Wilhelm Scherer, "H. Hettners Literaturgeschichte des 18. Jhs." (1878), in *Methoden der deutschen Literaturwissenschaft*, ed. V. Zmegac (Frankfurt: Äthenaum Fischer Verlag, 1974), 18; emphasis mine.

69. See Giovanni Getto, "La Storia letteraria," in *Problemi ed orientamenti critici di lengua e di letteratura italiana*, Tecnica e teoria letteraria 2 (Milan: Marzoratti, 1942), 26.

70. Geoffrey Hartman, "Reflection on Romanticism in France," *Romanticism. Vistas, Instances, Continuities*, ed. D. Thorburn and G. Hartman (Ithaca: Cornell University Press, 1973), 54.

71. Wilhelm Dilthey, "Die Auslegung oder Interpretation" (1909-10), in *Der Aufbau der geschichtlichen Wel in den Geisteswissenschaften. Gesammelte Schriften* 7 (Stuttgart: G. Teubner Verlagsgesellschaft, 1958), 219.

72. For a treatment of Schliermacher's hermeneutics, see my "Hermenêutica e Experiência Literária," *Teoria da Literatura em Suas Fontes* (Rio de Janeiro: Francisco Alves, 1983), 1:52-83.

73. Georg Lukács, *Megjegyzések az irodalomtörténet elméletehez* (Budapest: Franklin, 1910).

74. Roman Jakobsen, "Du réalisme artistique," *Theorie de la littérature*, ed. T. Todorov (Paris: Éditions du Seuil, 1965), 98-108; an incomplete note on the original 1921 publication can be found on p. 309.

75. Walter Benjamin, "Literaturgeschichte und Literaturwissenschaft," *Literarishe Welt* (17 Apr. 1931).

76. Paul Hernadi, "The Erotics of Retrospection: Historytelling, Audience Response, and the Strategies of Desire," *New Literary History* 12, no. 2 (1981): 243-52.

77. Hans Ulrich Gumbrecht, "Das in Vergangen Zeit Gewesne so gut erzählen als ob in der eigenen Welt wäre," in *Theorie der Geschichte Formen und Geschichtschreibung* 4, ed. R. Koselleck, H. Lutz, and J. Rüsen (Munich: Deutscher Taschenbuch Verlag, 1982), 480-513, esp. 501ff.

78. Paul Hazard, "As Origens do Romantismo no Brasil," *Revista da Academia Brasileira de Letras* 25 (Sept. 1927): 30.

79. Gonçalves de Magalhães, "Discurso sobre a História da Literatura no Brasil" (1836), in *Obras de Domingos José Gonçalves de Magalhães* 8: *Opúsculos Históricos e Literários* (Rio de Janeiro: Garnier, 1865), 245.

80. Antônio Cândido, *Formação da Literatura Brasileira*, 2 vols. (São Paulo: Livraria Martins Editora, 1959), 2:324.

81. Léon Bourdon, "Lettres familières et fragment du journal intime *Mes sottises quotidiennes* de Ferdinand Denis à Bahia (1816-1819)," *Brasília* (Coimbra: Faculdade de Letras da Universidade de Coimbra, Instituto de Estudos Brasileiros, 1958), 191.

82. Affonso Arinos, "Algumas Cartas Copiadas no Arquivo de Ferdinand Denis," *Brasília* (Coimbra, 1943), 652.

83. Ferdinand Denis, "Résumé de l'histoire littéraire du Brésil," in *Historiadores e Críticos do Romantismo* 1: *A Contribuição Europeia: Crítica e História Literária*, ed. G. César (São Paulo: Edições da Universidade de São Paulo, 1978), 36.

84. Gilberto Freyre, *Sobrados e Macumbos*, 2 vols. (Rio de Janeiro: Livraria José Olympio, 1968), 2:590.

85. Gama e Castro, "Correspondência (Satisfação a um Escrupuloso)," in *Historiadores* 1:124.

86. Almeida Garrett, "História Abreviada da Língua e Poesia Portuguesa," in ibid., 90.

87. Carl Schlichthorst, *Rio de Janeiro wie es ist. Beiträge zur Tages—und Sitten—geschichten der Haupststadt von Brasilien* (1829), from a passage translated in ibid., 99.

88. Alexandre Herculano, "Futuro Literério de Portugal e do Brasil," in ibid., 90.

89. Ferdinand Wolf, *Le Brésil littéraire—histoire de la littérature brésilienne* (1863), [Portuguese] translation: *O Brasil Literário* (São Paulo: Cia. Editora Nacional, 1955), 352.

90. Heron de Alencar, "José de Alencar e a Ficção Romântica," in *A Literatura no Brasil* 1, ed. Afrânio Coutinho (Rio de Janeiro: Editorial Sul Americana, 1955), part 2, 880.

91. Haroldo de Campos, "*Iracema*: Uma Arqueografia de Vanguarda," *Jornal da Tarde*, "Caderno de Programas e Leituras" (2 Jan. 1982), 3.

92. Sousândrade, *O Guesa*, in Augusto de Campos and Haroldo de Campos, *ReVisão de Sousândrade: Textos Críticos, Antologia, Glossário, Biobibliografia*, 2d ed. (Rio de Janeiro: Nova Fronteira, 1982), 243.

93. Cândido, in Haroldo de Campos, "Da Razão Antropofágica: a Europa sob o Signo da Devoração," *Colóquio/Letras* 62 (Lisboa, 1981): 14.

94. Pereira da Silva, "Estudos Sobre a Literatura," *Niterói* 2 (Paris): 238.

95. Santiago Nunes Ribeiro, "Da Nacionalidade da Literatura Brasileira," *Minerva Brasiliense* 1, no. 1 (Rio de Janeiro, 1843): 19.

96. Francisco A. Varnhagen, "Introdução" to *Florilégio da Poesia Brasileira*, in *Textos que Interessam à História do Romantismo* 1, ed. J. A. Castelo (São Paulo: Conselho Estadual de Cultura, 1961), 77.

97. José de Alencar, "Última Carta sobre *A Confederação dos Tamoios*," in *A Polémica sobre A Confederação dos Tamoios*, ed. J. A. Castelo (São Paulo: Universidade de São Paulo, 1953), 33-34.

98. M. de Auaújo Porto-Alegre, "*A Confederação dos Tamoios*. Ainda uma Palavra às Cartas do Sr. Ig . . .," no *Diário de Notícias*," in ibid., 71.

99. De Alencar, "Primeira Carta sobre *A Confederação dos Tamoios*," in ibid., 5.

100. Alceu Amoroso Lima, *Afonso Arinos*, Anuário do Brasil (Rio de Janeiro-Lisboa: Seara Nova, 1922), 138-39.

101. Santiago Nunes Ribeiro, "Da Nacionalidade da Literatura Brasileira," *Minerva Brasiliense* 1, no. 4 (Rio de Janeiro, 1843): 115.

102. Machado de Assis, "Instinto de Nacionalidade," *Obra Completa*, 3 vols., ed. Afrânio Coutinho (Rio de Janeiro: Aguilar, 1962), 3:804.

103. Gz, "Os Monumentos em Ruína," *Ostensor Brasileiro. Jornal Literário e Pictorial* 1 (Rio de Janeiro, 1845-46): 130.

104. Macedo Soares, "Gonçalves Dias," in *Caminhos do Pensamento Crítico* 1, ed. Afrânio Coutinho, (Brasília: Pallas/Institutio Nacional do Livro, 1980), 294.

105. Urbano Duarte Oliveira, "A Propósito da Chamada Poesia Científica," *Revista da Sociedade Phenix Literária*, no. 1 (Rio de Janeiro, 1878): 4.

106. Pedro Ivo, "O Realismo na Arte," in ibid., no. 2:30.

107. Dantas Barreto, "A Poesia no Século XIX," in ibid., no. 3:56.

108. Licínio Cardoso, "O Destino do Realismo," in ibid., no. 3:52.

109. João Salomé Queiroga, "Advertência" to his *Maricota e o Padre Chico*, in *Textos que Interessam à Historia do Romantismo* 1, ed. J. A. Castelo (São Paulo: Conselho Estadual de Cultura, 1961), 63; emphasis mine.

110. [Costa Lima makes ironic use of this Wilson Martins quote, which is from an unidentified newspaper article.]

Chapter 3. What Are the Building Blocks of History?

1. Jules Michelet, *Journal de Jules Michelet*, 4 vols., ed. Paul Viallaneix (Paris: Gallimard, 1959-76), 1:592.

2. See Michelet, *Histoire du XIXe siècle*, 3 vols. (Paris: Marpon et Flammarion, 1880), 2:163.

3. Michelet, *Histoire de la révolution française. Les Fédérations* (Paris: Calmann-Lévy, 1925), 205.

4. Michelet, *History of the French Revolution*, ed. Gordon Wright, trans. Charles Cocks (Chicago: University of Chicago Press, 1967), 12. [An edited translation of the first three of Michelet's 21-volume *Histoire de la révolution française*.]

5. Michelet, *The People*, trans. J. McKay (Urbana: University of Illinois Press, 1973), 84.

6. Voltaire, *Encyclopédie, ou Dictionnaire raisonné des sciences, des arts et des métiers* (Genève: 1779), tome 15, 1010.

7. Robert Darnton, "The *Encyclopédie* Wars of Prerevolutionary France," *The American Historical Review* 78, no. 5 (1973): 1344.

8. Hayden White, *Metahistory. The Historical Imagination in Nineteenth-Century Europe* (Baltimore: The Johns Hopkins University Press, 1973), 136.

9. Paul Viallaneix, "Notes" to the *Journal de Jules Michelet* 2:857.

10. Richard Harvey Brown, "The Position of the Narrative in Contemporary Society," *New Literary History* 11, no. 3 (1980): 548.

11. Françoise Gaillard, "An Unspeakable (Hi)story," *Yale French Studies* 59 (1980): 149.

12. Meyer H. Abrams, *The Mirror and the Lamp. Romantic Theory and Critical Tradition* (New York: Oxford University Press, 1953), 22.

13. Michelet, *Histoire de la révolution française. La Gironde et la Montagne* (Paris: Calmann-Lévy, 1925), 141-42.

14. Michel de Certeau, *L'écriture de l'histoire* (Paris: Gallimard, 1975), 47.

15. Ilya Prigogine and I. Stengers, *La Nouvelle alliance: Métamorphose de la science* (Paris: Gallimard, 1979), 51-52.

16. Johann Gustav Droysen, *Historik. Vorlesungen über Enzyklopädie und Methodologie der Geschichte* (1857); modern ed., ed. R. Hübner (Darmstadt: Wissenschaftliche Buchgesellschaft, 1971).

17. Werner Heisenberg, *The Physicist's Conception of Nature*, trans. Arnold J. Pomezans (New York: Harcourt, Brace and Company, 1958), 16; emphasis mine.

18. Robert Nisbet, *Sociology as an Art Form* (New York: Oxford University Press, 1976), 10.

19. Brown, *A Poetic For Sociology. Toward a Logic of Discovery for the Human Sciences* (Cambridge: Cambridge University Press, 1977), 96.

20. See Luiz Costa Lima, "Representação Social e *Mimesis*," *Dispersa Demanda* (Rio de Janeiro: Francisco Alves, 1981), 216-36.

21. White, *Tropics of Discourse. Essays in Cultural Criticism* (Baltimore: The Johns Hopkins University Press, 1979), 85.

22. Hans Robert Jauss, "Der Gebrauch der Fiktion in Formen der Anschauung und Darstellung der Geschichte," in *Formen der Geschichtsschreibung*, ed. R. Koselleck (Munich: H. Lutz und J. Rüsen, dtv., 1982), 417.

23. Alfred Schütz, "On Multiple Realities," *Collected Papers* 1, ed. Maurice Natanson (The Hague: Martinus Nijhoff, 1973), 210.

24. Wolfgang Iser, *The Act of Reading: A Theory of Aesthetic Response* (Baltimore: Johns Hopkins University Press, 1978).

25. Iser, "Zur Problemage gegenwärtiger Literaturtheorie. Das Imaginäre und die epochalen Schlüsselbegriffe," in *Auf den Weng gebracht. Idee und Wirklichkeit der Gründung der Universität Konstanz*, ed. H. Sund and M. Timmerman (Konstanz: Universität Konstanz, 1979), 371.

Chapter 4. In the Backlands of Hidden Mimesis

1. João do Rio, *O Momento Literário* (Rio de Janeiro: Garnier, 1908), 2.

2. Oliveira Lima, *Memórias (Estas Minhas Reminiscências . . .)* (Rio de Janeiro: José Olympio, 1937), 64.

3. Afrânio Peixoto, "Euclides da Cunha: O Homem e a Obra," *Poeira da Estrada. Ensaios de Crítica e de História* (Rio de Janeiro: Jackson Editores, 1944), 36.

4. José Veríssimo, "Campanha de Canudos" (1902). Reprinted in *Estudos de Literatura Brasileira*, 2d ed. (Belo Horizonte: Itatiaia-Universidade de São Paulo, 1977), 46.

5. Gilberto Freyre, "Euclides da Cunha, Revelador da Realidade Brasileira," in Euclides da Cunha, *Obras Completas*, 2 vols. (Rio de Janeiro: Aguilar, 1966), 1:22.

6. João Cabral de Melo Neto, "O Engenheiro," in *Poesias Completas (1940-1965)*, 2d ed. (Rio de Janeiro: Livraria José Olympio Editora, 1975), 344.

7. José Maria Bello, *História da República. Primeiro Período: 1889-1902* (Rio de Janeiro: Civilização Brasileira Editora, 1940), 31.

8. Medeiros e Albuquerque, *Minha Vida (Da Infância à Mocidade)* (Rio de Janeiro: Calvino Filho, 1933), 93.

9. Oliveira Vianna, *O Ocaso do Império* (Rio de Janeiro: José Olympio, 1959), 114.

10. Euclides da Cunha, *À Margem da História* (1909). Reprinted in *Obras Completas* 1:375.

11. Sílvio Rabelo, *Euclides da Cunha* (Rio de Janeiro: Civilização Brasileira, 1966), 82.

12. Cunha, *Obras Completas* 2:641.

13. Olímpio de Sousa Andrade, *História e Interpretação de* Os Sertões, rev. ed. (São Paulo: EDART, 1966), 55.

14. Raymundo Faoro, *Os Donos do Poder*, 2 vols., rev. ed. (Porto Alegre-São Paulo: Editora Globo-Editora da Universidade de São Paulo, 1975), 2:557.

15. Walnice Nogueira Galvão, *No Calor da Hora. A Guerra de Canudos nos Jornais. 4.ᵃ Expedição* (São Paulo: Àtica, 1974), 56.

16. Cunha, "A Nossa Vendéia" (14 March 1897), in *Obras Completas* 2:578.

17. Sílvio Romero, *Ensaios de Sociologia e Literatura* (Rio de Janeiro: Garnier, 1901), 4-5.

18. Cunha, *Os Sertões (Campanha de Canudos)* (1902), in *Obras Completas* 1. English is transcribed from the translation *Rebellion in the Backlands*, intro., trans., and notes Samuel Putnam (Chicago: University of Chicago Press, 1944), 225.

19. J. P. Fávila Nunes, "Na Roça," *Revista da Sociedade Fénix Literária*, no. 1 (Rio de Janeiro, Jan. 1878): 15-16.

20. Ataliba Nogueira, *António Conselheiro e Canudos* (São Paulo: Cia. Editora Nacional, 1974).

21. Araripe Júnior, *"Os Sertões (Campanha de Canudos)"* (1903). Reprinted in *Obra Crítica de Araripe Júnior* 4 (Rio de Janeiro: Ministério de Educação e Cultura, Casa de Rui Barbosa, 1966), 106.

22. Araripe, "Dois Grandes Estilos: *Contrastes e Confrontos*." Reprinted in *Obra Crítica*, 244.

23. See Thomas Kuhn, *The Structure of Scientific Revolutions* (Chicago: The University of Chicago Press, 1962), 44.

24. Umberto Peregrino, *Os "Sertões" como História Militar* (Rio de Janeiro: Biblioteca do Exército, 1956), 67-69.

25. Gilberto Amado, *Mocidade no Rio e Primeira Viagem à Europa* (Rio de Janeiro: José Olympio, 1956), 177, 180.

26. For a detailed examination of Siqueira de Menezes's actions at Canudos, see José Calasans, *No Tempo de Antônio Conselheiro* (Salvador: Progresso, 1959), 25-43.

27. See Brito Broca, *A Vida Literária no Brasil—1900* (Rio de Janeiro: Ministério de Educação e Cultura, 1957).

28. Afrânio Peixoto, "Euclides da Cunha: Dom e Arte de Estilo" (1919). Reprinted in *Poeira da Estrada*, 72.

29. Cunha's phrase is confirmed in Nina Rodrigues's statement:

> The backlands population is, and will for some time continue to be, monarchistic, because in the inferior evolutionary stage in which it finds itself, it lacks precisely the mental capacity necessary to understand and accept replacement of the concrete representative of power with the abstraction that that representative incarnates, namely law. The backlanders instinctively require a king, a leader, a figure to direct them, to

lead them, and for some time yet the President of the Republic, State Presidents, local political leaders will be kings for them, just as, in their religious inferiority, the priest and the images continue to be their gods. They will be monarchists just as they are fetishists less because of ignorance than because of insufficient or incomplete intellectual, ethical, and religious development. ("A Loucura Epidêmica de Canudos" [1897]. Reprinted in *As Coletividades Anormais* [Rio de Janeiro: Civilização Brasileira, 1939], 69-70)

30. Reference is to the short story "O Alienista," Machado de Assis, *Obra Completa*, 3 vols. (Rio de Janeiro: Aguilar, 1962), 2:253-88 .

31. M. Cavalcanti Proença, "O Monstruoso Anfiteatro. Sobre Os Sertões de Euclides da Cunha," *Estudos Literários* (Rio de Janeiro: José Olympio, 1971), 56.

32. John Searle, "The Logical Status of Fictional Discourse," *New Literary History* 6, no. 2 (1975): 320.

33. Antônio Cândido, "Euclides da Cunha Sociólogo," in "O Cinqüentenário de *Os Sertões*," *O Estado de São Paulo* (13 Dec. 1952; emphasis mine).

34. Mario Vargas Llosa, *La guerra del fin del mundo* (Barcelona: Seix Barral, 1981).

Chapter 5. Machado de Assis and the Veto's Inversion

1. Machado de Assis, *Obra Completa*, 3 vols., ed. Afrânio Coutinho (Rio de Janeiro: Aguilar, 1962), 2:176.

2. In a certain sense Freud defends himself from his own discovery through the reservation that the "navel" can be ignored because it adds nothing to interpretation. Had he not so stipulated, we could say that the navel can be seen as the limit point of a semantically motivated interpretation. The navel would, then, set the scene for the imaginary, i. e., for that which has no redeemable semantic basis of its own. But it surely would not be a part of the analyst's task to analyze the dream as a discourse that includes imagination, for, were that to be the case, he or she would be prevented from postulating the possibility of a correct, true interpretation of the dream, as Freud does. Conversely, that line of thought becomes vital if, in opposition to Freud, we today suggest the possibility of a *rigorous investigation* of certain discursive objects, such as the discourse of the patient undergoing psychoanalysis and fictional discourse, no longer constituting them as objects of *scientific research*. Since the basic feature of the discourses in which the imaginary resides is that they have no basis for semantic stabilization, being interpretatively *dispersive*.

3. Machado, "Pílades e Orestes," in *Obra Completa* 2:708. The English is reproduced from *The Devil's Church and Other Stories* by Machado de Assis, trans. Jack Schmidt and Lorie Ishimatsu (Austin: University of Texas Press, 1977), 130.

4. For further development of this point, see Luiz Costa Lima, "Sob a Face de um Bruxo," *Dispersa Demanda* (Rio de Janeiro: Francisco Alves, 1981), 102ff.

5. Ian Watt, *The Rise of the Novel: Studies in Defoe, Richardson, and Fielding* (Berkeley: University of California Press, 1971), 53.

6. Antônio Cândido, "O Escritor e o Público," *Literatura e Sociedade* (São Paulo: Companhia Editora Nacional, 1973), 81.

7. Raymundo Faoro, *Os Donos do Poder*, 2 vols., rev. ed. (Porto Alegre-São Paulo: Editora Globo-Editora da Universidade de São Paulo, 1975).

8. José Murilo de Carvalho, *A Construção da Ordem. A Elite Política Imperial* (Rio de Janeiro: Editora Campus, 1980); Simon Schwartzman, *Bases do Autoritarismo Brasileiro* (Rio de Janeiro: Editora Campus, 1982); and Fernando Uricoechea, *O Minotauro Imperial. A Burocratização do Estado Patrimonial Brasileiro no Século XIX* (Rio de Janeiro-São Paulo: Difusão Europeia do Livro, 1978).

9. A. L. Machado Neto, *Estrutura Social da República das Letras (Sociologia da Vida Intelectual Brasileira—1870-1930)* (São Paulo: Grijalbo, 1973), 84.

10. José Veríssimo, "Das Condições da Produção Literária no Brasil," *Estudos da Literatura Brasileira* (Rio de Janeiro: Garnier, 1903), 79.

11. Oliveira Vianna, *Instituições Políticas Brasileiras*, 2 vols. (Rio de Janeiro: José Olympio, 1949), 2:22.

12. That the lack of a separation between the public and the private continues to be present in Brazilian political representation is demonstrated by a passage from a recent presidential speech: "The people of Goiás are far, very far, from repeating the example of those who yesterday came to my home, or to the Planalto Palace, to praise me or my administration and, as soon as they saw their personal interests not followed by the government or myself, began to treat me and the government as though we had been opposed to them all along. I would say that, more than a bit of civic sense, not to mention patriotism, what they lack is modesty, or something worse: a sense of shame" (*Jornal do Brasil* [Rio de Janeiro, 16 July 1982], 4). I do not mean to say that our country still exists in a patrimonialism like that under the Empire, but the fact is that an indistinguishability between public and private is today still bound up with national power's unwillingness to make itself truly representative. The passage reproduced above thus agrees with, and further illuminates, the seemingly commonplace comment published today, while I finish the typescript of these pages: "The decision-making center remains hermetic and restricted and has not widened by even one centimeter the participation of intermediate and popular institutions in the definition of government policy" (Carlos Castello Branco, "Baixo Grau de Participação," *Jornal do Brasil* [12 Sept. 1982], 2).

13. René Dumesnil, introduction to Flaubert's *Madame Bovary* (Paris: Belles Lettres, 1945), clxxxi.

14. Émile Montégut, "Le Roman intime de la littérature réaliste," *Revue de Deux Mondes* 18 (Paris, 1 Nov. 1858): 210; emphasis mine.

15. Sílvio Romero, *Machado de Assis* (1897); ed. cit. (Rio de Janeiro: José Olympio, 1936), 35.

16. Veríssimo, "Letras e Literatos: Estudinhos Críticos da Nossa Literatura do Dia," *José Veríssimo. Teoria, Crítica e História Literária*, ed. João Alexandre Barbosa (São Paulo: Edições da Universidade de São Paulo, 1936), 109.

Afterword: Can the Imagination be Mimetic under Conditions of Modernity?

1. See Richard Kearney, *The Wake of the Imagination* (Minneapolis: University of Minnesota Press, 1988), which contains informative chapters on the Hebraic, Hellenic and medieval imagination.

2. See André Breton, *What is Surrealism? Selected Writings*, ed. and introd. F. Rosemont (New York: Monad, 1978), 227.

3. In addition to offering a concise survey of the history of the concept, in its last chapter Kearney's *The Wake of the Imagination* attempts an ambitious rethinking of the imagination in postmodernity. See also two books by Dietmar Kamper: *Zur Soziologie der Imagination* (München: Hanser, 1986) and *Zur Geschichte der Einbildungskraft* (München: Hanser, 1981).

4. Alexander Gerard, *An Essay on Genius* (London, 1774), 81.

5. Ibid., 56.

6. Friedrich Schlegel, *Gespräch über die Poesie*, ed. Hans Eichner (Stuttgart: Metzler, 1968), 319.

7. Samuel Tyler Coleridge, *Biographia Literaria*, ed. James Engell and W. Jackson Bate (Princeton: Princeton University Press, 1983), 304-5.

8. Immanuel Kant, *Critique of Judgment*, trans. J. H. Bernard (New York: Hafner and London: Macmillan, 1951), 89.

9. Novalis, *Schriften*, 2nd ed., 4 vols., ed. P. Kluckhohn and R. Samuel (Stuttgart: Kohlhammer, 1960-75), vol. III, 460.

10. Writers suggested as possible authors of this anonymous document include, besides Hegel, Hölderlin and Schelling.

11. *Mythologie der Vernunft. Hegels "ältestes Systemprogramm des deutschen Idealismus,"* ed. Christoph Jamme and Helmut Schneider (Frankfurt/Main: Suhrkamp, 1984), 12-13. My translation.

12. Gotthard Heidegger, *Mythoscopia Romantica* (Zurich, 1698), 13-14. All Heidegger quotes are my translation.

13. Ibid., 176.

14. Ibid., 183.

15. Ibid., 50-51.

16. See, for instance, L'Abbé Prévost, *The History of Manon Lescaut and the Chevalier des Grieux* (London and New York, 1925), 50-52.

17. Johann Christoph Gottsched, *Versuch einer Critischen Dichtkunst vor die Deutschen*, 4th ed. (Leipzig, 1751), 91. My translation.

18. Johann Christoph Gottsched, *Die vernünftgen Tadlerinnen* (Leipzig and Hamburg, 1738), part 2, issue 19, 178-79. My translation.

19. Niklas Luhmann, *The Differentiation of Society*, trans. Stephen Holmes and Charles Larmore (New York: Columbia University Press, 1982), 234-35.

20. Panajotis Kondylis, Die Aufklärung im Rahmen des neuzeitlichen Rationalismus (Stuttgart: Klett-Cotta, 1981).

21. Luhmann, *The Differentiation of Society*, 236, 239 and 245.

22. Ibid., 249.

23. Ibid., 249.

24. Joseph Addison, "On the Pleasures of the Imagination" (1712), in *The Spectator* no. 411.

25. Adam Bergk, *Die Kunst, Bücher zu lesen* (Jena, 1799), 2-3. All Bergk quotes are my translation.

26. Ibid., 6-7 and 9.

27. Ibid., 21.

28. Ibid., 105-6.

29. Jean-Jacques Rousseau, *Politics and the Arts. Letter to M. D'Alembert on the Theatre*, ed. Allan Bloom (Ithaca: Cornell University Press, 1968), 24-25.

30. Ibid., 26.

31. Dietmar Kamper, *Zur Soziologie der Imagination* (München: Hanser, 1986), 19. My translation.

32. Luhmann, *The Differentiation of Society*, 242.

33. See for romanticism Philippe Lacoue-Labarthe and Jean-Luc Nancy, *The Literary Absolute. The Theory of Literature in German Romanticism*, trans. Philip Barnard and Cheryl Lester (Albany: State University of New York Press, 1988) and for the historical avant-garde Peter Bürger, *Theory of the Avant-Garde*, trans. Michael Shaw (Minneapolis: University of Minnesota Press, 1984).

34. Samuel Tyler Coleridge, *Biographia Literaria*, ed. James Engell and W. Jackson Bate (Princeton: Princeton University Press, 1983), 304-5.

35. Walter Benjamin, *Gesammelte Schriften*, ed. Rolf Tiedemann and Hermann Schweppenhäuser (Frankfurt/Main: Suhrkamp, 1974), vol. I,1, 51.

36. I deal with this problematic in more detail in my introduction to Géza von Molnár's *Romantic Vision, Ethical Context: Novalis and Artistic Autonomy* (Minneapolis: University of Minnesota Press, 1986).

37. Benjamin, *Gesammelte Schriften*, 26 and 29.

38. Michel Foucault, *The Order of Things. An Archeology of the Human Sciences* (New York: Vintage, 1973), 59.

39. Ibid, 43.

40. Ibid.
41. Neil Flax, "The Presence of the Sign in Goethe's *Faust*," in *PMLA* 98 (1983): 187.

Index

Index

Theory and History of Literature
Edited by Wlad Godzich and Jochen Schulte-Sasse

Luiz Costa Lima has written nine books, including *Sociedade e discurso ficcional* (1986), *Dispersa demanda* (1981), *Mimesis e modernidade* (1980), and *Estruturalismo e teoria da literatura* (1973). Many of his works in literary theory have been published in Portuguese and German. He has contributed to *New Literary History*, and this is his first book to appear in English. A native of Brazil, he received his doctorate in literary theory and comparative literature at the Universidade de São Paulo (1972), was a visiting professor at Ruhr-Universität Bochum (West Germany) and was associate professor of Portuguese at the University of Minnesota (1984-86). Currently, he is professor of literary theory at Pontificia Universidade Catolica (Rio de Janeiro).

Ronald W. Sousa, a faculty member at the University of Minnesota since 1974, is now department chairman of comparative literature and professor of Spanish and Portuguese. He has also worked at the University of Texas and the University of California, Berkeley. Sousa received his master's degree (1968) and doctorate (1973) in comparative literature at the University of California, Berkeley. He is author of *The Rediscoverers: Major Figures in the Portuguese Literature of National Regeneration* and editor of *Problems of Enlightenment in Portugal*, Sousa contributes to *Ideologies and Literature, Luso-Brazilian Review* and *Bulletin of Hispanic Studies*.

Jochen Schulte-Sasse is director of graduate studies in the department of comparative literature and professor of German at the University of Minnesota. He is co-editor, with Wlad Godzich, of the series Theory and History of Literature.